MILITARY AIRCRAFT, Origins to 1918

AN ILLUSTRATED HISTORY
OF THEIR IMPACT

Other Titles in ABC-CLIO's
WEAPONS AND WARFARE SERIES

MILITARY AIRCRAFT, Origins to 1918

AN ILLUSTRATED HISTORY OF THEIR IMPACT

Justin D. Murphy

A B C 〰 C L I O

Santa Barbara, CA   Denver, CO   Oxford, England

Library of Congress Cataloging-in-Publication Data
Murphy, Justin D.
Military aircraft, origins to 1918 : an illustrated history of their
impact / Justin D. Murphy.
p. cm. — (Weapons and warfare series)
Includes bibliographical references and index.
ISBN 1-85109-488-1 (hardback : alk. paper) — ISBN 1-85109-493-8
(ebook) 1. Airplanes, Military—History--20th century. 2.
Aeronautics, Military—History—20th century.   I. Title.   II. Series.
UG1240.M88 2005
623.74'6'09041—dc22
2005003596

08 07 06 05 04 / 10 9 8 7 6 5 4 3 2 1

This book is also available on the World Wide Web as an eBook.
Visit abc-clio.com for details.

ABC-CLIO, Inc.
130 Cremona Drive, P.O. Box 1911
Santa Barbara, California 93116-1911

This book is printed on acid-free paper.
Manufactured in the United States of America

CONTENTS

CHAPTER SIX
Naval Aircraft   183

INTRODUCTION TO
WEAPONS AND WARFARE SERIES

WEAPONS BOTH FASCINATE AND REPEL. They are used to kill and maim individuals and to destroy states and societies, and occasionally whole civilizations, and with these the greatest of man's cultural and artistic accomplishments. Throughout history tools of war have been the instruments of conquest, invasion, and enslavement, but they have also been used to check evil and to maintain peace.

Weapons have evolved over time to become both more lethal and more complex. For the greater part of man's existence, combat was fought at the length of an arm or at such short range as to represent no real difference; battle was fought within line of sight and seldom lasted more than the hours of daylight of a single day. Thus individual weapons that began with the rock and the club proceeded through the sling and boomerang, bow and arrow, sword and axe, to gunpowder weapons of the rifle and machine gun of the late nineteenth century. Study of the evolution of these weapons tells us much about human ingenuity, the technology of the time, and the societies that produced them. The greater part of technological development of weaponry has taken part in the last two centuries, especially the twentieth century. In this process, plowshares have been beaten into swords; the tank, for example, evolved from the agricultural caterpillar tractor. Occasionally, the process is reversed and military technology has impacted society in a positive way. Thus modern civilian medicine has greatly benefitted from advances to save soldiers' lives, and weapons technology has impacted such areas as civilian transportation and atomic power.

Weapons can have a profound impact on society. Gunpowder weapons, for example, were an important factor in ending the era of the armed knight and the Feudal Age. They installed a kind of rough democracy on the battlefield, making "all men alike tall." We can only wonder what effect weapons of mass destruction (WMD) might have on our own time and civilization.

This series will trace the evolution of a variety of key weapons systems, describe the major changes that occurred in each, and illustrate and identify the key types. Each volume begins with a description of the particular weapons system and traces its evolution, while discussing its historical, social, and political contexts. This is followed by a heavily illustrated section that is arranged more or less along chronological lines that provides more precise information on at least 80 key variants of that particular weapons system. Each volume contains a glossary of terms, a bibliography of leading books on that particular subject, and an index.

Individual volumes in the series, each written by a specialist in that particular area of expertise, are as follows:

Ancient Weapons
Medieval Weapons
Pistols
Rifles
Machine Guns
Artillery
Tanks
Battleships
Cruisers and Battle Cruisers
Aircraft Carriers
Submarines
Military Aircraft, Origins to 1918
Military Aircraft, 1919–1945
Military Aircraft in the Jet Age
Helicopters
Ballistic Missiles
Air Defense
Destroyers

We hope that this series will be of wide interest to specialists, researchers, and even general readers.

Spencer C. Tucker
Series Editor

PREFACE AND ACKNOWLEDGMENTS

The heavens are their battlefields; they are the cavalry of the clouds. High above the squalor and the mud, so high in the firmament that they are not visible from the earth, they fight out the eternal issues of right and wrong. . . . Every flight is a romance; every report is an epic. They are the knighthood of the war, without fear and without reproach. They recall the old legends of chivalry, not merely by the daring of their exploits, but by the nobility of their spirit, and amongst the multitudes of heroes, let us think of the chivalry of the air.

David Lloyd George
29 October 1917

PERHAPS NO ASPECT OF THE First World War has left such a lasting impression upon the public memory than did that of the daring pilots who fought against one another in the skies over Europe. Ask people to identify the "Red Baron," and the vast majority, even if they do not know his name was Manfred von Richthofen, will at least know he was the leading ace of the war; his image, after all, has been used to sell frozen pizza and he has served as the arch nemesis of the *Peanuts* character Snoopy. The Red Baron is remembered for what he did and because air power fascinated people during the First World War and has continued to fascinate them since for a few simple reasons. For one thing, air power was something new. The first heavier-than-air flight had taken place just 11 years before the outbreak of the war. In addition, civilians, who heretofore were removed from the battlefield, experienced its awesome power, as they became its targets. Finally, when the armies of Britain, France, and Germany became bogged down in the trenches of Europe, in an impersonal war of attrition that took millions of lives, the exploits of aviators gave the press something to publicize.

Although military balloons had been used since 1794—and they would be relied upon heavily in the First World War when the Western Front became stalemated—airplanes and airships had only recently become part of each nation's war arsenal before the outbreak of the First World War. Consequently, even though a few, mainly younger, officers were air power enthusiasts and were developing theories that were way ahead of technology, many officers were somewhat skeptical of aviation's value. Indeed, in the opening stages of the war, a few commanders dismissed aviators' reports of troop movements unless they could be verified by such traditional sources as the cavalry. The first few months of the war were to change that totally as aviation proved its worth in reconnaissance.

As the war advanced, so too did the roles played by military aircraft. In addition to reconnaissance, aircraft were used as bombers to strike targets behind enemy lines and, in the case of the German zeppelin raids on Great Britain, civilian targets that would have been considered uncivilized just a few decades before the war. Aircraft also took on the role of combating other aircraft as depriving the enemy of the ability to conduct aerial reconnaissance became a matter of the utmost importance. As the roles of aircraft changed, so too did aircraft themselves evolve. By war's end aircraft capabilities had undergone a quantum leap, with aircraft bearing little resemblance to the frail wooden and cloth war birds that had entered the war. In many respects, the course of the air war itself was determined in large measure by the economic battle being waged on the home fronts. Whereas the aviation industry was relatively small in all countries prior to the war, the most industrialized nations were at a decided advantage when it came to mobilizing the resources that were necessary for wartime production. For lack of a better term, aviation was a key part of the emerging "military-industrial-complex"—a position it has maintained ever since.

As the capabilities of aircraft changed during the war, so too did aviation's relationship to other branches of service. Commanders increasingly relied upon aircraft to play a more integral part of the battle plan. From photographing the entire front on a continual basis so that staff officers could look for any changes or signs of weakness, to keeping track of forces once the battle was launched, aircraft were vital to military intelligence. Furthermore, aircraft could assist the artillery in softening up the enemy prior to attack by striking at targets beyond the reach of the artillery. In particular, bombers were sent to attack rail stations and rail junctions in the hope of disrupting the enemy's ability to move manpower and materiel. Finally, by war's end, aircraft played a critical part of any attack or defense against an attack, moving ahead of advancing troops to strafe enemy lines, or swooping in to stop an advance in order to give troops time to rally. At sea, aircraft served to extend both the navy's horizon and its reach. Airships and seaplanes were vital to waging war against German U-boats, if only because they were able to spot them in advance of a convoy of ships. By war's end, aircraft were gaining the ability to strike and sink ships by themselves. As a result, the era of the battleship was about to become the era of the aircraft carrier.

As aircraft evolved in these roles, so too did its organizational role within the military structure evolve. Where aircraft had been considered at the least as a weapon to be employed by the army or navy, or at the most as a junior partner whose purpose was to serve the needs of the senior partner, the war would end with the British having organized its air power as a separate, equal branch of service. This happened even though the British Army had fought to subordinate the use of aircraft to meeting the needs of the British Expeditionary Force on the Western Front. Anything else was regarded as a diversion. The war demonstrated, however, that the British Army could not override the public's demand that something be done to defend Great Britain from German bombers and zeppelins and that the British take retaliatory action against the Germans, even though more soldiers could be killed or wounded in a day during a battle on the Western Front than British civilians would be killed or wounded from German bombs during the entire war. The public demanded action, the politicians responded, and the result was the creation of the Royal Air Force. Other powers would follow suit in the aftermath of the war—the United States not until after the Second World War—firmly establishing the importance of military aircraft in modern warfare.

As the first of three volumes on military aircraft, this encyclopedia will trace the history of military aviation from the origins of flight through the end of the First World War. Chapter One examines the origins of aviation, paying close attention to the pioneers of aviation and the technological changes that ultimately made human flight a reality. It also focuses on the origins of military aviation, from the use of military balloons since the French Revolutionary Wars to the first uses of airplanes and airships in military conflicts prior to the First World War. Chapter Two examines the role of air power in the First World War, demonstrating its impact upon the overall conduct of the war as well as the technological innovations that transformed aviation. Special attention is also placed on the personal or human side of military aviation by examining the life of aviators and the role of aces, and by emphasizing the importance of the home front in mobilizing air power. Each of the remaining chapters are devoted to different types of military aircraft based upon the roles they played: Chapter Three, Reconnaissance and Auxiliary Aircraft; Chapter Four, Fighter and Attack Aircraft; Chapter Five, Bomber Aircraft; and Chapter Six, Naval Aircraft. It would be impossible to deal with all aircraft of this era in the space allotted to this volume; however, more than 200 aircraft, including variants and types, are either mentioned or discussed in varying degrees of depth within these four chapters.

For simplicity's sake, aircraft are presented in alphabetical order of country of origin with subheadings noting transitions to each country. Placing individual aircraft within the respective chapters was sometimes difficult because some aircraft performed different roles during the course of the war. As a result, I have placed aircraft in the chapter that corresponds to their primary role; thus, the Sopwith 11/2 Strutter, which originated as a fighter, ultimately served longer as a bomber, so it is in the chapter on bombers. In a few cases, however, where aircraft played equally important roles, they have been discussed in more than one chapter. The best example of this occurrence is the Sopwith Pup, which served as one of the most important British fighters in the war, yet also was crucial as part of the navy's effort to develop aircraft that could take off from and land onboard ships; therefore, the Sopwith Pup is discussed in both the fighter chapter and the naval aircraft chapter.

The illustrated appendix is an important part of the encyclopedia, but space considerations forced it to be limited to 80 aircraft, and it was no easy task choosing which ones to include, or conversely which ones to exclude. An attempt was made to choose the most important aircraft in terms of numbers produced or the difference it made in the war, while at the same time choosing aircraft from different phases of the war and giving an equitable number for the countries involved. It is not to slight the French that more German and British aircraft are included than French aircraft, but merely a reflection that the French tended to mass produce particular aircraft, whereas the British and Germans produced more types. It must also be noted that statistics on production are in some cases difficult to come by, either because of conflicting information from a variety of sources or because of a lack of information altogether. Where conflicting numbers existed, an attempt has been made to go with an average, to use the number from the latest source, or to go with the best reasonable estimate. Numbers have been converted from metric to standard with the exception of references to climbing rate, where I have used meters if that was a base to measure performance, and altitude, where I have provided both meters and feet as a basis for comparison. The glossary contains an altitude conversion chart to assist readers.

It would have been impossible to undertake a project of this type without the able assistance of the librarians at Howard Payne University. They both rushed to help me acquire interlibrary loan books, and forgave me when I was late in returning them. I must also thank the series editor, Dr. Spencer C. Tucker, for giving me this opportunity. Having previously guided me in obtaining my doctorate at Texas Christian University and allowing me to work with him on other projects, I feel so very humbled that he asked me to work on this one. Words cannot adequately express how much I value him as a mentor, a colleague, and a friend. His words of encouragement as I worked through the manuscript helped propel me to the finish line. Any errors or omissions, however, are mine. Finally, I must express my appreciation and apology to my wife, Jessica, and my sons, Jonathan and Jason, for bearing with me as I have worked on this project and not given them the time that they so richly deserve.

Justin D. Murphy

CHAPTER ONE

The Origins of Flight and Military Aviation

FROM THE DAWN OF TIME MAN has been fascinated with flight, as indicated by its importance in ancient mythology and religion. For the ancient Egyptians, the sky-god Horus, symbolized by the falcon or a human with a falcon head, was originally revered as a creator god, and the pharaoh portrayed himself as the incarnation of Horus on earth. Judaism and Christianity are replete with stories of winged angels, and Psalm 91:4 refers to God as having wings, saying, "He will cover you with his feathers, and under his wings you will find refuge." In Psalm 55:6–8, David expressed a desire to fly to safety, declaring, "Oh, that I had the wings of a dove! I would fly away and be at rest. I would flee far away and stay in the desert; I would hurry to my place of shelter, far from the tempest and storm." The mythology of ancient peoples is filled with stories of flight, such as the Greek tale of Daedalus and Icarus, who fashioned wings from feathers and wax in order to escape from Crete, or the Chinese legend of Emperor Shun, who used reed hats to fly or parachute from a burning tower. One African legend featured a military use of flight as the Ugandan warrior, Kibaga, flew over his king's enemies, reporting their position and hurling rocks down on them.

Although the preceding accounts are the stuff of faith and mythology, history accords the Chinese with developing the first manmade object to fly with the invention of the kite, possibly as early as 1000 B.C. Whereas kites were used for pleasure and ceremonial purposes, they were also used for such practical purposes as dropping fishing

1

lines farther from shore or from boats. According to one legend the Chinese general, Han Xin, employed a kite in the second century B.C. to calculate the distance to a palace that he was attacking. Chinese armies are also reported to have used kites for sending signals. In addition, the Chinese experimented with man-lifting kites, primarily as a means of punishing criminals. According to Marco Polo, kites were used to lift humans from ships in order to secure divine blessings for a safe voyage. Kites eventually made their way to Europe, where they may have been used for more ominous purposes. An illustration in a medieval manuscript, *The Noble, Wise and Prudent Monarch,* composed by Walter de Milemete in 1326, depicts knights using a kite to drop a firebomb over the walls of a besieged city. It is not certain whether or not this depicts an actual event, but Milemete, who served as chaplain to England's King Edward III, also depicted early cannon, which are known to have been used at the time.

In addition to the kite, the Chinese also invented the rocket, which, like their invention of the draw-string helicopter toy, demonstrated the possibility of mechanical flight. After developing black powder in the mid-ninth century, the Chinese invented a number of military weapons, including fire lances that used bamboo poles to shoot flames at approaching enemies. At some point in the late twelfth century the fire lance was adapted into the rocket, by turning it around and allowing the expulsion of gas and flame to serve the purpose of propulsion. The Chinese first used the rocket against Mongol forces besieging the Chin Dynasty's capital of K'ai-feng. By the sixteenth and seventeenth centuries the Chinese had developed two-stage rockets, which were capable of dispersing arrows after reaching their apogee, and boxed multirocket launchers. By the mid-thirteenth century knowledge of black powder and rockets had spread to the Arabs and western Europeans. Although the use of rockets by European armies gave way to cannon by the sixteenth century, British artillerist Sir William Congreve reintroduced the rocket in the British arsenal with great results in the Napoleonic Wars and the War of 1812. The development of rifled cannon resulted in the disuse of rockets until more effective means of propulsion were developed in the Second World War.

THE PURSUIT OF HUMAN FLIGHT

The earliest documented attempts at human flight date back to the Middle Ages, when various individuals sought to emulate birds.

Such is the case of the ninth-century Spanish Moor, Abu'l-Quasim'Abbas b. Firnas, who attempted to leap with feathered wings from a high tower in Cordoba, Spain. Whereas he supposedly glided a short distance, his "flight" ended in a crash landing, severely injuring his back. Subsequent attempts to mimic his efforts in Khorosan and Constantinople resulted in fatal landings.

Perhaps the most well-known attempt at early flight was that by the early-eleventh-century Benedictine monk, Eilmer of Malmesbury, who in 1010 fashioned wings that were attached to his arms and feet and succeeded in leaping from the watchtower of his abbey and gliding for approximately 600 ft. His wings were most likely constructed of ash or willow wands and covered with light cloth. After a steady descent that lasted about 15 seconds, Eilmer stalled and crashed, breaking both of his legs. He is said to have later attributed his fall to his failure to provide a tail. Because this would undoubtedly have added stability, it indicated that Eilmer had an understanding of some of the basics of flight.

Four centuries after Eilmer's ill-fated glide, the Renaissance artist, engineer, and scientist, Leonardo da Vinci, lent his keen intellect to the human quest for flight. An astute observer of nature, da Vinci carefully studied birds and became convinced that it would be possible for humans to replicate their movement. Toward that end, he designed numerous ornithopters, whose wings were to be flapped by cranks and pulleys, as well as helicopters and parachutes. Although there is no evidence that Leonardo ever attempted to build one of his models, he expressed little doubt that humans could successfully replicate the movement of birds. In the late seventeenth century, however, another Italian, Giovanni Alphonso Borelli, would conclusively demonstrate that humans lacked the muscular structure or strength for human-powered flight. Despite this, countless inventors would remain devoted to the ornithopter concept.

In 1670, a decade before Borelli published his treatise demonstrating that a human-powered ornithopter was impossible, Lana de Terzi, a Jesuit professor at the University of Ferrara, proposed creating a vacuum balloon-ship by evacuating the air from four thin copper spheres, each of which were to be approximately 24 ft and 7 in. in diameter. Terzi calculated that the displaced air from each sphere would weigh approximately 240 lbs more than each sphere itself; therefore, he concluded that the four spheres would provide a net buoyancy of 960 lbs that would be sufficient to lift passengers in a small ship. The craft would use a sail to capture the wind and soar through the air. More important, he recognized the military potential of such a devise, noting that it would be useful both for reconnaissance and for dropping bombs on enemy forces below. Although the spheres would have collapsed had the design been attempted, Terzi's concept of a balloonlike airship was sound, provided a lifting agent could be discovered.

Within four decades of Terzi's proposed airship, Bartolomeu Lourenço de Gusmão would arrive at the answer after watching a soap bubble pass through the air. Born in Brazil in 1685 and educated by Jesuits, Gusmão had left the order and traveled to Portugal to study at the University of Coimbra. Gusmão, who was most likely aware of Terzi's treatise, conceived of an airship, dubbed the *Passarola,* and obtained an audience with King João V on 8 August 1709. Before a stunned crowd of courtiers and the king, he successfully demonstrated a model, consisting of a small paper balloon and attached brazier, that lifted from the ground and floated through the air. Although reports of his feat soon appeared as far away as London and Vienna, there is no evidence that a larger version was attempted. This may in part have been because of King João's declining health and lack of interest among his administrators, but it may also have been a result of the Portuguese Inquisition. Although accounts vary, Gusmão was at least briefly imprisoned on charges of sorcery sometime around 1720. After either escaping or being released, he burned all of his papers and fled to Spain, where he died in Toledo on 19 November 1724. With the abrupt end of Gusmão's experiments and destruction of his papers, knowledge of his work gradually faded. Indeed, when human flight was achieved in 1783 by the Montgolfier brothers and Jacques Alexandre César Charles, it was apparently done with no knowledge of Gusmão's experiments.

The invention of balloons in 1783 both captured public attention and was almost immediately seen as something that had a practical application for military observation. Indeed, Joseph Montgolfier, the son of a prosperous paper manufacturer, first conceived of the hot air balloon in November 1782 while contemplating a picture that depicted Spanish forces trying to besiege British fortifications at Gibraltar. Since a fire could send sparks, ashes, and particles up a chimney, Joseph reasoned that it might be possible to capture the rising flux of hot air[1] and use it to lift a vessel over the walls of a fortress. He constructed a small taffeta balloon and on 4 November 1782 succeeded in making it rise to the ceiling. He then immediately wrote to his brother, Étienne, who soon joined him and began experiments at Avignon. On 14 December one of their balloons soared to about 1,000 ft and drifted nearly a mile before landing. In a 4 June 1783 public demonstration at Annonay, a 35-ft-diameter balloon rose before an astonished crowd to approximately 3,000 ft and drifted for 2 miles before landing. After this success, the brothers traveled to Paris, where they hoped to gain royal support.

By the time the Montgolfier brothers arrived in Paris, they found that they would be engaged in a race with noted French scientist Jacques Alexandre César Charles, who was attempting to build a hydrogen balloon. After British chemist Henry Cavendish successfully isolated hydrogen in 1766, Joseph Black and Tiberious Cavallo discovered that this inflammable gas could also be used as a lifting agent. The Montgolfier brothers were aware of this, but they lacked the financial resources to produce hydrogen in the quantities that would be needed; therefore, they remained committed to their hot air experiments. Money was not an issue, however, for Charles, who had the support of influential members in the Académie Royale des Sciences. With the assistance of Jean and Noël Robert, Charles constructed a 12-ft spherical balloon out of latex-covered taffeta and dubbed it the *Globe*. The Robert brothers then experimented with different means of producing hydrogen, ultimately resorting to pouring sulfuric acid over iron filings that had been deposited into an oak cask. The resulting chemical reaction released hydrogen into the balloon—a somewhat dangerous process because it also produced tremendous heat, which could have ignited the balloon. On 27 August the *Globe* was released amid great fanfare from the Champ de Mars in Paris. It landed 45 minutes later, after a tear in the fabric, 15 miles away in a field near the village of Gonesse, where startled villagers, convinced it was a creature from space, attacked it with knives, pitchforks, and muskets, much to the later amusement of their more sophisticated countrymen in Paris who read about the account in Parisian newspapers.

Having arrived in Paris in time to see Charles's accomplishment, the Montgolfier brothers, working at the Reveillon wallpaper factory, hurriedly completed a massive 70-ft-tall balloon that unfortunately was destroyed in heavy rainfall on 12 September. They quickly produced another one, the *Martial*, that was launched from Versailles on 19 September 1783, as approximately 100,000 spectators watched it carry a sheep, a duck, and a rooster on a flight of 8-minutes duration and a distance of 2 miles. With this accomplishment behind them, the Montgolfier brothers then raced to beat Charles in getting the first human aloft. By mid-October they had constructed a massive 56,000-cubit-ft-capacity balloon. Although

Étienne tested it by rising in a tethered ascent to 50 ft, Jean François Pilâtre de Rozier made the first official ascents before the Académie Royale over a 3-day period beginning on 15 October. This included experimenting with a small heater in an effort to keep the balloon aloft. Finally, on Friday, 21 November 1783, Pilâtre de Rozier and François Laurent, Marquis d'Arlandes, an infantry captain in the French Army, made the first untethered flight in human history, rising from the estate of the Duc de Polignac to a height of approximately 3,000 ft and slowly drifting across Paris before landing gently on its outskirts 25 minutes later after traveling approximately 4 miles.

Although the Montgolfiers had won the race to be the first to achieve human flight, Charles and the Robert brothers would soon demonstrate the superiority of the hydrogen balloon over the hot air balloon of the Montgolfier brothers. After constructing a 26-ft diameter balloon, the *Charlière* and using a multi-barrel system for generating enough hydrogen to fill its 9,200-cubit-ft envelope—a process that took 3 days—Charles and Noël Robert were ready for their ascent on 1 December 1783. Launching from the gardens of the Tuilleries palace in Paris, they rose quickly to a height of approximately 2,000 ft and drifted more than 30 miles before landing near Nesle, where Robert got out and Charles made a solo ascent to an altitude of more than 9,000 ft before descending an hour later a short distance away at Tour le Lay. The success of the hydrogen balloon compared with the Montgolfière was further emphasized the following year, on 19 September 1784, when the Robert brothers made a flight of approximately 150 miles in just over 6 hours.

The success of the Montgolfier brothers and Charles ignited an enthusiasm that swept across Europe and even reached America. The ease of constructing a Montgolfière, compared with the cost of a hydrogen balloon, gave hot air ballooning an initial advantage. In February 1784, Paolo Andreani, Agostino Gerli, and Carlo Gerli ascended in a Montgolfière outside Milan. On 4 June 1784, Élisabeth Thible became the first female aeronaut when she ascended over Lyons. On 24 June 1784, 13-year-old Edward Warren ascended over Baltimore. Much more spectacular, however, was Jean Pierre Blanchard and Dr. John Jeffries's daring crossing of the Straits of Dover on 7 January 1785. Attempting the same feat in reverse, Pilâtre de Rozier constructed an ill-conceived joint balloon that featured a hydrogen cylinder tied to the top of a Montgolfière. He and Pierre Romain ascended from the Pas de Calais on 15 June 1785, but after a few minutes the hydrogen envelope exploded, resulting in both

Pilâtre de Rozier and Romain plummeting to their deaths before horrified onlookers.

THE USE OF MILITARY BALLOONS

Although some observers saw the balloon as a novelty, others quickly saw its military potential as Lana de Terzi had anticipated a century earlier and as Joseph Montgolfier had envisioned when he began his experiments. Indeed, on 17 October 1783, two days after Pilâtre de Rozier made the first manned ascent, André Giraud de Vilette accompanied Pilâtre de Rozier on a tethered ascent and immediately recognized the balloon's potential for military reconnaissance. Three days later, on 20 October, he published an account of his flight in *Journal de Paris,* and emphasized how the balloon could provide commanders with useful information on the location of enemy positions and recognition of enemy movements. The Englishman William Cooke published a pamphlet that reiterated the balloon's value in reconnaissance and stressed its importance as a first-line observation and communication post that could provide early warning of an invasion force landing on the English coast. By 1784 anonymous pamphlets were predicting that the balloon could also potentially serve offensive purposes by transporting troops and equipment. Indeed, Benjamin Franklin, who was serving as the United States ambassador to France, even speculated that balloons could be used to carry troops across enemy lines and noted that the cost of building a thousand balloons equaled that of a single ship-of-the-line. Despite these observations, no effort would be made to incorporate balloons for military purposes until after the outbreak of the French Revolution and the wars that it unleashed.

With the outbreak of war in 1792, the new revolutionary regime in France faced enormous pressures and thus turned to extraordinary means of defending itself. Joseph Montgolfier developed a plan for using balloons to drop bombs on Toulon, which had been occupied by the British. Encouraged by a report made by the famous mathematician Gaspard Monge, Lazare Carnot, known as "the Organizer of Victory," and his fellow members of the Committee of Public Safety authorized chemist Jean Marie-Joseph Coutelle to construct balloons for reconnaissance and observation, signaling, and disseminating propaganda. Based at the Château de Meudon, located on the outskirts of Paris, Coutelle and his crew eventually developed twelve balloons, using the Lavoisier-Meusnier method—which had been developed in 1784 by Antoine-Laurent Lavoisier and Lieutentant Jean-Baptiste Meusnier—to produce hydrogen by heating iron tubes filled with metal filings and then separating hydrogen from steam—a process that was cheaper than using sulfuric acid and that produced enough hydrogen to fill a balloon in approximately 15 hours.[2] In addition, Coutelle also developed a special varnish to seal the envelope and prevent the loss of hydrogen. By March 1794 Coutelle perfected the first military observation balloon, *L'Entreprenant,* which was to be anchored at approximately 1,700 ft and manned by two passengers, one to observe enemy positions and movements with a telescope and the other to signal to ground crews either by flag signal or dropped messages. Coutelle's successful demonstration of *L'Entreprenant* convinced the Committee of its feasibility and on 2 April 1794 it pushed through the National Convention an act creating a balloon company (the Première Compagnie d'Aérostiers). Appointed Brevet-Captain, Coutelle was given command of the First Company and put in charge of organizing new recruits, many of whom were chosen for their technical and scientific backgrounds. By the first of June, Coutelle and the First Company had brought *L'Entreprenant* to Maubeuge, headquarters of the French Army of the North, which was commanded by General Jean Baptiste Jourdan.

Although Jourdan was initially skeptical, asserting that he needed battalions not balloons, Carnot and the Committee of Public Safety insisted that he cooperate with Coutelle. After an initial military reconnaissance of enemy positions around Maubeuge on 2 June proved the balloon's usefulness, Coutelle's company moved to Charleroi, where Jourdan's adjutant, General Antoine Morelot, accompanied Coutelle on ascents to observe Austrian positions. The information gained convinced Morelot that the Austrian garrison was on the verge of collapse; in fact, it surrendered on 24 June 1794. Much more significant, however, was the role played by *L'Entreprenant* on 26 June 1794 at Fleurus, where Coutelle and Morelot remained aloft for approximately 9 hours and reported on the position of Austrian forces by dropping messages in small bags that were weighted with sand and equipped with rings that allowed them to slide down the tether cable. These aerial reports gave Jourdan an important advantage in the disposition of his troops and were used to direct French artillery fire against the enemy, contributing greatly to the French victory at Fleurus, which in turn helped secure the Revolution. In addition to the intelligence acquired in these engagements, the use of the balloon also raised the morale of French troops, who cheered upon its ascent. Its value can also be seen in the attempt of Austrian forces to shoot it down with artillery.

Although the extent to which the use of *L'Entreprenant* contributed to the French victory at Fleurus was debated at the time, most authorities recognized that it was at the least a useful tool for observing enemy positions and movements. As a result, the Convention, which had actually ordered the creation of a second balloon company prior to Fleurus, decided in October to establish the first military school devoted to aviation, the École Nationale Aérostatique, in order to train balloonists, repair and construct balloons, and develop balloon tactics. Once the Second Company joined the Army of the Rhine in 1795, it participated in the Battles of Mayence and Mannheim in 1795 and Rastadt, Stuttgart, and Donauwerth in 1796. The First Company was captured by the Austrians at Würzburg in 1796. Although Coutelle and his company joined Napoleon's Egyptian Exhibition in 1797, their equipment was left on ship, resulting in its destruction by the British in the Battle of Aboukir Bay. The mixed results of balloons and the lack of support given by military commanders, who preferred using cavalry for reconnaissance, led the Directory to disband the Second Company in 1799, a fate that befell the First Company in 1802.

Despite the demise of the French balloon companies, the idea of aerial warfare continued to inspire theorists, who saw the potential for using balloons for offensive purposes. In 1807 Denmark attempted to devise a hand-propelled dirigible that could be used to bomb British ships blockading Copenhagen. Although the plan failed, the Danes did use balloons for dropping propaganda leaflets into Sweden in hopes of inciting a revolt against the Swedish government. In 1808 Major Nicolas Lhomond, who had earlier served under Coutelle, attempted to convince Napoleon that it would be possible to construct a fleet of huge hot air balloons that could transport an army across the Channel for an invasion of England. Napoleon never seriously considered the proposal.

In the decades between the end of the Napoleonic Wars and the outbreak of the American Civil War, balloons were primarily used for pleasurable excursions or scientific experiments. On occasion, however, their military use was considered. During the Second Seminole War, for example, the United States faced such a difficult task in locating the Seminoles in the dense swamps of Florida that Colonel John H. Sherburne recommended in 1840 that the War Department consider using balloons at night to identify the campfires of hostile Seminoles. Although Major General Edmund P. Gaines gave a tentative endorsement to Sherburne's plan, the war ended in 1842 before it could be further acted upon. During the Mexican War, Pennsylvania aeronaut John Wise publicized a plan of using balloons for an aerial bombardment of Veracruz. Even though the army never acted on Wise's plan, his promotion of balloons during the 1850s would play an important role in leading the Union Army to establish the Balloon Corps during the Civil War. In Europe, British commanders rejected recommendations from lower level officers that balloons be used during the Crimean War, and although the French revived the use of balloons during the Italian War of 1859, they had little impact upon that war.

The one occasion in which balloons were used for a military purpose during the period between the Napoleonic Wars and the American Civil War came during the Revolutions of 1848 in Italy. When Austrian forces besieged Milan in 1848, Italians sent up paper Montgolfières that carried anti-Austrian leaflets designed to arouse the countryside to the city's defense. It is more significant that during their siege of Venice, the Austrians organized two aerial battalions that in July 1849 attempted to float approximately 200 small Montgolfières over the city. Each Montgolfière was designed with a time fuse that was to drop a 24–30-lb bomb. Making careful calculations based upon wind speed and direction, the Austrians attempted to insure that the bombs would drop at the appropriate moment and force Venice to capitulate. A few of the balloons were launched from the sea by the Austrian side-wheel steamer, the *Vulcano*. Unfortunately for the Austrians, a sudden change of wind caused the balloons to drift away from their intended target. At least one bomb fell in the city, but most were off target, and some even drifted back over the Austrian positions and the *Vulcano*. While this first attempt at "strategic bombing" created little damage, it would be repeated by the Japanese during the Second World War.

After the outbreak of the American Civil War in 1861, Northern balloonists Thaddeus Lowe, John LaMountain, and John Wise tried to convince Federal officials that aerial observation could give the Union Army a decisive advantage against the South. Although Brevet Lieutenant General Winfield Scott, commanding general of the Union armies, was reluctant to consider such innovations, President Abraham Lincoln personally endorsed Lowe's offer to form a balloon corps within the Union Army after a June 1861 demonstration in which Lowe ascended 1,000 ft above the White House and then successfully sent a telegraph message to the president. With Lincoln's blessing, the balloonists entered the Union Army's service, accompanying Federal forces to provide observation of Confederate forces and operating off naval ships (the *George Washington Parke Curtis* and the *Fanny*) in the Potomac and York Rivers. Lowe helped avoid panic after the First Battle of Manassas by ascending to a height of 3 miles and reporting that no Confederate forces were advancing on Washington. LaMountain carried out the first successful reconnaissance mission of the war after an ascent above Fort Monroe revealed two Confederate camps. Using a telegraph to signal messages from his balloon to the ground, Lowe helped direct artillery fire at Falls Church on 24 September 1861. In addition, Lowe developed a mobile hydrogen generator, using sulfuric acid and iron filings, that allowed for filling a balloon in less than 3 hours. During the Peninsular Campaign, Lowe's timely reconnaissance reports helped avoid military disasters at Four Oaks and Gaines's Mill. In addition, the presence of his balloons delayed Confederate attacks by forcing commanders to take extraordinary means, often long, out-of-the-way marches, to avoid detection.

Although Confederates used signal balloons along the Potomac throughout 1861, their first use of manned balloons did not come until the Peninsular Campaign of 1862. Major E. P. Alexander, a young Confederate artillery officer who had trained as a signal officer at West Point before resigning upon the outbreak of war, convinced Confederate General Joseph E. Johnston to bring a balloon to the York Peninsula for observing Union movements. Using a coated cotton hot air balloon, Captain John Randolph Bryan, a native of the peninsula, made three ascents before his balloon was lost after its moorings were severed. Alexander next used a hydrogen balloon that Captain Langdon Cheves had constructed in Savannah, where local women donated silk dresses to provide the materials needed for construction. Alexander used the balloon during the Seven Days' Battles to report Union troop movements at Gaines's Mill. The Confederate balloon was captured on 4 July 1862 after the tugboat on which it was being transported ran aground in the James River. Because of its meager resources, the Confederacy was forced to abandon further use of balloons.

Although balloons had proved their usefulness as a platform for observing enemy forces above and over the terrain, the Union Army would dissolve the Balloon Corps after the Battle of Chancellorsville in 1863. Most Union commanders, including general-in-chief of the army Major General Henry Halleck, discounted their effectiveness altogether. For one thing, even though balloons worked well for defensive or siege operations, they were ineffective for offensive operations when an army was on the move. Indeed, while en route to Manassas on 21 June 1861, John Wise's balloon became lodged in trees, which eventually tore the fabric. There were other limitations as well. Whereas telescopes allowed observers to see approximately 15–25 miles depending on visibility, observers needed to be within 5 miles to count tents and make accurate troop estimates, something that was not always possible. Confederate commanders also learned to use false campfires and wooden "Quaker" cannon to mislead enemy observers, resulting in faulty intelligence. Balloonists also faced problems with high winds, which had the effect of lowering altitude, not to mention jostling them around. Finally, although balloons could identify enemy positions, their presence both gave away one's position and attracted enemy artillery fire, much to the chagrin of nearby troops.

Although many European military observers had noted the value of balloons during the American Civil War, their use in the Franco–Prussian War probably had a greater impact upon their future use by European armies. After France suffered a crushing military defeat at Sedan, which left Paris under siege and isolated, French ballooning enthusiast Gaspard Félix Tournachon, known popularly as Nadar, approached officials of the new Third Republic and convinced them to use balloons in the defense of Paris and as part of the postal service so that Paris could remain in contact with the rest of France. On 23 September 1870 the balloon *Neptune* succeeded in escaping from the city and drifting over Prussian lines before finally descending 11 hours later some 60 miles away at Evreux. Two weeks later, on 7 October, Minister of the Interior Léon Gambetta escaped Paris in *L'Armand Barbès,* then made his away around Prussian lines to organize a citizen army in an effort to lift the siege. The French also perfected a microfilm system in which a small roll containing as many as 5,000 letters could be attached to a carrier pigeon and returned to Paris. Although balloonists had no control over their direction, 58 of the 66 that left Paris during the siege made it safely to friendly territory, carrying 102 passengers, more than 400 pigeons, and approximately 2.5 million letters.

The success of the Paris airlift, combined with the lessons from the American Civil War, convinced the major European powers to add a balloon corps to their military arsenal. The French were the first to do so in 1874, and all of the major powers followed suit within 10 years. Their primary use was for aerial observation, particularly in colonial campaigns, where the innovation of portable hydrogen cylinders made them more practical than before. Balloons operating in the U.S. Signal Corps also played an important role in the Spanish–American War, carrying out both reconnaissance and observation roles as balloons confirmed that the Spanish Fleet lay in Santiago harbor, located a trail for American forces to move through the dense jungle approaching San Juan Heights, and directed American artillery fire against Spanish positions. Balloons would also be used by the British in the Boer War, by the French in various colonial conflicts in Africa, and by the Russians and Japanese in the Russo–Japanese War.

To combat the problem of using observation balloons during high winds, in 1898 German Army Major August von Parseval and Captain H. Batsch von Siegsfeld designed the *drachen* balloon, a kite-balloon that was sausage-shaped and had a fin or vane, which acted like a kite in a heavy wind. This allowed it to take a diagonal altitude to the wind and maintain its position in winds up to 45 mph. The *drachen* design was soon adapted by the major powers, and these would play an important role during the military stalemate of trench warfare along the Western Front during the First World War. Despite the improved design that the kite-balloon offered, they remained ineffective as offensive weapons because they were at the mercy of the winds; however, by the time the *drachen* balloon was introduced in 1898, inventors were well on their way to achieving steerable flight with the airship.

THE DEVELOPMENT OF THE AIRSHIP

Whereas balloons had proven their usefulness as observation platforms in the American Civil War and as means of escaping Paris during the Franco–Prussian War, they were handicapped by their inability to maneuver, making them a prisoner of the wind, which, as the Austrians had discovered during the siege of Venice, was subject to change. In addition, balloons provided stationary targets that, at the very least, revealed to the enemy the position of its ground crew, who came to curse the inevitable artillery barrage. Even though a sphere was the best shape for maintaining stability and gas volume, it was next to impossible to navigate. The spherical shape of balloons also presented problems in the face of gusting winds, which could cause the balloon to bob and weave, sometimes to the danger of the crew in the gondola. This problem was recognized early on; in fact, French military engineer Lieutenant Jean-Baptiste Meusnier had suggested, prior to his death in 1793, that an elliptical or cigar-shaped airship equipped with some means of propulsion would provide a solution; unfortunately, the technology at the time did not provide the means. By 1850, however, successful demonstrations had been made with models using clockwork mechanisms.

The quest for steerable, powered flight was first fulfilled by Henri Giffard in 1852. Giffard, a brilliant steam engine designer, who had seen earlier demonstrations of model airships, constructed a nonrigid airship that was 140 ft long with a maximum diameter of 40 ft that tapered down to two conical points on each end and that held a volume of 88,287 cubic ft of hydrogen. The gondola was suspended beneath a 66-ft-long pole that was attached to netting that covered the envelope. The pole also included a large triangular sail rudder at its end that allowed for steering. The airship was powered by a 3 hp steam engine that Giffard had specially designed to turn an 11-ft, three-bladed propeller. To minimize the risk of sparks from the coke-fired boiler igniting the airship, Giffard had taken the precaution of venting the exhaust downward through wire gauze and with a mixture of released steam. On 24 September 1852, Giffard successfully flew his airship a distance of approximately 15.5 miles from the Paris Hippodrome to Trappe, averaging approximately 6 mph and reaching an altitude of nearly 5,000 ft. Although Giffard managed to steer a complete circle around the Hippodrome in subsequent trials, this could only be accomplished in absolutely calm conditions because his craft was not capable of flying against the wind. Giffard's attempts to build large airships ended in failure, partly because of flawed designs and partly because of lack of funds. Despondent over his perceived failure, he would commit suicide in 1882 at age 57.

In addition to Giffard, several other early attempts at powered flight deserve mention. During the Franco–Prussian War, French naval engineer Henri Dupuy de Lôme began work on an egg-shaped airship that was 49 ft 2.4 in. long, with a maximum diameter of 46 ft 10.8 in., and a 123,600-cubit-ft capacity. The most interesting feature of the design was that it was powered by a crew of eight men who operated hand cranks to turn a huge four-bladed, 29-ft, 6-in.-diameter propeller. Although the war ended before Dupuy de Lôme could demonstrate his ship, on 2 February 1872 he succeeded in averaging 6 mph on a short flight with a crew that had been "fueled" with liberal portions of rum. In 1883 Gaston and Albert Tissandier designed a 91-ft, 10-in.-long airship that had a maximum diameter of 30 ft and 2.4 in., and a capacity of 37,434 cubit ft that was powered by a 1.5 hp electrical engine. The extreme weight of the batteries, however, resulted in a 1:400 power/weight ratio. As a result, the design was capable of no more than 3 mph.

Although these first attempts at building steerable airships had resulted in aircraft that were capable of operating only in calm conditions, French Army Captains Charles Renard and Arthur Krebs would produce the first truly successful airship, *La France,* in 1884. After the French government reestablished its aeronautics research facility at Chalais Meudon in 1877, Renard, a graduate of the École Polytechnique, began researching various means of powering an airship and ultimately decided that an electrical motor presented the best option. Although army leaders expressed little interest in funding his design plans, Renard succeeded in 1881 in winning the support of French Premier Léon Gambetta, who personally provided 400,000 francs for research and development. By 1883 Krebs, who had joined Renard's efforts, had succeeded in producing an 8.5 hp electrical motor, while Renard had developed a lightweight battery system. In the meantime, with the assistance of Renard's brother, Paul, they had designed and constructed a streamlined envelope that was 165 ft long with a maximum diameter of 27 ft and a capacity of 66,000 cubic ft. A 108-ft-long, 4.5-ft-wide, and 6-ft-deep, torpedo-shaped gondola, constructed of lightweight bamboo and canvas, was suspended underneath the envelope to house the batteries and motor, which powered a 23-ft, four-bladed tractor propeller. Renard and Krebs relied upon a rudder, elevator, ballonnets, and sliding weight to provide steering and maintain stability. *La France* made its debut on 9 August 1884, taking off from Chalais Meudon and making a circular 23-minute flight, reaching a maximum speed of 15 mph, before landing at the same spot from which it had departed. Although the power of the batteries limited her range, *La France* demonstrated that a dirigible was practical. Although Renard later developed an internal combustion engine, lack of funding from the French government, which had become mired in the Panama Scandal and the Dreyfus Affair, left his efforts unfulfilled. Like many other frustrated aviation pioneers, Renard would commit suicide in 1905.

The year 1885 brought two innovations that would transform the quest for powered flight: the development of an effective internal combustion engine by Gottlieb Daimler and the electrolytic process for producing aluminum by P. L. T. Heroult and C. M. Hall. The first successful application of an internal combustion engine to aviation was made in 1888 by German clergyman Friedrich Wölfert, who used a Daimler engine to power a small airship of his own design. Although Wölfert's experiments eventually won the attention of Kaiser Wilhelm II and the Prussian Balloon Corps, Wölfert and an assistant were tragically killed on 12 June 1897 when the hydrogen in his balloon was ignited by the hot-tube, open-flame ignition system used by early Daimler engines. Meanwhile, the Austrian engineer David Schwarz had designed a rigid airship out of aluminum, which was completed in 1897 after his death. Although the airship succeeded in ascending, its inexperienced pilot panicked when the motor malfunctioned and released too much gas, resulting in a crash that damaged the airship beyond repair.

One of the most interesting figures in early aviation, Alberto Santos-Dumont, the eccentric son of a wealthy Brazilian coffee grower, would gain international fame after settling in Paris in 1892 and developing a series of small airships powered by internal combustion engines. Beginning with his first airship in 1898, Santos-Dumont became a frequent sight in Parisian skies, mooring his *Number 9* outside his apartment and his favorite restaurants. On 19 October 1901 he won a 129,000-franc prize sponsored by Henry Deutsch de la Meurthe for the first person to make a 7-mile round-trip from the Aéro-Club de France headquarters in St. Cloud to the Eiffel Tower and back within 30 minutes. He even made an in-flight repair on his engine by walking out on the keel of his airship. Although Santos-Dumont's interests were primarily for pleasure, he recognized the military potential of his blimps and predicted that they would be used at sea to spot U-boats. As will be noted later, Santos-Dumont would subsequently contribute to the development of heavier-than-air flight.

By far the most significant contributor to the development of airships for military purposes was Ferdinand Graf von Zeppelin. As a military observer for the Württemberg army during the American Civil War, Zeppelin had recognized the role that balloons had played for the Union Army. After retiring from the German Army in 1890, Zeppelin devoted his energies to developing a rigid, steerable airship, hiring a staff of engineers to assist him. Even though the German Army expressed some interest in both Zeppelin's ideas and those of his rival, David Schwarz, it was unwilling to fund an unproven product. Undeterred, Zeppelin raised 800,000 marks, 300,000 of which he provided himself, and began construction of his first airship (LZ-1) in June 1898 on Lake Constance. Completed 2 years later, the LZ-1 was a 420-ft-long, 38-ft-diameter rigid airship of aluminum-zinc alloy construction, containing nearly 400,000 cubic ft of hydrogen within 17 gas cells. It was powered by twin Daimler 14 hp engines, used a rudder for directional control, and relied upon a 220-lb weight that could be moved forward or backward for up-down control. On 2 July 1900 it made its maiden flight, lifting off from Lake Constance, with Zeppelin and four others on board, and landing 18 minutes later. The LZ-1's aluminum-zinc alloy structure proved to be understrengthed, forcing Zeppelin to ground it in October after just two additional flights. Nevertheless, Zeppelin had proven that a large rigid airship was practical and almost immediately began making design modifications for a larger, faster airship, the LZ-2.

Although Zeppelin obtained some funds from private investors and received grants from the Prussian government and the proceeds of a lottery in Württemberg, he ultimately had to expend the bulk of his own fortune to complete the LZ-2 in 1905. When the LZ-2 was destroyed in 1906 after making just two flights, patriotic Germans contributed enough funds to complete the LZ-3 by October 1906. Although the German General Staff had considered Zeppelin a quack for attempting such huge rigid airships and had begun developing smaller nonrigid dirigibles, the German Army suddenly became interested in Zeppelin's design after the LZ-3 completed a nonstop flight of 208 miles, purchasing the LZ-3 and ordering another. Despite the fiery crash and destruction of LZ-4 upon landing after a 24-hour test flight on 4 August 1908, the German government had seen enough to see potential in the airship. With government assistance, Zeppelin formed the Deutsche Luftschiffahrts-Aktien-Gesellschaft (DELAG). By the following year, DELAG had identified and solved most of the design problems in the early models in the new LZ-6, which made a successful cross-country flight on 25 August 1909. After the LZ-3 and the LZ-5 were both destroyed in 1910, however, some military leaders began to raise serious questions about continued funding for zeppelins.

Although the series of mishaps that befell zeppelins was an important factor in the army's reluctance to continue funding after 1910, another equally important factor was disagreement on how best to employ them. Although Zeppelin advocated a strategic reconnaissance role, deep behind enemy lines, army leaders were more interested in tactical reconnaissance. For that reason they favored the use of smaller nonrigid and semi-rigid dirigibles. In addition, the development of airplanes offered another alternative. As a result, the army did not order another zeppelin until mid-1913, by

which time the commercial airships of Zeppelin's DELAG had captivated public attention through their successful passenger and shipping operations. As will be discussed in later chapters, the zeppelin
would play an important role with the German Army and Navy during the First World War.

In the immediate aftermath of Zeppelin's test of LZ-1, other powers began their own airship programs. Inspired in part by Santos-
Dumont's blimps, French engineer Henri Julliot designed a semi-
rigid airship, using a steel-rod frame and calico covering, for the
Lebaudy Airship Company, owned by Paul and Pierre Lebaudy.
Named the *Lebaudy-Julliot I,* it successfully made its maiden voyage
on 13 November 1902 and would undergo several design modifications over the next few years. In 1905 the Lebaudy brothers donated
it to the French Army after the outbreak of the First Moroccan Crisis almost provoked war between France and Germany. Although the
French War Ministry subsequently approved a plan calling for a
fleet of 20 airships to be used as artillery spotters and for both short-
and long-range reconnaissance, the development of the airplane, as
will be discussed later, led the War Ministry to reallocate funds for
airplanes; thus, only 4 airships were available for use in 1914. In
1902 Stanley Spencer built the first British airship, a nonrigid 75-ft-
long and 20-ft-diameter airship that was powered by a 3 hp engine
and used for aerial advertising. E. T. Willows developed a series of
semi-rigid airships, which the Royal Flying Corps examined for
adoption, but ultimately rejected. The British Army's Balloon section, under Colonel J. E. Capper, designed the *Nulli Secundus* (Dirigible No.1) in 1907, a 122-ft-long and 26-ft-diameter nonrigid design that was powered by the 50 hp Antoinette engine. This was
followed in 1910 by the *Gamma,* which was powered by a 100 hp
engine and employed tail fins and swivel propellers to maintain excellent stability in the air. In Italy, Count Almerigo da Schio constructed the first Italian airship, *Italia I,* in 1905, but the Italian military did not begin using airships in maneuvers until 1911.
Nevertheless, Italy did successfully use airships against the Turks in
the Tripolitan War of 1911.

Of all the reactions to the zeppelin, the most intense by far came
from Great Britain, where the British press, led by Lord Northcutt's
Daily Mail, raised public fears to a fever pitch by pointing out the
dangers of an aerial attack. This was depicted in H. G. Wells's *The
War in the Air,* which was written in 1907 and published in 1908.
Wells captivated audiences with his depiction of strategic bombing,
arguing that aerial warfare would inevitably blur the lines between

combatants and civilians as warring nations targeted each other's major cities. Indeed, in the last paragraph of chapter seven, Wells used one of his protagonists to warn that air warfare could lead to the collapse of Western civilization itself:

> Think of it, Smallways: there's war everywhere! They're smashing up their civilisation before they have made it. The sort of thing the English did at Alexandria, the Japanese at Port Arthur, the French at Casablanca, is going on everywhere. Everywhere! Down in South America even they are fighting among themselves! No place is safe— no place is at peace. There is no place where a woman and her daughter can hide and be at peace. The war comes through the air, bombs drop in the night. Quiet people go out in the morning, and see air-fleets passing overhead—dripping death—dripping death![3]

While Wells's account focused on airships, a new development in humanity's quest for flight had already arisen—the heavier-than-air airplane—and it would be dramatically demonstrated a year later by Louis Blériot's flight across the English Channel on 25 July 1909.

THE QUEST FOR HEAVIER-THAN-AIR FLIGHT

Although the achievement of lighter-than-air flight was in many ways an application of science—the discovery of hydrogen as a lifting agent—to technology, the achievement of heavier-than-air flight would result more from advances in technology and their application to science. In particular, three major steps had to be completed before heavier-than-air flight could become a reality: first, an understanding of aerodynamics derived from physical experimentation and the development of new instruments; second, an efficient means of propulsion to achieve flight; and third, an understanding of the basic mechanics of flight (i.e., knowing how to fly). Until all three of these factors were mastered, heavier-than-air flight would remain a dream.

Where Leonardo da Vinci had relied upon observation and reason to develop theories of aerodynamics, a true understanding of aerodynamics did not begin to develop until scientific experimentation began to be carried out in the seventeenth and eighteenth centuries. Experiments on fluid mechanics in relation to ship design (i.e., calculation of forces resulting from a shape moving through a fluid) helped lay the foundation of aerodynamics. In addition, aerodynamics was advanced by the development of such new instruments as the pitot tube, which was invented by Henri Pitot in 1732 to measure the speed at which a fluid flowed. This is still used today to measure airspeed. There was also the whirling arm, which was invented by English military engineer Benjamin Robbins to measure air resistance in order to improve artillery projectiles.

Although Pitot and Robbins had no interest in aviation, early-nineteenth-century English aristocrat Sir George Cayley would have a tremendous impact on the science of aerodynamics. Although Cayley lacked a formal education, he was well read and greatly interested in science and technology. As a young man, he had developed an interest in aviation after experimenting with a draw-string helicopter toy. Even though he was also fascinated with lighter-than-air balloons and airships, he spent most of his time trying to develop a heavier-than-air flying machine. More important, unlike his predecessors and some of his successors, Cayley was not obsessed with trying to imitate the flight of birds; rather, he applied aerodynamic studies to the problem of flight. As Richard Hallion notes in *Taking Flight: Inventing the Aerial Age from Antiquity through the First World War*:

> He [Cayley] recognized winged aviation as a balancing act among the four forces of flight: one had to use *power* to overcome *drag* so that wings could produce *lift* to overcome *gravity*, or as he put it . . . "to make a surface support a given weight by the application of power to the resistance of the air." . . . Thus, . . . Cayley distinguished between the problem of *sustaining* a plane in the air via the lifting power of its wings and *propelling* a plane through the air via the power of its engine.[4]

Through a combination of theoretical contemplation and practical experimentation—he was the first to use the whirling arm for aerodynamic studies—Cayley came to understand the importance of lift, thrust, and drag as early as 1799. By 1800 he had even conceptualized the basic shape of an airplane with fuselage, cockpit, and fixed wings. His experiments also revealed the importance of dihedral—an upward angle of the wing—and wing camber—curvature of the wing—to provide greater lift and stability. With these concepts in place, in 1804 Cayley successfully designed and flew a 5-ft-long glider. In 1809 he constructed a glider that carried a 10-year-old boy aloft for a few yards. This was followed in 1853 by an even larger glider that carried his coachman aloft for a short distance. Cayley published several works on aviation in the interval between his successful experiments with gliders. In addition, he devoted research to airships, possibly because he recognized the ease of their lifting capability compared with the lack of a power system capable of providing lift to a fixed-wing airplane.

Influenced by Cayley's writings, Englishmen William Henson and John Stringfellow obtained a patent for a steam-powered aerial carriage, dubbed the *Ariel*, in 1842 and formed the Aerial Transit Company in 1843 in an effort to raise capital. Although their design featured many elements of a modern airplane—cambered wings, an elevator, a rudder, tricycle landing gear—attempts to build a model that could actually fly failed because of the lack of an engine with a low weight-to-power ratio.

In the mid-nineteenth century, aeronautical enthusiasts in France and Great Britain founded popular societies designed to promote aeronautical research and raise public interest. One of the founding members of the Aeronautical Society of Great Britain, Francis Herbert Wenham—a marine engineer—is significant for two major achievements that ultimately contributed to heavier-than-air flight. First, he correctly hypothesized that a wing would provide greater lift if it were broader in span. Second, he developed the first wind tunnel, which offered a far more accurate instrument for aerodynamic measurements than the whirling arm. In addition, the wind tunnel conclusively proved his hypothesis that a wing with a broad span and narrow chord would provide greater lift. Wenham's work was later furthered by Horatio Phillips, who constructed a more powerful wind tunnel and experimented with a variety of cambered (i.e., curved) winged surfaces, proving that cambered surfaces provided greater lift than did flat surfaces.

In 1871 Alphonse Pénaud, the son of a French naval officer, successfully demonstrated a model airplane that flew approximately 130 ft before his fellow members of the Société Générale de Navigation Aérienne. The model, which consisted of a 20-in. dowel rod to which Pénaud had affixed cambered wings and a small diamond-shaped tail, was driven by a rear-mounted propeller that was powered by twisted rubber cords. The wings, which spanned approximately 18 in., and tail were set at an upward angle (dihedral) and provided stable flight. Pénaud's demonstration proved that powered, heavier-than-air flight was possible provided that the problems of scale, power, and control could be solved. With the assistance of Paul Gauchot, Pénaud designed and patented a plan for a steam-powered aircraft in 1876. Whereas Pénaud's design most certainly would not have succeeded, it offered great promise; unfortunately, failure to win financial backing and criticism from his contemporaries drove Pénaud to commit suicide in 1880.

In 1883 Alexandre Goupil designed a bird-shaped aircraft with highly cambered wings, which spanned approximately 19 ft and 8 in. and had a wing area of 292 square ft. In a December 1883 test of an engine-less version that was tethered to the ground, it succeeded in lifting two men in the face of a 14-mph breeze. His most important contribution was the invention of elevons on each wing, which provided for both pitch and roll control. Although Goupil abandoned his research because of lack of funding, in 1916 Glenn Curtiss, who was involved in a bitter patent suit against the Wright brothers, would install a 100 hp Curtiss OXX engine in an aircraft based on Goupil's design and briefly fly it in an effort to improve his case.

By far the most controversial figure in the early quest for flight was the Frenchman Clement Ader, who was born near Toulouse in 1841 and educated at the École Industrielle in Toulouse. Although he exhibited interest in observing flying insects and birds as a child, it was France's defeat in the Franco–Prussian War that launched his interest in aviation. For Ader, military aviation was more than a matter of patriotism; it was a matter of national survival in France's struggle against Germany. Although Ader shared success as a bicycle manufacturer with the Wright brothers, his similarities ended there. Where the Wrights would conduct long experiments with models and gliders before attempting to construct an airplane, Ader gave these steps only precursory efforts before leaping toward constructing an aircraft. In doing so, he attempted to follow the example of nature, rather than of science, designing a steam-powered airplane with batlike wings that spanned more than 50 ft and a four-bladed tractor propeller that had been carved to resemble bird feathers. Named the *Éole* after the Greek god of the winds (Aeolus), the craft possessed a highly efficient 20 hp engine that weighed just 200 lbs, but it lacked any practical aerodynamic controls—indeed, Ader planned on increasing or decreasing the power to provide pitch control. Worse, the boiler and condenser were placed in front of the pilot's seat and both obstructed the pilot's forward view and created immense drag.

After working in secret for some 5 years, Ader unveiled the *Éole* on 9 October 1890 before the public at Armainvilliers, making a series of high-speed runs before briefly skimming above the ground for a distance of 165 ft. Although this hardly qualifies as a successful flight in that it was not sustained and certainly not controlled, Ader nevertheless attracted the attention of the French government and military leaders, most especially Minister of War Charles-Louis de Freycinet, who on 3 February 1892 issued the first military contract in history for an airplane. At a price of 550,000 francs, Ader was to construct an airplane that could fly 35 mph and reach an altitude of 1,000 ft, while carrying either a pilot and observer for aerial reconnaissance duties or a pilot and 165 lbs of bombs to attack enemy forces. Over the next 5 years, Ader toiled in secrecy—leading to allegations of fraud—before finally producing the *Avion III-Aquilon* in 1897, which was basically a larger, twin-engine version of the *Éole* that possessed the same basic aerodynamic flaws as its predecessor. Even worse was Ader's design for a circular runway to demonstrate the *Avion III*. Deprived of the benefit of taking off into a constant headwind, the *Avion III* lost what little chance it might have had and its 14 October 1897 trial was an absolute failure. Although the tail lifted from the ground, the front failed to lift. Furthermore, the *Avion III* was heavily damaged after being blown off course by crosswinds—an adverse result of the faulty runway configuration. Even on a straight runway, however, the *Avion III* would not have flown.

Although Ader attempted to gloss over the *Avion III*'s failure, blaming the adverse weather conditions of the trial, and appealed for additional government funding, the French government, which had been discredited by the Panama Scandal and was now mired in the Dreyfus Affair, had little time or political standing to provide further funding for what Ader's contemporary, Samuel Langley, director of the Smithsonian Institute, described as an enormous bat. Thus, after spending 550,000 francs of government funds and an additional 700,000 francs of his own, Ader ended his aviation research, turning instead to automobiles. Several years later he would re-emerge to dispute the Wright brothers' place as the first to fly, claiming that he had made a flight of some 300 ft in the *Éole* in September 1891—a claim that has never been substantiated and has generated controversy over his place in aviation history. Although Ader had succeeded in developing steam engines with a low weight-to-power ratio—those for the *Avion III* were 6.4 lbs per 1 hp—he had neglected the aerodynamics research of predecessors such as Cayley, Pénaud, and Phillips. Ader consequently failed, despite the advantages of his financial resources, initial government support, and engineering skill. Another casualty was that France, which had given birth to the balloon and the airship, would not give birth to heavier-than-air airplanes.

During the same time that Ader was working on the *Avion III*, Hiram Maxim, an American-born inventor who had moved to Great Britain and had won international fame and great wealth with the Maxim machine gun, was conducting his own aviation experiments. Unlike Ader, who had simply started building an airplane, Maxim first attempted to solve the problems of lift and propulsion. Believing that greater size would provide greater lift, Maxim constructed a test vehicle of gargantuan proportion—it weighed 8,000 lbs, its biplane configuration had a wing area of approximately 4,000 square ft, and its twin 180 hp steam engines turned 17-ft-diameter propellers. Designed to run along a rail track that was laid at Baldwyns Park in Kent, Maxim's test rig was restricted from rising more than 2 ft. Through his experiments, Maxim was able to measure lift and test a variety of propeller designs to obtain higher thrust. Although Maxim succeeded in raising it off the ground during a 31 July 1894 test run, the test rig was damaged and was never used again, in part because Maxim was unwilling to bankroll continued experiments by himself. Nevertheless, his experiments on propeller design and his use of steel-tube construction proved to be important for future inventors.

Where Maxim had sought to solve the problem of propulsion first, his contemporary, the German Otto Lilienthal, like the Wright brothers, believed that one must first understand flight itself and that this could be achieved only by actually flying. Born in Berlin into a working-class family in 1848, he had attended several technical schools, becoming a skilled machinist. After briefly serving in the Prussian Army during the Franco–Prussian War, Lilienthal, through hard work and dedication, became the owner of his own machine shop in 1880, which would provide him the financial means and technical expertise to pursue his interest in flying. Like Ader and many of his other predecessors, he had been keenly interested in birds and hoped to apply the knowledge gained from studying bird flight to the problem of heavier-than-air flight. Toward that end, between 1891 and 1896 he would test aerodynamic theories by building a series of hang gliders (eighteen different designs) and making almost 2,000 flights. He even went so far as to build an artificial hill outside Berlin so he could test his gliders. Lilienthal unfortunately relied upon his shifting body weight as a means of control, which ultimately proved fatal. During his final glide on 9 August 1896, a heavy gust of wind induced a stall from which he could not recover, causing him to plummet to the ground from a height of 50 ft. He died of his injuries the next day. Although his aerodynamic tables would prove to be incorrect, primarily because he relied upon a whirling arm instead of a wind tunnel for his calculations, and he remained committed to a powered ornithopter approach, his inspiration was immense. In particular, his influence on the Wrights was crucial because it convinced them of the need to master the art of controlling an aircraft before actually attempting to build one. Indeed, the Wrights were so determined to avoid a fatal stall similar to Lilienthal's that they would persist in using a canard design (tail first), which placed the elevator in the front of their gliders and aircraft, even though this resulted in a poor center of gravity and hence an inherently unstable aircraft.

Like Lilienthal, Octave Chanute, a French-born, naturalized American citizen, who had become a successful, wealthy civil engineer, believed that knowledge of flight was a prerequisite to building a heavier-than-air flying machine. After retiring at age 57 in 1889, Chanute devoted his energies, his intellect, and his resources into compiling all known data on aviation, both publishing his research and hosting conferences that would bring together aviation pioneers from around the world to share their knowledge. Assisted by Augustus M. Herring and William Avery, Chanute began building a series of gliders in 1895. Drawing in part from his experience in building railroad bridges, Chanute's gliders featured Pratt trussing and wire-braced wings that provided strength to its lightweight spruce and silk construction. His most successful version was a biplane configuration completed in 1896. Although Chanute still relied upon the pilot's shifting weight to control the glider, it was far more advanced than Lilienthal's gliders. More important, Chanute would serve as a sounding board for the Wright brothers, encouraging them in their research and publicizing their achievements. In many ways, their success was a culmination of his efforts.

Whereas the Wrights would work in relative obscurity in the quest for flight, one of their contemporary aviation enthusiasts, Samuel Langley, had both the fortune and misfortune of working in the limelight. As secretary of the Smithsonian Institution, Langley brought a high profile to his efforts to solve the problem of heavier-than-air flight. After conducting exhaustive tests with a whirling arm, Langley constructed and successfully launched a series of steam-powered model aircraft from a houseboat anchored in the Potomac River. His most successful model, *Aerodrome No. 5*, had a 13-ft wingspan, was powered by a 1 hp steam engine, and on 6 May 1896 flew approximately 90 seconds in a circular pattern for almost 3,300 ft.

Although Langley's experiments drew widespread attention, in part because of his prestigious position, it was not until the approach of the Spanish–American War in early 1898 that Washington officials, especially Assistant Secretary of the Navy Theodore Roosevelt, became interested in building an aircraft capable of carrying a person. After a special Army–Navy review board evaluated Langley's work and issued a 29 April 1898 report calling upon the War Department to provide funding, Langley received $50,000 in grants for developing an airplane. Assisted by Charles Manley, a engineering student at Cornell University, Langley began work on the *Great Aerodrome,* a scaled-up version of the *Aerodrome No. 5,* which was to be powered by a 52 hp gasoline motor. Langley unfortunately failed to consider that a larger version would require a far stronger structure and design. In addition, he provided few control features on the plane other than a pivoting tail and small rudder. After 5 years and $73,000, Langley's *Great Aerodrome* proved to be an utter disaster that resulted in two highly publicized failed attempts to launch it from the houseboat on 7 October 1903 and again on 8 December 1903. Langley was pilloried in the press by reporters and politicians, many of whom ridiculed his waste of taxpayers' money and scoffed at the very idea that heavier-than-air flight would be possible in the near future, even if at all. Indeed, whereas the *New York Times* was somewhat kinder than most in its editorial, it nevertheless warned others of the futility of pursuing the quest and took a backhand slap at the eccentric Santos-Dumont, concluding:

> We hope that Prof. Langley will not put his substantial greatness as a scientist in further peril by continuing to waste his time, and the money involved, in further airship experiments. Life is short, and he is capable of service to humanity incomparably greater than can be expected to result from trying to fly. Men like Santos-Dumont should have this field all to themselves. For students and investigators of the Langley type there are more useful employments, with fewer disappointments and mortifications than have been the portion of aerial navigators since the days of Icarus.[5]

Ironically on 17 December 1903, just 9 days after Langley's failure and 8 days after the *Times* editorial, Orville and Wilbur Wright would prove the skeptics wrong and usher in the era of heavier-than-air flight at Kitty Hawk, North Carolina.

Although it is certainly true that Orville and Wilbur Wright achieved their success on the pioneering work of others and the availability of technology that their predecessors had lacked, the fact remains that they succeeded after years of intense study and practical experimentation. In addition, it is wrong to think of the Wrights as mere mechanics or skilled craftsmen; their approach to the problem of flight was scientific. Although neither attended college—Wilbur (born in 1867) had been admitted to Yale but was unable to attend after being injured by a baseball bat and Orville (born in 1871) did not graduate from high school—both brothers were well read, skilled in mathematics, and possessed keen analytical minds. They combined this with a hard work ethic and determination to succeed in whatever task they were undertaking. Furthermore, they had an uncanny ability to get to the heart of a problem and seek a solution. Most important, the Wrights understood that the most critical issue that had to be solved was learning how to control a plane in the air, not power it. In this, they followed the example of Lilienthal and Chanute, both in the sense of understanding that actual experience in the air was necessary and that shifting the pilot's weight was no solution to the problem of control, as Lilienthal's tragic death had proven. This also indicated another quality—extreme self-confidence. They firmly believed that if they mastered the art of controlled flight, the problem of propulsion could be easily remedied.

Like many other aviation pioneers, the Wrights had developed an interest in flight at an early age, specifically when their father, a bishop in the Church of the United Brethren in Christ, brought home a rubber-band powered helicopter in 1878. Like Ader, the brothers operated a successful bicycle business, beginning with a repair shop in 1892 and venturing into manufacturing in 1896. Their success would give them the time needed to devote to research and the financial means to conduct it. Newspaper accounts of Lilienthal's exploits renewed their interest in aviation and news of his death left them determined to solve the problem of heavier-than-air flight. After reading everything on flight that was available locally, in 1899 Wilbur wrote the Smithsonian Institution, seeking and receiving a packet of materials on aviation. In addition, the Wrights initiated a fruitful correspondence with Octave Chanute, who would encourage them in their work, observing their experiments, and who in 1901 warmly introduced Wilbur when he gave a presentation about his and Orville's experiments to a meeting of the Western Society of Engineers.

From their readings the Wrights became the first to grasp fully the three-dimensional nature of flight and therefore sought to insure that the pilot had control over those three dimensions: pitch (up and down flight); yaw (left and right flight); and roll (banking left and right flight). Of the three dimensions, roll would prove to be the most critical, for making a controlled turn in an aircraft would require a rolling, or banking turn. By the end of 1899 the Wrights were on their way to solving this issue by experimenting with wing-warping on kites. They then turned to building gliders, borrowing heavily from Chanute, but incorporating wing-warping to provide control. After consulting the U.S. Weather Bureau about the best place for sustained winds in which they could test their gliders, they selected Kitty Hawk, North Carolina. After testing flying gliders in 1900 and 1901 with mixed results, the Wrights reached the conclusion that Lilienthal's aerodynamic calculations were incorrect. Based on their practical experience in the air and the use of a wind tunnel that they constructed themselves, they gained a thorough understanding of lift and drag and incorporated this in the design of their 1902 glider before returning to Kitty Hawk in August 1902. The 1902 glider had a longer wingspan of 32 ft (compared with 22 ft for the 1901 glider and 15 ft for the 1900 glider) and 2 ft less chord. Tests quickly revealed that it provided greater lift and better overall performance. Most important, however, after attempting several modifications to the control system, the Wrights developed an integrated control system that utilized the elevator, rudder, and wing-warping to control pitch, yaw, and roll.

Having obtained success with their 1902 glider—they made more than 1,000 flights, including one of more than 600 ft by Wilbur—they returned to Dayton, convinced that all they needed now was a means of power to achieve ultimate success. This would involve acquiring an engine with a low weight-to-power ratio and an effective propeller. Their most significant breakthrough was to think of the propeller as a moving wing. After building a larger wind tunnel to test propeller designs and developing new aeronautical tables, they succeeded in hand carving two propellers from spruce, with each having a 66 percent efficiency ratio (power of thrust compared with the power output of the engine), where Maxim had achieved an efficiency ratio of less than 50 percent. In the meanwhile, the Wrights had written ten engine manufacturers seeking an internal combustion engine with a low weight-to-power ratio. When none responded favorably, the Wrights, who had already built a one-cylinder engine to run equipment within their bicycle shop, simply designed their own with the able assistance of their shop foreman Charlie Taylor. Together, they produced a four-cylinder engine that weighed approximately 200 lbs and provided 16 hp for a weight-to-power ratio of 12.5 to 1. They then designed a larger version of their 1902 glider—it would have a 40-ft wingspan—and on 23 September 1903 departed for Kitty Hawk, prepared to make history.

After arriving at Kitty Hawk on 25 September 1903, the Wrights set to work repairing their hangar and building a new workshop in order to assemble the *Flyer* once all the parts arrived. Although the *Flyer* was assembled by early November, the Wrights experienced problems with their engine, which damaged the propeller shafts, resulting in a 5-week delay as first Charlie Taylor attempted to repair them in Dayton and ship them back, then Orville finally went back to Dayton and built new ones. After winning a coin toss to determine who would fly first, Wilbur made the first attempt on 14 December. He unfortunately pulled back on the elevator too soon, resulting in a quick take off stall and crash after traveling just a few feet. After making repairs to the *Flyer* over the next 2 days, the brothers waited for a break in the weather. Finally, at 10:35 on the morning of 17 December 1903, Orville made history by taking off and flying 120 ft in 12 seconds. Of the four flights made that day, the last, with Wilbur manning the wing, was the longest at 852 ft and 59 seconds; unfortunately, while readying it for a fifth flight, a heavy gust of wind rolled the *Flyer* over and destroyed it.[6]

Although the press was somewhat skeptical at the initial reports of the Wright Brothers' success, understandably so in the aftermath of Langley's well-publicized failure, there was no doubt by the summer of 1904 that the brothers had succeeded as they continued testing a new version of the *Flyer* near their home in Dayton. Although Dayton did not offer the high winds available at Kitty Hawk, the Wrights were able to solve the problem of low wind by developing a trebuchet-launching system that used a falling counterweight to accelerate the *Flyer* quickly down its rail track. After making 105 flights in 1904, the vast majority of which were short hops, many of which ended in crashes, the Wrights realized that further modifications to their design were needed. By enlarging the elevator and extending it further forward of the wings, they finally achieved the world's first practical airplane in the summer of 1905; one that was capable of long sustained flight (limited only by the fuel capacity of the tank) and that possessed great maneuverability. Having achieved success with the 1905 *Flyer* and realizing that they possessed a monopoly on heavier-than-air flight, the Wrights were now ready to market their aircraft and toward that end, they turned to the armies of the world's great powers.

MILITARY AVIATION ON
THE EVE OF WORLD WAR I

From the beginning the Wrights had understood that their airplane had potential as a military weapon, especially in light of the international rivalries of the time, such as the tensions between France and Germany during the First Moroccan Crisis in 1905. After the U.S. Army rejected their initial offer on the grounds that they had not yet demonstrated its operational practicality—indeed the U.S. Patent Office would not issue a patent until 1906 for the same reasons—the Wrights then pursued negotiations with foreign powers, attempting to play one against the other in order to drive up the price. The French expressed the most interest because Octave Chanute had promoted the Wrights' successes before the Aéro-Club de France. French Artillery Captain Ferdinand Ferber immediately recognized the potential of their airplane for military purposes and encouraged the French War Ministry to accept the Wrights' price of $200,000 (1 million francs). Although the French government was reluctant to pay such an amount, Ferber enlisted the support of Henri Letellier, son of the publisher of *Le Journal,* who succeeded in bringing enough public opinion to bear upon the government that it opened negotiations with the Wrights. French demands for long-term exclusive rights and that the Wrights reach an altitude of 300 meters by 1 August 1906 eventually caused negotiations to break down. Two other factors also contributed to the collapse of negotiations: the peaceful resolution of the First Moroccan Crisis removed the military pressure for a quick agreement and the Brazilian Santos-Dumont managed to make two brief takeoffs in a heavier-than-air craft in Paris on 23 October and 12 November 1906, respectively. Although Santos-Dumont achieved a flight of just 722 ft on the last attempt, he demonstrating that the Wrights might not have a monopoly for long.

Once negotiations with the French broke down, the Wrights engaged Charles Flint, a leading arms manufacturer, as their agent for selling the *Flyer* outside the United States. Although they had moral reservations about Flint's unscrupulous business dealings, they needed his contacts in Europe. After joining Flint in France, the Wright brothers grew increasingly exasperated with the French because of the political and economic intrigues involved in the negotiations; so much so that they attempted to enlist interest among the Germans. Although 1907 ended without an agreement to sell the *Flyer,* the following year would bring the Wrights success and international acclaim. It would also prove to be the high point of their career.

In December 1907, just 4 months after establishing an Aeronautical Division, the U.S. Signal Corps issued specifications for its first military aircraft, demanding that it have a range of 125 miles, that it possess an average speed of 40 mph, and that it be easy to disassemble and reassemble for transportation. After receiving 41 bids, most from crackpots, the War Department accepted the $25,000 bid made by the Wright brothers—a price that was far less than what they had demanded from the French. By then the Wrights had improved their *Flyer* by adding two seats and an improved motor, capable of 35 hp. Orville arrived in Fort Meyers, Virginia, in August 1908, and began flight demonstrations the following month. After making several flights, including some with passengers, Orville crashed on 17 September, killing his passenger, Lieutenant Thomas E. Selfridge—the first air crash victim. Despite the accident, which also severely injured Orville, the press provided favorable coverage of the *Flyer* and the U.S. Army proceeded to purchase the *Wright Military Flyer* the following year on 2 August 1909, becoming the first military power to possess an airplane. Meanwhile, Wilbur had headed to France to demonstrate the *Flyer* before a skeptical French public. After his successful flight at Hunaudièrs on 8 August 1908, Wilbur became a public celebrity, winning numerous awards, including membership in the Legion of Honor.

Although 1908 was certainly a banner year for the Wrights, the state of aviation technology was soon to pass them by as new designers entered the field of competition. Indeed, by 1908 they were no longer the only American aircraft designers. In that year the *Scientific American* magazine awarded Glenn Curtiss the first aviation prize offered in the United States for his *June Bug*—primarily because the Wrights had avoided public demonstrations for fear their design would be copied. Curtiss had already established a reputation as an aviation engineer, having designed an internal combustion engine in 1905 to power Thomas Scott Baldwin's semi-rigid airship, which was later purchased by the Signal Corps. Curtiss, therefore, quickly emerged as a major rival to the Wrights, and in 1910 formed the Curtiss Aeroplane Company. During an air show on Long Island later that summer, Curtiss made the first public military display of an aircraft, when an expert army marksman, Lieutenant Jacob E. Fickel, successfully struck a target while riding as a passenger in a Curtiss aircraft piloted by Charles Willard. This successful demonstration contributed to Congress authorizing $125,000 to purchase additional aircraft for the Signal Corps. As previously mentioned, Curtiss's success would lead to prolonged litigation in which the Wrights claimed that he had copied their control system.[7]

The rise of European firms was much more significant than the competition from Curtiss, however, because European militaries were to provide the primary market for aircraft. Even as Wilbur wowed French crowds in 1908, the French were making significant strides of their own through the pioneering efforts of Charles and Gabriel Voisin, Henry and Maurice Farman, Léon Lavavasseur, Armand Deperdussin, Léon Delagrange, Raymond Saulnier, and Louis Blériot. Based in part on their spirit of cooperation in sharing ideas and designs, the French would soon eclipse the Wrights. The biggest thing contributing to French success was their development of engines, which was partly the result of their thriving automobile industry. In particular, Lavavasseur's Antoinette engine (a water-cooled 8 cylinder V-type that provided 50 hp), introduced in 1905 for use in his powerboats, provided the French with a power plant that was readily adapted for their first aircraft. This was soon followed in 1908 by the revolutionary Gnôme Omega (an air-cooled 7 cylinder rotary engine that provided 50 hp but weighed less than half that of the Antoinette). Its unique design featured a fixed crank-shaft, which the engine spun around, cooling itself in the air, and moving in conjunction with the propeller. The Gnôme Omega truly revolutionized the aircraft industry as newer, larger versions would offer greater power with a low weight-to-power ratio. It is not surprising that rotary engines were one of the most popular power plants for early WWI aircraft, as will be noted in Chapter Two. As a result of these changes, 1909 would prove to be a critical turning point in aviation history, one that was dramatized by two spectacular events—Blériot's crossing of the English Channel on 25 July and the first international air competition held at Reims between 22 and 29 August—that clearly revealed that Europe had surpassed the United States as the home of aviation and would have an important impact on military aviation.

Even before Wilbur Wright's flights in 1908, Captain Ferber had predicted that some daring pilot would soon cross the English Channel. When Wright's final flight in 1908 lasted some 2 hours and 40 minutes and covered approximately 75 miles, it was clear that crossing the English Channel was a practical goal. Lord Northcliffe, publisher of the *Daily Mail,* offered a £1,000 prize for the first to accomplish a cross-Channel flight. After Henry Latham, a wealthy Englishman who resided in France, was forced to ditch his

Antoinette IV after his engine failed just 7 miles into the trip, attention turned to Louis Blériot, who had made himself a serious candi-
date for the Channel crossing after winning a 14,000-franc prize for
completing a 42-kilometer flight from Etampes to Orléans in less
than 45 minutes in early July. Upon learning of Latham's failed
flight on 19 July, Blériot set out for the coast, establishing his flight
base at Sangatte. Poor weather forced him to delay his attempt until
the early morning hours of 25 July. Informed around 2:00 a.m. that
the weather was clearing, Blériot arose quickly, determined to take
off before Latham. At 4:35 a.m. his Blériot XI monoplane lifted off
and carried him across the Channel, where he crash-landed—something he was prone to do—36 minutes later near Dover. The reaction to Blériot's flight was significant and overwhelming. Although
Blériot received a hero's welcome for his courageous flight, the
British press and public recognized the implications. England was
no longer an island cut off from the continent and protected by its
fleet. The *Daily Mail* and other papers emphasized that Britain was
behind in the air race and needed to take immediate steps in developing air power.

The second significant event of 1909 was the Reims air competition, which featured more than 38 aircraft competing for 200,000
francs in prize money. The air competition attracted the top names
in French aviation as well as such prominent politicians as Britain's
David Lloyd George. The competition quickly revealed that European designers had not only caught up with the Wrights and Curtiss, but had surpassed them. Of the eight top prizes offered, the
French won seven. The sole non-French victor was Curtiss in the
fastest plane category. Far more significant, the Reims air competition, combined with the excitement over Blériot's cross-Channel
flight, proved the airplane's viability to military leaders.

Blériot's crossing and the Reims air show also greatly increased the
public's fascination with aircraft, a fascination that was increasingly
focusing on its military potential. Throughout Europe, patriotic citi-
zens and wealthy and influential individuals formed such organiza-
tions as the Air Fleet League in Germany and the Aerial League of
the British Empire, whose purpose was to lobby for air power. Inspired by nationalism, Germans contributed more than 7 million
marks, Frenchmen more than 6 million francs, and Italians more
than 3.5 million lire to develop their country's air power in 1912
alone. Even Greeks contributed sufficient funds to purchase four
planes, which went operational in 1913. By 1912 air shows were also
developing military tones with demonstrations of aerial bombing.

The close cooperation of civilian aviators and military officials was furthered by agreements that provided for pilots and their planes to enter military service in the event of an outbreak of war. Civilian pilots also participated in prewar military games, demonstrating the effectiveness of aerial observation and reconnaissance, although the difficulty of relaying information remained to be settled.

The French were the first to begin making aircraft purchases, in part because French military leaders saw that the aircraft might give them an edge over the Germans and that purchases were necessary for stimulating the fledgling industry. By the end of 1910, the French military possessed thirty planes and had ordered an additional sixty-one. In November 1911 the French held their first military air show, in which a Nieuport monoplane won the top prize for achieving an average speed of 70 mph. The following year tire manufactures André and Edouard Michelin, acting with the full support of the French War Ministry, funded an international competition in order to spur aviation development. In a series of aerial games held between January and September 1912, aircraft demonstrated their usefulness for artillery spotting. Lieutenant Riley Scott, whose bombsight had failed to win the approval of the U.S. War Department, demonstrated that aerial bombardment was also feasible, winning a large cash prize for bomb-dropping. By 1912 the other European great powers, and even smaller states like Greece and Romania, were following the French example, purchasing or developing aircraft of their own and training pilots.

Although Germany had concentrated most of its early efforts in aviation on airships, the success of French aviators in the 1911 French air games convinced the German General Staff to begin a heavier-than-air program. Nevertheless, the German War Ministry issued few contracts for aircraft until 1913, in sharp contrast to their French rivals. As a result, German aircraft firms remained small. Indeed, many remained in existence only because of their contracts to train German pilots. One of the key figures in Germany's aviation industry was Franz Schneider, who became chief designer for Luft-Verkehrs Gesellschaft (L.V.G. or Air Transport Company) in 1912. Schneider had previously worked in France with the Nieuport firm. Prior to the outbreak of war in 1914, Schneider designed excellent aircraft as well as several innovative inventions, including an interrupter gear for firing a machine gun through the arc of the propeller, a method for firing through a hollow shaft of the airscrew, and a ring-mounting system that allowed an observer to swing a machine gun onto a moving target. Despite these innovations, the General Staff failed to see any other role for aircraft than reconnaissance. By 1913, the War Ministry finally began to increase the number of contracts for aircraft, and, as will be seen in Chapter 2, this would allow Germany to narrow the French lead, in part because many of the early French military aircraft were already becoming obsolete.

Compared with the other European powers, the British government provided little support for prewar aviation. Up until the time of Louis Blériot's cross-Channel flight in 1909, the British War Department had invested a mere $10,000 on military aircraft. Indeed, the only British military aircraft available in 1910 were two Farman biplanes owned by Lieutenant L. D. L. Gibbs and Captain Bertram Dickson and one Blériot monoplane owned by Captain J. D. B. Fulton. It was not until after Dickson and Gibbs demonstrated the reconnaissance value of their aircraft during the army's 1910 military exercises that the War Department belatedly saw the need for military aviation. On 1 April 1911 it officially created the Air Battalion within the Royal Engineers, creating an airship company and an airplane company. At the time the airplane company possessed just five aircraft, designated only for reconnaissance use. After the Second Moroccan Crisis almost produced war between Germany and France in the fall of 1911 and the Italians used aircraft to drop bombs on the Turks in the Tripolitan War, however, the British War Department felt more pressed to act, creating the Royal Flying Corps in April 1912. Although it had earlier reconstituted the Royal Balloon Factory as the Royal Aircraft Factory in 1911, the British government relied upon it primarily for design and experimentation, rather than construction—it would construct just 48 aircraft by 1914. More important, without the same level of government contracts as received by their continental counterparts, British aviation firms, such as those established by the Short brothers, T. O. M. Sopwith, and A.V. Roe, remained small and lacked the resources needed for technological innovation. As a result, the British were destined to enter the First World War with both an inadequate air service and an inadequate private aviation infrastructure.

Whereas the prewar Russian military has generally been depicted as being technologically backward compared with the other great powers, this was not entirely true when it came to air power. After Louis Blériot's flight across the English Channel in 1909, Tsar Nicholas II's cousin, Grand Duke Mikhail Alexandrovich, played an instrumental role in promoting aviation in Russia and was named the first commander of the Department of the Air Fleet, soon known as the Russian Imperial Air Service. In addition to raising funds for the purchase of French Blériots and Farmans, Grand Duke Mikhail sent Russian military officers to France for pilot training. By 1911, the Volkov Field Balloon School outside St. Petersburg had been expanded to include airplanes. Because harsh Russian winter conditions resistricted the length of training, Grand Duke Mikhail saw the need to relocate to the warmer climate of the Crimea, opening the Sevastopol School of Aeronautics for army and navy officers. More significant, Russia possessed an innovative aircraft designer of its own in Igor Sikorsky, who prior to the First World War had designed one of the world's first successful, large multiengine aircraft, the four-engine *Ilya Muromet,* which in June 1914 successfully completed a 1,600-mile round-trip flight from St. Petersburg to Kiev. As will be indicated later, however, Russia unfortunately lacked the industrial infrastructure needed to fulfill its own aircraft needs once the war began.

Like their Russian counterparts, Austro-Hungarian military leaders recognized the potential of aircraft early on, but they were unable to implement their grandiose plans because of the lack of funds and industrial infrastructure. After Louis Blériot's flight across the English Channel in 1909, the Austro-Hungarian Army transferred the Militär Aeronautishe Anstalt (MAA, balloon section), which had formerly been under the Fortress Artillery Command, to the Transport Troops Command, and began acquiring a few airships and airplanes from foreign suppliers. A further reorganization took place in October 1911 as the MAA was renamed the *Luftschifferabteilung* (LA, airship section). Even this proved to be somewhat of a misnomer, however, because the army and War Ministry had already recognized that the cost of building and maintaining airships was prohibitive compared with that for airplanes. Indeed, in October 1910 Chief of the General Staff Franz Conrad von Hötzendorff had initiated grandiose plans for fielding an air force of 200 airplanes and 400 pilots. The army held its first aircraft competition in 1910, setting specifications of a minimum 2 hours endurance and a 70-km/h (44-mph) average speed with a 210-kg (463-lb) load and minimum 30-meter altitude. Only domestic firms were allowed to compete in hopes of stimulating an Austro-Hungarian aircraft industry. Of all the aircraft to compete, Igo Etrich's *Taube,* which was produced by Lohnerwerke GmbH, exceeded the specifications. It was both easy to fly, and it could be disassembled in 8 minutes and reassembled in 30 minutes. After purchasing its first *Taube* monoplanes, the army established its first flying school at Wiener-

Neustadt in April 1911. By the end of 1911, 16 pilots had completed their training and entered service. Despite Conrad von Hötzendorff's demands for greater spending for military aviation and the threats raised by the outbreak of the First Balkan War in 1912, however, Austria-Hungary continued to lag behind the other great powers in aviation spending with just $472,244 spent in 1912, 1913, and 1914. During these same 3 years, Germany spent $26,676,962 compared with $23,668,841 for France and $8,660,098 for Great Britain.[8] As a result, Austria-Hungary would be ill-prepared for the First World War.

The United States, which ironically had given birth to heavier-than-air flight in 1903 and had purchased the first military airplane in 1909, did little to advance its air power compared with the European great powers. Nevertheless, the United States did achieve some aviation firsts prior to the war. After observing an international air meet held at Belmont Park, New York, in October 1910, Captain Washington Irving Chambers convinced the navy to appropriate $25,000 for purchasing two airplanes. Just 1 month later, on 14 November 1910, Eugene Ely, a pilot from the Curtiss firm, made the first ship-to-shore flight, taking off in a 50 hp Curtiss Pusher from an 83-ft-long, 24-ft-wide, 5-degree downward sloped platform that had been constructed over the forecastle of the cruiser U.S.S. *Birmingham,* which was operating offshore from Old Point Comfort, Virginia. This feat was followed 2 months later, on 18 January 1911, when Ely landed on a similar platform on the U.S.S. *Pennsylvania.* The following year, Lieutenant John H. Towers conducted a reconnaissance flight of slightly more than 6 hours in a Curtiss A-2 floatplane after taking off from the water at Annapolis. Despite these successes, it was not until January 1914 that the U.S. Navy opened its first Naval Air Station. Furthermore, the U.S. Army, which had purchased its first aircraft in 1909—a *Wright Military Flyer*—for the U.S. Signal Corps, did not purchase a second one until 1911 and would have just 20 airplanes by 1914.

Although Italy was slow to begin developing its own aircraft industry—indeed, as late as January 1915 Italy had just 100 skilled aircraft workers—it was the first European power to use airplanes and airships in a war. Upon the outbreak of the Tripolitan War on 28 September 1911, the Italians entered Libya with two airships, two *drachen* balloons, and nine foreign-built airplanes. Italian pilots carried out the first heavier-than-air aerial reconnaissance mission on 23 October, when Captain Carlo Piazzo flew his Blériot approximately 1,000 ft above the Turkish lines and signaled the location of the enemy to Italian artillery. On 1 November Second Lieutenant Giulio Gavotti conducted the first aerial bombardment from an airplane, dropping four 2-kg grenades on Turkish forces. Italians also made successful use of aerial photography and wireless transmission. Although most foreign observers downplayed the offensive role of Italian aircraft in the conflict, Giulio Douhet, commander of Italy's small aeronautical division, published *Rules for the Use of Aircraft in War,* predicting that the line between civilians and combatants would be erased as belligerents would use aircraft to bomb their enemy's centers of armament production. In doing so, civilians would inevitably suffer from aerial bombardment and become casualties of war. Although almost all of his contemporaries dismissed him as a fanatical theorist and barbarian—indeed, he would be court-martialed for insubordination by his superiors—Douhet received a lot of attention and won a few admirers. In part in response to his predictions about the role of aerial bombardment, Giovanni Caproni would begin developing a three-engine bomber, which was ready to fly by October 1914.

In addition to the Tripolitan War, the world would get a vision of things to come in a series of other prewar conflicts. Although the First and Second Balkan Wars of 1912 and 1913 would see more widespread use of aircraft than did the Tripolitan War, including Greek attempts to drop bombs on Turkish ships in the Dardanelles, the lessons were the same: aircraft were best suited for reconnaissance and they were vulnerable to ground fire when flying under 1,000 meters. After the outbreak of the Mexican Revolution in 1911, the U.S. Army increased its military presence along the border and used aircraft for aerial reconnaissance, forming its first airplane squadron in 1913 by dispatching eight airplanes (Curtiss JN-3s and R-4s) to Columbus, New Mexico—these would later accompany Brigadier General John J. Pershing during his 1916–1917 Punitive Expedition into Mexico. In its actions against Veracruz in April 1914, the U.S. Navy used aircraft (an AB-3 flying boat and Curtiss C-3 floatplane) launched from the U.S.S. *Mississippi* to conduct reconnaissance operations, including photographic reconnaissance, to search for mines and report on Mexican troop positions. The various factions in Mexico, including General Victoriano Huerta, who seized power in 1913, Pancho Villa, and General Venustiano Carranza, would use aircraft against one another. The French and the Spanish would also use aircraft to help suppress an uprising in Morocco in early 1914.

Through their use in these conflicts and in military war games, aircraft had more than proven their potential by 1914—they had demonstrated their necessity and contributed to the growing arms race within Europe. It is ironic that, because aviation was a new innovation, prewar aviators and aircraft manufactures tended to consider themselves a close-knit fraternity, despite the international rivalries that existed at the time. Indeed, despite opposing military alliances, it was common for designers to share information and for companies to lease patents to manufacturers in other countries. In August 1914, for example, the Halberstadt factory in Germany was working in close operation with the Bristol Works in Britain, and the Oberursel plant in Germany was licenced to produced Gnôme engines, which had been developed in France. Through international air meets and competitions aviators from across Europe knew each other by reputation and in many cases on a first-name basis. This spirit of cooperation and comradery would begin coming to a swift end, however, after Serbian nationalist and terrorist Gavrilo Princip assassinated Austro-Hungarian Archduke Franz Ferdinand and his wife Sophie in Sarajevo on 28 June 1914 and the ensuing diplomatic crisis gave way to war in late July and early August 1914.

NOTES

1. It is important to note that the Montgolfier brothers falsely believed that the type of combustion materials used—they preferred raw wool and moist straw—released a mysterious gas that caused the balloon to rise. In reality, lift is provided because the hot air within the envelope is less dense than the surrounding atmosphere.

2. The Lavoisier-Meusnier method was also used because the Committee of Public Safety had restricted the use of sulfuric acid for the production of gunpowder.

3. H. G. Wells, *The War in the Air,* available online through The Literature Network at *http://www.online-literature.com/wellshg/warinair/*.

4. Richard P. Hallion, *Taking Flight: Inventing the Aerial Age from Antiquity through the First World War (New York: Oxford University Press, 2003),* p. 108.

5. *New York Times,* 10 December 1903, p. 8.

6. Where Langley had spent $73,000 on his failed *Aerodrome,* the Wrights' 1903 *Flyer* had been produced for approximately $1,000.

7. The suit would drag on for years, consuming time and money from both parties, until it was temporarily suspended during the First World War

as part of the U.S. government's effort to coordinate aircraft production. In the meanwhile, Wilbur had died in 1912 and Orville had sold the Wright Company to a group of New York investors. After the war ended, the case was dropped.

8. These amount are in 1914 dollars. Examined more closely, it is important to note that Germany spent $14,836,726 on aviation in 1914 alone and that this was more than the combined total of $14,107,621 spent by France ($9,181,513) and Great Britain ($4,926,108).

CHAPTER TWO

Military Aviation in World War I, 1914–1918

IN NORMAL CIRCUMSTANCES THE DESIRE OF Austria-Hungary to punish Serbia for its suspected role in the assassination of the Archduke Franz Ferdinand would have been understandable, even to be expected, and should not have produced a general European war felt around the world. These were not normal times, however, because the assassination came on the heels of a series of international crises that had pushed Europe ever closer to the brink of war. Indeed, by 1914, the dynamics of international rivalries and imperial ambitions had resulted in Europe becoming an armed camp of opposing alliances. Germany and Austria-Hungary were allied through the Dual Alliance, whereas France and Russia were allied through the Franco–Russian Military Convention. Although Italy was nominally allied with Germany and Austria-Hungary through the Triple Alliance, its territorial aspirations in Europe could be fulfilled only at Austria-Hungary's expense; thus, Italy was moving increasingly closer to France. Great Britain, threatened by Germany's naval buildup, was in the process of abandoning its "splendid isolationism" and had reached a series of ententes (understandings) with France and Russia. As indicated in Chapter One, this situation had contributed greatly to the development of airships and airplanes and their incorporation into European armies. Indeed, from the outset, aircraft were seen as valuable because of their military potential—a potential that was first demonstrated in European war games and in the Tripolitan War and the First and

Second Balkan Wars, and that would soon prove to be decisive in the opening stages of the war to come.

The actions of Austro-Hungarian officials in the aftermath of the assassination revealed that they considered that more was at stake than merely retaliating against Serbia for its presumed role in killing the heir to the throne. They believed that, if left unchecked, Serbian nationalism in particular and Slavic nationalism in general would result in the collapse of the multiethnic Austro-Hungarian empire; however, military action against Serbia was no simple task because Russia could be expected to support, at least diplomatically and possibly militarily, a fellow Slavic country. Emperor Franz Josef therefore appealed to his German ally for support, and Kaiser Wilhelm II responded on 5 July 1914 by issuing the famous "blank check," pledging Germany's full support even if it risked a general European crisis. Reassured by German support, Austria-Hungary ignored informal warnings by Russian and French diplomats and presented Serbia with an ultimatum on 23 July, threatening war if all the conditions were not accepted by 25 July. Although Serbia accepted most of the conditions before the deadline, it refused, as Austria-Hungary had anticipated it would, to allow Austro-Hungarian officials to conduct investigations within Serbia. Austria-Hungary and Serbia therefore both began mobilizing their militaries—including reconnaissance aircraft—on 25 July. Three days later, on 28 July, Austria-Hungary declared war against Serbia, and on 29 July began bombarding Belgrade.

In the meanwhile, European diplomacy was quickly spinning out of control, fulfilling the great German Chancellor Otto von Bismarck's prediction that "some damned fool thing in the Balkans" would provoke the next general war. On 25 July, after receiving assurances from France, Tsar Nicholas II had ordered a "partial mobilization" of the Russian Army.[1] It was this situation, more than anything else, that triggered a general European war because it effectively triggered Germany's war plan, the Schlieffen Plan, named after its originator, General Alfred von Schlieffen, who had served as chief of the German General Staff from 1891 to 1905. Although it had undergone some modifications under Schlieffen's successor, General Helmuth von Moltke "the Younger," the Schlieffen Plan sought to deal with the dilemma of a two-front war by concentrating German forces against France and defeating her before Russia could complete its mobilization—a process that the Germans believed would take approximately 6 weeks. After defeating France, German forces could then be transferred via Germany's excellent railroad network back to the East in time to deal with the Russians, who conceivably might sue for peace once their ally had been defeated. More important, the knockout blow against France was to be delivered by concentrating German forces on the right wing and striking through Belgium, whose neutrality and territorial integrity Germany, along with other European great powers, had earlier guaranteed.[2] Thus, with no consideration of the diplomatic consequences—Germany should have expected British military intervention—the German General Staff had devised a plan whose clocklike precision required action once Russia began its mobilization. When Russia rejected German demands that it stop its mobilization, on 1 August Germany mobilized its forces and declared war on Russia; however, as dictated by the Schlieffen Plan, German troops headed west, not east, moving through Luxembourg on 2 August and entering Belgium on 3 August, on which day Germany also declared war against France, who had mobilized its army 2 days earlier. It is important to note that Germany justified its declaration of war against France in part on the false claim that French aircraft had bombed Nuremberg on 2 August. Germany's rejection of a British ultimatum that it stop its invasion of Belgium resulted in a British declaration of war at midnight on 4 August.

Even though the vast majority of Europeans enthusiastically entered the war and firmly believed that it would be over by Christmas, events would soon prove otherwise, in part because of the role that aircraft were to play in the opening phases of the war. Instead of a short war, Europe would endure a 4-year nightmare of death and destruction on a scale never before witnessed—one that would draw in nations from around the globe. The war would take the lives of approximately 10 million people, redraw the maps of the world, alter the fate of nations and peoples, and also change the nature of warfare itself. Aircraft would both contribute to that change and undergo a tremendous transformation. It is to that subject that this chapter now turns.

THE MOBILIZATION AND IMPACT OF AIR POWER IN 1914

Compared with the millions of troops mobilized upon the outbreak of the war, the number of aircraft mobilized was minuscule. It must be noted that different scholars give different numbers—proving the adage that there are lies, damned lies, and statistics—for the aircraft available in 1914, primarily because of imprecise records and differences over what constituted a "front-line" aircraft. In terms of aircraft attached to the armies that were being mobilized in 1914 (e.g., naval aircraft will be considered later), perhaps the best estimates are that Germany mobilized approximately 250 airplanes and 9 airships, compared with France with 141 airplanes and 4 airships, Russia with 244 airplanes and 14 airships, Great Britain with 63 airplanes attached to the British Expeditionary Force, and Austria-Hungary with approximately 50 airplanes. It is important to note a few qualifications when considering these numbers. First, with the exception of Sikorsky's *Ilya Muromet,* Russia's aircraft were qualitatively inferior because most were older aircraft of foreign design that had already been decommissioned elsewhere, and the great variety of aircraft employed by the Russians created a logistical nightmare in terms of procuring parts and engines. Second, whereas Germany concentrated most of its aircraft on the Western Front—a policy that would continue throughout the war—its forces were outnumbered by the combined strength of Great Britain and France. Third, France was the only power that attempted to organize its squadrons (escadrilles) around aircraft type, which gave it somewhat of a logistical advantage, something that other powers would attempt to replicate as much as possible. Despite these small numbers, aircraft would quickly make their presence felt in the opening weeks of the war.

Although the German High Command attempted to use its zeppelins to bomb Belgian fortresses resisting the German invasion as well as French forces attacking in Alsace, the primary role played by aviation in the opening stages of the war was in providing long-range reconnaissance. Indeed, one of the first lessons learned was that airships were extremely vulnerable to ground fire, as demonstrated in Germany's loss of three zeppelins by the end of August. The Germans would also learn another lesson from their mistake of initially placing observers in the front seat of reconnaissance aircraft, which left their view partially obstructed by the wings, struts, and wires of the aircraft. As a result, German reconnaissance flights failed to detect the arrival of the British Expeditionary Force in France.

The French made mistakes of a different kind. Although France possessed an adequate force of reconnaissance aircraft, its organization for disseminating information almost proved its undoing. Rather than report directly to the French High Command, French observers sent their reports to French Military Intelligence, the Second Bureau, which interpreted and summarized information before sending it on to the High Command. Because French Military Intelligence did not expect the brunt of the German attack to come through Belgium and Luxembourg, it discounted the information that it was receiving from French aviators—a mistake that almost proved fatal.

The reconnaissance efforts of the British Expeditionary Force's (BEF's) Royal Flying Corps, which conducted its first reconnaissance mission on 19 August, flying over the Nivelles-Genappe area to locate the Belgian cavalry, were much more successful. Three days later, on 22 August, the British flew twelve reconnaissance missions that identified the direction of the German advance even though they resulted in the loss of one plane downed by ground fire. British aviators observed General Alexander von Kluck, commander of the German First Army, initiate the turning movement of the German Army's right wing, which Schlieffen had designed to wheel behind the French forces. Based on their reports, BEF Commander-in-Chief Field Marshal Sir John French ordered a holding action at Mons, which delayed the German advance for 24 hours and allowed the French Fifth Army under General Charles Lanrezac to escape what would have been certain envelopment and destruction.

During the week that followed Mons, the British and French continued to retreat in the face of the overwhelming numbers in the German Army's right wing, all the while flying reconnaissance missions that allowed them to keep track of the German Army's movement. Meanwhile, the French armies that had invaded Alsace and Lorraine under French War Plan XVII had been thrown back by the German Army's left wing. Moltke and the German General Staff began to see visions of a grand Cannae—Hannibal's double envelopment of the Romans in 216 B.C. It was at this critical point that the Germans made a fatal error that might have gone unnoticed if not for reconnaissance aircraft. On 30 August, Kluck ordered the German First Army to swing to the southeast to maintain contact with General Karl von Bülow's German Second Army, which had been slowed down by a vicious counterattack conducted by the French Fifth Army. The movement, which would cause the German First Army to pass in front of Paris rather than behind it—a critical deviation from the Schlieffen Plan—was spotted by the Royal Flying Corps on the next day. The French, whose government had already panicked and relocated from Paris to Bordeaux, now had an opportunity to snatch victory from the jaws of defeat. General Joseph Joffre, commander-in-chief of French forces, had already begun the process of forming the French Sixth Army in front of Paris. On

2 September Louis Breguet, flying his own airplane, spotted a gap that developed when Kluck swung further to the southeast along the Marne River, unknowingly exposing his flank to the Sixth Army. As a result, the Allies counterattacked, stopping the German advance in the Battle of the Marne, which was fought between 5 September and 10 September.

Whereas numerous factors contributed to the failure of the Schlieffen Plan (e.g., the unanticipated resistance of the Belgians, the swift intervention of the BEF, the logistical problems inherent in moving such vast numbers of men over such vast distances, Molte's decision to dispatch two army corps to meet the Russians in East Prussia), British and French aerial reconnaissance (and the willingness of commanders to act upon it) can arguably be considered one of the most significant factors. This is especially true when one contrasts the success of British and French reconnaissance aircraft with the failure of German reconnaissance aircraft to identify the presence of the BEF and to recognize the formation of the French Sixth Army. The results were profound. Paris was saved and German hopes for a quick victory were crushed. The results of the Marne ironically might have been even more profound, if not for the role that German aerial reconnaissance had played in producing victory over the Russians at Tannenberg less than 2 weeks earlier.

As mentioned earlier, one of the major premises behind the Schlieffen Plan was that it would take Russia at least 6 weeks to complete its military mobilization. In part this was correct, but in 1913 the Russian General Staff had promised its French counterpart that in the event of war, the Russian Army would invade Germany's East Prussian provinces within 15 days of mobilization if at all possible. As a result, on 17 August the Russian First Army under General Pavel K. Rennenkampf invaded East Prussia to the north of the Masurian Lakes and headed toward Königsberg, and on 19 August the Russian Second Army under General Aleksandr V. Samsonov invaded East Prussia to the south of the Masurian Lakes and headed toward Danzig. Although the speed of the Russian advance meant that many of the 600,000 men, divided roughly equally between the two armies, would not be fully equipped, the sheer force of numbers was daunting. Indeed, General Maximilian von Prittwitz und Graffon, commander of the German Eighth Army, which was outnumbered more than two to one, became so panic-stricken after elements of his army clashed with Rennenkampf at Gumbinnen on 20 August that he ordered a general withdrawal to the Vistula. Astounded, Moltke replaced Prittwitz with General Paul von Hindenburg and transferred General Erich Ludendorff from the Western Front to be Hindenburg's chief of staff.

By the time Hindenburg and Ludendorff arrived at the Eighth Army's headquarters on 23 August, they found that Prittwitz's deputy chief of staff, Colonel Max Hoffmann, had already developed a plan to concentrate German forces against Samsonov's Second Army. This was based in part on German intercepts of Russian wireless transmissions, which were broadcast "in the clear" (not coded) and revealed that Rennenkampf had ordered a halt so that Samsonov could catch up. Of equal importance, aerial reconnaissance had confirmed the validity of the intercepted transmissions. Based on reports from the zeppelin L-4 and German *Taubes*, the Germans learned that Samsonov was badly spread out over a 60-mile front. In the resulting Battle of Tannenberg, fought between 26 and 31 August, the Germans turned both flanks of Samsonov's army, resulting in Russian casualties of 130,000 men, 90,000 of whom were taken prisoner.

As would be the case on the Marne, numerous factors contributed to the outcome—Russia's mistake of rushing its armies forward without adequate supplies, the incompetence of Rennenkampf and Samsonov, and the broadcast of Russian messages "in the clear." German aerial reconnaissance, however, proved to be of the utmost importance, especially because the vast distances of the Eastern Front prevented effective cavalry reconnaissance. By enabling the Germans to confirm the location of the two Russian forces and to track their movements, Hindenburg, Ludendorff, and Hoffmann were willing to run the risk of concentrating their forces against Samsonov's Second Army. It was indeed a risk because the Germans left just one cavalry division to oppose Rennenkampf's First Army. Without the reconnaissance reports from German aircraft, the gamble might not have been taken. Indeed, no less a figure than Ludendorff attributed the German victory at Tannenberg to the intelligence gathered by aerial reconnaissance.

The results of Tannenberg were just as profound. It allowed the Germans to shift their forces back to the north and defeat Rennenkampf's First Army in the First Battle of the Masurian Lakes, fought between 9 and 14 September with the Russians being forced to retreat after losing an additional 140,000 men. Most important, however, the German victory at Tannenberg offset the German defeat at the Marne. Had the Germans been defeated and the Russian advance continued, the Germans would have been forced to transfer large numbers of troops from the Western Front to the Eastern Front.[3] Such a course might have allowed the British and French to achieve a breakthrough following the Marne or, at the least, compelled the Germans to retreat in the West. As it turned out, the Germans engaged the British and French in a race to the English Channel, each trying to turn the other's flank, but without success, in large measure because reconnaissance aircraft alerted commanders to enemy movements. Indeed, even though other factors certainly contributed to the resulting military stalemate of trench warfare on the Western Front, reconnaissance aircraft were at least partially responsible because they prevented either side from concealing the disposition of troops that might have otherwise achieved a breakthrough had they caught the opposing force off guard.

THE EVOLUTION OF
AIR POWER DURING THE WAR

Just as the role of reconnaissance aircraft contributed to the stalemate on the Western Front, the nature of trench warfare would have a major impact on the evolution of air power during the war as the role of aircraft evolved. First and foremost, aircraft continued the reconnaissance role that had proved so important in the opening phases of the war. Second, the need to prevent the enemy from conducting aerial reconnaissance gave rise to the fighter, which was also used to escort and protect one's own reconnaissance aircraft. Third, the desire to strike behind enemy lines and at the enemy home front gave rise to the bomber, which was intended to be used as a tactical weapon on the battlefield and as a strategic weapon against the enemy's productive capacity and will to fight. Fourth, the desire to break the military stalemate in the trenches would eventually result in the use of aircraft to provide close air support to ground troops. Fifth, the need to project naval power and protect shipping lanes led to a greater reliance upon aircraft at sea. By the time the First World War ended, the role of air power had changed and its importance had been clearly demonstrated. Each step of this evolution will now be examined in detail.

Aerial Reconnaissance and Observation

One of the ironic results of the stalemate of trench warfare on the Western Front is that it breathed new life into the use of balloons.

As demonstrated in Chapter One, balloons had been used for military observation as early as 1794, but their effectiveness had been limited by weather conditions and the difficulty of keeping up with marching forces. Although the introduction of kite-balloons prior to the turn of the century had effectively dealt with the first issue as far as high winds were concerned, the advent of the airplane had definitely solved the second issue to the point that armies had begun phasing out their balloon corps prior to the war—indeed, the French had abandoned balloons altogether in 1911. That changed, however, with the advent of trench warfare on the Western Front, which remained fairly stationary until the spring of 1918, by which time as many as 300 balloons could be found on both sides of the front. Although the Germans had an initial advantage with their *drachen* balloons, the Allies soon developed the Caquot balloon, which French engineer Albert Caquot had adapted from the *drachen* design. The Italians developed the Avorio-Prassone, which could reach altitudes of 7,000 ft, something that was necessitated by the mountainous terrain along the Italian Front. By war's end the Allies had produced approximately 4,000 balloons, compared with approximately 2,000 for the Central Powers (Germany and Austria-Hungary).

Balloons were normally used at an altitude of 4,000 ft, which allowed observers to see up to 15 miles in good conditions. The advantage over airplanes was that balloons were stationary, thereby allowing time for a more detailed analysis by observers. The incorporation of telephone lines with the tethering system allowed observers to communicate directly and immediately with ground forces. In addition to gathering information on enemy troop movements, observers proved invaluable to artillery, which relied upon indirect fire and thus required confirmation that its guns were registered on their intended targets. Because observation balloons played a critical role in gathering information along the stalemated Western Front, both sides increasingly targeted their opponent's balloons with artillery fire or aircraft fire. The Germans lost 315 *drachens* to aircraft in 1918 alone. At first pilots used everything from flare guns to air-to-air rockets to strike at balloons, but gradually fighters equipped with incendiary bullets were sent out to target balloons. Indeed, the United States' second-leading ace of war, Second Lieutenant Frank Luke, achieved fourteen of his eighteen kills against German balloons, winning the nickname "the Arizona Balloon Buster."[4] Although observers were virtually helpless to defend themselves because much of their line of fire was obstructed by their balloon—there is only one recorded instance of an observer down-ing an airplane—antiaircraft guns provided some protection while ground crews attempted to lower the balloon; however, because it took some time to lower a balloon, observers often had to parachute to "safety," which was not necessarily a "safe" alternative because the observer could easily drift toward opposing forces and come un-der small arms fire. In addition, the flammable hydrogen gas used to inflate balloons posed a great risk to the observer and its ground crews if a flaming balloon collapsed upon them or, worse, enemy ar-tillery struck the gas canisters used to fill the balloons.

Although balloons were effective along a stationary front, ob-servers were limited in how far behind the lines they could see. This is where aircraft proved especially effective, as demonstrated early in the war, because observers could fly far behind enemy lines and take note of changes in troop and supply buildup, which might indi-cate a change in enemy plans. As early as February 1916, for exam-ple, German reconnaissance aircraft were observing signs of British plans for an offensive along the Somme. Likewise, in 1918 Italian reconnaissance aircraft detected the Austrian Army's intention to launch an offensive along the Piave River by noting that the Austri-ans had increased the number of artillery pieces there and changed their disposition.

Because observers might be limited in understanding and remem-bering everything that they saw, the use of photography proved ex-tremely important. By the end of 1914 the Germans were already using more than 100 aerial cameras, including a serial camera that allowed for continuous photographs along the front. By war's end cameras were able to take detailed photographs at altitudes as high as 20,000 ft. Photography allowed military commanders to see the battlefront for themselves, which helped in assessing enemy activity and dispositions and the effectiveness of artillery bombardments on enemy positions. Aerial photography also played an important role in preparing battle plans. Prior to attacking the Germans at Neuve Chapelle on 10 March 1915, for example, the British took detailed photographs of the German trenches and distributed copies to unit commanders leading the assault. Photo-reconnaissance also con-tributed to strategic bombing in that it helped determine such tar-gets as railroad junctions, ammunition depots, and artillery posi-tions for bombers to attack.

Reconnaissance aircraft played a critical role in helping artillery find the range to its intended target. By early 1915 the use of the wireless transmitter enabled either the observer or pilot to report the location of hits to the target. The British introduced the "clock code" with 12:00 representing due North, 3:00 due East, 6:00 due South, and 9:00 due West. Imaginary circles from the center of the target were designated Y, Z, A, B, C, D, E, and F and represented distances of 10, 25, 50, 100, 200, 300, 400, and 500 yards, respectively. Thus, the pilot or observer noting that a shell burst fell 100 yards due East of the target would signal B3. The French used intersecting 90-degree lines at the center of the target and references to "over" or "short of" and/or "left" or "right" of center. The Germans, on the other hand, used a grid system, in which imaginary squares located about the target indicated where a shell fell. Because opposing guns were almost always out of the view of those stationed on the ground, aircraft came to play vital counterbattery roles, reporting the position of enemy artillery. Indeed, counterbattery work consumed as much as two-thirds of British activity on some days during the Battle of the Somme in 1916.

The need to maintain contact between troops at the front and commanders in the rear was another important role of reconnaissance aircraft in the First World War because infantry more often than not became bogged down in no-man's-land without effective lines of communication with the rear. Thus, the contact patrol, involving flight at low altitude, which was a risky endeavor, was crucial to infantry attacks. By the Festubert Offensive in May 1915 the RFC was using three wireless-equipped Maurice Farmans to report on the progress of ground forces, which were to communicate with white cloth strips placed on the ground. (The noise of aircraft at the time prevented two-way wireless communication.) Although viewing conditions greatly limited communication with ground forces in this manner, contact patrols became a standard feature of future offensives, allowing commanders to monitor the progress of their troops. This was especially crucial because staff officers who planned attacks often had no concept of conditions at the front and devised timelines for advances that were utterly impossible to meet. Contact patrols could also help prevent "friendly artillery fire" by informing commanders in the rear that their guns were shelling their own troops. In addition, contact patrols were often the first to report enemy counterattacks and provide information for directing artillery fire to oppose them.

In consideration of their roles, it is clear that reconnaissance aircraft had a dramatic impact upon the war, especially since they helped eliminate strategic surprise and thereby limited the possibility of a successful offensive. To a degree, therefore, reconnaissance aircraft contributed to a continuation of the very stalemate to which they owed their *raison d'être* (reason of being). In addition, their importance to military operations led directly to the development of the fighter as both sides sought to deprive the enemy of the ability to conduct operations with reconnaissance aircraft. The rise of the fighter forced both sides to introduce armed reconnaissance aircraft to provide crews a measure of self-defense or to utilize fighters for escort service.

The Rise of Fighters and their Role in the War

Although the primary danger pilots faced at first was from enemy (and friendly) ground fire, the need to prevent the enemy from carrying out reconnaissance became just as important as carrying out one's own reconnaissance after a few weeks of war. As a result, the days of opposing pilots waving at each other in the air came to a quick end, as both sides resorted to a variety of weapons (e.g., bricks, large steel darts, grenades, pistols, rifles, and even grappling hooks) in an effort to drive the enemy from the skies. On 25 August 1914 pilots and observers in Royal Flying Corps No. 2 Squadron armed themselves with rifles and pistols. Within three days the British had forced three German *Taubes* to land. Although Germans would achieve similar successes of their own, the odds of hitting a moving target with a rifle or pistol were extremely small. Of all the weapons available, the most practical one was the machine gun.[5]

The idea of firing a machine gun from an airplane actually predated the war. Early aircraft, however, lacked the power to carry a water-cooled machine gun, a pilot, and an observer. By 1912, however, technology was beginning to change as lighter-weight machine guns became available. On 7 and 8 June 1912 Captain Charles DeForest Chandler of the U.S. Army Signal Corps fired a new air-cooled machine gun, designed by Colonel Issac Newton Lewis, from the air in his Wright Type B airplane, placing 14 of 45 rounds into a 6-ft-tall, 18-in.-wide target from an altitude of 500 ft. Although the U.S. War Department failed to appreciate the significance of the demonstration, because it continued to see the airplane's role as providing the eyes of the army, other European powers took notice. Well before the outbreak of the war, aircraft designers had recognized that the most practical method of firing a machine gun from an airplane would be to fire through the arc of the propeller, thereby allowing the pilot to use the airplane to aim the gun. German designer Franz Schneider and French designer Raymond Saulnier had both independently developed an interrupter gear prior to 1914, but like the American War Department, the German and French General Staffs did not see any role for aircraft other than reconnaissance. In addition, the French War Ministry failed to adopt Saulnier's design because the added weight of the water-cooled Hotchkiss gun—the French stubbornly refused to consider the air-cooled Lewis gun—adversely affected aircraft performance.

As mentioned earlier, the need to prevent enemy reconnaissance aircraft from conducting their missions would quickly lead to the incorporation of the machine gun on aircraft by the end of 1914. Pusher aircraft, which had the propeller in the rear, had an initial advantage in that the machine gun could be placed in the nose and used to fire forward. On 5 October, for example, French Corporal Louis Quénault downed a German Aviatik while firing a Hotchkiss gun from the observer's seat in a Voisin III pusher piloted by Sergeant Joseph Frantz. The British would introduce a similarly designed pusher, the Vickers F.B.5 Gunbus, in February 1915. Although pusher aircraft allowed observers to fire forward, they left the rear of the airplane vulnerable to attack and they were not as fast or maneuverable as tractor-driven aircraft (propeller in the front). It was for these reasons that the Germans opted for tractor-driven aircraft and began installing their ring-mounted Parabellum gun in the observer's seat. This offered a greater range of fire and the Parabellum's drum had twice the capacity of the Lewis gun and four times the capacity of the Hotchkiss. The German ace, Oswald Boelcke, would get his first kill in such an aircraft. A few enterprising pilots mounted a Lewis gun on the top wing of their aircraft in order to fire over the arc of the propeller, but this presented its own hazards, as British pilot Louis Strange discovered on 10 May 1915 when his Martinsyde Scout turned upside down while he was attempting to change the drum on his Lewis gun, which was mounted on his upper wing. Strange somehow managed to hang on while the plane plummeted from 9,000 ft down to 1,500 ft before he was able to get back into the cockpit and right his plane.

As indicated earlier, the techniques improvised for using machine guns had their limitations, but this was soon to change. In March 1915 Roland Garros, a French pilot who had obtained fame for crossing the Mediterranean prior to the war, had been sent from the front to work with Saulnier in trying to perfect the process of firing through the propeller's arc. Because the Hotchkiss gun was notorious for firing irregularly, Saulnier's interrupter gear could not guarantee that a bullet would not strike the wooden propeller. After many experiments, Garros and Saulnier affixed wedge-shaped metal deflectors on the propeller and found that on average five in six shots passed through the propeller with the wedges deflecting the other. Although this presented some danger in that a deflected bullet could damage the engine or strike the pilot, Garros was undaunted and returned to the front in late March with a Hotchkiss gun affixed to his Morane-Saulnier monoplane. Beginning on 1 April 1915, Garros shot down five German planes in less than 3 weeks. On 18 April, however, he was forced down by ground fire behind enemy lines. Able to examine Garros's plane, the Germans had the propeller at the Fokker factory within 24 hours.

After inspecting Garros's plane, Dutch aircraft designer Anthony Fokker, who had begun aircraft construction in Germany just prior to the war, determined that the deflector shields provided only a partial solution. In any event, he had already been experimenting with Franz Schneider's prewar interrupter design, and by late Spring 1915 had perfected it by synchronizing the interrupter gear with the camshaft of his new Fokker E.I monoplane, the Eindecker. In this way the interrupter gear could be timed to prevent the gun from firing when a bullet would otherwise strike a propeller blade. Although German authorities were impressed with Fokker's demonstration of the mechanism at the factory, they demanded that he personally demonstrate it in flight against an Allied aircraft before they would adopt it, even though this would violate his status as a neutral noncombatant. After making several flights over the next 8 days, Fokker refused to fly further. German officials finally relented and allowed Fokker to instruct Lieutenant Oswald Boelcke how to operate the gun.

The introduction of the Eindecker with its synchronized machine gun in late July 1915 transformed air combat. Although the E.I had a relatively slow speed at 81 mph compared with the Morane-Saulnier Type N's 90 mph and took 7 minutes to climb to 3,000 ft, it had good maneuverability and its round fuselage and thin wings made it hard to detect. The first two Eindeckers were sent to Feldfliegerabteilung 62 at Douai, where both Boelcke and Max Immelmann were based. Although the Germans had eleven Eindeckers in service by the end of July, they made a tactical error of distributing two to each Abteilung rather than concentrate them in a single squadron, which would have had a more devastating impact upon the Allied air forces.

After Boelcke and Immelmann began shooting down Allied planes in fairly rapid fashion, an enthusiastic German High Command pressed Fokker to speed up production of Eindeckers as fast as he could.

Although the Germans had relatively few Eindeckers in service on the Western Front—just 55 at the end of October and just 86 at the end of December 1915—their impact revolutionized the war in the air. Armed with this technologically superior aircraft—an updated version, the E.II, replaced the 80 hp Oberusel rotary engine with a 100 hp version, increasing speed to 87 mph and the ceiling to 12,000 ft—Immelmann and Boelcke would formalize air combat tactics into a science. Immelmann introduced the turn named after him. After diving to attack an enemy plane, he pulled back up into a loop and upon reaching the top, half-rolled to an upright position, above and behind and in the opposite direction of the enemy target. By executing a stall turn, the pilot could then execute a second dive attack on the enemy plane. Boelcke developed his famous Dicta that remained relevant for decades to come: attack from above with the sun at your back; use clouds to conceal your approach; pull within close enough range to hit the target but avoid being hit yourself; turn toward an oncoming attacker to close the distance; and back sharply from a rear attack. Although the Allies would introduce a new generation of fighters in the late spring of 1916—the Nieuport 17 was the first with a synchronized gun—that were more than a match for the Eindecker, the Germans would soon respond with a new generation of fighters of their own—the Albatross D.I—setting off a continuing technological race that would cause the advantage to swing back and forth until the war ended. The generations of fighters that succeeded the Eindecker will be discussed in greater detail in Chapter Four, but it is important to note how the introduction of the Eindecker impacted tactics, strategy, and organization.

In response to the so-called Fokker scourge, in which the British lost 43 aircraft between August 1915 and January 1916, the Allies were forced to change tactics until they could introduce a comparable fighter. Where pilots had previously been given a tremendous amount of discretion in search-and-destroy missions, the Eindecker forced Allied units to begin flying in formation and provide escort for reconnaissance aircraft. More significant, after taking over command of the RFC in France on 19 August 1915, Major General Hugh Montague Trenchard emphasized the need for taking aggressive offensive action in the air by concentrating Allied fighters into fighter squadrons rather than scattering them piecemeal among squadrons. Even though Allied fighters were still inferior to the Fokker Eindecker, their concentration in numbers offered a better defense until new fighters were introduced.

By 1916 all powers had gained enough experience to issue tactical guidelines. One of the most important lessons learned and applied was the importance of formation flying and fighting in groups rather than venturing out alone. Mutual support, particularly against attack from the rear and in identifying enemy planes, was another major advantage of fighting in groups. Squadrons generally flew in a "V" formation with the flight leader in front and those behind flying at different altitudes. Stacked squadrons flying above each other provided protection from overhead attacks. Needless to say, coordination was crucial to success, especially because communication was limited to hand or wing signals. Whereas dogfights involving squadrons or groups of squadrons against one another are the most remembered aspect of the air war in the First World War, fighters were more frequently engaged in less spectacular activity: patrolling the line and escorting bombers or reconnaissance aircraft. Escort duty was generally reserved for junior pilots, whereas more experienced fighters preferred flying in small groups of two to three planes to hunt for victims. In addition, fighters sometimes provided support to ground troops by strafing enemy lines—a role that will be discussed in greater detail later. Although the fighter had definitely changed the war in the air by the start of 1916, the two epic battles of Verdun and the Somme would provide new directions in their use.

Prior to launching their offensive against Verdun on 21 February 1916, the Germans had conducted highly detailed photographic reconnaissance of French positions and concentrated their Fokker Eindeckers, including Boelcke's squadron, in the area around Verdun in order to deny the French aerial reconnaissance of the massive German troop buildup. This policy of conducting an aerial blockade (Luftsperre) initially proved to be successful. Although a few French aircraft managed to get through the screen of German fighters, they were unable to gather enough information to convince the French High Command that the Germans were preparing a winter assault on Verdun. The critical mistake that the Germans made was to continue the aerial blockade after the onset of the battle. Even though doing so helped to protect German artillery positions, the Germans wasted aerial resources that could have been better used to disrupt the French supply line up the one road—*La Voie Sacree* (The Sacred Way)—that allowed the French to send reinforcements and supplies into Verdun. The way in which the French employed their fighters is much more significant.

General Henri Philippe Pétain, commander of French forces at Verdun, recognized that seizing air supremacy from the Germans was crucial if the French were to hold Verdun. The French increased the number of escadrilles in the Verdun sector from four to sixteen—including six fighter escadrilles—as well as the number of aircraft per escadrille to twelve. Just as important, Commandant Tricornot de Rose, placed in overall command of the air forces in the Verdun sector, demanded that his fighter pilots fly in formation. Some of the most famous fighter escadrilles of the war, the *Storks* (*Les Cigognes*) and the *Lafayette Escadrille* (composed of American volunteers), established their reputations at Verdun. By August, French fighters had regained control of the skies above Verdun, because of the introduction of new aircraft and because of their superiority in numbers and concentration of force. By tying down German fighters in combat, French reconnaissance aircraft were able to perform their vital role in counterbattery work. Although numerous factors prevented the Germans from achieving their goal of bleeding the French white at Verdun, their misuse of aircraft combined with the successful French use of aircraft was certainly an important factor.

Just as the German attack at Verdun produced a change in French fighter tactics and organization, the British attack on the Germans along the Somme in the summer of 1916 would force the Germans to take similar steps. In preparation for the Somme Offensive, the British had reorganized the RFC, assigning a reconnaissance wing to each corps to photograph the front lines within 5 miles of the corps and a fighter wing and long-range reconnaissance wing to each army. Although the long preliminary barrage that the British carried out gave the Germans ample warning to shift aircraft to that sector before the battle began, the Allies still enjoyed a numeric advantage of 185 British and 200 French aircraft against 130 German aircraft at the start of the offensive. In addition, the British and French had introduced new aircraft that were superior to the Eindecker and would give them air supremacy for the first 2 months of the campaign. Having observed the success of the French at Verdun, Trenchard was convinced that a policy of relentless and incessant offensive against German fighters would produce victory. Although the British did enjoy initial success in the skies over the Somme, this had more to do with deficient German resources and organization, something that could be and would be remedied. When circumstances should have dictated a change in policy, Trenchard stubbornly persisted in his relentless offensive despite heavy losses. As a result, RFC pilots were to endure a similar level (comparative in scope) of fruitless attrition as that suffered by the infantry under Field Marshal Sir Douglas Haig's command.

Confronted at the Somme by an enemy with superior numbers and organization, the Germans responded by centralizing the command of their air service, concentrating single-seat fighters into their own squadrons (Jagdstaffeln or Jastas), increasing the number of aircraft attached to artillery units, and converting four bomber units into heavy-armed escorts for artillery spotters. The British would lose 782 aircraft compared with 369 for the Germans during the Somme Offensive (1 July through 27 November) as the creation of Jastas by the end of August began to have a most telling impact. In September and October, for example, the reorganized Germans shot down 211 Allied aircraft while losing just 39 of their own. Boelcke's Jasta 2, which included Manfred von Richthofen, was particularly effective, shooting down 76 British aircraft at the loss of just 7 planes between 17 September and 31 October.

By the end of 1916 the basic organizational structure and tactical use of fighter aircraft were set. One major advantage enjoyed by the Germans was that prevailing westerly winds forced Allied planes to fly into the wind upon returning to their bases and allowed crippled German planes to glide back to the German side of the line. The introduction of newer generations of fighters would cause the battle for air supremacy to shift back and forth. In the spring of 1917, for example, the Germans enjoyed huge successes against the British, culminating in the first few weeks of April when the British lost 75 aircraft between 4 and 8 April alone. One of the reasons for such attrition, however, is that prior to the start of the Battle of Arras in April 1917, the British had purposely held back such new aircraft as the S.E.5, the F.2.B Bristol fighter, and the Sopwith Triplane in order to concentrate them for the offensive and catch the Germans by surprise. By the end of April 1917 the tide had begun to turn. British losses for the month were 151 aircraft compared with Germany's 119. For the remainder of 1917 the fighter advantage lay with the Allies, although the Germans did limit the damage somewhat by combining Jastas together to form Jagdgeschwaders, the most famous of which was Richtohofen's "Flying Circus," Jagdegeschwader No. 1, which operated in the Ypres sector. By the last year of the war Germany had introduced perhaps the best fighter of the war with the Fokker D.VII, but the quantitative advantage enjoyed by the Allies more than compensated for the qualitative advantage of the last generation of German fighters. As will be demonstrated later in this chapter, productive capacity was an absolutely critical component of air power.

The Rise of Bombers and their Role in the War

Although the rise of fighter aircraft was a product of the war itself— the need to attack enemy reconnaissance aircraft and protect one's own—the idea of using aircraft and airships for bombing the enemy had been sown in the public's imagination by journalists and novelists prior to the war. As seen in Chapter One, novelists like H. G. Wells reflected the belief that aerial bombardment would destroy both the enemy's capacity to fight and will to fight. Although the reality of aerial bombardment during the First World War did not live up to the prewar hype, it was not because of a lack of effort. Even before the war, air power enthusiasts, like E. Joynson Hicks, a British M.P., had conceived of strategic missions for the bomber: attacks against an enemy's military plants and transportation infrastructure; attacks against an enemy's command and control centers; and attacks against the civilian population. By 1913 the French, Germans, British, and Italians were conducting bombing exercises and experimenting with bombsights and bomb release equipment. The advent of trench warfare gave new impetus to these ideas, as aircraft would be used tactically on the battlefield to bomb targets beyond the range of artillery and as both sides turned to strategic bombing and (in the case of the German zeppelin raids on Great Britain) terror bombing to weaken the enemy.

Most prewar aspirations for bombers centered upon airships, because they were capable of greater range and heavier bomb loads. When the Germans and French attempted to use their airships in the opening stages of the war, they soon discovered how vulnerable airships were to ground fire, as the Germans lost three zeppelins in 1 month's time to enemy ground fire and the French had two of their airships damaged by their own infantry fire. As a result, both the French and Germans grounded their airships until 1915 and turned to the airplane. The Russian Igor Sikorsky and the Italian Giovanni Caproni ironically were far ahead of the aircraft designers among the other European powers. By the time war broke out in 1914 Sikorsky's four-engine *Ilya Muromet* had successfully completed a 1,600-mile round-trip flight between St. Petersburg and Kiev. Meanwhile, Caproni was putting the finishing touches on a three-engine bomber that was ready to fly by October 1914. Lacking anything similar to what the Russians and Italians possessed, the French, British, and Germans were forced to rely upon reconnaissance aircraft until they developed bombers of their own. Indeed, by November commanding generals had authorized that all reconnaissance aircraft be equipped to carry bombs. At the time the government munition plants had not yet developed aerial bombs, so airmen generally improvised by adding tail fins to surplus artillery shells and converting them into bombs, at first dropped over the side by the observer and later fitted to bomb racks and released by either the pilot or observer.

Although Article 25 of the 1907 Hague Convention had outlawed the bombardment of nonmilitary targets, the inaccuracy of aerial bombardment made it impossible not to violate this provision. On the night of 26 August, for example, German zeppelins, operating out of Düsseldorf, began a series of bombing raids on Antwerp, Belgium. In the first raid, the Germans dropped 1,800 lbs of shrapnel bombs, partially destroying a hospital and killing twelve civilians. On 8 October the British launched a retaliatory raid with two Sopwith Tabloids, each carrying two 20-lb bombs. Although one of the planes succeeded in destroying Z-9 in its Düsseldorf shed, the other dropped its bombs on the Cologne railway station, killing three civilians. A similar, far more daring raid was carried out by four Avro 504 biplanes, each carrying four 20-lb bombs, against the zeppelin works at Friedrichshafen. Although only three of the planes reached their destination, they struck the hydrogen works and inflicted minor damage to the sheds. Although several German soldiers and workers were killed or wounded, neither of the two zeppelins were damaged and the gasworks was operational within a week.

Although these initial raids had been somewhat ad hoc affairs in which pilots of reconnaissance aircraft were given little to no instructions, the military high commands began issuing directives as to tactics by early 1915, such as releasing bombs at low altitude in order to improve accuracy, and specifying missions. Most bombing missions centered on enemy positions that were out of artillery range, but other targets included industrial centers far behind the lines. The French, for example, attempted to sever the rail lines in the Briey basin in Lorraine in hopes of disrupting Germany's supply of iron ore. In addition, both sides conducted raids against enemy cities, often justifying them as retaliatory raids. The Germans, having occupied northeastern France, were better placed to defend attacks against German cities because they were too far out of range from enemy bases to carry out attacks against Britain, France, and Russia. Although Italy was well equipped to carry out bombing raids on Austrian territory, its leaders were reluctant to do so because the targets lay in the heavily Italian populated areas that Italy hoped to annex.

Before the end of 1914 powers also began to organize units specifically intended to carrying out bombing missions. The French had formed Groupe de Bombardement No. 1 (G.B. 1) from three escadrilles composed of the new Voisin pusher aircraft, and the Germans had established the Brieftauben-Abteilung Ostende (B.A.O.) or "Ostend Carrier Pigeon Flight" for duty along the English Channel. In December 1914 aircraft from the B.A.O. carried out bombing attacks on Channel ports, whereas G.B. 1 bombers attacked the Badische Analin und Soda Fabrik the following spring after receiving reports that it had produced the deadly chlorine gas used at Second Ypres. Field Marshall Joffre even issued orders for an attack against Thielt after receiving intelligence reports that Kaiser Wilhelm II was scheduled for a visit on 1 November 1914. Although a change in the Kaiser's schedule resulted in canceling the attack, it is significant to note that it would have been impossible to contemplate such a move a decade earlier. Similar attempts were made by the Germans against Nicholas II and by the French against Crown Prince Wilhelm and Bavarian Crown Prince Rupprecht.

The Battle of Neuve Chapelle, launched with a preliminary bombardment on 10 March 1915, marked the beginning of a new phase in the use of air power. Whereas aerial reconnaissance had provided British First Army Commander General Sir Douglas Haig with detailed information about the German defenses and led him to designate the salient around Neuve Chapelle as the target for his first assault, tactical bombing was attempted for the first time as part of a battle plan. Where bombs had previously been dropped sporadically by reconnaissance pilots, military commanders ordered strikes against a reported divisional headquarters in Fournes; the key railway stations at Menin, Douai, Lille, and Don; and the railway junction at Courtai. Flying a B.E.2 c, Captain Louis Strange dropped three 20-lb bombs on a stationary troop train at Courtai, reportedly killing or wounding seventy-five soldiers and disrupting traffic for 3 days. On the other hand, Captain Edgar Ludlow-Hewitt mistakenly dropped a 100-lb bomb on the railway station at Wavrin, thinking he was over Don. Because pilots lacked an effective bombing sight, they had to fly extremely low over their targets, which exposed them to enemy ground fire. When Strange returned from his bombing raid on Courtai, his plane was found to have at least forty bullet holes. Lieutenant William Rhodes-Moorhouse was not as fortunate. While dropping a 100-lb bomb at an altitude of 100 ft over Courtai, he was mortally wounded; an action for which he received the RFC's first Victoria Cross.

Despite a few spectacular successes, such as the destruction of zeppelin sheds and Strange's bombing at Courtai, the initial results of tactical and strategic bombing were extremely limited. Of 483 bombing attacks that the British and French launched against German targets between 1 March and 20 June 1915, only seven were considered successful. In addition, bombers proved extremely vulnerable to ground fire, antiaircraft guns, and enemy bombers. By late 1915 experience dictated the development of tactical guidelines for bombing, such as attacking targets downwind and flying in formation to minimize the impact of antiaircraft guns. In addition, daytime bombing raids were increasingly restricted to short runs or to entice enemy fighters into a trap, while nighttime bombing raids were used to fly deep into enemy territory. It should be noted that nighttime flying presented a host of problems because of the lack of training and instruments—obstacles that would not be overcome until the last 2 years of the war.

By far the most significant legacy of bombing in the war—one that would shape postwar air power theory—was the German bombing campaign against Great Britain, which began in 1915 and continued until the end of the war, and was by far the most extensive use of strategic bombing during the war. Although Kaiser Wilhelm II at first proved reluctant to sanction attacks against London and other British cities, the German public clamored for taking the war directly to the British, who had imposed a naval blockade of all items—including food—into Germany. As a result, the Kaiser gradually relented to public pressure and the demands of his military subordinates who saw aerial bombardment as a legitimate means of destroying the English will to fight. The first attacks were carried out on the night of 19 January 1915 by naval zeppelins L-3 and L-4 against Yarmouth and King's Lynn. The attacks destroyed a few homes and shops, killing six civilians and injuring twenty (including three children) in the process. Although the Germans justified the raid as an attack on "fortified places," the British denounced them as an act of barbarism. The success of the raid finally led the Kaiser to lift restrictions on London.[6]

Attempting to launch their zeppelins against London was no easy task for the Germans. Attacking at night without adequate instruments was difficult enough; adverse weather only compounded problems. Captain Ernst Lehmann, commander of the newly commissioned Z-12, which could carry a bomb payload of 12 tons, devised an ingenious method of lowering an observation car as much as 2,700 ft beneath his zeppelin so it could remain above the clouds, where an observer below could communicate via telephone to the wheelhouse and guide the airship to its intended target. When Lehmann attempted his first raid against London on 17 March 1915, however, he turned back because of heavy fog, refusing to drop his bomb load on an unseen target below. Because the naval zeppelins were based in Germany and thus were stretching their range, the task of bombing London in 1915 ultimately fell to the army, which could use bases in Belgium. After making several attempts to find London in April and May 1915, Captain Erich Linnarz, commander of the LZ-38, finally succeeded on 31 May. Dropping a payload of five 110-lb bombs and forty-eight small incendiary bombs from 7,000 ft, the LZ-38 destroyed approximately $100,000 of property, killing seven civilians and injuring thirty-five.

Although the attack did not induce the British to panic, as the Germans expected, First Lord of the Admiralty Winston Churchill did order the Royal Naval Air Service (RNAS) to divert resources to defending civilians against further zeppelin attacks. When the Germans attempted their second raid against London on the night of 6–7 June with three zeppelins—LZ-37, LZ-38, and LZ-39—the British were ready. After naval intelligence intercepted German radio signals and notified the RNAS wing stationed at Dunkirk, two Morane-Saulniers and two Farmans were dispatched to attack the zeppelins upon their return. Although Lieutenant John Rose had to return to base after the engine on his Morane-Saulnier malfunctioned, his companions were far more successful. Lieutenant Alexander Warneford, flying the other Morane-Saulnier, intercepted LZ-37 on its return to Ghent, destroying it after releasing six bombs from above as it descended to its base. Lieutenants John P. Wilson and John S. Mills used their Farmans to bomb and destroy LZ-38 as it was entering its shed at Évère. As a result of their losses, the Germans temporarily halted raids by their army zeppelins, waiting instead for Captain Peter Strasser to assembly his fleet of naval zeppelins for a major raid.

In an attempt to carry out a mass raid against London, Strasser postponed further probes of the English coast in June and July, awaiting the arrival of nine new zeppelins, each of which had a gas capacity of 1.1 million cubic ft and were capable of 61 mph with their four Maybach engines. Although Strasser carefully planned his first mass raid against London for 9 August 1915, it proved to be an absolute failure with not a single ship finding its target. In subsequent attacks the Germans enjoyed little success, with the exception of an attack carried out by Captain Heinrich Mathy in L-13 on 8 September. The L-13, which had a payload of fifteen high-explosive bombs and some fifty incendiary bombs, accounted for approximately 25 percent of the damage that London would suffer in the entire war, resulting in $2.5 million of property damage, thirty-five deaths, and thirty-seven injured civilians.

In response to the zeppelin raids, Arthur Balfour, who had replaced Churchill as first lord of the admiralty in the aftermath of the Gallipoli debacle, placed Admiral Sir Percy Scott in charge of London's antiaircraft defenses. Believing that antiaircraft guns were the key to defense, Scott established batteries of high-angle cannon and a network of high-power spotlights around London. More important, he acquired motorized 75 mm guns from the French, which allowed for a mobile antiaircraft system. In addition, Scott established continual air patrols over London at night and had the RNAS increase its coastal patrols. The improved British antiaircraft defenses led Strasser to suspend attacks in late 1915 until new, improved zeppelins could enter service. As a result, the British enjoyed a 3-month respite until 31 January 1916, when Strasser dispatched nine zeppelins on a raid intended to strike Liverpool. Although only one of the zeppelins, L-21, reached its destination, its bombs did minimal damage. The other eight, however, dropped their loads across the English countryside, killing 70 civilians and injuring 113. Although this was the deadliest raid thus far in the war, it achieved no real military objective. To the extent that the raids had tied up British manpower and resources at an enormous expense, the German raids were worthwhile, even if they did not achieve their intended result.

On 2 September 1916 Strasser launched what he hoped would be the climactic air raid of the campaign, sending a flotilla of twenty zeppelins against England—two in a diversionary attack over the Humber and eighteen (including five of the newest zeppelins) against London; however, British antiaircraft defenses had by then become much stronger. In particular, British aircraft were now armed with much improved incendiary ammunition designed to penetrate the zeppelin's outer skin and explode the hydrogen. In addition, cryptographers working in Room 40 of naval intelligence had obtained German code books, which allowed them to decode intercepted messages sent between zeppelins on the night of 2 September, thereby providing ample warning to the antiaircraft defense network. Lieutenant Leefe Robinson intercepted SL-11 (Schutte Lanz airship) with his B.E.2 and used his new incendiary shells to shoot it down, for which he would receive the Victoria Cross. Whereas the fiery descent of SL-11 cheered British onlookers, it shook the confidence of the other zeppelin crews who witnessed it in the air, leading all but one—LZ-98 commanded by Lehmann—to turn abruptly around before dropping their payload on their intended targets. On 23 September Strasser carried out a new raid with four of his new super zeppelins (L-30, L-31, L-32, and L-33), which were to attack London, and six older types, which were to carry out diversionary raids. British antiaircraft defenses once again proved their worth against these lumbering giants. Caught in a web of spotlights east of London, the L-32 provided an easy target, as Lieutenant John Sowrey pulled underneath it with his B.E.2 and emptied three canisters of incendiary and tracer bullets fired from his Lewis gun into the belly of the great ship, striking a fuel tank, which then produced a tremendous explosion that brought the L-32 down in a ball of flames. Although the remaining zeppelins completed their mission, dropping bombs that killed 39 and injured 131, the Germans suffered the loss of a second super zeppelin, L-33, after Lieutenant Alfred de Bath Brandon punctured its gas bags so severely that it was forced to land near Colchester.

Although the disasters that befell German zeppelins in September 1916 were held from the public, the German High Command demanded that the Kaiser order an end to the navy's raids, considering them a waste of manpower and precious resources that could be used elsewhere. The navy naturally resented the army's interference, but naval leaders did remove the autonomy that Strasser had previously enjoyed. In addition, production of new zeppelins was gradually curtailed. More important, all subsequent zeppelin attacks, which were carried out until August 1918, were limited to the British east coast and industrial midlands in order to avoid the air defenses around London. Nevertheless, German losses continued to mount. Of seven zeppelins launched on a raid against Harwich and Yarmouth on 27 October 1917, for example, only three returned home. Whereas the numerical losses of German zeppelin crews paled in comparison to those suffered by the men in the trenches, the percentages are quite astonishing. In March 1918 Strasser reported a casualty rate of more than 40 percent, as 70 officers and more than 250 crewmen had died and 150 had been wounded or taken prisoner. In the last zeppelin raid of the war, on the night of

5 August 1918, Strasser himself would go down in L-70, the largest zeppelin built during the war.

The Germans carried out forty zeppelin raids during the war, dropping 220 tons of bombs that left 557 dead and 1,538 wounded, destroying $30 million of property. In doing so, however, the Germans paid a heavy price. Of the 140 airships that participated in the raids, approximately two-thirds were destroyed by enemy fire, storms, or accidents. Given the enormous costs of building and maintaining the airships, the zeppelin raids must be considered a failure because each airship cost approximately $500,000 to build, and the monthly maintenance cost for the fleet could have funded four infantry brigades. They failed to inflict the physical damage that the Germans expected and did not create the desired psychological trauma that had been anticipated. They must also be considered a public relations disaster in that attacks on nonmilitary targets led neutral powers, particularly the United States, to sympathize with the British.

Although the zeppelin raids proved the futility of using hydrogen-filled airships as a strategic bomber, the Germans did not give up on strategic bombing. Instead, they turned to a new weapon that came available in Spring 1917, the twin-engine Gotha G-IV bomber. The Germans hoped that this new weapon, when combined with a resumption of unrestricted submarine warfare in 1917, would drive Britain from the war. In the first Gotha raid, conducted on 25 May 1917, a fleet of 23 bombers led by Captain Ernst Brandenburg headed toward London, but because of heavy fog ended up dropping their payloads over Folkestone, killing 95 civilians and injuring 195, more casualties than any single zeppelin raid. On 13 June Brandenburg led 20 Gothas in a noontime attack on London, dropping 7 tons of bombs that destroyed the Liverpool Street Station, killed 162 people, injured 432 others, and caused more than $600,000 in property damage. Every single Gotha returned to Ghent unscathed. More significant, this one single raid inflicted more damage on London than did all the earlier airship raids combined. The British responded by withdrawing two of their top squadrons (No. 66 and No. 56) from the Western Front for the defense of London—a move that allowed the Germans to shift their attacks to British positions on the front. When the British sent the squadrons back to France, the Germans shifted back to London on 7 July, sending a formation of 22 Gothas that inflicted 252 casualties. To defend against the raids that followed, none of which comprised more than 43 Gothas, the British were forced to maintain almost 800 aircraft—approximately

50 percent were top of the line fighters—at home to reassure the public. This commitment deprived the British of much-needed aircraft for their Passchendaele Campaign and contributed at least in part to the British suffering twice as many casualties in the air as did the Germans.

These attacks both outraged Englishmen and absorbed the British High Command's attention, leading to the appointment of Lieutenant General Jan Smuts as chair of the Committee on Air Organization and Home Defense against Air Raids. By 17 August, when the Smuts Committee issued its report, a combination of poor weather and improved British air defenses, which included the use of barrage balloons and suspended cables, was turning the tide against Germany as some missions lost as many as 50 percent of their Gothas. More important, German hopes that the civilian population would be terrorized into forcing their government to abandon the war never materialized.

In 52 attacks on Great Britain, German Gothas and Staken R.VI bombers had dropped 73 tons of bombs, killed 857 British subjects, wounded another 2,400, and left more than $7 million in property damage. Although the bombing campaigns far exceeded any success enjoyed by the zeppelins, they did not achieve as much as they could have. Failing to recognize the extent of their success, especially in terms of forcing the British to reallocate resources, the Germans neither dedicated as many bombers nor conducted as many raids as they could have. As a result, the British gained time to improve their defenses, developing high-altitude fighters and high-altitude antiaircraft guns. More important, the bombing campaign compelled the British to merge the RFC and the RNAS together into the new Royal Air Force (RAF). By May 1918 the toll on German bombers reached the point that cross-Channel attacks were dropped altogether. If anything, the German bombing raids only strengthened British resolve, something that would be repeated in 1940.

In the meanwhile, the British, desiring to strike back at the Germans, had organized the 41st Wing in October 1917 to carry out strategic bombing raids against German industrial targets. It should be emphasized that Field Marshal Sir Douglas Haig, commander-in-chief of the BEF, and Trenchard, commander of the RFC, bitterly opposed this as a misallocation of resources that should be used first and foremost to support the army's needs on the front. Their objections had been overridden, however, because politicians—Prime Minister David Lloyd George among them—were feeling the public's demand for revenge. Equipped with D.H.4s, F.E.2bs, and

Handley-Page 0/100s, the 41st Wing began operations in the fall. It was restructured as VIII Brigade in February 1918 and as the Independent Bombing Force on 6 June 1918. By then the first Handley-Page 0/400s had begun to enter service, allowing the British to carry out highly successful raids against Rhineland cities such as Coblenz, Cologne, Karlsruhe, Mainz, and Mannheim. By the Armistice the British had carried out 675 raids against German targets, dropping more than 14,000 bombs, killing 746 Germans, injuring 1,843 others, and causing approximately $6 million in damage. Had the war continued, the massive Handley-Page V/1500 bomber would have given the British the ability to strike Berlin. Although the British bombing campaign had not really begun in earnest until the creation of the Independent Bombing Force, the British had seen enough results over such a short period of time that they would be firmly convinced of the value of strategic bombing.

The Development of Close Air Support

One of the important roles that aircraft of all types came to play as the war continued was providing close air support to ground forces. As mentioned earlier, this had first been demonstrated with the RFC's use of contact patrols during the Festubert Offensive in May 1915. In addition to maintaining contact with ground troops, aircraft were used to lay smoke screens and drop ammunition and supplies. By the time the British launched the Somme Offensive in the summer of 1916 air power was becoming an integral part of planning and execution. Observation aircraft and artillery cooperated together on key sectors of the battle area, bombers were used to target German communication and transportation centers in the rear, and fighters were used on line patrols to strafe enemy positions and assist in ground assaults.

By 1917 all powers were using their aircraft to provide close support to ground forces. On 23 May, for example, Italy followed a 10-hour artillery barrage by sending 34 Caproni bombers against Austrian front lines in advance of an infantry assault during the Tenth Battle of the Isonzo. Although the inaccuracy of aerial bombardment limited the extent of physical damage, the impact upon morale—positive for the Italians and negative for the Austrians—was significant. Likewise, the Italians employed 280 aircraft—including 85 Caproni bombers—on the first day of the Eleventh Battle of the Isonzo (18 August). Whereas the Caproni bombers hit targets in the rear, reconnaissance aircraft and fighters strafed Austrian positions. After the failed Nivelle Offensive in the spring of 1917 produced mutinies in the French Army, General Henri Philippe Pétain assumed command of the French Army and specifically ordered that aircraft restrict their activities to the battle zone. In this way, fighters, bombers, and armed reconnaissance aircraft played a vital role in supporting French troops at a time when French morale had been shattered. To a degree, therefore, close air support enabled the French to recover their fighting spirit so that they were able to launch limited offensives by the end of 1917 and play a leading role in the Allied counteroffensive of 1918. Likewise, both the British and the Germans relied upon fighters for ground support during the Passchendaele Campaign that dominated fighting along the Western Front in the late summer and fall of 1917. The experience gained from these campaigns would have an even greater impact in 1918.

By the spring of 1918 Germany had knocked Russia and Romania out of the war, allowing the German General Staff, under the direction of Hindenburg and Ludendorff since August 1916, to transfer massive numbers of troops from the Eastern Front to the Western Front in hopes of bringing a swift end to the war before the United States, which had entered the war in April 1917, could make a difference. In preparation for the spring offensive, German reconnaissance aircraft had photographed a 50-mile stretch of the British lines, allowing for a detailed plan of attack. Ludendorff, the architect of the offensive, amassed approximately 730 aircraft to assist in the attack. Up to the eve of the attack, however, German fighters were instructed not to increase engagements with British aircraft for fear of revealing the German plans. The Germans also organized an new type of air unit, the Schlachtstaffeln, a ground-attack squadron, comprised of specially designed aircraft to provide close coordination with ground forces to bring a concentration of firepower upon key positions along the front. These included the all-metal Junkers J.I, which had been introduced the prior year, and the Halberstadt CL.IV, a two-seater that placed the pilot and observer back to back and was ideal for strafing enemy trenches with machine-gun fire, grenades, and mortar bombs. Once the offensive began, German aircraft traced the movement of both enemy and German troop movements and provided close support as German storm troops advanced on Allied lines, strafing and bombing Allied positions, knocking out communication centers, clearing out machine-gun posts, and demoralizing hard-pressed Allied defenders.

With a resumption of mobile ground warfare after the Germans achieved initial breakthroughs, the tasks imposed upon both German and Allied aircraft increased dramatically, particularly in terms of scouting enemy movements and attempting to shield such endeavors. Whereas aircraft played a critical role in the German success, they proved to be a two-edged sword, as the British, despite losing 478 aircraft in the first 10 days of the German offensive (21 March to 31 March 1918), successfully used aircraft to disrupt the German advances and thereby give the British Army time to regroup. On 4 June 1918, French bombers from Escadrille 12 dropped 7,200 bombs on German troops concentrated in a ravine near the Forest of Villers-Cotterets, virtually annihilating the entire force. More important, aircraft proved vital when the Allies (now including fresh American troops) launched a counterattack at Château-Thierry on 18 July 1918 by providing detailed reports on German positions and movements in the sector.

Although the Germans had pretty much exhausted themselves by the time the Allied counteroffensive got underway at Amiens on 8 August 1918—a date that Ludendorff called the "black day of the German Army"—aircraft played a critical role in the Allied success. Even though Allied aircraft were unable to destroy German communication and supply lines and prevent the German Army's retreat, despite repeated efforts, they played an important role in strafing German troop columns and in providing support to Allied tanks. As tanks advanced, aircraft would patrol forward to identify enemy artillery before it could fire on them. Indeed, in one of the decisive battles of the Allied counteroffensive, the Battle of Saint-Mihiel, which was fought between 12 and 16 September, aircraft were employed as an integral part of the offensive, rather than just playing an auxiliary role.

Although General John J. Pershing, commander of the American Expeditionary Force (AEF), had originally been somewhat skeptical about the value of aircraft based on their poor performance during his Punitive Expedition into Mexico in 1916, he had come to appreciate their worth on the battlefield by the summer of 1918. In preparing for the Saint-Mihiel Offensive, Pershing assigned Colonel William "Billy" Mitchell with the task of organizing the 1,500 Allied aircraft that Supreme Allied Commander Field Marshal Ferdinand Foch had put at the AEF's disposal. By the start of the battle, Mitchell had developed an aerial battle plan unparalleled in the war. Assigning approximately one-third of his force to support ground operations, Mitchell divided the remaining two-thirds into two brigades of 500 planes each. These were used in a variety of strategic missions unprecedented in the war: achieving air superiority; attacking German troops, supply depots, and communication centers; and bombing enemy air bases to force them into the open. Employing his brigades as aerial cavalry, Mitchell ordered strafing and bombing attacks on German infantry to reinforce Allied attacks and to cut off lines of retreat. Mitchell's success in helping the AEF win the battle led to his promotion to brigadier general.

Mitchell followed up his success at Saint-Mihiel by organizing aircraft for the Meuse-Argonne Offensive that was launched on 26 September and would continue until the Armistice on 11 November. Although Mitchell had just 800 Allied aircraft—approximately two-thirds flown by American pilots—for the start of the Meuse-Argonne Offensive, his brilliant use of them proved critical to success. Despite the inferiority of the Liberty D.H.4s—one of the few American aircraft to see action in the war—at his disposal, Mitchell launched massive bombing raids on German positions to overcome them with sheer force of numbers. On 9 October a force of 253 bombers and 110 fighter escorts crossed the Germans lines and dropped more than 30 tons of explosives on a staging area where the Germans were attempting to organize a counterattack. Losing just one plane in the attack, the Americans shot down twelve German aircraft. Indeed, in a 2-week period, American pilots shot down more than 100 German aircraft and destroyed 21 observation balloons. It was also during the Meuse-Argonne Offensive that Mitchell organized an airdrop to supply the famous Lost Battalion—the First Battalion, 308th Infantry, 77th Division—which had become isolated and surrounded by Germans, until it could be relieved by Allied troops. Although many other factors contributed to the ultimate success of the Allied counteroffensive, the advantage that the Allies had gained in air power by the time it was launched certainly helped expedite the military successes that forced the Germans to sign the Armistice on 11 November 1918 and bring 4 years of war to an end.

The Use of Air Power in Other Theaters

Although the nature of trench warfare on the Western Front had made it unique compared to other theaters of the war and had contributed greatly to the evolving role of aircraft as described earlier, aircraft would also play important roles in other theaters of the war. It is important to note that even though the British, French, and

Germans concentrated the bulk of their air forces over the Western Front, their aircraft and their pilots played important roles on other fronts. Whereas Austria-Hungary attempted to become self-sufficient in aircraft, she had to rely increasingly upon Germany to provide aircraft to her forces. Likewise, Russia, although possessing an excellent aircraft in the *Ilya Muromets,* relied heavily upon imported French motors for its domestically produced aircraft as well as on French aircraft that had become obsolete on the Western Front. The British and French would also dispatch squadrons to Italy and the Balkans to support the Italians, Serbs, Greeks, and Romanians in those theaters, just as the Germans would do the same for Austria-Hungary, Turkey, and Bulgaria.

By far the most important role of air power on the Eastern Front was reconnaissance and observation. Indeed, air combat was far rarer on the Eastern Front than was the case on the Western Front. Only 358 of Germany's claim of 7,425 air victories occurred on the Eastern Front. Because the Eastern Front was more fluid compared with the West, with such breakthroughs as the German advance through Galicia in the spring and summer of 1915 making it more difficult to stabilize the front, pilots of reconnaissance aircraft faced different challenges in that they were not always flying over familiar terrain. Indeed, the vast scope of the front and the poor quality of maps made it difficult for pilots to orient themselves. Nevertheless, reconnaissance aircraft played an important role in many campaigns. Russian photo-reconnaissance of Austro-Hungarian forces during the spring of 1916, for example, contributed greatly to the initial success of the Brusilov Offensive by allowing Russian artillery to knock out many of the Austro-Hungarian guns in the preliminary barrage of 4 June, thereby clearing the way for the infantry assault launched on 5 June. Russia unfortunately lacked the resources to exploit its breakthrough before German reinforcements arrived. The outbreak of the Russian Revolution in March 1917 tilted air power on the Eastern Front decisively in Germany's favor by almost completely disrupting Russia's fledgling aircraft industry. A combination of Russian deserters and German aerial reconnaissance gave the Germans plenty of advance knowledge of Russia's last offensive in the war—the ill-fated Kerensky Offensive launched on 1 July 1917. Although the Russians achieved initial success against Austro-Hungarian forces, they were caught totally off guard by a well-planned German counteroffensive. The ensuing military collapse of the Russian Army contributed to the Bolshevik Revolution on 7 November and ultimately to the Treaty of Brest-Litovsk (3 March 1918), by which Russia left the war.

Despite the limited number of aircraft involved on the Balkan Front, they played an important role, especially in reconnaissance. A German reconnaissance flight over the Dardanelles on 18 March 1915 helped foil the Allied Fleet's attempt to force the Turkish Straits by providing sufficient warning to Turkish fortifications. British reconnaissance aircraft provided spotting duties for British ship-to-shore fire during the ensuing British and ANZAC (Australian and New Zealand Army Corps) landings at Gallipoli in late April. Had the British possessed fighters and bombers at Gallipoli and been able to employ them in support of ground forces, the ultimate outcome might have been different. After Serbia's near collapse in 1915, both the French and British would dispatch aircraft, which helped secure the bridgehead at Salonika. Germany would also send aircraft to support its Turkish and Bulgarian allies. Aircraft proved especially crucial in enabling armies to maintain communications in the rugged terrain of the Balkans, where telegraph and telephone lines were largely nonexistent. It should be noted, however, that the use of air power in the Balkans was severely limited by logistical problems of bringing up fuel and supplies.

Aircraft played a variety of roles on the Italian Front, where the principal combatants—Italy and Austria-Hungary—were augmented by their respective allies. The lack of available aircraft, the difficulty of terrain, and the failure to advance greatly limited the Italian military's use of aircraft during the numerous battles along the Isonzo River in 1915 and early 1916. By late 1916, however, the Italians did possess sufficient Caproni bombers to carry out strategic bombing campaigns against Austro-Hungarian bases along the Adriatic. As mentioned previously, the Italians were using aircraft by 1917 to provide close ground support of troops in the Tenth and Eleventh Battles of the Isonzo River. Italy's initial successes against Austria-Hungary, however, led Germany to dispatch both troops and aircraft to the Italian Front. As a result, the Germans and Austro-Hungarians would gain air superiority, which contributed to their tremendous victory over the Italians in the Battle of Caporetto (Twelfth Battle of the Isonzo). Augmented by British and French forces after Caporetto, the Italians would recover in time for the Battle of the Piave River in June 1918. For weeks leading up to the battle, Allied aircraft had systematically bombed Austrian airfields and supply depots. In addition, the Allies dropped Lieutenant Camillo de Carlo behind Austrian lines on the night of

30 May 1918. Based upon his intelligence gathering, the Allies were prepared well in advance of the Austrian attack and had amassed more than 700 aircraft (mostly Italian) along the front. When the Austro-Hungarian Army launched its attack on 15 June, the Allies quickly seized control of the skies, using their fighters to strafe enemy positions and their bombers to disrupt enemy supplies. The Battle of the Piave River marked the last Austro-Hungarian offensive of the war and paved the way for the decisive Battle of Vittorio-Veneto (24 October to 4 November), which knocked Austria-Hungary out of the war.

Although only a handful of aircraft were employed in the Middle Eastern, African, and Asian theaters, they played important roles in the conflict there. In January 1915, for example, British aircraft provided warning to General Sir John Maxwell, commander of British forces in Egypt, that a Turkish force was advancing across the Sinai Peninsula in an attempt to seize the Suez Canal. As a result, by the time the Turks arrived at the canal on 2 February, the British were more than prepared and successfully drove them off. Enjoying air supremacy throughout the Middle East, the British used aircraft to bomb Turkish forces around oases in the Sinai in 1916 and to provide effective reconnaissance and ground support during their advance into Palestine in 1917 and Syria in 1918. The British enjoyed similar successes against the Turks in Mesopotamia (modern Iraq), where their so-called Lewis-gun detachments, comprised of aircraft and armored cars working together, served the role traditionally played by cavalry in striking at Turkish flanks as the British advanced north of Baghdad in late October 1918. Although both the Germans and the British would use aircraft for reconnaissance purposes in Africa, the British had a decisive advantage. Its prosperous dominion, the Union of South Africa, had established an aviation corps in 1912 and would use aircraft to provide effective reconnaissance during its January 1915 invasion of German Southwest Africa (modern Namibia). More important, German forces were cut off from supplies and fuel needed to support their few aircraft. Perhaps the most interesting use of aircraft in Africa was Germany's attempt in November 1917 to use a naval zeppelin (L-59) to supply its forces in East Africa by ferrying some 14 tons of goods from Bulgaria. After reaching Khartoum, Lieutenant Commander Ludwig Bockholt received a radio message ordering him to return, although there is some dispute about whether the message was misinterpreted. Although the mission was a failure, when the L-59 returned to Bulgaria it had been aloft for 95 hours and had traveled 4,200 miles. In

China, which had earlier ceded spheres of influence along its coast to the European powers and Japan, the Japanese took advantage of the war in Europe to lay siege to the German fortress of Quingdao (Tsingtao) between 23 August and 7 November 1914.[7] During the siege the Germans used an observation balloon and an airplane for artillery spotting, whereas the Japanese employed four seaplanes in a similar fashion and also attempted to drop small bombs on German gunboats.

The Use of Air Power at Sea

Although the technological limitations of aviation at sea were certainly much greater than that on land, aviation nevertheless played just as important a role in transforming warfare at sea as it did on land during the First World War. In addition to helping fulfill the traditional naval objective of control or command of the seas, naval aviation also offered the possibility of projecting naval power inland through the air, thereby greatly enhancing its strength and importance. Upon the outbreak of the war, the navies of the belligerent powers employed three main types of naval aircraft: airplanes and airships operating from land bases; seaplanes (airplanes fitted with floats) and flying boats operating from coastal ports; and seaplanes that were either towed from or carried aboard ship and hoisted into or out of the water.[8] By war's end, naval aviation had evolved to include airplanes and seaplanes that were capable of taking off from and landing on a ship's deck, something that was rather hazardous until the British launched the first purpose-built aircraft carrier, the H.M.S. *Argus*, in 1918.

Compared with their counterparts flying over the battlefields of the First World War, naval aviators faced a number of difficulties that were unique to their area. Weather conditions could change more rapidly and violently at sea than over land. Engine failure over land allowed the pilot at least a fighting chance of landing safely, whereas ditching a plane at sea, especially in rough waters, was dangerous, and search-and-rescue missions were often like looking for a needle in a haystack, particularly if the downed plane lost its wireless communication. Naval pilots also faced a more difficult challenge in navigation because they did not have the convenience of recognizable landforms, roads, and railways to guide them once they departed the coastline and headed into the open sea. The mind-numbing task of flying over vast stretches of water made it easy for pilots to lose their bearings, especially in cloudy or foggy conditions. As a result of these factors, endurance was one of the most critical factors in naval aircraft because time aloft determined the type of missions that could be carried out. Airships were consequently used extensively for naval reconnaissance. The lack of a stationary front also increased the difficulty of naval aerial reconnaissance. Because warships could move quickly, unlike the armies bogged down in the trenches of the Western Front, locating the enemy's presence was more difficult. Although the wireless made it possible to report ship sightings in real time, it could not guarantee accurate information. Navigational inaccuracy and misidentification of ships often produced faulty reports, and naval aircraft conducting such operations were sometimes the victim of friendly fire, as in the Battle of Heligoland Bight in 1914 when a German destroyer shot at one of its own navy's zeppelins.

Although air enthusiasts had boldly predicted before the war that aerial attacks would take a toll on surface vessels, the early use of aircraft in the opening stages of the war provided no evidence to support them. Despite the repeated efforts of Japanese seaplanes to bomb German ships during its siege of Quingdao, it took several weeks before a target was hit, and even then not a single German ship was lost to aerial attack. Likewise, an Austro-Hungarian flying boat failed to strike the French cruiser *Waldeck Rousseau* in an attack carried out in the Adriatic in October 1914. There were several factors that contributed to the lack of success. In the initial stages of the war belligerents lacked effective aerial bombs; indeed, they were forced to rely upon improvised ordnance. Belligerents also did not possess accurate delivery systems (i.e., bomb sights, racks, and release mechanisms were crude at best). Until more powerful engines were developed, early naval aircraft did not have the lifting capacity to carry a bomb load sufficient for sinking enemy ships. In addition to these equipment problems, naval targets proved more difficult to locate and hit than did stationary targets on land.

As a result of these difficulties, naval aircraft were used primarily for reconnaissance duties. German zeppelins provided reconnaissance when the High Seas Fleet launched its cruisers and destroyers on raids against the British coast and during the Battle of Jutland, when the L-12 located the British Fleet on 1 June 1916. In the Adriatic, Austro-Hungarian Lohner flying boats successfully maintained surveillance over Italian seaports and air superiority over the Adriatic until the last year of the war, when the Italian Macchi M.5 flying boat shifted the balance to Italy's favor. In addition to providing reconnaissance against opposing naval forces, naval aircraft were useful in identifying minefields and submarines. Aircraft equipped with wireless also performed spotting duty for battleships, which now had the capability of firing beyond the range of sight. Whereas they were used mainly for directing ship-to-shore fire, as in the case of the Gallipoli Campaign, aircraft occasionally directed ship-to-ship fire, as in the case of the British monitors that fired upon the German light cruiser *Königsberg* and forced her crew to scuttle her in the Rufji River delta in East Africa.

Of all of its roles at sea, naval aircraft proved most effective in antisubmarine warfare. Indeed, Royal Navy Lieutenant Hugh Williamson had outlined a proposal as early as March 1912 for using aircraft to drop specialized depth charges against enemy submarines. Because submarines of the First World War era had an extremely limited capacity for underwater propulsion, the mere threat of an aerial attack could have an important impact on the war by forcing them to remain submerged. This would become especially important after the Allies adopted the convoy system. One of the most famous instances of aerial antisubmarine warfare came on 15 September 1916, when Austrian Lohner seaplanes forced the French submarine *Foucault* to surface after spotting it and dropping depth charges. To be most effective against the U-boat menace, the Allies needed aircraft capable of greater range and endurance. The Felixstowe flying boat proved to be very effective in the North Sea and English Channel, whereas the SS (Submarine Scout) blimp, a nonrigid airship that relied upon an RAF B.E.2 fuselage for power, could remain aloft for as long as 24 hours and reach speeds up to 55 mph. Although Allied aircraft sank just one German submarine and permanently disabled just two, they greatly enhanced the success of the convoy system because they could identify the thin oil line exhaust from German submarines and report their position to naval destroyers accompanying a convoy. While U-boats managed to sink 257 convoyed ships during the last 18 months of the war, only two of these ships were operating in convoys that were accompanied by aerial escort. From a strategic level, therefore, naval aircraft enjoyed far greater success in antisubmarine warfare than it did on a tactical level.

Whereas aircraft proved more successful in a defensive rather than offensive role on the high seas, aircraft had demonstrated potential as offensive weapons against unarmored shipping by the end of the war. Beginning in 1915, the Germans used aircraft from their Belgian bases to attack Allied shipping in the English Channel and the North Sea. In one incident that had international repercussions, a German seaplane damaged the American tanker, the *Cushing*, on 29 April 1915. This incident would be cited in the American protests that followed the sinking of the *Lusitania* by a U-boat. Even though at least three British merchant ships were sunk by German torpedo planes in 1917, German naval aircraft proved more effective in interdicting neutral vessels and forcing them to dock in German or German-controlled ports. One of the most successful German commerce-raiders, the *Wolf*, which was active in the South Pacific and Indian Ocean for much of 1917, employed a Friedrichshafen FF 33e floatplane to assist it in locating targets. Russia also successfully used seaplanes in the Black Sea to attack Turkish and Bulgarian coastal installations and Turkish shipping. The Russian Black Sea Fleet designated the *Imperator Nikolai I* and the *Imperator Alexandr I* as *gidrokreisera* (hydrocruisers) to carry seaplanes in order to extend the area in which they could operate. Russian seaplanes would account for approximately 5 percent of the 1,000 ships that the Turks lost between 1914 and 1917, including the 6 February 1916 sinking of the collier *Irmingard*, the largest merchant ship lost to air attack during the war.

With the development of primitive carriers by the end of the war, the possibilities of using naval aircraft to launch attacks against enemy naval ships and installations became practical. The British Navy had taken the lead in designing aircraft carriers, primarily because its seaplanes and flying boats were ineffective in challenging German zeppelins. Realizing that land-based aircraft would be more effective, the British began installing ramps on the decks and over the turrets of ships such as the H.M.S. *Campania* and H.M.S. *Furious* to allow airplanes like the Sopwith Pup and Sopwith Camel to take off. On 19 July 1918, for example, seven Sopwith Camels were launched from the *Furious* on a mission to destroy zeppelin sheds at Tondern. Even though they succeeded in destroying the L-54 and L-60 in their sheds, the pilots had to ditch their aircraft upon completing their mission. With the H.M.S. *Argus*, however, the British successfully overcame the difficulty of landing onboard ship. The *Argus* featured a full-deck landing platform with a command island to the starboard side and with a retractable charthouse to allow for unobstructed take-offs and landings. In addition, the *Argus* vented exhaust gases through ducts on each side of the vessel, rather than through vertical funnels, thereby reducing air instability for landing aircraft. Whereas the war ended before the *Argus*'s capabilities could be demonstrated in battle, the future of naval aviation and naval warfare were clearly in the process of changing. Although postwar theorists perhaps overstated the role that aircraft had played in making battleships obsolete insofar as examples from the First World War are concerned, the importance of aircraft to naval warfare would make the aircraft carrier the critical component in the naval arsenal, something that remains true to this day.

THE ORGANIZATION AND MOBILIZATION OF AIR POWER DURING THE WAR

As demonstrated in the preceding sections, the First World War had transformed the nature of air power as aircraft developed new roles and gained greater importance in the overall scheme of the war itself. It is not surprising that the war had an important impact upon the organizational structure of air power as each belligerent attempted to find a more efficient and effective way in wielding this new weapon. Just as important, if not more important, was the impact that the war would have upon aircraft production, as each power sought to mobilize the resources necessary to meet the ever-increasing need for greater numbers of aircraft and the ever-increasing demands for better-performing aircraft. In addition, the expansion of air power involved training thousands of pilots to fulfill the growing roles played by aircraft and produced the aces who captivated public attention like no other figures of the war.

The Organization of the Air Services

When the European powers entered the First World War, their air services were divided between their armies and their navies, as in the case of the British RFC and the RNAS. This is understandable because the needs of each service and the types of aircraft needed to fulfill those needs were somewhat different. As the demands for aircraft increased, however, this often resulted in interservice rivalries over the procurement and allocation of new aircraft and the missions that each were to pursue. During the course of the war the various powers gave aviation increased presence within the respective high commands so that intelligence gathered from the air could be communicated to top commanders faster. Coordination between artillery and the air services became an important part of daily operations on the stalemated Western Front. Planning for ground offensives also involved coordination with the air services, as seen earlier in the 1916 Battles of Verdun and the Somme and the 1918 German spring offensive and Allied counteroffensive. As indicated earlier, the French granted local autonomy to the air units stationed around Verdun during that epic battle, and the Germans would grant a similar level of autonomy to the Jagdgeschwaders, such as Richthofen's "Flying Circus." Despite these efforts, military commanders sometimes failed to heed the advice of aviators and the demands of political leaders to use aircraft in a more effective manner. As conflicts over missions and role increased, the air services increasingly demanded greater autonomy and even recognition as an independent branch of service. In addition, political debates over the role of air power could have an important impact upon military organization, especially in France and Great Britain, where the war ministries and the military high commands were more subject to parliamentary oversight.

In France, where the political structure of the Third Republic created a weak executive branch and left the Chamber of Deputies and Senate in a position to force changes in ministries rather frequently, the organization and mission of the air service became a subject of heated parliamentary debates and produced a lack of continuity in the air power command structure. Prior to the war, for example, the army's air service had first been organized in October 1910 as the Inspectorate of Military Aviation under Major General Pierre-August Rocques within the Directorate for Engineers. In April 1912 Brigadier General August Édouard Hirschauer replaced Rocques, but charges of collusion with leading aircraft manufacturers led to his resignation in September 1913. Brigadier General Félix Paul Antoine Bernard, who had experience in the artillery, replaced Hirschauer and began pressing for a greater degree of autonomy for aviation. On 4 April 1914 this was granted as the army reorganized aviation as the Directorate of Military Aeronautics (Twelfth Directorate) directly under the war minister. Bernard's decision to cut back production and release mechanics for front-line service upon the outbreak of the war proved to be a critical mistake, leading to Hirschauer's return in October 1914. When French aircraft proved inferior to the Fokker Eindecker the following year, a parliamentary commission blamed Hirschauer and demanded a reorganization of aviation, in part so that the political demands for a bombing campaign against Germany could be met. As a result, Hirschauer was sacked in mid-September and aviation was reorganized yet again, with Senator René Henri Besnard being appointed undersecretary for aeronautics with oversight of the Twelfth Directorate. This arrangement lasted just 6 months because his attempts to impose a reorganization of the procurement process disrupted production and resulted in widespread protests from aircraft manufacturers. After Besnard's forced resignation in February 1916 Minister of War General Joseph-Simon Galliéni restored military control by appointing Colonel Henry Jacques Régnier in charge of the Twelfth Directorate. After yet another cabinet change in March 1917, an undersecretary for aeronautics was reestablished under Socialist Deputy Charles Augustin Daniel Vincent, who had served as a reconnaissance observer. Vincent would last for approximately 5 months until yet another cabinet reshuffle resulted in his replacement by Jacques Louis Demesnil. Many scholars have argued that this constant administrative turmoil greatly hampered French air power, both in terms of overall production and in delaying the introduction of more technologically advanced fighters and bombers.[9]

Although Great Britain did not experience the same degree of political turmoil that France did, the interservice rivalry between the RFC and the RNAS intensified after the onset of the war because their dual demands for aircraft were greater than Britain's fledgling aviation industry could supply and because their objectives and priorities grew further apart. The RNAS initiated plans for an aggressive bombing campaign to attack both the German Fleet and dockyards as well as German arsenals and factories, whereas the RFC demanded that its tactical support of the BEF be given top priority. In an effort to promote cooperation between the RFC and RNAS, the British war cabinet appointed the Joint War Air Committee (chaired by the Earl of Derby and including RNAS Director of Air Service Rear Admiral C. L. Vaughn-Lee and RFC Director of Military Aeronautics Lieutenant General Sir David Henderson) on 15 February 1916. Although the Joint War Air Committee collapsed after 2 months of acrimonious infighting, one of the results of its failure was a slow but steady push toward creating an independent air service. The combination of German air raids and David Lloyd George becoming prime minister in December 1916 added new impetus in this direction. Public demands for better air defenses and a strategic bombing campaign against Germany (which Haig and Trenchard opposed as a waste of resources) led to the Smuts Committee's recommendation that the two forces be merged. More important, the heavy casualties Britain had suffered at the Somme and in the Passchendaele Campaigns left Lloyd George determined to break Haig's control over war policy, which also included Trenchard's control over the RFC. As a result, on 1 April 1918 the RFC and RNAS were merged into the Royal Air Force, which was the first independent air service in history. In practice, however, the birth of the RAF did not result in an immediate change in policy because the German spring offensive necessitated the concentration of air power for close air support.

Germany entered the First World War with a somewhat complicated command structure because both Prussia and Bavaria maintained separate armies and air forces, which in wartime fell under the German High Command.[10] In addition, the Germany High Seas Fleet jealously guarded its own aerial resources and, as indicated earlier, would spend an enormous amount of funds building a zeppelin fleet during the war as part of its campaign against Great Britain. It should be noted, however, that the interservice rivalry within Germany did not get as bitter as that within Great Britain, primarily because the German High Command exercised a virtual dictatorship over the country, especially after Hindenburg and Ludendorff assumed command of the general staff in August 1916. More important, unlike the French, the Germans profited from greater continuity within their command structure. In March 1915 the office of Chef des Feldflugwesens (Chief of Field Aviation) was established under Colonel Hermann von der Lieth-Thomsen to provide direction to the air service and coordination with the High Command. Whereas Lieth-Thomsen's proposal for creating an independent air service failed in 1916 because of naval and Bavarian resistance, the pressures of Verdun and the Somme led Hindenburg and Ludendorff to make aviation an autonomous branch of the army on 8 October 1916 when Lieutenant General Ernst von Höppner was named commanding general of the air service (Kogenluft) and Lieth-Thomsen was named his chief of staff. They would both remain in this position until the end of the war and would both be awarded Germany's highest military award, the Pour le Mérite, for their roles in organizing and leading German air power. Another key figure was Major Wilhelm Siegert (later promoted to Lieutenant Colonel), who had served as Lieth-Thomsen's deputy, before assuming the inspectorate of aviation in July 1916, a position in which he assumed responsibility for implementing Germany's aviation production program until the end of the war.

Germany's ally, Austria-Hungary, enjoyed a comparable degree of organizational continuity, largely through the leadership of one extraordinary individual, Major Emil Uzelac, who on 24 April 1912 was named commander of the *Luftschifferabteilung* (LA) or airship section of the army. Uzelac had previously served as an engineer in the transport corps and brought a good technical understanding of aircraft requirements to his position. Although he was 45 at the time of his appointment, he promptly began training and soon received his pilot's license. Promoted to colonel after the outbreak of the war, Uzelac proved to be a hands-on leader who often personally tested new aircraft and sought information from junior officers and enlisted men. After Italy entered the war against Austria-Hungary on 23 May 1915 and increased the demands upon the air service, Uzelac played a leading role in its reorganization as the *Luftfahrtruppen* (LFT) or aviation troops. Uzelac was promoted to major general in May 1918 and remained in command of LFT until 1 October 1918. Despite the limitations of Austria-Hungary's aircraft industry, Uzelac was successful in maintaining an operationally effective air service against the Russians and in keeping a surprising esprit de corps among his aviators, possibly because he was more willing to rely upon noncommissioned pilots than were most of his other counterparts. Despite suffering the same aircraft shortages as the LFT, the Austro-Hungarian Navy still managed to maintain air superiority over the Adriatic until the end of 1917. Even though Russia's exit from the war allowed Austria-Hungary to shift resources to the Italian Front, it was insufficient compared with the size of force that Italy, augmented by France and Great Britain, had amassed by 1918, and as mentioned earlier, this proved critical to Austria-Hungary's collapse in the fall of 1918.

Even though the Imperial Russian Air Service had entered the war with slightly more aircraft than did Germany, the bulk were by and large obsolete foreign aircraft that the Russians would have a difficult time finding spare parts for once Turkey entered the war on Germany and Austria-Hungary's side, thereby closing off the best access to Russia. The lack of skilled mechanics made the maintenance problems even worse, resulting in more Russian pilots dying from accidents in faulty planes than from aerial combat. Despite the limitations of its equipment and its industrial base, the Imperial Russian Air Service still managed to expand during the war. By the summer of 1915 it fielded 553 aircraft divided among 58 units, but this was hardly adequate for providing air cover along a front that stretched more than 1,000 km. In May 1916, for example, an average of seventy-two missions were flown each day with each mission averaging just 58 minutes. Indeed, by 1916 the Imperial Russian Air Service fielded more pilots than it had aircraft. The one major success story for the Imperial Russian Air Service was its organization of the *Eskadra Vozdushnykh Korablei* (EKV) or Squadron of Flying Ships, which was organized around Igor Sikorsky's *Ilya Muromets* and which provided excellent service for long-range reconnaissance and bombing duties. Russia unfortunately did not produce the Ilya Muromet in sufficient numbers to make a difference before the Russian Revolution of 1917 brought aircraft production to a virtual halt. With the outbreak of the Russian Civil War in the summer of 1918, the Bolsheviks nationalized control over Russian aircraft factories and reorganized Russia's remaining aircraft within the Red Army into some 30 squadrons. The Red Army would enjoy a major advantage in air power against the Whites, especially with the use of the Grigorovich M.9 flying boats along the Volga River.

Although Italy did not declare war on Austria-Hungary until 24 May 1915, it had begun preparations for entering the war, including the organization of an air service, soon after the outbreak of war in August 1914. Italy initially organized its air service to perform two roles, tactical and strategic reconnaissance, issuing a decree to that effect on 25 October 1914. By the start of 1915, however, the example of aerial observation for artillery on the Western Front indicated that a more thorough organization was needed. As a result, on 7 January 1915 the Il Corpo Aeronautico Militaire (Military Air Corps) was created, establishing a general directorate in the War Ministry and a division for balloons and airships and a division for airplanes. More important, a central aeronautical inspectorate assumed responsibility for jump-starting Italy's infant aircraft industry, which at the time consisted of approximately 100 skilled workers in five different firms that were capable of producing approximately 50 planes a year. This was hardly adequate. As the inspectorate swung into gear, it relied heavily upon a conversion of Italy's automobile industry to aviation manufacturing. By the time Italy entered the war, the aircraft industry had grown to 1,500 workers. As production increased dramatically in 1916, the Italian Navy divided its air service into directorates based at Taranto and Venice in order to better coordinate its activities in the Adriatic. It should be noted that Italy's leading air power theorist, Giulio Douhet, was court-martialed for insubordination and sentenced to 1 year in prison for openly criticizing Italy's war policy. After the Italian debacle at Caporetto in late 1917, the Italian Air Service was reorganized as a General Commissariat within the War Office and Douhet was appointed director of aviation in January 1918, a position he held until he retired in frustration in June 1918. Douhet would have a greater impact after the war, however, as one of the leading air power theorists.

After the outbreak of war in Europe in 1914 and the German sinking of the *Lusitania* in 1915, the United States slowly began a program of military preparedness by expanding the national guard, including funding for national guard aviation units. Many American pilots, however, rushed off to the Western Front to join the RFC and the French Foreign Legion. The most famous unit of American volunteers was the *Lafayette Escadrille,* officially designated as Squadron N. 124, which was organized in May 1916 as a joint force of American volunteers and French army pilots. After the United States entered the war and began organizing an air service for the AEF, almost all members of the *Lafayette Escadrille* transferred into the AEF with some of its leading pilots, such as William Thaw and Raoul Lufbery, being appointed squadron commanders; however, the U.S. Army was unwilling to welcome one pilot, Corporal Eugene Bullard, into its ranks, ostensibly because he had gotten into a fist-fight with one of his French officers, but primarily because he was an African-American. It should be pointed out that this incident did not prevent the French from awarding Bullard the prestigious Croix de Guerre or eventually naming him to the Legion of Honor.[11]

After the United States declared war on Germany in April 1917, Major William "Billy" Mitchell, one of five U.S. aviation officers stationed in Europe, headed to London to meet with Trenchard to discuss aviation strategy. By the time Pershing arrived in Europe with the first units of the AEF, Mitchell had prepared a detailed plan for developing two distinct types of air forces: fighter squadrons to attack enemy aircraft and bomber squadrons to conduct a strategic campaign against enemy targets. Pershing, however, refused to give the air service the degree of independence that Mitchell desired, believing that air power existed to provide tactical support to the ground forces. Nevertheless, in August 1918, Mitchell was promoted to brigadier general and assumed command as chief of air service, First Army. In addition to planning the use of air power in the Saint-Mihiel and Meuse-Argonne Offensives, Mitchell pressed for a major expansion of American air power, so much so that two additional army air services (Second and Third Army) were created before the Armistice. This expansion was made possible through the untiring efforts of Lieutenant Colonel George O. Squier, who established the air services training base at Kelly Field, near San Antonio, Texas, where a total of 5,182 officers and 197,468 enlisted personnel received their training during the war. Had the war continued into 1919, the United States would have had an even greater impact on the air war.

Aircraft Production during the War

The transformation of the aircraft industry and aircraft themselves during the First World War proves the adage that "necessity is the mother of invention." With aircraft conclusively demonstrating their value for reconnaissance and observation in the opening stages of the war and fighters and bombers becoming an essential part of the air war by 1915, aircraft production became a vital part of wartime industrial output. As demands upon the air services increased, manufacturers faced the difficulty of replacing losses and increasing quantity, as well as improving quality in order to keep up with or surpass the enemy. The result was a truly astounding technological revolution in aviation. Where the aircraft of 1914 were slow, flimsy, underpowered machines with limited carrying capacity and low ceiling capability, the aircraft of 1918 were capable of flying twice as fast and twice as high, and were powered by engines four times more powerful than were their 1914 counterparts. During the course of the war Britain, France, and Germany would produce a combined total of slightly more than 150,000 aircraft. By the end of the war, the French had 3,700 aircraft in service, the British 2,600, and the Germans 2,500. Although large numbers of aircraft were consumed in the war—the British lost 782 aircraft during the Somme Offensive—quite a few were simply withdrawn as they became obsolete with the introduction of new aircraft. Germany and France, for example, both introduced approximately 200 new design types during the course of the war. As a result, the average service life of most aircraft was a mere 6 months. Whereas the pace of development and production could be quite remarkable—it took just 3 months to transform the Liberty V-type engine from a design on paper (29 May 1917) to an engine-powering aircraft (29 August 1917)—such speed of production sometimes resulted in design flaws that were not detected until the aircraft were used in combat conditions.

Just as the military had issued specifications and relied upon private contractors to meet them prior to the war, the same procedures were used during the war. Once the air services set the specifications, private industry would develop designs to meet them, and production would begin under the supervision of air service technicians. It is important to note that Britain was somewhat of an exception to this general rule in that the RFC had established the Royal Aircraft Factory to design new prototypes, which would then be contracted out to private companies for production. Although demands for new designs often came from the front, at times the acquisition of an enemy plane revealed new technological breakthroughs that resulted in the introduction of new production models. German inspection of a captured Sopwith Triplane led to the Fokker Dr.1. Leaders also tried to anticipate future needs for aircraft based on anticipated changes on the front. In 1917, for example, the British began development of two specialized aircraft that could be used if they ever gained control of the air from German fighters: the Sopwith Salamander to assist in ground support combat and the Handley Page V/1500 for bombing Berlin.

Another major challenge confronting all powers, especially Germany, Austria-Hungary, and Russia, was procuring sufficient materials to meet the demands. As a result, all powers to varying degrees increasingly resorted to greater governmental control in the allocation of resources in an effort to meet production goals. This sometimes involved forcing companies to use subcontractors to produce aircraft. Although the demands for increased aircraft production resulted in a vast expansion in the number of workers in the aircraft industries of the various powers, the pace of production resulted in longer workdays that sapped the patriotism of workers, especially when wages did not keep pace with wartime inflation, and increasingly resulted in strikes. Between 11 and 26 September 1917, for example, more than 57,000 French aircraft workers went on strike, shutting down production at thirty-two factories. Whereas the extent of strikes varied from country to country, they definitely hampered production.

Several factors were critical to successful aircraft design. Machine guns had to be affixed to the plane to provide the pilot or gunner easy access to change magazines and remove jammed cartridges. Engines had to be installed to allow ground crews easy access both to make repairs and to replace engines. During the course of the war vast improvements in engines and airframes allowed for more durable, high-efficiency aircraft. Although the first all-metal airplanes were introduced by war's end, the vast majority of military aircraft flown during the war were constructed with wooden airframes and canvas covering. As a result, aircraft were susceptible to structural collapse in adverse weather conditions or in extreme maneuvers. In addition, fire was a major hazard. Other problems included the wooden propellers, which could be shot off if the synchronization gear failed on the machine guns (this most likely is what caused Max Immelmann's fatal crash on 18 June 1916).

By far the most important factor in a successful design was the engine. Demands for greater power and longer performance at full throttle quickly resulted in major differences as well as higher expense. By war's end, a Liberty V-12 400 hp motor cost approximately $2,500, compared with a total cost of $400 for the Ford Model T automobile. Aircraft engines were of two main types: the rotary engine, in which the engine revolved around a stationary crankshaft; and the fixed or stationary engine, which used either an inline (cylinders in a row), radial (cylinders configured in a star pattern), or V configuration of cylinders to turn the crankshaft. At the beginning of the war approximately 80 percent of all aircraft used rotary engines—the Gnome-Rhône being the most famous—because their lightness resulted in a higher power-to-weight ratio, they were air cooled, and they had little vibration. These advantages, however, came at the price of poorer fuel efficiency than fixed engines and the adverse torque effect produced by the rotating motor.[12] In addition, castor oil was the only type of lubricant that could be used in rotary engines and this ended up being spewed back on to the pilot, sometimes to the point of producing nausea. More important, the centrifugal force generated by a rotary engine limited its size to no more than 200 hp. As a result of these problems, manufacturers increasingly turned to the stationary engine. In addition to building larger engines, engineers also squeezed greater power out of engines by increasing compression rates, improving carburetors, and adding superchargers for high altitudes. Although the World War I–era Liberty Engine and World War II–era Rolls Royce Merlin were both approximately 1,650 cubic in. in size, the former was capable of only 400 hp, whereas the latter produced 2,000—approximately 40 percent of the difference was better fuel. Engine overhauls were required approximately every 300 hours of flight, compared with 2,000–3,000 hours in modern counterparts.

Although much depended upon the engine, other factors were just as important for a plane's performance. Ground crews had to take great care to inspect the propeller and airframe for even the slightest damage, which could prove disastrous in adverse weather conditions or combat flying. One of the reasons for increasing the size of air units was to insure that sufficient numbers of planes could be available for a mission because as many as one-fourth of a unit's planes might be unable to fly when called upon. Psychological factors also played an important role in an aircraft's success or failure. Whereas the performance and reputation of some aircraft, such as the Sopwith Camel, inspired courage in a pilot and fear in his enemy, the opposite sometimes occurred with pilots refusing to fly their assigned "death trap," such as the B.E.2c. At times, however, overrating an enemy's aircraft created just as strong a psychological impact. This was especially true of the Allied reaction to the Fokker Eindecker, which generated a scare in the popular press and debates in Allied governments.

As a general rule, those powers with a strong industrial base, such as France, Great Britain, and Germany, had a tremendous advantage in aircraft production compared with those with a limited industrial base, such as Russia and Austria-Hungary. There were, however, exceptions to this general rule. The United States, although being a leading industrial power and the birthplace of heavier-than-air flight, had made little effort to develop military aviation prior to entering the war in 1917 and the war ended before the industrial might of the United States had a significant impact upon the air war. Italy, although entering the war in 1915 with virtually no domestic aircraft industry, would make substantial gains in its productive capacity by war's end. The statistics for aircraft production of the various powers vary widely from source to source, primarily because of discrepancies in the production numbers reported by manufacturers and the numbers reported received by the various air services, and in some cases the lack of reliable records altogether. Table 2.1 relies upon either the most recent scholarly evidence or an average of accepted figures (statistics for Russian production are not readily available on a year-by-year basis and the United States is not included because the war ended before American production had a substantial impact upon the war).

TABLE 2.1
WORLD WAR I AIRCRAFT PRODUCTION[13]

	France	Great Britain	Italy	Russia	Germany	Austria-Hungary
1914	541	193		N/A	694	64
1915	4,489	1,680	382	N/A	4,532	281
1916	7,549	5,716	1,255	N/A	8,182	732
1917	14,915	14,832	3,861	N/A	13,977	1,272
1918	24,652	32,536	6,488	N/A	17,000	1,989
Totals	52,146	54,957	11,986	5,300	44,385	4,338

Of all the great powers, France had demonstrated the most interest in developing aircraft in the prewar years by issuing contracts to
spur production, research, and development. As a result, France
held a tremendous initial advantage, especially in terms of engine
production—indeed as late as 1916 France supplied nearly 24 percent of the engines that powered British aircraft. Like the other
powers, however, the French expected a short war and cut production to release workers and mechanics for military service at the
start of the conflict. Beginning in October 1914 the French
launched their first wartime plan to increase production. This and
subsequent plans emphasized standardization of aircraft types and
the use of subcontractors for licensed-built aircraft. Whereas just
16.2 percent of aircraft were produced by subcontractors in 1916,
43.7 percent were subcontracted in 1917 and 61 percent were subcontracted in 1918. Companies were offered advances on production and guaranteed contracts, resulting in more firms entering production and increasing the number of aircraft workers from 12,650
in 1914 to 68,920 in 1916 to 185,000 in November 1918. France
would see steady increases in aircraft production, especially in
1918, which allowed the army to replace obsolete aircraft, so that
the percentage of new aircraft at the front increased to 61 percent
by April 1918 and 87 percent by July 1918. It is equally important
that the French would produce a total of 92,386 engines during the
war—more than the combined total for Germany (42,149 engines)
and Great Britain (41,025 engines).

Despite strong encouragement from the British press, the British
government showed little interest in military aviation prior to 1911,
when it formed the Royal Aircraft Factory, which was intended to be
a design and experimental institute that would not compete against
private industry. Unlike the French, however, the British issued so
few contracts that its aircraft industry was virtually nonexistent prior
to the outbreak of the war. The biggest critical shortage was in engine manufacturing. In 1915, for example, the British produced just
1,721 engines compared with 7,096 for the French. As a result,
Britain was almost totally dependent upon France for engines during the first 2 years of the war and would continue to rely heavily
upon French engines until war's end. Another result was that the
British continued to mass produce aircraft, such as the B.E.2,
which had been designed prior to the war by the Royal Aircraft Factory, long after they had become obsolete. Of 1,680 aircraft produced in 1915 by thirty-four different manufacturers, 710 were
B.E.2s. After Lloyd George placed the aircraft industry under the

Ministry of Munitions and empowered the Air Board to allocate resources, production would begin to soar in 1917 both in quantity—despite labor strikes that resulted in the loss of 281,600 workdays—and in quality, with the introduction of such aircraft as the Sopwith Camel. One factor behind British production success in 1917 was reducing the number of types produced from 53 to 30. Similar reductions in aircraft and engine types in 1918 would result in even greater efficiency as the British aircraft industry had expanded by war's end to employ 347,112 workers—the world's largest aircraft industry—resulting in the production of 32,536 aircraft in 1918. As a result, Britain and France would enjoy a 4:1 ratio advantage over the Germans in aircraft on the Western Front during the last year of the war.

Like Great Britain, Germany did not make a substantial investment in military aircraft prior to the war. In part, this was because the German military hierarchy was divided over whether to rely upon airships, which cost substantially more to produce, or airplanes, which in the prewar years did not match the carrying capacity or flight duration of airships. Although the army came to prefer airplanes, the War Ministry was unwilling to issue contracts until aircraft manufacturers produced a proven product, which they could not easily do without the influx of funds from government contracts. With the outbreak of the war, however, the German government moved quickly to increase production, encouraging large industrial firms to begin producing aircraft. As indicated in Table 2.1, Germany would see substantial gains in aircraft production during the course of the war. Germany also introduced the war's first practical fighter with the Fokker Eindecker in 1915. With the British blockade limiting Germany's access to raw materials, the German aircraft industry increasingly relied upon plywood airframes, rather than canvas-covered airframes, and in 1917 would introduce the first all-metal airplane with the Junkers J1. Rather than introduce a variety of new engine types, the Germans relied primarily upon inline, water-cooled engines, steadily improving their performance. This did, however, result in an overreliance upon the Daimler firm, and aircraft production generally exceeded engine production, forcing the Germans to shift engines from older planes into new planes.

During the last 2 years of the war, Germany would embark on two ambitious production programs: the Hindenburg Program, which set a goal of producing 1,000 aircraft per month; and the America Program, which set a goal of producing 2,000 aircraft per month.

Although the German aircraft industry grew to more than 100,000 workers by the end of the war and was considered extremely efficient, it fell short of its objectives. Even had the Hindenburg Program of 1917 and the America Program of 1918 succeeded, neither would have offset the combined production of France and Great Britain, not to mention Italy. Whereas German fighters such as the Fokker D.VII and D.VIII are generally regarded as the best produced in the war, their qualitative advantage could not overcome the quantitative advantage enjoyed by the Allies.

Although Italy had successfully employed foreign-built aircraft during the Tripolitan War (1911–1912), it had failed to develop a domestic aircraft industry; however, even though Italy had just 100 skilled aircraft workers in January 1915, it would made substantial gains after entering the war. In part, this was possible because of the strong Italian automobile industry. Fiat, for example, began producing aircraft engines in 1915 and in 1917 introduced the 300–320 hp A.12bis, of which approximately 13,000 would be produced by war's end. Although Italy remained dependent upon French fighters, it was more than self-sufficient in reconnaissance aircraft and bombers. Indeed, Gianni Caproni's multiengine bombers were some of the best produced in the war. Whereas Italy's production paled in comparison to France, Britain, and Germany, it far surpassed that of Austria-Hungary, its principal opponent, and that would prove decisive in 1918, allowing Italy to gain air superiority over the Adriatic and contributing to its victory at Vittorio-Veneto.

Although Russia had introduced the world's first large bomber, Igor Sikorsky's four-engine *Ilya Muromets* in 1913, and had twenty-four aircraft manufacturers operating in 1914, the Russian aircraft industry lacked the materials and personnel to replace the aircraft lost in 1914, much less fulfill demands for new aircraft. In particular, Russia's great weakness was its reliance upon foreign engines. Although Russia produced 1,893 aircraft and imported just 883 aircraft between August 1914 and November 1916, it produced just 920 engines while importing 2,326 during the same period. Nevertheless, Russia did experience some gains in productivity. By 1916, for example, 73 percent of its aircraft were delivered from domestic producers. Russian factories unfortunately generally operated at below capacity because of supply shortages. Whereas Russia reached a peak of 352 aircraft produced in February 1917, the outbreak of the Russian Revolution at the end of the month resulted in a sharp decline in production and the virtual end of production by the time Russia left the war in March 1918.

Whereas Austria-Hungary had developed one of the world's first successful reconnaissance aircraft—the *Etrich Taube*—it lacked the financial resources and industrial infrastructure to see substantial increases in aircraft production until the last 2 years of the war. One reason for its problems was that its overreliance upon Lohnerwerke GmbH before the war had left Austria-Hungary without a strong domestic industry, forcing it to allow German firms (Albatros, Aviatik, and Deutsche Flugzeug Werke) to establish subsidiary divisions within the country, something it had been reluctant to do before the war. In addition, Austria-Hungary allowed the somewhat unscrupulous financier Camillo Castiglioni to obtain a virtual monopoly over the aircraft industry when he purchased Igo Etrich's Brandenburg company (later known as Hansa-Brandenburg) and gained controlling interest in Phönix Flugzeugwerke A.G. and the Ungarische Flugzeug Werke AG (UFAG). Compared with their German counterparts, Austro-Hungarian firms were far less efficient, with approximately twice as many workers being required to build an airplane in 1918. As a result, Austria-Hungary had no choice but to import aircraft from Germany to meet its wartime needs. Nevertheless, the Austro-Hungarian aircraft industry did produce one of the war's better fighters in the Phönix D.I, but it unfortunately came too late.

Although the United States had given birth to heavier-than-air flight and had issued the first contract for a military airplane, the U.S. government had made little investment in military aviation prior to entering the war. Indeed, the United States had less than 250 aircraft when it declared war on Germany on 9 April 1917. Nevertheless, the United States possessed such a large industrial base that Secretary of War Newton D. Baker had little difficulty in convincing Congress to appropriate $640 million to fund his plan to construct approximately 22,000 aircraft and 44,000 engines over an 18-month period. The outcome, however, proved that a sudden influx of funds could not create an entire new industry from scratch overnight. While American designers would quickly come up with the 400 hp Liberty V-12 engine, the United States produced only 1,300 of its 4,500 goal by June 1918 and less than 4,000 by war's end. One of the problems inherent in American manufacturing was that American factories were not tooled to produce parts on the metric system, which was used by the French and British. As a result, the United States had some difficulty in replicating its automobile industry's assembly-line approach for the production of license-built D.H.4s, which were to be powered by the Liberty V-12. Of the

3,227 Liberty D.H.4s that were constructed in the United States, only 1,885 arrived in France by the war's end and just 667 saw action at the front before the Armistice.

The Pilots and Aces of the First World War

Just as the production of aircraft was crucial to air power, so too was the production of pilots. Most pilots were young, unmarried men, who were prepared to undertake the obvious risks involved, some for higher pay, but most for the notoriety they received. Medical standards, especially for vision, had been adopted by all powers prior to 1914, but the initial demand for pilots at the outset of the war forced many belligerents, especially the French, to ignore earlier criteria that would have resulted in denials of applicants for military service. Weight considerations also became less important as aircraft performance increased. Although there does not appear to have been an overt cultural bias in the selection process, there appears to have been more pilots from the upper and middle classes than from the lower class.

Although a number of civilian flight schools had arisen prior to the First World War, they were insufficient to meet the demands for producing military pilots once war broke out in 1914, forcing all sides to increase their training programs. Whereas the military took over this responsibility, the lack of instructors often resulted in inadequate preparation. France produced approximately 18,000 pilots during the war: 134 in 1914, 1,484 in 1915, 2,698 in 1916, 5,608 in 1917, and 8,000 in 1918. Just as important as quantity of pilots trained was quality of pilots trained. Whereas the British used in-air instructors, the French simply turned their student pilots loose, beginning with taxiing exercises on the ground before sending them aloft in a trainer. Because the Germans had a smaller recruiting base than did the Allies, they generally placed more emphasis upon training, both in flying and in combat tactics. By war's end training emphasized the specialized missions that pilots would be expected to fulfill on the front. British pilots, for example, entered service in 1918 after an average of 50 hours training, compared with just 5 hours in 1914. In addition to flying lessons, pilot training included general military instruction, navigation basics, and an overview of aircraft design. Most flight instructors were former combat pilots, many of whom had experienced nervous breakdowns. Although flight schools have often been cited for high fatality rates, the available evidence does not support the allegations of poor training. The French, for example, lost just 300 students out of 18,000 trained.

Observers generally agree that the military pilot lived in a far more glamorous atmosphere than did his counterpart in the trenches. The accommodations and meals were better, and the esprit de corps was higher than it was among other branches of military service. Without a long military tradition and older officers, the air units of all sides sometimes resembled a fraternity house more than a military base. Some squadrons, such as the *Lafayette Escadrille,* which was composed of wealthy American volunteers, developed distinctive personalities because of their unique composition; others achieved this through the persona of a key leader, such as Manfred von Richthofen, who presided over the "Flying Circus." Pilots were close knit both because of the common mission and common danger, and because of the isolation of the air bases and large amount of leisure time spent together during inclement weather. Airmen, often to the chagrin of military authorities, adopted their own dress in violation of established military codes. In addition, pilots were allowed to personalize their planes. Air units were also noted for their casual, informal atmosphere, although pilots with long experience and greater victories commanded greater respect. Despite this collegiality, however, units underwent almost constant change as replacements filled the ranks of pilots who had been shot down or who had transferred to other units. New arrivals often faced a difficult time winning acceptance. Personal jealousies and rivalries occasionally created strife within squadrons.

The physical conditions that World War I pilots faced were quite harsh. Flying at altitudes approaching 14,000 ft in an open cockpit presented risks of frostbite and lack of oxygen. In addition, the exhaust fumes from engines and the castor oil spewed by rotary engines could leave pilots nauseated. If that were not enough, they faced problems with their machine guns jamming and aircraft that were prone to spin or stall during combat. One of the biggest hazards that confronted pilots was combat fatigue caused by prolonged flying, which was both physically and mentally challenging even in noncombat conditions. Add to that prolonged exposure to death— that of colleagues and his own brushes with death—and any pilot was susceptible to combat fatigue. Many pilots came to accept that they themselves would soon meet the same fate as their fallen comrades. Indeed, at many points in the war, such as in 1916 when the air battles over Verdun and the Somme were raging, the average life expectancy of a pilot on the Western Front was a mere 3 weeks from

entering service, the majority of victims being pilots of slow reconnaissance planes that provided easy targets to enemy fighters. Needless to say, such a death toll had an impact upon squadron effectiveness and caused many a pilot to lose his nerve. Although parachutes
were available and may have eliminated as many as one-third of all
air combat casualties, senior officers refused to issue them on the
premise that airmen would lose their will to fight and would abandon their planes at the first sign of trouble. A few German pilots
were allowed to use parachutes only toward the very end of the war.

From the very beginning of the conflict the public was fascinated
by the role of pilots, often comparing them with medieval knights.
Although military officials were slow to recognize the individual
achievements of military pilots, the press, which was desperate to
provide its readers military heroes, took the initiative in glorifying
successful pilots as aces. Indeed, H. G. Wells advocated that
knighthood be bestowed on any British pilot who downed a zeppelin or an enemy airplane, whereas the French tire manufacturer
André Michelin established a 1-million-franc fund to reward aviators. Most military officials disapproved of the latter practice, viewing it as an insult to men who were simply fulfilling their duty, and
by 1917 the practice of private prizes and awards had been forbid-
den. Although the British maintained an official "no publicity" policy, by 1916 the German and French High Command came to understand the propaganda impact of publicizing the successes of
aces because, with the ground war stalemated, the air war provided
clear victors in the form of aces who shot down enemy planes.
Whereas the infantry often resented the favors and publicity lav-
ished upon airmen—12 percent of Germany's Pour le Mérite were
awarded to airmen, who comprised just 0.1 percent of the army's
personnel—by war's end ground troops grew to appreciate the
ground support provided by airmen.

As the number of combat flights increased, the various powers increased the criteria for designating aces and making decorations.
The French were the first to promote a system of recognition, with a
fifth victory (tenth by 1917) giving a pilot official recognition in the
daily military communique and the "unofficial" designation of ace.
The requirement for Germany's coveted Pour le Mérite (Blue Max),
which Kaiser Wilhelm II had personally awarded to Immelmann and
Boelcke after both scored their eighth victory, was gradually raised
to sixteen by early 1917 and thirty by 1918. One of the difficulties
faced in recognition was confirming kills. When numerous planes
were involved in a dogfight, it was sometimes difficult to determine

who should get the credit for a victory. It should also be stressed that aces were an elite group. French aces comprised just 4 percent of French fighter pilots yet accumulated 50 percent of the victories. In addition to their sense of duty, aces were noted for loving the thrill of combat and the risks involved. As a result, the very best aces took risks that often led to their own demise. Twenty-five percent of French aces were lost compared with just 16 percent of French pilots as a whole. The loss rate for aces from other countries was equally high: 25 percent for Germans, 28 percent for Austrians, and 30 percent for Italians.

Aces were viewed both as heroes and arguably as the most enduring figures still remembered from the war. Indeed, as any reader of comic strips knows, Manfred von Richthofen, the Red Baron, is the great nemesis of one of the most famous pilots of all, the *Peanuts* cartoon character Snoopy. The high command even encouraged aces to publish their memoirs, as in the case of Richthofen, whose autobiography sold 500,000 copies in the first two editions. Fallen aces like Oswald Boelcke were accorded a hero's funeral, worthy of royalty. Even opposing aces were given a grudging respect, as demonstrated in press coverage and reaction to fallen enemy aces and as demonstrated when a British pilot dropped a wreath over Boelcke's burial site. Aces also occasionally challenged one another to single combat like medieval jousts, even though military commanders strictly forbade this. Indeed, while single combat was common early in the war, superiors required that pilots fly and fight in formation from 1916 onward.

Most of the early aces of the First World War had established reputations as aviators prior to the war. Roland Garros, for example, had made the first flight across the Mediterranean. In one of the great ironies of the war, Garros was in Berlin for an air show when war broke out in August 1914. On the night of 3 August, he made a daring escape, flying his Morane-Saulnier monoplane to France and immediately enlisting in the French Army. Posted to Escadrille Morane-Saulnier No. 23 in Nancy, Garros achieved ace status after shooting down five aircraft in less than 3 weeks in April 1915 after applying metal deflectors to his propeller so he could fire a machine gun through its arc. Garros was unfortunately forced down behind enemy lines and taken prisoner on 18 April. Although he returned to duty after making a daring escape from prison in January 1918, he was ill-prepared for the technological changes that had transformed aircraft during his 3-year confinement. Although he somehow managed to survive for 9 months, on 5 October 1918 he was shot down and killed. Lionized by the press, Garros's memory was honored by bestowing his name to the red-clay tennis courts on which the French Open is played.

In addition to Garros, other notable French aces include George Guynemer, Charles Nungesser, and René Fonck. Guynemer had initially been rejected for military service because of his frail physique, but his father, a wealthy French aristocrat and former officer, used his connections to secure his son admission to a French military flight school. After obtaining his wings in June 1915, Guynemer became a member of the most famous French fighter squadron, *Les Cigognes (Storks)* and achieved fifty-four victories before disappearing in a cloud bank on 11 September 1917. Nungesser, who had first served in the cavalry upon the outbreak of the war, transferred to the air service in early 1915. Noted for his good looks, athleticism, and love of Parisian nightlife, Nungesser survived the war with forty-five kills to his credit, but died while trying to cross the Atlantic in May 1927. A member of the *Storks*, Fonck was noted for his skilled marksmanship and pulling to within close range of his victim before opening fire. His economical use of ammunition allowed him many multiple-victory flights, including six kills on 9 May 1918. He ended the war as the leading Allied ace with seventy-five confirmed kills, though he claimed 127.

Although the British Army was slow to recognize their aces, the press quickly brought their names to the public's attention. Notable British aces include Albert Ball, James McCudden, and Edward Mannock. Ball volunteered for the army in 1914 and obtained his wings at his own expense, before joining the RFC in January 1916. Despite inferior aircraft, he quickly gained notoriety in the press, achieving forty-four kills before he was shot down on 7 May 1917. With a total of fifty-seven victories, McCudden received the Victoria Cross and the *Croix de Guerre,* among other medals, before dying on 9 July 1918 in a crash caused by mechanical failure shortly after takeoff. Britain's leading ace in the war, Mannock had been working as a telephone-cable layer in Turkey upon the outbreak of the war and was briefly imprisoned (along with other British subjects) after Turkey entered the war on Germany's side. Liberated through American arbitration, Mannock returned to England with an intense hatred against Germany, entered the RFC and rose through the ranks to achieve seventy-three victories before he was shot down by ground fire in June 1918. The British also benefited from several aces who came from the dominions, most notably the Canadian William "Billy" Bishop, who gained seventy-two kills and survived the war to serve as director of the Royal Canadian Air Force in the Second World War.

Other Allied aces of note included Willy Coppens of Belgium, Francesco Baracca of Italy, Alexander Kazakov of Russia, and Raoul Lufbery and Edward Rickenbacker of the United States. Coppens, who had entered the war with the Belgian Army and served in the Ypres sector, paid for his own flight training in England and entered the tiny Belgian Air Service in July 1916. He would end the war as Belgium's leading ace with thirty-seven kills. Although Baracca had entered the Italian Air Service in 1912, the lack of capable Italian fighters delayed his first victory until 7 April 1916. He went on to achieve thirty-four victories before he was shot down on 19 June 1918, when he mistook an Austrian armed reconnaissance plane (a Phönix C.I) for a fighter (a Phönix D.I) and attacked from the rear, only to be gunned down by the observer. Kazakov entered the Russian Imperial Air Service in February 1915 and quickly gained notoriety on 18 March 1915 when he attempted to snag a German Albatros two-seater with a weighted grapnel on a suspended cable, only to ram it with his own plane and force it down. Promoted to command a squadron, Kazakov would win seventeen victories by the time Russia left the war. He went on to shoot down fifteen Red Army aircraft while flying for the Whites during the Russian Civil War before dying in a crash landing on 3 April 1919. Lufbery became the first prominent American ace of the war while flying for France in the *Lafayette Escadrille*. After the United States entered the war, he was commissioned as a major in the American Air Service and achieved seventeen total victories by the time he was shot down on 19 May 1918. Having won fame as a race car driver prior to the First World War, Rickenbacker served as Pershing's personal driver before being allowed to transfer to the American Air Service. He survived the war with twenty-six victories and received the Congressional Medal of Honor.

Germany would produce several of the most famous aces of the war. As previously mentioned, Oswald Boelcke (forty victories) and Max Immelmann (fifteen victories) were the first prominent German aces and contributed greatly to the development of fighter tactics and maneuvers that would be used by both sides. Both Boelcke and Immelmann were army cadets prior to the war and both volunteered for flight training upon the outbreak of the war. Immelmann was lost on 18 June 1916 when the synchronizing gear on his Eindecker malfunctioned, causing him to shoot off his propeller. Shortly after achieving his fortieth victory, Boelcke was killed after a midair collision with Erwin Böhme, a member of his own squadron who managed to land his plane. Boelcke's funeral was held in the cathedral at Cambrai with all the pomp and ceremony that would have been accorded a royal prince. Indeed, the service was filmed so that the German public could view it in cinemas. By far the most famous ace of the war was Manfred von Richthofen, who had entered the war as a cavalry officer before transferring to the air service in 1915. Selected by Boelcke for service on the Somme, Richthofen went on to command Jagdgeschwader No. 1, known as the Flying Circus because he and other pilots flew different colored planes. By his death in April 1918, Richthofen had won eighty victories, the most confirmed kills of any ace in the war, and achieved everlasting fame as the "Red Baron." Two other German aces deserve mention. Ernst Udet, who ended the war with sixty-two kills, would develop the dive bomber as the chief of the Luftwaffe's Technical Office prior to World War II. Hermann Göring would end the war with twenty-two victories and would serve as one of Hitler's chief henchmen in the Nazi Party and as commander of the Luftwaffe during the Second World War.

Austria-Hungary's leading ace of the war, Godwin Brumowski, achieved a total of thirty-five victories. Born to Polish parents in the province of Galicia, he began the war as an observer in the Austrian air service. Although he received no formal training, he learned by observing his pilots. By late 1915 he was appointed the commander of a mixed squadron of fighters and reconnaissance aircraft. Even though he was not promoted beyond noncommissioned officer rank and despite his Polish ancestry, he would remain in the small Austrian air service after the First World War.

By the end of the First World War, aircraft had redefined the nature of warfare by making it three dimensional. Whereas such postwar air power theorists as Douhet and Mitchell would overexaggerate their decisiveness in the bloody conflict that had just ended, aircraft had clearly played a determining factor in the outcome of the war. Although hints and indications of things to come were certainly demonstrated, particularly in the last year of the war, technology had not quite caught up to the theories of men like Douhet and Mitchell. Once the war was over and the pressure for innovation eased, the time for fulfilling their visions would be extended, as will be discussed in the second volume on military aircraft in this series.

Having discussed the origins of flight in Chapter One and the evolution of military aviation in the First World War in this chapter, the remaining chapters of this volume will focus on the aircraft that fulfilled the various roles that have been discussed.

NOTES

1. Although the Russian mobilization order was ostensibly partial, meaning against Austria-Hungary, the Russian military had made no prewar plans for such a contingency; thus the order was in effect a general mobilization, which was made official on 29 July.

2. Schlieffen had originally planned on sweeping through the Netherlands as well, but this had been abandoned by Moltke, who also increased the number of forces on the left wing to meet the anticipated French attack on Alsace-Lorraine.

3. Indeed, some scholars argue that Moltke's transfer of two army corps and one cavalry division to the Eastern Front in late August caused the defeat at the Marne.

4. Luke obtained his eighteen victories over a 17-day period in 1918, beginning on 12 September and ending on 29 September when he was shot down behind German lines and killed when he refused to be taken prisoner. For his exploits, Luke was posthumously awarded the Congressional Medal of Honor.

5. It is somewhat ironic that the first practical machine gun had been introduced by Hiram Maxim, who later conducted experiments in a vain effort to achieve heavier-than-air flight.

6. Wilhelm II's reluctance to bomb London was primarily based on his relationship to the British royal family. The grandson of Queen Victoria, Wilhelm was a first cousin to Britain's wartime monarch, George V.

7. The British assisted Japan with approximately 1,500 troops and a battleship.

8. In the early stages of the war, most seaplanes were simply land-based airplanes that had been fitted with floats.

9. It is interesting to note that French aircraft production did not greatly outpace German production until the last year of the war, after a degree of stability had been established by Vincent and Demesnil.

10. Indeed, one can argue that Bavaria's military autonomy in peacetime placed German air power in a weaker position upon the outbreak of the war than should have been the case because the Bavarian War Ministry had stubbornly favored the Munich-based Otto Works in order to escape reliance upon the Prussian Army and Prussian-controlled North German aircraft firms. The technologically inferior pusher aircraft produced by the Otto Works proved to be so inferior that the firm collapsed just a few months into the war.

11. To add insult to injury, Dr. Edmund Gros, one of the organizers of the *Lafayette Escadrille* (though not a pilot), wrote AEF officials to prevent Bullard from being admitted as a pilot, and used his influence after the war to prevent Bullard from having his name included on a memorial to the *Lafayette Escadrille*.

12. Although the Sopwith Camel's 130 hp Clerget rotary engine produced so much torque that novice pilots often entered a violent—and too
often deadly—spin, an experienced pilot was able to use this to his advantage by being able to make a 360-degree right circle in the same time that it
took opponents to turn 90 degrees.

13. The statistics for this chart are derived from the following sources:
Malcolm Cooper, *The Birth of Independent Air Power: British Air Policy in
the First World War* (London: Allen & Unwin, 1986); James J. Davilla and
Arthur M. Soltan, *French Aircraft of the First World War* (Mountain View,
CA: Flying Machines Press, 2002); Alan Durkota, Thomas Darcey, and Vic-
tor Kulikov, *The Imperial Russian Air Service: Famous Pilots and Aircraft of
World War One* (Mountain View, CA: Flying Machines Press, 1995); Peter
M. Grosz, George Haddow, and Peter Schiemer, *Austro-Hungarian Army
Aircraft of World War One* (Mountain View, CA: Flying Machines Press,
1993); John H. Morrow Jr., *German Air Power in World War I* (Lincoln:
University of Nebraska Press, 1982); and John H. Morrow Jr., *The Great
War in the Air: Military Aviation from 1909 to 1921.* Smithsonian History of
Aviation (Washington: Smithsonian Institution Press, 1993).

CHAPTER THREE

Reconnaissance and Auxiliary Aircraft

FROM THE BEGINNINGS OF MILITARY AVIATION and until the last stages of the First World War, the primary role played by aircraft was to provide aerial observation and tactical and strategic reconnaissance. As previously noted, reconnaissance aircraft had proven to be crucial in the opening phases of the war, contributing to the German victory over the Russians at Tannenberg and the Franco-British victory over the Germans at the Marne. Reconnaissance aircraft proved equally important in the Race to the Channel by alerting commanders to enemy movements. Although other factors certainly contributed to the resulting military stalemate of trench warfare on the Western Front, reconnaissance aircraft were at least partially responsible because they prevented either side from concealing the disposition of troops that might otherwise have achieved a breakthrough had they caught the opposing force off guard. The primacy of indirect artillery fire in trench warfare also made aircraft essential as an artillery spotter.

The value of aerial reconnaissance proved to be so significant after the opening of the war that the high commands recognized that gaining control of the air space over the battleground was critical to the course of the war. As a result, both sides developed fighters in an effort to prevent the enemy from conducting reconnaissance and observation flights by shooting down his planes and to provide escort protection for one's own reconnaissance aircraft against enemy fighters. On the other hand, the advent of the fighter revealed the essential weaknesses of the first generation of unarmed reconnaissance aircraft, forcing both sides to develop the Type-C armed reconnaissance airplane, which was equipped with a pivot or ring-mounted machine gun for the observer to fire at attacking aircraft. By war's end, armed reconnaissance aircraft, such as the Armstrong Whitworth F.K.8, were equipped with a pilot's forward-firing machine gun in addition to the observer's gun, thereby providing an aircraft capable of holding its own against enemy fighters.

AUSTRO-HUNGARIAN RECONNAISSANCE AND AUXILIARY AIRCRAFT

Although Austria-Hungary was hampered by its weak industrial structure, it nevertheless produced one of the world's first successful and widely produced reconnaissance airplanes in the *Taube* (*Dove*), which was noted for its elegant birdlike wings. Designed by Igo Etrich after more than 6 years of experimentations with monoplane designs, the *Taube* made its maiden flight at Wiener Neustadt on 29 November 1909. Subsequent modifications resulted in a military prototype that Etrich's assistant, Karl Illner, used to carry a passenger on a cross-country flight in May 1910. After Chief of the General Staff Franz Conrad von Hötzendorff flew as an observer during a September 1910 meet at Wiener Neustadt, he enthusiastically called for purchasing 200 airplanes and training 400 pilots. Although the War Ministry remained reluctant to commit its limited funds for aviation, Conrad was successful, after lobbying Emperor Franz Josef personally, in winning a commitment to purchase a *Taube* as long as it passed the army's standard of a minimum 2-hour range, 45-mph speed, and 300-lb payload. After the *Taube* passed the army trial in March 1911, the War Ministry purchased it and issued an order for seven more by awarding a 175,000 crown contract to Austria-Hungary's first aircraft firm, *Motorluftfahrzeuggesellschaft* (MLG), which had been formed by financier Camilo Castiglioni and Daimler Motor Company and had purchased the rights to the *Taube*. MLG ironically was not ready to begin production, so it contracted with Lohner to construct them. Subsequent army attempts to increase speed and climbing standards resulted in delays in production. In addition, the War Ministry became unwilling to issue further contracts to MLG because it merely held the rights and did not actually produce the aircraft.

As a result, Austria-Hungary would not get the full benefit of its first domestically produced aircraft.

The *Taube* would have a bigger impact on the German air service, comprising approximately half of the aircraft that Germany mobilized in 1914. Because *Taubes* were built by several German and Austro-Hungarian firms, there were slight variations in the some 500 that were produced through 1914. Engines varied from the original 120 hp Austro-Daimler inline to the 85 hp Austro-Daimler inline to the 100 or 120 hp Mercedes inline engines, resulting in differing speeds, with a top speed of 70 mph. Wingspans varied from 44 ft and 11 in. to 48 ft, and length varied from 34 ft 10 in. to 37 ft. Whereas most were constructed from wooden airframes, those built by Deutsche Flugzeugwerke (D.F.W.) utilized steel-tube airframes, resulting in varying weights, with 1,900 lbs being a good average for loaded weight. Although it was not very maneuverable, the *Taube*, which used wing-warping, was easy to fly and stable in flight. By early 1915 *Taubes* were withdrawn from frontline service and relegated to use as trainers.

In addition to the *Taubes* it produced, the Lohner firm produced a number of its own reconnaissance aircraft for Austria-Hungary both before and during the war. After the success of the Lohner Pfeilflieger ("Arrow Flyer," because of its swept-back biplane wing configuration) in competition with other European aircraft and a national fundraising campaign by the Austro-Hungarian Aero Club, Lohner began production of military versions in late 1912 and early 1913. After placing an initial order for 28 Lohner B.I aircraft, the LA required modifications that lengthened the fuselage, strengthened the undercarriage, and added an additional 37.7 sq ft of wing area. The added weight unfortunately resulted in wing stress failures. Subsequent attempts to strengthen the fuselage and wings under guidelines developed by Professor Richard Knoller were not completed by the time war broke out in 1914.

After several failed attempts to develop a reliable military version of the Pfeilflieger (the B.II–B.VI), Lohner finally provided the military with its most successful version when the B.VII was introduced in August 1915. Powered by a 150 or 160 hp Austro-Daimler inline motor and designed to carry heavier loads than its predecessors, the B.VII was especially well suited for the mountainous areas of the Tyrol. It featured a canvas-covered fuselage that provided a single cockpit for the pilot and observer and allowed for an 80-kg (176-lb) bomb load. Many were later retrofitted with a pivot-mounted machine gun for the observer, and new versions were introduced as the Lohner C.I. The B.VII and C.I (approximately 140 of which entered service) together provided the *Luftfahrtruppen* (LFT) with an aircraft that was capable of providing long-range reconnaissance and conducting light bombing raids against Italian targets. On 14 February 1916, for example, twelve Lohner B.VII aircraft based at Pergine conducted a 236 mile round-trip raid that successfully damaged the Porta Volta power station at Milan, while one observer shot down an Italian aircraft. Similar attacks were conducted throughout 1916. The B.VII version had a wingspan of 50 ft 6 in., a length of 31 ft 2 in., a loaded weight of 3,177 lbs, and a speed of 75 mph, compared with the slightly smaller C.I, which had a wingspan of 42 ft, a length of 30 ft 4.2 in., a loaded weight of 2,939 lbs, and a speed of 82 mph.

Although Austria-Hungary had originally prevented German firms from establishing branches within the Dual Monarchy in hopes of building up its own industry, it changed its policy by early 1914 in order to increase production. As a result, Austria-Hungary would enter the war with a two-seat reconnaissance biplane, the Albatros B.I, manufactured by the Oesterreichische Albatros Werke (later Phönix Flugzeugwerke). Modeled after the German Albatros, the Austrian Albatros B.I went through four series of production (the Series 21, 22, 23, and 24) that varied slightly in span and length and were powered by either a 145 hp Hiero inline engine or 160 hp Austro-Daimler inline engine. The Albatros B.I employed a wooden-framed and ply-skinned fuselage, and the two halves of its top wings were joined together above the trestle-type cabane and braced to the lower wing by three bays of struts. The Series 22, known as the "Knoller-Albatros" because its swept-back top wing was designed by Professor Richard Knoller, employed a more powerful 160 hp Austro-Daimler motor and provided a Schwarzlose gun for the observer. The new design, with a span of 45 ft 7 in. and length of 27 ft 5 in., proved to be an effective climber over mountainous terrain. As more improved armed reconnaissance aircraft, such as the Hansa-Brandenburg C.I, became available, the Austrian Albatros B-types were either shifted to the Balkans or served as trainers after being fitted with dual-control systems.

Although Austria-Hungary did not enjoy as much success with its version of the Albatros as did Germany with its versions, it would eventually produce an excellent armed reconnaissance aircraft with the Aviatik C.I biplane. Like Albatros, Aviatik had been allowed to open a branch (Oesterreichishe-Ungarische Flugzeugfabrik Aviatik) within Austria-Hungary shortly before the outbreak of war in 1914.

Its first aircraft, the B.II, was modeled closely after the same version in Germany. It had a top wing that was swept back slightly with sloping struts, supporting the top wing extensions. Instead of a center section, it had a cabane consisting of a trestle constructed from steel tubing to which a gravity fuel tank was attached. With the exception of the area around the cockpits (the pilot in the rear, the observer in front), the wooden-framed, canvas-covered fuselage was rectangular in shape. Powered by a 120 hp Austro-Daimler inline engine, the B.II could reach 68 mph and a maximum ceiling of 2,500 m (8,202 ft) while carrying two 22-lb bombs. An improved version of the B.II, powered by a 150 hp Austro-Daimler inline motor, was introduced in the fall of 1915. In addition to a ring-mounted Schwarzlose machine gun, it could carry up to three 44 lb bombs and could reach a ceiling of 5000 m (16,404 ft).

The Aviatik C.I, which had been designed by new chief engineer Julius von Berg in the spring of 1917 and which was produced by both Aviatik and on license by such other Austro-Hungarian firms as Lohner, was far more successful. At first, the Aviatik C.I was not well received because its smaller frame with a span of just 27 ft 6.7 in. and length of 22 ft 6 in., its lighter construction (loaded weight of just 2,152 lbs), tight seat compartments, and sensitive controls made it a more difficult aircraft to fly than the Hansa-Brandenburg C.I aircraft that pilots were accustomed to flying. In addition, the C.I still placed the pilot in the rear seat, which did not leave the observer with a good field of vision or a good range of fire. Later versions would reverse the seating configuration. Despite the problems with its seating configuration, pilots came to appreciate the power provided by its 185 hp Daimler inline engine, which produced up to 111 mph, and the protection provided by its forward-firing machine gun and observer's ring-mounted machine gun. At least 28 Aviatik C.I aircraft were converted into single-seat photo-reconnaissance fighters because without the observer's weight they proved as effective as the Aviatik D.I.

Manufactured by Ungarische Lloyd Flugzeug und Motorenfabrik, the Lloyd C-type biplane went through four main production series during the course of the war. The C.I, introduced in 1914, reached an astonishing height of more than 20,000 ft during an airshow before the war, but only a few were produced before the C.II (series 42) was introduced in early 1915. Powered by a 145 hp Hiero inline motor, which was enclosed in a pointed cowling with only the cylinder heads exposed and which was cooled by a box radiator mounted on the trestled cabane, the C.II was a sturdy airplane because both its wings and the fuselage were wooden framed and plywood covered. The wings were swept back and the fabric-covered ailerons extended behind the trailing edge of the top wing. The observer fired a semi-circular ring-mounted Schwarzlose machine gun. Whereas the C.II and C.III had a wingspan of 47 ft 11.6 in., length of 28 ft 11.2 in., and loaded weight of 2,888 lbs, the C-V, which was introduced in mid-1917, was a much more streamlined and slightly lighter machine with a wingspan of 36 ft 8.5 in., a length of 23 ft 8.3 in., and a loaded weight of 2,613 lbs. Powered by a series of more powerful engines—the 185 hp MAG Austro-Daimler inline engine, the 200 hp Benz inline engine, and the 220 hp Benz inline engine—it could reach a maximum speed of 106 mph and climb to 3,000 m (9,843 ft) in just more than 16 minutes with the 220 hp Benz inline motor. A total of 205 Lloyd C-types were built during the war, with almost half being the C.V variety.

Although Hansa-Brandenburg was a German company, the Hansa-Brandenburg C.I biplane was unique in that it was constructed only within Austria-Hungary. With a total of 1,258 built under license in eighteen different series by Phönix and Ufag, the Hansa-Brandenburg C.I was Austria-Hungary's most widely produced and used reconnaissance aircraft during the war. Designed by Ernst Heinkel, who would gain greater fame for his World War II–era aircraft, the C.I was a high-powered aircraft, using ever-increasing powerful engines from the 160 hp Austro-Daimler inline motor to the 230 hp Hiero inline motor that increased its speed from 87 mph in the former to 99 mph in the latter. Its quick takeoff ability made it well suited for the small airfields in the mountainous areas along the Italian, Balkan, and Carpathian Fronts. Despite its span of 40 ft 2.25 in., length of 27 ft 8.6 in., and loaded weight of 2,888 lbs, it was highly maneuverable and well armed with one forward-firing Schwarzlose machine gun and one ring-mounted, observer-fired Schwarzlose machine gun. As a result, the Hansa-Brandenburg C.I was more than capable of evading enemy fighters and defending itself. In addition, its ability to carry a 200-lb bomb load made it useful as a light bomber. It also proved to be an effective ground attack plane because of its forward- and rear-firing machine guns and because it could carry eight fragmentation bombs under its wings. It was used heavily in this role during the June 1918 Piave Offensive.

Influenced somewhat by its production of the Hansa-Brandenburg C.I, Phönix Flugzeugwerke A.G. would introduce one of the best-armed reconnaissance aircraft of the war in April 1918 with the appearance of the Phönix C.I biplane. With a wingspan of 36 ft 1 in., length of 24 ft 11.2 in., loaded weight of 2,734 lbs, and powerful 230 hp Hiero inline engine, the Phönix C.I received universal praise because of its speed (109 mph), climb rate (5,000 m or 16,404 ft in 55 minutes), and ease to fly. In addition, its synchronized forward-firing machine gun and ring-mounted observer's machine gun made it one of the most well-armed aircraft produced in the war. Based on enthusiastic reports from its pilots, on 31 August 1918 LFT proposed orders for 565 additional Phönix C.I aircraft. Because it was so heavily armed, was very maneuverable, and was faster than even the Sopwith Camel at high altitudes, the Phönix C.I did not require fighter escorts. As a result, some enemy pursuit aircraft occasionally mistook it for a fighter only to be shot down by the observer when they attacked from the rear, such as happened when leading Italian ace Francesco Baracca was shot down on 19 June 1918. In addition to its defensive armament, the Phönix C.I could also be equipped with bomb racks, camera systems, wireless equipment, and exhaust silencers. Only 98 Phönix C.I aircraft were delivered before the war ended. After the war, the Swedish government built 32 versions of the Phönix C.I.

Like the Phönix works, Ungarische Flugzeugwerke A.G. (Ufag) had constructed the Hansa-Brandenburg C.I on license and incorporated some of its features in its own reconnaissance aircraft, the Ufag C.I biplane, which was introduced in early 1918. Designed by Béla Oravecz, the Ufag C.I featured separate cockpits for the pilot and observer and a rather compact design with a wingspan of just 31 ft 2 in., length of 24 ft 3.7 in., and loaded weight of just 2,494 lbs. Powered by a 230 hp Hiero inline motor, it could reach a maximum speed of 118 mph and could climb to 4,000 m (13,123 ft) in just 31 minutes. In addition, it was extremely well armed with two forward-firing synchronized Schwarzlose machine guns and one that was ring mounted for the observer. A total of 126 were produced by Ufag, and another 40 were licensed-built by Phönix before the war ended.

BRITISH RECONNAISSANCE AND AUXILIARY AIRCRAFT

Although the British had been slower than their continental counterparts in starting their aircraft industry and hence had to rely heavily upon French-built aircraft (and especially upon French aviation engines) for the Royal Flying Corps (RFC), they had started to produce a few aircraft of their own prior to the outbreak of the war. By far the most significant of these in terms of numbers produced was the Royal Aircraft Factory B.E.2 biplane designed by Geoffrey De Haviland and first introduced in 1912. As had been intended when the Royal Aircraft Factory (R.A.F.) was founded, it was to design aircraft to meet military specifications, although private contractors would then construct them. As a result, there was a degree of variation among the earliest B.E.2 aircraft that were produced by such firms as Handley-Page and Vickers, before it became more standardized. During late 1912 and 1913 the B.E.2 proved its worth in British Army maneuvers (including the use of wireless transmissions from the air) and won over such officers as General Sir Douglas Haig to the value of aircraft. When the RFC dispatched its forces to France in August 1914, the B.E.2 supplied three squadrons and played a critical role in the early reconnaissance that allowed the Allies to defeat the German Schlieffen Plan.

Although the B.E.2 gained a reputation as a stable, easy to fly aircraft and had played an important role in 1914, it would fail its baptism by fire when German fighters (and even German armed reconnaissance aircraft) entered the skies over the Western Front in 1915. Its inherent stability translated into an almost utter lack of maneuverability, making it easy fodder for the Germans. Worse, the 70 hp Renault rotary motor of the early B.E.2, B.E.2a, and B.E.2b was too underpowered to allow a machine gun to be carried onboard. Despite these abundantly apparent weaknesses, the British stubbornly persisted in trying to improve the B.E.2 by upgrading its engines. In 1915, the B.E.2c was introduced with a 90 hp R.A.F. 1a V-type engine. Although it could now be fitted with a spigot-mounted Lewis gun, the observer had to manhandle it from side to side. If that were not bad enough, the observer, who sat in the front seat, had a limited range of fire because of the struts and wires that surrounded him. Needless to say, the B.E.2c was a sitting duck for German fighters, yet they remained in service until as late as 1917. By far the most widely produced version (a total of 1,801 aircraft) was the B.E.2e, which was introduced in mid-1916. Although a few of the later issues were fitted with the 105 hp R.A.F. 1b V-type motor or the 150 hp Hispano-Suiza V-type motor, the majority still relied upon the 90 hp R.A.F. 1a V-type motor. This "improved" version featured a new wing design with a longer span for the top wing and only one set of struts on each side of the fuselage to support the wings, but it still placed the observer in the front seat with a spigot-mounted Lewis gun. With a span of 40 ft 9 in., length of 27 ft 3 in., and weight of 2,100 lbs, the B.E.2e remained a slow aircraft with a speed of 70 mph at its 10,000 ft (3,048 m) ceiling. It was just as outclassed when it was introduced in 1916 as its previous versions had been. Forced to keep the B.E.2 in service until it could produce an effective C-type reconnaissance aircraft, the British would suffer more air casualties in the B.E.2 than in any other aircraft.

Another early British aircraft that enjoyed a long life in service was the Avro 504, which was designed by Alliot Verdon Roe and introduced in 1913. The first prototype was powered by the 80 hp Gnôme rotary engine, which was covered by a square-engine cowling. Its fuselage employed a wire-braced wooden box-girder construction with straight upper longerons that terminated in a vertical stern-post to which the rudder and tail skid, but no fin, were attached. A long central skid was attached between the wheels. The wings were equal in length, but they were staggered and included warping ailerons. After modifying the engine cowling to make it more streamlined and replacing the warping ailerons with hinged ailerons, the Avro 504's performance improved markedly, with its 80 hp Gnôme rotary engine providing approximately 82 mph, climbing to 1,000 ft (304 m) in just under 2 minutes, and gaining the ability to reach an altitude of 15,000 ft (4,572 m) by February 1914. With a span of 36 ft, length of 29 ft 5 in., and a loaded weight of 1,574 lbs, the Avro 504 was far more maneuverable than its contemporary, the B.E.2. It proved to be a versatile aircraft that was used primarily for reconnaissance in the opening stages of the war, but also was among the first British aircraft to be fitted with a Lewis gun on the top wing and used as a fighter. It even served as a light bomber and anti-zeppelin aircraft. As better aircraft became available, the Avro 504 saw duty as Britain's primary trainer, a role that it would continue to play until 1933 with a total of 8,970 having been constructed in Great Britain and some 2,000 in the Soviet Union.

Although the Sopwith Tabloid biplane did not enjoy the longevity of the B.E.2 or the Avro 504, it deserves honorable mention as an early aircraft that saw service with both the RFC and the Royal Naval Air Service (RNAS) in the first 2 years of the war, albeit in limited numbers. The Tabloid, which was originally designed to be a high speed racer, made a spectacular debut in November 1913 at the Hendon Air Show, catching the attention of both the public and army and navy officials. It was much smaller than the B.E.2 and Avro

504, having a wingspan of just 25 ft 6 in., a length of 20 ft 4 in., and a loaded weight of just 1,120 lbs. This compact size, combined with its 80 hp Gnôme rotary motor, gave it a maximum speed of 93 mph and a service ceiling of 15,000 ft (4,572 m), while carrying a pilot, passenger, and enough fuel to remain aloft for 2.5 hours. Although the original version relied upon wing-warping for lateral control, the approximately forty Tabloids that entered military service between the fall of 1914 and summer of 1915 used ailerons. One reason for its limited production was that its side-by-side seating arrangement was not ideally suited for reconnaissance. Nevertheless, the Tabloid's endurance made it ideally suited for carrying out specialized missions, including one of the war's most spectacular early bombing raids by an airplane. On 8 October 1914 two Tabloids, each carrying two 20-lb bombs, took off from Antwerp with the objective of bombing the German zeppelin sheds at Cologne and Düsseldorf.[1] First Lieutenant Reggie Marix succeeded in bringing his Tabloid down to within 600 ft above the Düsseldorf shed before dropping his bombs over the side. The resulting explosion destroyed the L-9 in its shed, demonstrating the vulnerability of hydrogen airships. Although the other Tabloid, piloted by Commander Spenser Grey, became lost in the fog and missed the zeppelin shed in Cologne, he dropped his bombs on the Cologne railway station, killing three civilians.

The Bristol Scout biplane was another British reconnaissance aircraft that entered service just as the First World War broke out. Designed in 1913 by Frank Barnwell and intended to be a one-seat racer, it was a trim machine with a wingspan of just 24 ft 7 in., a length of 20 ft 8 in., and a loaded weight of 1,440 lbs. Powered by a 110 hp Clerget rotary engine that gave it a maximum speed of 110 mph and a ceiling of 16,404 ft (5,000 m), it could outperform most enemy fighters during the first 2 years of the war. Although its primary duty was reconnaissance, a few enterprising pilots rigged it to carry a Lewis gun, which Captain Lanoe George Hawker used to shoot down two German Albatros armed reconnaissance aircraft on 25 July 1915, a feat for which he became the first pilot to receive the coveted Victoria Cross. A later version, known as the Scout D, was fitted with a synchronized forward-firing machine gun and saw service as a fighter until 1916. Bristol Scouts were also used for home defense as an anti-zeppelin aircraft equipped with explosive Ranken darts that could be dropped on enemy airships.

As one of the many firms that produced the B.E.2, Armstrong Whitworth soon introduced a much-improved version of its own, the F.K.3, named after lead designer Frederick Koolhoven. Work began on the F.K.3 in August 1915 with the first production type resembling the B.E.2c with a separate front seat for the observer and rear seat for the pilot. Later versions employed one large cockpit with dual controls for the pilot, who sat in front of the observer to allow for more effective range of fire for the mounted Lewis gun. With a wingspan of 40 ft 1 in., a length of 29 ft, and a loaded weight of 2,056 lbs, the F.K.3 (or "Little Ack") was a rugged aircraft that could reach a maximum speed of 87 mph with its 90 hp R.A.F. 1a V-type motor. Although it was a marked improvement over the B.E.2, the British employed it only in the Mediterranean and Middle East theaters, primarily because the need for aircraft there arose at about the time the F.K.3 entered production in 1916. A total of approximately 500 were produced and were used for artillery spotting, patrol reconnaissance, and light bombing.

By far the best British C-type reconnaissance aircraft of the war, the Armstrong Whitworth F.K.8, dubbed the "Big Ack," entered service in 1917 at about the same time as the R.A.F. R.E.8. Powered at first by the 120 hp Beardmore inline engine, the F.K.8 was later outfitted with a 160 hp Beardmore inline motor (although a few used the 150 hp R.A.F. 4a V-type or 150 hp Lorraine-Dietrich inline engine), which gave it a maximum speed of 95 mph and ceiling of 13,000 ft (3,962 m). Like the F.K.3, it was a rugged aircraft with a wingspan of 43 ft 6 in., a length of 31 ft, and a loaded weight of 2,811 lbs. In addition, its undercarriage came equipped with oleo shock absorbers. Unlike most wooden biplanes, the upper wings were attached to the fuselage with inverted V-struts instead of a central section. The F.K.8 also featured dual controls (although the observer could control only the elevator and rudder, not the ailerons). Later versions utilized an enclosed engine cowling and long exhaust pipe. By December 1917 Armstrong Whitworth was producing approximately 80 F.K.8 aircraft per month. On the Western Front, the F.K.8 proved vital to the British efforts to disrupt the German spring offensive of 1918, dropping bombs and firing on advancing troops and directing artillery fire. In July 1918 F.K.8s equipped with radio transmitters were assigned to the Tank Corps in an effort to coordinate air-to-ground operations. In October 1918 F.K.8s in Squadron No. 35 were used to lay down and maintain a smoke screen in front of the British XIII Corps as it attacked German positions west of Serain. On the Macedonian Front, F.K.8s and D.H.9s in Squadron No. 47 dropped more than 5,000 lbs of bombs on Bulgarian forces retreating over the Kosturino Pass. Approximately 1,500 were produced during the war.

The R.A.F. R.E.8, intended as a replacement for the long-suffering B.E.2, and nicknamed the "Harry Tate" after a popular contemporary comedian, was introduced in 1917. Armed with a forward-firing Vickers machine gun and a rear-firing, ring-mounted Lewis gun, the RE.8 was powered by a 150 hp R.A.F. 4a V-type motor and was capable of reaching 103 mph. Although it was an improvement to the B.E.2 in terms of firepower and was noted for being easy to fly, the R.E.8's size (wingspan of 42 ft 7 in., length of 32 ft 7 in., and loaded weight of 2,869 lbs) caused it to lack the maneuverability necessary to evade the last generation of German fighters. As a result, it suffered the same fate as its predecessor—easy fodder for the Germans. Despite this, the British pressed on with production of the R.E.8, even though the better-performing F.K.8 was available, producing slightly more than 4,000 and keeping them in service to war's end.

FRENCH RECONNAISSANCE AND AUXILIARY AIRCRAFT

Because the French had issued numerous contracts for aircraft in the prewar years in order to stimulate their aircraft industry, they would come to possess a number of aircraft that had become obsolete and been withdrawn from front-line service by the time war broke out in 1914. Nevertheless, French reconnaissance aircraft supplied the needs of France in 1914 as well as those of its British and Russian allies.

Among its many early aircraft, the Blériot XI monoplane was undoubtedly the most famous French aircraft because its manufacturer, Louis Blériot, had won international acclaim by flying it across the English Channel on 25 July 1909. Whereas Blériot's 1909 craft had been powered by a 25 hp Anzani engine and was capable of approximately 40 mph, as the Blériot XI began to enter French service in 1910 it was fitted with ever-increasing more powerful engines. The Blériot XI first saw military action in Italian service during the Tripolitan War, proving their worth for artillery spotting and reconnaissance patrols. By 1914, the 70 hp Gnôme rotary motor had become its standard engine and gave it a maximum speed of 66 mph. Much smaller than the contemporary *Taube* and B.E.2, the Blériot XI had a wingspan of 29 ft 7 in., length of 25 ft 7 in., and loaded weight of 1,378 lbs. Its wooden airframe was covered with cloth and its wings were braced by wires and used wing-warping for maneuvering. Because its 3,000 ft (914 m) ceiling made it susceptible to ground fire, the Blériot XI was withdrawn from front-line service by early 1915 and relegated to service as trainers. An estimated 800 aircraft were produced.

Whereas the Blériot XI was among the most numerous French reconnaissance aircraft at the start of World War I, it was quickly superseded by a series of aircraft produced by Morane-Saulnier that had entered service just prior to the start of the war. Introduced in 1913, the Morane-Saulnier Type L was a parasol monoplane (high wing above the pilot) that provided the pilot and observer an unobstructed view of the ground below. Its wings were braced by wires that were attached to the fuselage and to a pylon located above the center of the wing and warping was used for lateral control. Both the Type L and the Type LA (the latter used ailerons instead of warping) were powered by an 80 hp Gnôme or Le Rhône rotary motor and were capable of reaching 75 mph. Both had a wingspan of 33 ft 9 in., length of 10 ft 3 in., and loaded weight of 1,496 lbs. Faster and more maneuverable than their German counterparts, the Morane-Saulnier monoplanes, although used primarily for reconnaissance, also attacked German aircraft as the pilot could pull within range and his observer could use a rifle to shoot down or force down the enemy plane. Roland Garros converted his Morane-Saulnier into a primitive fighter by affixing deflector wedges to his propeller so that he could fire a forward-mounted machine gun.

Another earlier French aircraft that saw service as a reconnaissance aircraft in the early stages of the war was the Caudron G.III biplane produced by early French aviation pioneers Gaston and Rene Caudron. Although only a few were ready for service when the war began, production increased dramatically with approximately 2,600 ultimately being produced both for reconnaissance and training purposes. The G.III featured a wingspan of 43 ft 11 in. (its lower wing was much shorter at 25 ft 1 in.) and four long booms that affixed its twin rudder tail to the wings and fuselage, giving it a length of 21 ft. Its fabric-covered wings were wooden ribbed and heavily braced with struts and wires, and it relied upon wing-warping for maneuvering. The vast majority were powered by a 90 hp Anzani radial engine, which gave it a top speed of 69 mph and provided a service ceiling of 10,000 ft (3,048 m). It was gradually replaced beginning in March 1915 by the much bigger Caudron G.IV, which was powered by two 80 hp Le Rhône rotaries or two 100 hp Anzani radial motors and was capable of 82 mph. As a result of its twin-engine configuration, the observer who sat in the front of the nacelle could fire forward with a movable Lewis gun or Vickers gun. A few models were also equipped with a machine gun that was affixed to the top wing and allowed the observer to stand and fire at aircraft in the rear. With a wingspan of 56 ft 4 in., length of 23 ft 6 in., and loaded weight of 2,915 lbs (which included a 250-lb bomb load), the G.IV soon proved to be too cumbersome to evade German fighters. As a result, they were gradually converted to light bombers and were eventually withdrawn from the Western Front in 1916. Both the Russians and the Italians continued to use them well into 1917. A total of 1,358 were constructed during the course of the war.

Maurice and Henri Farman introduced a series of pusher aircraft before and during the war that saw service as reconnaissance aircraft. The F.20 biplane, designed by Henri Farman, was introduced in 1913 and was serving in British, French, and Belgian units at the start of the war. The F.20 had a wingspan of 44 ft 10 in. (the lower wing was just 24 ft 7 in.), a length of 27 ft 9 in., and a loaded weight of 2,105 lbs. Powered by an 80 hp Gnôme or Le Rhône rotary motor that was mounted to the rear of the wooden-framed, aluminum-covered nacelle, the F.20 was capable of 60 mph and had a service ceiling of approximately 2,750 m (9,000 ft). Because the pilot sat in the nose of the nacelle and the observer sat directly behind him, the F.20 offered an outstanding forward and side range of observation. Although the French attempted to mount a Lewis gun in the front of the nacelle and use the F.20 as a fighter, its slow speed and lack of maneuverability quickly demonstrated that this was not feasible. Once the Fokker Eindecker appeared on the Western Front, the F.20 was withdrawn from service, although they would continue to be used in Russia, Africa, and the Middle East until late in the war. Approximately 3,300 F.20 aircraft were constructed with slight variations in different production series.

The M.F.7 and the M.F.11 biplanes, designed by Maurice Farman, were both pusher aircraft that served well into 1916. Introduced in 1913, the M.F.7 still used a forward elevator, giving it a somewhat "primitive" appearance to other aircraft issued at this time. Powered primarily by a 70 hp Renault inline engine, the M.F.7 was relatively slow at 60 mph, but it had a service ceiling of 4,000 m (13,123 ft). Approximately 380 M.F.7 aircraft were produced before they were gradually replaced by the M.F.11, which began to enter service in mid-1915. The M.F.11 replaced the forward elevator of the M.F.7 with a more standard rudder-elevator tail and its front nacelle resembled that of the F.20. The M.F.11 had a wingspan of 53 ft, a length of

31 ft, and loaded weight of 2,105 lbs. It was powered by a variety of engines, but the most widely used version was the 130 hp Renault in-line motor, which gave it a top speed of 80 mph and a service ceiling of 3,850 m (12,631 ft). Armed with an observer-fired Hotchkiss or Lewis gun, the M.F.11 was able to defend itself against German fighters into early 1916. It also had sufficient lifting capacity to serve as a light bomber. In addition to serving with the French, who pro-duced several thousand to fill 37 squadrons with them by the end of 1915, the M.F.11 served with the Italians, who also licensed-produced 601 of them with either a French-supplied Renault engine or 100 hp Fiat A10 inline motor, and the RFC, which employed them on the Western Front, the Balkans, and the Middle East. Once they were withdrawn from front-line service, many M.F.11 aircraft were equipped with dual controllers and used as trainers.

Although the French would use a variety of other pusher aircraft for reconnaissance, including the Farman F.40 and Voisin Type 3, which also served as bombers, their lack of maneuverability ulti-mately made them vulnerable to German fighters, leading the French to search for a tractor C-type reconnaissance aircraft. Their first major attempt came with the Dorand AR.1 and AR.2, which were introduced in early 1917, but these proved to be far too under-powered. The French would ultimately develop one of the best-armed reconnaissance aircraft of the war with the Salmson 2A2, which entered production in the fall of 1917. Powered by a 260 hp Salmson Canton-Unné liquid-cooled radial engine and protected by three 7.7 mm machine guns, the Salmson 2A2 could reach 115 mph and was more than capable of defending itself for artillery ob-servation and photo-reconnaissance duties. With a wingspan of 38 ft 7 in., length of 27 ft 11 in., and loaded weight of 2,798 lbs, it proved to be very maneuverable and had a service ceiling of 6,250 m (20,505 ft). By war's end it supplied twenty-four French squadrons as approximately 3,200 Salmson 2A2 aircraft were produced, in-cluding 705 purchased by the United States to supply the American Expeditionary Force.

GERMAN RECONNAISSANCE AND AUXILIARY AIRCRAFT

Although the Austrian-designed *Taube*, which was licensed-produced by several German firms, would comprise approximately half of the

Germany's reconnaissance aircraft when war broke out in 1914, Germany had already developed a series of very effective B-type unarmed reconnaissance aircraft of its own. Unlike the French, who had issued contracts in order to stimulate their aircraft industry and consequently ended up with almost half of their aircraft being obsolete by 1914, the Germans had waited until aircraft manufacturers reached the specification requirements that the army needed. This, in addition to the production of the *Taube*, would give the Germans a slight advantage over the French in the number of aircraft mobilized in 1914, as previously noted.

By far the most successful German reconnaissance aircraft at the outset of the war was the Albatros B.II, which was designed by Ernst Heinkel and was just being introduced when the war began. Like the earlier B.I, the Albatros B.II was a sturdy airplane that featured a wooden airframe in which the fuselage was covered by plywood, making wire braces unnecessary, and fabric-covered wings, that used ailerons instead of wing-warping. Where the B.I had employed three bays of struts for its wings, the B.II employed just two bays of struts, thereby reducing drag. The B.II had a wingspan of 42 ft, a length of 25 ft, and a loaded weight of 1,591 lbs. Most were powered by a 100 hp Mercedes inline motor and could reach a maximum speed of 66 mph and had a service ceiling of 3,000 m (9,840 ft). Although it gave good performance, it was somewhat limited by the practice of placing the pilot in the rear seat and the observer in the front seat. Approximately 250 were constructed and entered service into 1915 before they were replaced by C-type armed reconnaissance aircraft.

By the end of the war, Albatros would produce approximately 2,100 C-type armed reconnaissance biplanes, beginning with the Albatros C.I, which was introduced in early 1915. A slightly enlarged version of the B.II with a wingspan of 42 ft 4 in., a length of 25 ft 9 in., and loaded weight of 2,618 lbs, the C.I sported a much more powerful motor, first the 150 hp Benz Bz.III inline engine and later the 160 hp Mercedes D.III inline engine or 180 hp Argus As.III inline engine. This resulted in a maximum speed of 82.5 mph and climbing rate of 1,000 m (3,281 ft) in approximately 10 minutes in the former to a speed of 107.5 mph and a climbing rate of 1,000 m in 6 minutes in the latter. In addition, the Albatros C.I was equipped with a ring-mounted Parabellum machine gun and it placed the observer in the rear. This change in seating arrangement, which the French and British were slow to adopt, allowed the observer to protect the rear against attack and to shoot down enemy reconnaissance aircraft when the pilot pulled alongside them. It was in this fashion that Oswald Boelcke obtained his first kill. The Albatros C.I and its variants proved to be so successful that the High Command ordered that they be subcontracted to meet demand.

In the fall of 1915 Albatros introduced the C.III, which gradually replaced the C.I. Similar to the C.I, the Albatros C.III was slightly smaller with a wingspan of 38 ft 4 in. and length of 26 ft 3 in. Although heavier at a loaded weight of 2,976 lbs, the C.III was more aerodynamic, using a rounded tailplane and rudder, which allowed the pilot to take greater evasive maneuvers than had been possible earlier. As was the case with the C.I, the plywood fuselage could absorb a lot of punishment and still fly. More important, however, its 150 hp Benz Bz.III inline motor or 160 hp Mercedes D.III inline motor provided enough power to allow it to be equipped with a synchronized forward-firing machine gun in addition to the ring-mounted observer's gun. Even though this resulted in a slight sacrifice of speed, down to 87.5 mph in the C.III, the added firepower more than compensated. The C.III design was the most widely produced version of the Albatros.

As technology improved and more powerful engines became available, subsequent versions of the Albatros C-type were introduced. All followed the same basic design, though some modifications were made to improve performance. The Albatros C.V was introduced in 1916 and was powered by the 220 hp Mercedes D.IV inline motor, which allowed it to reach 106 mph and climb to 1,000 m in just 8 minutes. The Albatros C-types culminated with the introduction of the C.X in early 1917 and the C.XII in late 1917. The wingspan for both was the same at 47 ft 1.5 in., but the C.XII was a foot shorter at 29 ft and weighed 63 lbs less at a loaded weight of 3,606 lbs. Both the C.X and C.XII were powered by the 260 hp Mercedes D.IVa inline engine, which produced a maximum speed of slightly more than 109 mph and an outstanding climbing rate at 1,000 m in just 5 minutes. Capable both of reaching a ceiling of 5,000 m (16,404 ft) and maintaining it for an extended period, both the C.X and C.XII came equipped with oxygen to enable its crew to conduct high-altitude photo-reconnaissance. Several hundred were built by a number of contractors.

Like Albatros, other German aircraft manufacturers began replacing their B-type aircraft in 1915 or introducing C-type aircraft of their own. One of the earliest to do so was Luft Verkehrs Gesellschaft (L.V.G.), whose chief engineer, Franz Schneider, had previously worked for the Farman brothers. Prior to the outbreak of war in 1914, Schneider had already designed several B-type aircraft and had patented an interrupter gear for firing a machine gun through the arc of the propeller. In mid-September 1914 he patented a ring-mounting system that allowed an observer to swing a machine gun onto a moving target. These were soon installed on strengthened versions of his B-type design, which were designated as the C.I. In the fall of 1915 Schneider introduced the much-improved L.V.G. C.II biplane, which was used for both armed reconnaissance and light bombing duties. With a wingspan of 42 ft 2 in., length of 26 ft 7 in., and loaded weight of 3,091, the L.V.G. C.II featured plywood covering around the cockpit and fabric covering on the rest of the aircraft. Powered by a 160 hp Mercedes D.III inline motor, it could reach 81 mph and had a service ceiling of approximately 3,050 m (10,000 ft). A synchronized, forward-firing Spandau was later added for additional firepower. Although an exact number is not available, approximately 250 L.V.G. C.I and C.II aircraft were in service by spring 1916. Later versions, the C.V and C.VI, which were introduced in 1917 and 1918, respectively, were slightly larger and were powered by a 200 hp Benz Bz.IV inline engine, which provided a maximum speed of 106 mph and a service ceiling of 6,500 m (21,325 ft.) In addition, they were equipped with both a forward-firing synchronized Spandau machine gun and a ring-mounted Parabellum machine gun and could carry up to 250 lbs of bombs.

Another prominent manufacturer of C-type aircraft was Deutsche Flugzeugwerke (D.F.W.). Indeed, the 2,340 D.F.W. C-types produced during the war were the most of any German aircraft type. Of these, the most important in this series were the C.IV biplane, which was introduced in early 1916, and the C.V biplane, which was introduced in late summer 1916. Both were similar in design and dimensions with a wingspan of 43 ft 7 in. and length of 25 ft 10 in. The C.IV was powered by a 150 hp Benz Bz.III inline engine and was capable of 96 mph, whereas the C.V was powered by a 220 hp Benz Bz. IV inline motor and capable of 100 mph. Both were equipped with a forward-firing synchronized machine gun and a rear-firing, ring-mounted machine gun. They were relatively fast and highly maneuverable, and they were capable of steady performance at high altitudes (in 1919 a C.V set a world record by reaching 9,620 m or 31,561 ft), which made them effective for prolonged photo-reconnaissance. At the same time, their plywood-covered fuselage made them sturdy enough to withstand the punishment that came with artillery spotting and infantry contact patrols.

RECONNAISSANCE AND AUXILIARY AIRCRAFT

Allgemeine Elektrizitäts Gesellschaft (A.E.G.), which was Germany's leading electrical firm and which had been urged by the German War Ministry to enter aircraft production in 1910, had produced a small number of B-types and C-types early in the war before introducing its most widely produced model, the A.E.G. C.IV biplane in 1916. Unlike the Albatros C-types and most other C-types, the A.E.G. C.IV used wood only for its wing ribs. Virtually everything else—the airframe, struts, wing spars, ailerons, undercarriage, and tail structure—were manufactured out of varying diameter light-gauge steel tubes over which fabric was stretched. With a wingspan of 44 ft 2 in., length of 23 ft 5.5 in., and loaded weight of 2,464 lbs, the A.E.G. C.IV was a sturdy aircraft that performed well in combat conditions. Powered by a 160 hp Mercedes D.III inline engine, it was capable of a maximum speed of almost 99 mph, could climb to 1,000 m (3,281 ft) in 6 minutes, and operate at a service ceiling of 5,000 m (16,404 ft). Although an exact number produced is not available, a majority of the 658 A.E.G. C-types built were of the C.IV series, including some that the High Command required the Fokker Company to produce.

Luftfahrzeug Gesellschaft (L.F.G.), which in 1912 had taken over the defunct German firm that had been licensed to produce aircraft for the Wright brothers, eked out a living producing licensed-built aircraft, including Albatros B-types and the Albatros C.I, before introducing its own aircraft, the L.F.G. Roland C.II biplane in early 1916. It featured a unique semi-monocoque construction that involved wrapping several layers of plywood veneer strips around a light wooden frame before covering it with fabric. Although this was very labor intensive, it provided a smoother curved surface with a high strength-to-weight ratio that held up well in combat conditions and adverse weather. Although one of the smallest C-type German reconnaissance aircraft, with a wingspan of 33 ft 9.5 in. and a length of 25 ft 3.25 in., its rugged construction resulted in a loaded weight of 2,824 lbs. Because of its aerodynamic design, however, its 160 hp Mercedes D.III inline motor produced a top speed of 103 mph and allowed it to climb to 1,000 m (3,281 ft) in just 6 minutes. The L.F.G. Roland C.II was also well armed with a ring-mounted Parabellum machine gun for the observer and a forward-firing synchronized Spandau machine gun. Its one major defect was that the pilot's seat was so low in the fuselage that he had to land almost blindly. Approximately 275 were constructed.

Although several other German C-types were constructed, including ground support models that will be discussed in Chapter

Four, the Rumpler C.VII (Rubilt) deserves special mention because of its outstanding performance as a high-altitude photo-reconnaissance aircraft. Based on several successful earlier designs, the Rumpler C.I, which had been the first photo-reconnaissance aircraft of the war, and the C.IV, the Rumpler C.VII (Rubilt) featured a high-compression 240 hp Maybach Mb.IV inline engine that allowed it to maintain a speed of 100 mph at 6,100 m (20,013 ft) and operate at a service ceiling of nearly 7,300 m (3,950 ft), which was far beyond the capacity of Allied fighters. For the crew to operate at such heights, the C.VII Rubilt provided oxygen generators and electrically heated flying suits.

ITALIAN RECONNAISSANCE AND AUXILIARY AIRCRAFT

With an almost nonexistent aircraft industry when it entered the war in 1915, Italy at first relied heavily upon French aircraft until its own industry, which drew heavily upon its automobile manufacturing base, began producing aircraft. One of the first Italian-produced aircraft to be used in the war was the Macchi Parasol, which had first been introduced in 1913. Although it was used as an artillery spotter in the First Battle of the Isonzo (June 1915), its poor climbing rate limited its effectiveness in the mountainous terrain of the Italian Front. Italian copies of the German Aviatik B.I were more successful. A total of 423 of them were manufactured by the Società Anonima Meccanica Lombarda (S.A.M.L.). Powered by the French-built 140 hp Canton-Unné radial motor, the S.A.M.L. Aviatik was capable of 71.5 mph and had a decent rate of climb. It was protected by a pivot-mounted, observer-fired Revelli machine gun.

In late 1916 S.A.M.L. introduced a replacement for its Aviatik copy with an aircraft of its own design, the S.A.M.L. S.1. It was powered by a 260 hp Fiat A-12 bis inline motor capable of 100 mph, had a wingspan of 45 ft 3 in., a length of 27 ft 10 in., and a loaded weight of 3,080 lbs. It was protected by a pivot-mounted, observer-fired Revelli machine gun. In 1917 an enhanced version, the S.A.M.L. S.2, was introduced. The S.2, which was similar in design—its wingspan was shorter at 41 ft—was powered by a 300 hp Fiat A-12 bis inline engine capable of 104 mph and included a second Revelli machine gun mounted to the top wing and fired by the pilot. Both the S.1 and the S.2 were noted for their power and for being easy to fly. A total of 657 were produced by war's end.

Although it was unpopular with Italian airmen, Fiat's aircraft subsidiary, Savoia-Pomilio, introduced a series of pusher biplanes that were modeled after Farman types that had been in service in Italy since 1915. The first was the S.P.2, which entered service in fall 1916. Although powered by the 260 hp Fiat A-12 bis inline motor, which gave it a top speed of 91 mph and a ceiling of up to 6,200 m (20,341 ft), the S.P.2 lacked maneuverability because of its wingspan of 48 ft 3 in. and length of 31 ft 2 in. The pilot and observer, although protected by one or two Revelli machine guns, were vulnerable when attacked from the rear. A later reconnaissance version, the S.P.3, was powered by a 300 hp Fiat A-12 bis inline engine, but still suffered the same weaknesses. In the fall of 1917 a twin-engine version, the S.P.4, was introduced for reconnaissance and light bombing. Powered by two 200 hp SPA inline engines, it carried three crewman, was protected by two machine guns, and carried a 781-lb bomb load. Approximately 800 of all three types (half of which were S.P.2s) were produced.

Like Savoia-Pomilio, the Società Italiana Aviazione (S.I.A.), was a subsidiary of Fiat, but it produced far more effective reconnaissance aircraft. In 1917, S.I.A. introduced the 7B.1, which was constructed with a combination of wood and steel-tube framing and which had a wingspan of 43 ft 7 in., a length of 29 ft 8 in., and a loaded weight of 3,460 lbs. Powered by the 260 hp Fiat A-12 bis inline motor, it was fast at 116 mph and it was an excellent climber that could reach 4,000 m (13,123 ft) in 25 minutes. It had a service ceiling of 7,010 m (23,000 ft). It was protected by a forward-firing Revelli machine gun that was mounted on the top wing and a hinged-mounted Revelli for the observer. Because severe stress could cause the wings to collapse during combat maneuvers, a second version, the 7B.2, was introduced in May 1918; unfortunately, it failed to solve the wing problems. Of the 572 constructed, 501 were of the 7B.1 variety.

The Pomilio PC was introduced in March 1917 and quickly proved to be one of the best reconnaissance aircraft of the war. Powered by the 260 hp Fiat A-12 bis inline motor and capable of reaching 112 mph, the Pomilio PC was faster than most opposing fighters and thus did not require escort aircraft. It had a wingspan of 36 ft 4 in., a length of 30 ft 6 in., and a loaded weight of 3,469 lbs; however, it was unstable in gusty winds, forcing the manufacturer to make such modifications as adding a curved fin to the lower rear fuselage in the more stable, final versions, the PD and PE. The later versions also included a forward-firing synchronized gun fired by the pilot as well as a ring-mounted Lewis gun for the observer. More than 1,600 of all types were manufactured by war's end, and it comprised 112 of the 199 Italian aircraft used when Italians launched their offensive in the Battle of Vittorio Veneto.

The final Italian reconnaissance aircraft to enter the war was the Ansaldo S.V.A.5 "Primo," which began entering service in February 1918. It was originally intended as a fighter, but its lack of maneuverability compared with other 1918 fighters resulted in its being used primarily as an armed reconnaissance and photo-reconnaissance aircraft. The S.V.A.5 was powered by either a 220 hp SPA.6A inline engine or 265 hp SPA.6A inline engine, which produced a maximum speed of 143 mph in the latter and gave it a service ceiling of 7,000 m (22,965 ft). It had a wingspan of 29 ft 10.25 in., a length of 26 ft 6.8 in., and a loaded weight of 2.315 lbs. The S.V.A.5 was protected by two fixed forward-firing, synchronized Vickers guns, which also enabled it to provide ground strafing duties in support of infantry. In addition to carrying a light bomb load, the S.V.A.5 and its variants were used to drop propaganda leaflets behind enemy lines because its range could be extended up to a maximum of 650 miles, which enabled the Italians to reach Vienna and return to their bases. Production continued until 1927 with approximately 2,000 aircraft being produced.

RUSSIAN RECONNAISSANCE AND AUXILIARY AIRCRAFT

Although Russia had produced the world's first large multiengine aircraft with the *Ilya Muromet*, which was used for long-range reconnaissance, it had more in common with bombers and thus will be discussed in that chapter. Its designer, Igor Sikorsky, had experimented with a variety of smaller aircraft prior to 1914 and after the war, but only one of these, the Sikorsky 16, which was intended as an escort for the Ilya Muromet, entered production in limited numbers before the end of the war. As a result, Russia had to rely primarily upon its prewar purchases of French aircraft (most of which were obsolete by the start of the war), importing French and British aircraft (which had to enter through the port of Archangel in the White Sea after Turkey entered the war and closed the Turkish Straits), or producing licensed-built foreign aircraft (which presented logistical problems in procuring needed parts and supplies). Russia, however, eventually would have some success in producing its own aircraft, of which the Anatra V.I, the Anatra D and DS, and the Lebed 12 were the most important reconnaissance types.

Located in Odessa, Ukraine, the Anatra factory began production in late 1915 of a modified Voisin pusher biplane, the Anatra V.I (Voisin Ivanov), which was named after its Russian designer, Piotr Ivanov. It had a wingspan of 48 ft 2 in., a length of 31 ft 2 in., and a loaded weight of 2,656 lbs. The observer sat in the front seat of its plywood nacelle and operated a mounted Colt machine gun. Powered by a 150 hp Salmson Canton-Unné radial engine, it had a top speed of 78 mph and a service ceiling of 3,500 m (11,482 ft). Approximately 150 were constructed up to 1917, and a few remained in service during the Russian Civil War.

Although front-line pilots complained that the Anatra V.I was difficult to fly, they would find the Anatra D and DS far more to their liking. A tractor-driven aircraft that was modeled after the German and Austro-Hungarian Aviatik, the Anatra D (or Anade) entered service in 1916. It had a wingspan of 37 ft 8 in., a length of 25 ft 3 in., and a loaded weight of 1,910 lbs. In addition, it was protected by a rear-mounted Colt machine gun. Powered by a 100 hp Gnôme rotary motor, it was capable of 82 mph and could climb to 2,000 m (6,562 ft) in 15 minutes. Despite the abundance of wood in Russia, the Anatra factory had such difficulty in obtaining quality lumber that it eventually had to resort to manufacturing wing spars out of two parts that overlapped and were glued and taped together. Needless to say, this caused structural collapses in many of the 205 Anatra D aircraft that were produced. An improved version, the Anatra DS, was introduced in the summer of 1917. It was powered by a 150 or 160 hp Salmson Canton-Unné radial engine, capable of a maximum speed of 89.5 mph, and was armed with a forward-firing, synchronized Vickers gun fired by the pilot and a rear-firing, ring-mounted Lewis gun fired by the observer. Although the Anatra DS matched up well against German and Austro-Hungarian fighters, the Russian Revolution disrupted and limited production to approximately 100 aircraft.

Located in St. Petersburg, V. A. Lebedev Aeronautics was organized prior to the war by Vladimir A. Lebedev. After building several prototypes as well as licensed-built French aircraft, it began producing the Lebed 11 and Lebed 12 after the Russian Imperial Air Service provided the company with a captured Albatros C-type in 1915. Although only 10 Lebed 11 aircraft were produced, a total of 214 Lebed 12 aircraft were produced in 1916 and 1917. It had a wingspan of 43 ft 1 in., a length of 26 ft 1 in., and a loaded weight of 2,678 lbs. Powered by a 150 hp Salmson Canton-Unné radial motor, it was capable of reaching 83 mph and carrying a 220-lb bomb load. Armed with an observer's ring-mounted Colt gun, the Lebed 12 proved to be an effective armed reconnaissance aircraft; unfortunately, it came too late in the war to make a difference.

U. S. RECONNAISSANCE
AND AUXILIARY AIRCRAFT

Although the Wrights had achieved heavier-than-air flight on 17 December 1903, they did not develop a practical airplane until 1905 with the *Wright Flyer III*. When the U.S. Army Signal Corps issued specifications for a military aircraft in December 1907, demanding that it have a range of 125 miles, that it possess an average speed of 40 mph, and that it be easy to disassemble and reassemble for transportation, the Wrights submitted plans with a bid of $25,000 (far less than the $200,000 they had demanded from the French). After Orville made several demonstration flights at Fort Meyers, Virginia, in September 1908 (and despite a crash on 17 September that killed his passenger, Lieutenant Thomas E. Selfridge), the War Department accepted the bid. The Wrights made a few modifications before delivering and demonstrating the aircraft in the summer of 1909 and officially receiving payment on 2 August 1909.

Unlike their original flyers, which required the pilot to lay prone on the lower wing, the *Wright Military Flyer* (Type A) possessed two seats, allowing the pilot and passenger to sit upright; otherwise, it was fairly similar to the earlier versions in that it placed the elevator in the front of the aircraft (canard configuration) to minimize stalls, utilized a pusher configuration (with the engine and propeller in the rear), and required the use of a drop-weight launching system.[2] Constructed with a spruce and ash airframe and covered with cotton linen cloth, the *Wright Military Flyer* had a loaded weight of 1,200 lbs. It sported a four-cylinder water-cooled inline engine that was capable of producing up to 35 hp and that allowed it to reach 44 mph, surpassing the army's requirement of 40 mph and winning the Wrights a $5,000 bonus. Once adopted, it was first based at College Park, Maryland, where in October 1909 Wilbur instructed

Lieutenant Frederick E. Humphreys and Lieutenant Frank P. Laum to fly. Both men had to learn to fly literally "by the seat of the pants," since the flyer lacked any instruments, other than a strip of cloth tied to the land skid to indicate whether the plane was flying level. After just a few hours training, both Humphreys and Laum soloed. Over the next 2 years, Wilbur would teach five additional pilots to fly, including Lieutenant Henry "Hap" Arnold, who would later serve as the commander of the U.S. Army Air Forces during World War II. Even as the U.S. Army purchased the *Wright Military Flyer* in 1909, however, the Wrights were quickly being surpassed by a rival at home in Glenn Curtiss.

Having won several aviation prizes, including the award for the fastest airplane at the famous 1909 Reims Air Show, Curtiss had formed the Curtiss Aeroplane and Motor Company in 1910 and had already won U.S. Army and Navy contracts before introducing the Curtiss JN "Jenny" series in 1914. Designed to meet the U.S. Army's requirements for a tractor-driven reconnaissance aircraft and trainer, the first to enter major production was the JN-3, of which the British purchased ninety-seven as trainers for the RNAS. The JN-3 was among the first American aircraft to see combat service, as the eight JN-3 biplanes of the 1st Aero Squadron accompanied General John J. Pershing's Punitive Expedition into northern Mexico in 1916 after Pancho Villa raided Columbus, New Mexico. The harsh desert environment resulted in poor performance and gave Pershing an initial bad perception of the capabilities of aircraft. The JN-4 was far more successful.It was an improved version of the JN-3 that was powered by a variety of motors (those powered by the 150 hp Wright-Hispano liquid-cooled engine had a maximum speed of 93 mph). With a wingspan of 43 ft 7 in., a length of 27 ft 4 in., and loaded weight of 2,130 lbs, the JN-4 proved to be easy to fly and served as a basic trainer until 1927, with more than 6,000 being produced.

The Thomas Morse Aircraft Factory, founded in January 1917, began production of the Thomas Morse S-4 in late 1917. Designed by B. D. Thomas, who had previously worked for Glenn Curtiss, the S-4 was originally intended to be a fighter. With a wingspan of 26 ft 6 in., a length of 19 ft 10 in., and a loaded weight of 1,373 lbs, it was a highly maneuverable and acrobatic aircraft, but its 80 hp Le Rhône 9C rotary motor proved to be underpowered. With a ground speed of 95 mph and a ceiling of just 15,000 ft (4,572 m), the S-4 was not up to 1918 fighter standards. Nevertheless, approximately 600 were produced and proved to be useful as advanced trainers.

NOTES

1. The mission was both in retaliation for Germany's use of zeppelins based at Düsseldorf and Cologne to drop bombs on Antwerp and in hopes of preempting a German attack on Britain.

2. As previously noted, the Wrights persisted in using a canard configuration in order to avoid a fatal stall, but this resulted in poor center of gravity, making the *Wright Flyer* difficult to handle. In their later aircraft, beginning with the *Wright Military Flyer* Type B in 1910, the Wrights would employ a standard tail assembly with the rudder and elevator in the rear. They would also use a wheeled undercarriage in place of skids, allowing for a conventional takeoff without the aid of the drop-weight launching system.

CHAPTER FOUR

Fighter and Attack Aircraft

WITH RECONNAISSANCE AIRCRAFT PROVING their worth in the opening stages of the war, the need to deprive the enemy of the ability to conduct reconnaissance as well as the need to provide escort service for one's own reconnaissance aircraft became a top priority and resulted in the emergence of the fighter in the spring of 1915. Even though reconnaissance and observation remained the primary strategic role of air power, the fighter and the men who flew them would captivate the public imagination like no other aspect of the First World War. The press often compared fighter pilots to the medieval knights of old, who, instead of being mounted on horses, were now flying their mounts in bloody jousting matches over the battlefields of Europe. Whereas the skill and courage of individual pilots was extremely important, the quality of their aircraft was crucial to success because air combat gave little room for error or aircraft inferiority. The pace of technology brought successive generations of fighters to the forefront, causing the balance of air superiority to shift on several occasions as newer, faster, more maneuverable, and better armed aircraft were introduced. In addition, the application of the machine gun to aircraft also opened the possibility of using air power in direct support of ground troops. By war's end the fighter had proven that its tactical role was essential to the strategic purpose of air power.

AUSTRO-HUNGARIAN FIGHTER
AND ATTACK AIRCRAFT

Although Austria-Hungary had produced a number of reconnaissance aircraft types early in the war, it had to rely upon German manufacturers to supply its need for fighters until the last 2 years of the war, when Austro-Hungarian manufacturers began producing licensed-built German fighters and introduced fighters of their own. The most numerous German fighter to be produced in Austria-Hungary was the Albatros D.III biplane. After obtaining the rights to the Albatros D.II in December 1916 and producing 16 during the spring of 1917, Oesterreiche Flugzeugfabrik A.G. (Oeffag) would produce a total of 526 Albatros D.III fighters in three different series (distinguished by their engines) during the last 18 months of the war. Although similar in design to the German original, with a wingspan of 29 ft 6 in. and length of 24 ft 1.5 in., the Oeffag version of the Albatros D.III featured a sturdier fuselage and wing structure that allowed it to incorporate more powerful motors. Instead of the 160 hp Mercedes D.IIIa inline engine, which produced up to 108 mph, the first Oeffag-built Albatros D.III fighters sported a 185 hp Austro-Daimler inline motor that produced 112 mph and could climb to 1,000 m (3,281 ft) in just more than 3 minutes and 5,000 m (16,404 ft) in 32 minutes. Later versions powered by the 200 hp Austro-Daimler inline engine could reach 117 mph and climb to 1,000 m in 2 minutes and 35 seconds, whereas those powered by the 225 hp Austro-Daimler inline motor could reach 125 mph and climb to 1,000 m in just more than 3 minutes. They were well armed with two forward-firing synchronized Schwarzlose machine guns that were either buried in the fuselage or mounted above it.

The first purely Austro-Hungarian fighter to enter production was the Hansa-Brandenburg D.I biplane, which was designed by one of the German firm's top engineers, Ernst Heinkel. Although approximately fifty were produced at the German plant, they were used exclusively by the *Luftfahrtruppen* (LFT). An additional seventy were produced by Phönix[1] in late 1916 and began entering service in early 1917. The Hansa-Brandenburg D.I was a rather compact fighter with a wingspan of 27 ft 10.5 in., a length of 20 ft 8 in., and a loaded weight of 2,112 lbs and its 185 hp Austro-Daimler inline engine was capable of producing up to 115 mph. Nevertheless, pilots complained about its unstable flight characteristics and the poor forward visibility caused by its raised engine cowling, which made landing hazardous. Its most unique characteristic was the use of a star-strutter system, suggested by Austrian engineering professor Richard Knoller, in which four struts attached to the top wing and four struts attached to the bottom wing converged together in a central housing approximately midway in the gap between the wings, giving it the appearance of two pyramids joined together at the points. Although this provided a strong support system for the wings, the added weight and drag may have contributed to the aircraft's unwieldiness. Another problem of the Hansa-Brandenburg D.I was that (with the exception of some of the last produced by Phönix) it lacked a synchronized machine gun, relying instead upon a Schwarzlose mounted to the top wing—a firing system that was outmoded by the time it entered service in late 1916 and early 1917. As a result, only a few experienced pilots, such as Austro-Hungarian ace Godwin Brumowski, enjoyed success in the Hansa-Brandenburg D.I. Most pilots derisively referred to it as a flying coffin, which was an indictment against its lack of firepower as well as its tendency to enter deadly spins.

Intended as a replacement for the Hansa-Brandenburg D.I, the Aviatik D.I biplane was the first fighter to be designed in and produced entirely within Austria-Hungary. All four versions of the D.I were produced at the same time with the primary difference in series type being the size of the engine.[2] A wide variety of radiator types were randomly installed, leading to variations in appearance and pilot visibility. Despite these differences, the most important feature of the Aviatik D.I was that its wood-plywood construction made it easy to reproduce by licensed manufacturers. Thus, even though Aviatik produced 336 of the 677 total Aviatik D.I fighters, just more than 50 percent were manufactured by other Austro-Hungarian firms—121 by Ungarishe Allgemeine Maschinefabrik A.G. (MAG),[3] 110 by Lohner, 45 by Wiener Karosserie und Flugzeugfabrik (WFK), 36 by Flugzeug und Maschinenfabrik Thöne & Fiala, and 31 by Lloyd. The total of 677 produced by the end of the war made the Aviatik D.I the most widely produced Austro-Hungarian fighter of the war. Indeed, it comprised 43 percent of all fighters delivered to the LFT during the last 18 months of the war.

Designed by Julius von Berg, the Aviatik D.I was noted as a compact fighter that was fast and highly maneuverable. Its wingspan was 26 ft 3 in., its length was 25 ft 10.7 in., and its loaded weight was 1,878 lbs. Although it used engines varying from the 160 hp Austro-

Daimler inline motor up to a 225 hp Austro-Daimler inline motor, the majority of Aviatik D.I fighters were fitted with the 200 hp Austro-Daimler, which provided a maximum speed of 121 mph, an outstanding climbing rate of 1,000 m (3,281 ft) in 1 minute 42 seconds and 5,000 m (16,404 ft) in 16 minutes 26 seconds, and a service ceiling of slightly more than 6,000 m (19,685 ft). Despite the excellent performance characteristics of the Aviatik D.I, pilots complained about the steering wheel control system that Berg had designed—primarily because they were unaccustomed to it—leading to its replacement with a control stick about midway through production. Another problem in early versions of the Aviatik D.I was that it relied upon a wing-mounted Schwarzlose maching gun set at a 15-degree upward angle, which made aiming difficult and forced pilots to attack while in a dive, which placed them at a disadvantage by surrendering altitude. Beginning in December 1917, twin-synchronized guns were introduced, but these were mounted so far forward that pilots lacked access to the guns, which was a major problem because the Schwarzlose was prone to jam. As a result, by the summer of 1918 complaints led to further modifications in existing fighters and those being produced with the guns placed directly in front of the cockpit for easy access in the event of a jam. Had the armament problems been worked out in advance, the Aviatik D.I would have been one of the better fighters of the war. By the time the problems were solved and work on an improved fighter, the Aviatik D.II, had begun, it was too late to make a difference in the war.

Like the Aviatik D.I, the Phönix D.I biplane was intended as a replacement for the Hansa-Brandenburg D.I. Although it was produced in smaller numbers (120 D.I, 45 D.II, and 48 D.IIa fighters) than the Aviatik D.I and did not begin entering service until October 1917, the Phönix D-series fighters are generally considered the best fighters designed and produced in Austria-Hungary. Its fuselage resembled that of the Hansa-Brandenburg D.I, which Phönix had earlier produced, but it used a more standard strutter and wire brace wing assembly than the star-strutter employed on the Hansa-Brandenburg D.I. Although its 200 hp Hiero inline engine made it slightly slower at 110 mph than the Aviatik D.I and it could not climb as well as the Aviatik D.I or the Allied aircraft it fought against, its wooden-framed, plywood-covered fuselage made it a sturdy aircraft capable of diving at high speeds and absorbing a lot of damage. The Phönix D.I was also praised for being easy to fly and fairly maneuverable. Its wingspan was 32 ft 1.8 in., its length was 22 ft 1.8 in., and its loaded weight was 2,097 lbs. The D.II series was lightened by approximately 100 lbs and featured a more aerodynamic wing design, resulting in improved maneuverability. The D.IIa was powered by a 230 hp Hiero inline motor, which increased maximum speed to 115 mph and slightly improved its rate of climb. All versions featured twin-synchronized Schwarzlose machine guns, but they were placed within the engine cowling, which denied the pilot access in the event of a jam. Nevertheless, it proved to be a match for Allied fighters. An improved model, the D.III, was entering production just as the war ended, but none saw service. Sweden purchased twenty-one Phönix D.III fighters after the war and later produced an additional seventeen after obtaining the license rights. It remained in service with the Swedish Army Air Force until 1933.

BRITISH FIGHTER AND ATTACK AIRCRAFT

From the beginning of the war, British pilots had been among the first to arm themselves with pistols and rifles in an effort to shoot down enemy planes. Recognizing the difficulty of trying to strike a moving target with a rifle, a few enterprising British pilots mounted Lewis guns on the top wing of their aircraft in an effort to use their airplane to aim at the enemy. Such a configuration had its drawbacks, however, because the pilot had to stand up to replace the cannister. As previously noted, Captain Louis Strange's Martinsyde Scout turned upside down and plummeted 7,500 feet before he managed to upright it. It was for this reason that the British initially turned to the pusher configuration for its fighters, until a practical synchronization gear became available.

The Vickers F.B.5 was the first British fighter to enter service. As early as 1913, the Vickers firm had demonstrated the use of a Maxim gun from one of its early pusher prototypes. With the outbreak of war in 1914 and the dual needs to deprive enemy aircraft from conducting reconnaissance missions and protect one's own reconnaissance aircraft, Vickers began production of the F.B.5 in the fall of 1914. The first units entered service on the Western Front in February 1915. Nicknamed the "Gun Bus," the F.B.5 featured a two-seat nacelle to which its motor was attached in the rear. The observer sat in the front seat and had an excellent range of view and field of fire with a pivot-mounted Lewis gun. With a wingspan of 36 ft 2 in., a length of 27 ft 2 in., and a loaded weight of 2,050 lbs, the

F.B.5 was powered by a 100 hp Gnôme Monosoupape rotary engine that provided a top speed of 70 mph, could climb to 5,000 ft (1,524 m) in approximately 16 minutes, and had a service ceiling of 9,000 ft (2,743 m). Although it was relatively slow and lacked maneuverability, it was easy to fly and enjoyed great success until the emergence of the Fokker Eindecker in the fall of 1915 proved its vulnerability to rear attack. Nevertheless, the F.B.5 remained in service on the Western Front until mid-1916, when it was withdrawn for service as trainers or service on the Middle Eastern Front. Approximately 200 were produced.

Like the Vickers F.B.5, the Royal Aircraft Factory (R.A.F.) F.E.2 biplane originated with a prewar design by Geoffrey de Havilland that first flew in August 1913. After the outbreak of war the R.A.F. immediately placed an order for twelve F.E.2a fighters. Although these were ready by January 1915, the original 100 hp Green engine proved to be so underpowered that they could not be used. As a result, it was May 1915 before a modified version, the F.E.2b, which was powered by a 120 hp Beardmore inline motor, entered service. Even so, these would not arrive at the front in large numbers until late 1915. Although it was a large aircraft with a wingspan of 47 ft 9 in., length of 32 ft 3 in., and loaded weight of 2,970 lbs, the F.E.2b's 120 hp Beardmore inline engine provided 80 mph (similar to the Fokker Eindecker) and a service ceiling of 9,000 ft (2,743 m). It was equipped with oleo shock absorbers on its landing gear, which made for smoother landings. Later F.E.2b fighters were equipped with a 160 hp Beardmore inline motor that increased speed to 91.5 mph and improved its rate of climb, and the F.E.2d introduced in mid-1916 came equipped with a 250 hp Rolls-Royce inline engine. Despite its pusher configuration, the F.E.2b and F.E.2d proved to be more than a match for the Fokker Eindecker, in part because the observer, who sat in the front of the nacelle, operated a forward-firing, bracket-mounted Lewis gun, and could also stand and fire to the rear with a Lewis gun that was mounted to fire over the top wing, thereby providing a degree of protection when attacked from the rear. By late 1916, however, the appearance of German biplane fighters forced the gradual withdrawal of the F.E.2 types as fighters and their reallocation to home defense or as night bombers, roles that they continued to play until the end of the war. Approximately 2,000 of all varieties were constructed by the R.A.F. and its many subcontractors.

Where the Vickers F.B.5 and R.A.F. F.E.2 series had been two-seat fighters, the Airco D.H.2 biplane was a single-seat pusher that was designed by Geoffrey de Havilland in the summer of 1915 and entered production later that fall. By year's end, the first D.H.2 fighters began to enter service. Far more compact than its predecessors, the D.H.2 had a wingspan of 28 ft 3 in., a length of 25 ft 2 in., and a loaded weight of 1,441 lbs. Powered by either a 100 hp Gnôme Monosoupape rotary motor or a 110 hp Le Rhône rotary motor, it had a maximum speed of 93 mph and could climb to 10,000 ft (3,048 m) in approximately 25 minutes. Pilots faced a somewhat difficult challenge in flying the airplane and firing its movable Lewis gun, leading many to improvise methods of fixing the gun to fire forward (albeit against regulations). Although many of Britain's early aces, such as Major Lanoe George Hawker, obtained great success in the D.H.2, which proved to be highly maneuverable for a pusher, it should be pointed out that many an inexperienced pilot lost their lives because of its tendency to enter a spin, leading to it being dubbed "The Spinning Incinerator" early in its service. Improved pilot training, however, would help minimize this problem. Although it was clearly outclassed by German biplane fighters that entered service in late 1916, the D.H.2 remained in use on the Western Front well into 1917, suffering great casualties in "Bloody April," before they were withdrawn with some being dispatched to the Middle East. Approximately 400 were produced.

The R.A.F. F.E.8 biplane, which was similar in design to the Airco D.H.2, was one of the last pusher fighters to enter the war. Although it had been designed by John Kenworthy in mid-1915, the F.E.8 did not enter production until early 1916 and did not begin arriving on the Western Front until July 1916. Like the D.H.2, its early reputation suffered from its propensity to enter spins, but after Major Frank W. Goodden conducted several spins on purpose on 23 August 1916 and demonstrated how to recover from them, pilots became more accepting of it. With a wingspan of 31 ft 6 in., a length of 23 ft 8 in., and a loaded weight of 1,346 lbs, the F.E.8 was powered by either a 100 hp Gnôme Monosoupape rotary engine, a 110 hp Le Rhône rotary engine, or a 110 hp Clerget rotary engine that produced an average 95 mph and could climb to 1,000 m (3,281 ft) in less than 5 minutes. Although its flight characteristics compared favorably with its predecessors, the F.E.8 was already outclassed by German fighters when it arrived on the front. Approximately 200 were produced before it was withdrawn from service in mid-1917.

The first effort of the British to match the Germans with a tractor-driven fighter led to the introduction of the R.A.F. B.E.12 biplane. The B.E.12, unfortunately, was just a larger version of the

R.A.F. B.E.2 two-seat reconnaissance biplane, which had already proven to be easy prey to the Germans. Although the B.E.12 possessed greater power with its 150 hp R.A.F. 4a inline motor, which was capable of producing a maximum speed of 102 mph, it proved to be a slow climber, taking almost 48 minutes to reach its service ceiling of 12,500 ft (3,810 m). With a wingspan of 40 ft 10 in., length of 27 ft 3 in., and loaded weight of 2,327 lb, it was stable and easy to fly, but it lacked maneuverability. It was armed with a single Lewis gun mounted to the top wing to fire over the arc of the propeller, which compared unfavorably with the synchronized guns of its German counterparts. A total of 468 were produced before they were withdrawn from the Western Front in 1917. An additional 100–150 aircraft that were powered by the 200 hp Hispano-Suiza V-type engine and armed with twin Vickers guns mounted on the top wing were constructed for home defense during the last 2 years of the war. Designated as the B.E.12b, they were also capable of carrying two 112-lb bombs and were used for antisubmarine patrols along the English coast.

The first British tractor-driven fighter to enjoy great success was the Sopwith Pup biplane, which entered service in the second half of 1916. The Sopwith Pup was derived from its larger predecessor, the Sopwith 11/2 Strutter, which had been introduced as a fighter early in 1916, but had soon been relegated to armed reconnaissance and light bombing duties. A compact fighter, the Pup had a wingspan of 26 ft 6 in., a length of 19 ft 3.75 in., and a loaded weight of 1,225 lbs. Most were powered by either an 80 hp Le Rhône rotary motor, an 80 hp Gnôme rotary motor, or an 80 hp Clerget rotary motor that produced a maximum speed of 110 mph and enabled it to climb to 15,000 ft (4,572 m) in 29 minutes 10 seconds. More important, the Sopwith Pup was noted for its superb maneuverability and was the first British fighter to be fitted with a synchronized gun, a .303 caliber Vickers. It should be noted that the Pup was originally intended for service with the Royal Naval Air Service (RNAS), but the demands of the Somme Offensive saw all but 290 of the 1,770 manufactured serve with the Royal Flying Corps (RFC). The Pup's role with the navy will be considered later.

Like the Sopwith Pup, the Sopwith Triplane had been designed by Herbert Smith for naval service, but it ended up serving on the Western Front, after its prototype enjoyed immediate success when demonstrated in July 1916. Unlike the Pup, however, the Sopwith Triplane was attached only to RNAS units that were stationed in France and Belgium. Patterned after the Pup, the Sopwith Triplane (nicknamed the "Tripehound") was designed to provide enhanced maneuverability. With a wingspan of 26 ft 6 in., a length of 18 ft 10 in., and a loaded weight of 1,541 lbs, the Sopwith Triplane was powered by a 130 hp Clerget rotary engine, could maintain 117 mph at 5,000 ft (1,524 m), climb rapidly (3,000 ft [914 m] in just 2 minutes 30 seconds), and had a service ceiling of 20,500 ft (6,280 m). Armed with either a single-, or twin-synchronized Vickers machine gun, the Sopwith Triplane proved to be such an agile and lethal fighter that, even though only 140 were produced and were in service for just a few months, German pilots were quickly demanding a similar aircraft.

The Bristol F.2a and F.2b biplane, nickednamed the "Brisfit," was designed by Frank S. Barnwell as a replacement for the much-maligned Royal Aircraft Factory B.E.2 two-seat reconnaissance aircraft. Equipped with a forward-firing, synchronized Vickers gun and one or two ring-mounted Lewis guns, the Brisfit proved to be one of the best two-seat fighters of the war. Although crews at first flew in formation and relied on the observer's gun or guns for defense, they soon learned that the surprising maneuverability of the Brisfit, combined with its firepower, made it more than an equal match for the German aircraft that it went up against. Despite its rather large size—a wingspan of 39 ft 3 in., a length of 25 ft 10 in., and a loaded weight of 2,779 lbs—the Brisfit was powered by ever-increasing more powerful engines, ranging from its original 190 hp Rolls-Royce Falcon inline motor to the 275 hp Rolls-Royce Falcon III inline motor. The latter gave it a maximum speed of 125 mph, a superb climbing rate of 10,000 ft (3,048 m) in 11 minutes 15 seconds, and a service ceiling of 20,000 ft (6,096 m). It should be noted, however, that the British engine industry was unable to keep up with demand, causing many of the Brisfits to be equipped with underpowered motors. By war's end, a total of 3,101 had been produced by Bristol and its many subcontractors, including Armstrong Whitworth. An additional 2,100 Brisfits were produced after the war with the Brisfit remaining in service with the Royal Air Force (RAF) until 1933.

Although the R.A.F. had failed with the B.E.12, it would produce one of the best British fighters of the war in the S.E.5 and S.E.5a biplane. Designed to utilize the powerful, yet lightweight 150 hp Hispano-Suiza V-type engine, which had become available in 1916, the S.E.5 sought to strike a balance between the stable, yet unmaneuverable B.E.2, with the more agile, but more difficult-to-fly Nieuports and SPADs used by the French. They quickly proved their worth upon entering service over the Western Front in the spring of

1917, leading to increased orders. Since the 200 hp Hispano-Suiza V-type engine was available by then, those equipped with it were designated as the S.E.5a. The S.E.5 and S.E.5a proved to be lethal fighters in the hands of aces like Edward Mannock, who achieved fifty of his seventy kills in an S.E.5. With a wingspan of 26 ft 7.4 in., a length of 20 ft 11 in., and a loaded weight of 1,988 lbs, it was a sturdy, compact aircraft that was capable of 138 mph, could climb to 10,000 ft (3,048 m) in 11 minutes 20 seconds, and had a service ceiling of 19,500 ft (5,943 m). It was well armed with a Foster-mounted Lewis gun that allowed upward fire from the top wing and a forward-firing Vickers gun that used the Constantinesco synchronizing gear, which relied upon hydraulic pressure to regulate the firing of the gun. Of the 5,205 S.E.5 types produced, 4,377 came in the last year of the war.

After achieving success with the Sopwith Pup and Sopwith Triplane, Herbert Smith introduced a fundamentally different design in March 1917 with the Sopwith F.1 biplane—better known as the Sopwith Camel because its twin, forward-firing Vickers guns, which used the Constantinesco synchronized gear, were covered, giving it the appearance of having a hump. A compact aircraft with a wingspan of 28 ft, length of 18 ft 9 in., and loaded weight of 1,453 lbs, the Camel was different from its predecessors in that its weight was concentrated in the front of the plane, with the engine, armament, and pilot being placed within 8 ft of the nose. When this weight placement was combined with the torque produced by the 130 hp Clerget rotary motor, the Sopwith Camel was capable of making a tight 360-degree right circle in the same time that it took opponents to turn 90 degrees. Even though it was slower at 113 mph than the S.E.5 and many of its German opponents, its turning ability gave it a huge combat advantage, as demonstrated by the nearly 1,300 victories it achieved during its 16 months of service, giving it more victories than any other single aircraft of the war. This advantage came with a price, however, because the Camel was an unforgiving aircraft whose inherent instability required constant attention from the pilot. Inexperienced pilots could easily enter a deadly spin from which many did not emerge. Of the 5,490 Camels produced during the war, 4,165 were constructed in the last year of the war.

Two other Sopwith aircraft that entered service in 1918 deserve mention. The Sopwith Snipe biplane, equipped with a 230 hp Bentley B.R.2 rotary engine, was a more powerful verison of the Sopwith Camel that was capable of 121 mph and possessed better climbing ability. With a slightly longer wingspan of 30 ft 1 in. and a more steamlined fuselage, the chief advantage of the Snipe was that it was just as maneuverable as the Camel, but was not as prone to enter deadly spins. Approximately 200 were produced by war's end, and the Snipe remained in service until 1926 with an ultimate total of 2,103 being produced. The Sopwith Dolphin biplane was powered by the 200 hp Hispano-Suiza V-type engine that provided a maximum speed of 112 mph. It was well armed with twin-synchronized, forward-firing Vickers guns, twin angle-mounted Lewis guns, and four 25-lb bombs. It proved to be an effective fighter and was an even more effective ground attack aircraft. The top wings were mounted low to the fuselage with the center section being cut to allow the pilot an outstanding range of vision. A total of 1,532 entered service by the end of the war.

FRENCH FIGHTER AND ATTACK AIRCRAFT

Although the Morane-Saulnier Type L monoplane had originally been intended as a reconnaissance aircraft when it entered service just as the war started (the first 50 were awaiting shipment to Turkey but were diverted to the French Army), it would make its mark as one of the first aircraft to be used for the purpose of shooting down enemy aircraft. Using a parasol wing that was raised above the fuselage and supported by a series of wire braces that were connected to a tall central pylon, making it a rather ugly aircraft, the original version relied upon wing-warping for control. In early 1915 modified versions were introduced with ailerons and received the designation LA. With a wingspan of 33 ft 9 in., a length of 20 ft 9 in., and a loaded weight of 1,444 lbs, the Type L and LA proved to be faster than early German two-seat aircraft as its 80 hp Gnôme or Le Rhône rotary motor provided 71 mph. As a result, pilots armed with pistols and rifles were soon able to force down slow-moving *Taubes* and Albatros B-types.

The key turning point in the Type L's development came in early 1915 when French pilot Roland Garros received permission to leave the front and join designer Raymond Saulnier in devising a method for firing a machine gun through the arc of the propeller. Unable to develop a reliable interrupter gear, Garros and Saulnier used the expedient of affixing metal wedges to the propellers and found that five of six rounds passed through with the other one being deflected. Beginning on 1 April 1915 Garros quickly proved the advantage of forward fire by shooting down five German aircraft in a 3-week period. Although Garros was forced down behind German lines on 18 April, the French would continue to enjoy success with similarly armed Type L and Type LA fighters until the appearance of the Fokker Eindecker, which had the first interrupter gear, inspired in part by Fokker's inspection of Garros's plane. Approximately 600 Morane-Saulnier Type L and LA aircraft were produced in France and an additional 400 were licensed-built by the Dux works in Russia.

Like the Morane-Saulnier Type L and LA, the Nieuport 10 biplane had originally been intended for reconnaissance duty when it entered service in the summer of 1915, but it was soon pressed into fighter service to combat the Fokker Eindecker. Designed by Gustave Delage, who had joined the Nieuport firm in early 1914, the Nieuport 10 was the first in a series of Nieuport aircraft to feature a sesquiplane design in which the chord of the bottom wing was much narrower than that of the top wing, making it as maneuverable as a monoplane but as strong as a standard biplane. In addition, it featured a V-strut on each side of the fuselage with the struts being attached to the bottom wing at a single point. The angle of the lower wing could also be adjusted on the ground depending on whether it was going to be used as a single-seat fighter or as a two-seat reconnaissance aircraft. With a wingspan of 25 ft 11.75 in., a length of 23 ft 1.5 in., and a loaded weight of 1,433 lbs, the Nieuport 10 was a compact aircraft that was very maneuverable, but its 80 hp Le Rhône rotary engine could produce just 71 mph and its top-wing mounted Lewis gun was not as effective as the synchronized guns of its German opponents. A later version, the Nieuport 12, was introduced in late 1915. It was slightly larger and was powered by either a 110 or 130 hp Clerget rotary motor, which increased its speed up to 96 mph. Although the Nieuport 12 was used primarily as a two-seat fighter escort, some of the last to be produced featured synchronized guns. Approximately 7,200 Nieuport 10s and 12s were produced in France and saw service with the French and their British, Russian, and Italian allies. An additional 240 Nieuport 10s were produced in Italy by Societa Nieuport-Macchi and approximately 325 were built in Russia by the Dux and the Lebedev firms.

Although its first fighters had originated as reconnaissance aircraft, the French would introduce their first specially designed fighter, the Nieuport 11 biplane, in January 1916. A sesquiplane like the Nieuport 10, the Nieuport 11 was dubbed the *Bébé* (Baby) because of its compact size—a wingspan of 24 ft 8 in., a length of 18 ft 1 in., and a loaded weight of just 1,058 lbs. Its 80 hp Le Rhône rotary engine produced 100 mph, enabled it to climb to 3,000 m (9,843 ft) in just 15 minutes, and gave it a service ceiling of 5,000 m (16,404 ft). Although it lacked the synchronized guns employed by the Fokker Eindecker and relied instead on a top-wing mounted Lewis gun or Hotchkiss gun, the Nieuport 11 proved to be a nimble aircraft that could outclimb and outmaneuver the Eindecker. As a result, the Nieuport 11 was critical both in helping the Allies bring an end to the "Fokker Scourge" and in giving them air superiority over the skies of Verdun and the Somme. It should be noted, however, that the Nieuport 11's V-struts made the wings prone to twist in a steep dive, often resulting in a crash.

The Nieuport 16 used the same airframe as the Nieuport 11, but it came equipped with a more powerful 110 hp Le Rhône rotary motor, which slightly increased its speed to 102 mph but made it somewhat nose heavy and difficult to fly. Although most Nieuport 16s were equipped with a top-wing mounted Lewis gun, some of the last to be produced featured a synchronized gun. Many Nieuport 16s were also armed with up to eight Le Prieur rockets for attacks against German balloons. After they were withdrawn from frontline service in late 1916, the remaining Nieuport 11s and 16s were reassigned as advanced trainers. Allied fighters who scored significant victories in the Nieuport 11 and 16 included Albert Ball, William Bishop, Charles Nungesser, and Georges Guynemer. Approximately 2,000 Nieuport 11s and 16s saw service with the Allies, including approximately 540 that were licensed-built in Italy and approximately 200 that were licensed-built in Russia.

Introduced in the summer of 1916, the Nieuport 17 featured several design improvements by Gustave Delage that improved upon the Nieuport 11 and 16. Although it retained the sesquiplane configuration used in the early models, the chord of the lower wing was increased and the V-struts and wing structures were strengthened. Its fuselage combined both steel-tube and wooden (spruce and ash) framing, and used both plywood and fabric covering. The result was a sturdier and better balanced aircraft, unlike the nose-heavy Nieuport 16. It had a slightly longer wingspan at 26 ft 9 in., length at 19 ft, and a slightly heavier loaded weight at 1,234 lbs. Powered by either a 110 hp Le Rhône 9JA rotary engine or 130 hp Clerget 9B rotary engine, the Nieuport 17 could reach 102 mph and climb to 3,000 m (9,483 ft) in 11 minutes 30 seconds in the former and reach 118 mph and climb to 3,000 m (9,483 ft) in 9 minutes in the latter. Although some Nieuport 17s were armed with twin-Lewis guns mounted on the top wing, most came equipped with synchronized Vickers guns, finally giving the French and British an aircraft that was equal in firepower to their German enemies. The Nieuport 17 became the mainstay of the French air service in late 1916 and early 1917, and its success prompted the Germans to copy many of its characteristics in their first generation of biplane fighters. Although a precise number for French Nieuport 17s is not available, the number produced probably exceeded 2,000 aircraft, including some 150 Italian-built versions. Approximately 300 Nieuport 17s were still in service in August 1917.

Although France had achieved great results from aircraft powered by rotary engines, including those used in its Nieuport fighters, by late 1916 the rotary engine was reaching its maximum level of performance because greater horsepower resulted in greater torque, which made them difficult to handle for inexperienced pilots. As a result, three rotary engine–powered fighters introduced by French manufacturers in late 1916 and during 1917—the Hanriot HD.1, the Nieuport 28, and the Morane-Saulnier A.1—would see only limited use in the French air service, as the French turned instead to the SPAD VII, which was powered by the V-type Hispano-Suiza stationary engine. Nevertheless, these three last rotary engine fighters deserve brief mention.

Designed by Emile Dupont, the Hanriot HD.1 biplane resembled the Sopwith 11/2 Strutter. Although the prototype, which was powered by a 120 hp Le Rhône rotary motor, received somewhat favorable reviews when it was demonstrated in late 1916, the French ultimately rejected it for service with the Aviation Militaire in order to concentrate production of the SPAD VII. Even though it was rejected for French service, Hanriot manufactured approximately 100 HD.1s for the Belgian and Italian air services. With a wingspan of 28 ft 6 in., a length of 19 ft 2 in., and a loaded weight of just 1,334 lbs, the Hanriot HD.1 proved to be a highly maneuverable and fast fighter that had a top speed of 114 mph. Althougth the HD.1 did not begin entering Belgium service until August 1917, Belgium's leading ace, Willy Coppens, would obtain the majority of his thirty-seven victories while flying an HD.1. They would remain in service in Belgium until 1927. The HD.1 proved to be so popular with the Italian air service that approximately 900 HD.1s would be licensed-built in Italy by Nieuport-Macchi with some slight modifications in design, which will be discussed later.

The Nieuport 28, which was designed by Gustave Delage and introduced in late 1917, was powered by a 160 hp Gnôme Monosoupape rotary engine. Although it was capable of a maximum speed of 122 mph, which was faster than the SPAD VII, and its compact size (a wingspan of 28 ft 8 in., a length of 21 ft, and a loaded weight of 1,625 lbs) made it highly maneuverable, the extreme torque produced by its engine made it even more unforgiving than the Sopwith Camel and led to its rejection by the French. When the American Expeditionary Force (AEF) began organizing its first squadrons, however, it was forced to purchase 297 Nieuport 28s because it was one of the few aircraft available and the French were unwilling to supply SPAD VIIs. Although Eddie Rickenbacker managed to succeed in the aircraft, he was the exception to the general rule. American pilots came to hate the Nieuport 28, viewing them as dangerous to fly, especially after tragic crashes claimed the lives of Raoul Lufbery, a leading ace from the *Lafayette Escadrille*, and Quentin Roosevelt, the son of former President Theodore Roosevelt.

The Morane-Saulnier A.1 monoplane was introduced in late 1917 and began entering service in January 1918. Like the earlier Type L and LA, the A.1 used a parasol wing configuration. The front part of the fuselage and engine cowling were covered with sheet metal, whereas the rear fuselage was constructed of spruce planks that were wrapped with fabric. The wing was constructed of wood, featured a slight swept-back design, and was attached to the fuselage and undercarriage by angled struts that were reinforced by auxiliary struts. Powered by a 150 hp Gnôme Monosoupape, the A.1 had a maximum speed of 129 mph. Its wingspan of 27 ft 11 in., length of 18 ft 6 in., and loaded weight of 1,431 lbs made it highly maneuverable, yet, as was the case with the Nieuport 28, the immense torque of its engine resulted in several crashes by novice pilots. As a result, the vast majority of the 1,210 A.1s that were produced ended up seeing service only as trainers. Indeed, their reputation was such that their wings were "clipped" to prevent them from flying, turning them into so-called penguins in which students learned the basics by taxiing at high speed.[4]

Faced with the need to increase performance and recognizing the hazards of high-powered rotaries, the French would turn to the eight-cylinder, V-type Hispano-Suiza to power its last generation of fighters. The first of these was the SPAD VII biplane introduced by the Société Anonyme Pour l'Aviation et ses Derives (SPAD) in the fall of 1916. With a wingspan of 25 ft 8 in., a length of 20 ft 3 in., and a loaded weight of 1,550 lbs, the SPAD VII was a maneuverable, sturdy aircraft. It quickly became the mainstay of the French air service in 1917 with more than 3,500 produced in France.[5] The first models were powered by a 150 hp Hispano-Suiza 8Aa V-type engine, which produced 119 mph and could climb to 3,000 m (9,843 ft) in 11 minutes 20 seconds. Later versions were powered by a 180 hp Hispano-Suiza 8Ab V-type engine, which produced 131 mph and could climb to 3,000 m (9,843 ft) in 8 minutes 10 sececonds The SPAD VII was armed with a synchronized Vickers gun. A modified version, the SPAD XII, was similar in design to the SPAD VII, but was powered by a 200 hp Hispano-Suiza V-type engine and included extra armament with a .37 mm cannon that fired through its hollow engine hub—an arrangement that had been suggested by French ace Georges Guynemer. Less than 300 of this variant were produced.

Introduced in the summer of 1917 as a successor to the SPAD VII, the SPAD XIII was better armed with twin-synchronized Vickers guns. Slightly larger and heavier with a wingspan of 27 ft, a length of 20 ft 8 in., and a loaded weight of 1,808 lbs, the SPAD XIII was powered by a series of Hispano-Suiza engines, beginning with the 200 hp Hispano-Suiza 8Ba V-type engine and ending with the 235 hp Hispano-Suiza 8Be V-type engine. Those powered by the former could reach 131 mph and climb to 2,000 m (6,562 ft) in 5 minutes 17 seconds, whereas those powered by the latter could reach almost 140 mph and climb to 2,000 m (6,562 ft) in 4 minutes 40 seconds. Although the SPAD XIII may not have been equal in quality to the more highly regarded Sopwith Camel and Fokker D.VII, it more than made up for any shortcomings in the sheer number produced, which reached approximately 8,400, compared with 5,490 for the Sopwith Camel and 1,000 for the Fokker D.VII. An improved version, the SPAD XVII, which was powered by the 300 hp Hispano-Suiza 8Fb V-type engine, was introduced toward the end of the war and supplied to France's most famous squadron, *Les Cigognes* (the *Storks*). Only twenty SPAD XVIIs were produced by war's end.

Introduced in late 1917, the Caudron R.11 biplane was a twin-engine fighter based upon the earlier R.4 bomber. With a wingspan of 58 ft 9 in., a length of 36 ft 9 in., and a loaded weight of 4,733 lbs, the R.11 was designed to provide escort service for French bombers and reconnaissance aircraft. Its two 215 hp Hispano-Suiza V-type engines provided a maximum speed of 114 mph, a service ceiling of 5,950 m (19,520 ft), and an endurance of 3 hours. Most important, it was armed with a total of five Vickers guns, which gave its pilot, tail gunner, and rear gunner a huge firepower advantage over German fighters. Its rugged construction also allowed it to absorb a great deal of punishment. In addition, the R.11 was fitted with dual controls that allowed the tail gunner to fly the plane if the pilot became incapacitated. Production continued until 1922 with approximately 500 being produced.

Had the war continued into 1919, the French air service would have been equipped with an outstanding aircraft in the Nieuport 29, which is sometimes referred to as the Nieuport-Delage Ni-D.29 after its designer Gustave Delage. Unlike previous Nieuports, which had used a sesquiplane layout and rotary motors, the Nieuport 29 featured a standard biplane configuration with a wingspan of 31 ft 10 in., a length of 21 ft 3 in., and a loaded weight of 2,535 lbs. Powered by a 300 hp Hispano-Suiza 8Fb V-type engine, the Nieuport 29 had a maximum speed of 146 mph and a ceiling of 8,500 m (27,887 ft). The prototype was demonstrated in June 1918 and received rave reviews, but with the end of the war on 11 November 1918 production was delayed until 1921. In addition to serving as France's main fighter until 1928, it would also be licensed-produced in Italy and Japan for their air forces.

GERMAN FIGHTER AND ATTACK AIRCRAFT

Although Germany had enjoyed some success by using its Albatros C-type armed reconnaissance aircraft to shoot down Allied aircraft, Roland Garros's demonstration of the advantage of forward fire through the arc of the propeller of his Morane-Saulnier monoplane convinced the Germans of the need to develop an aircraft with similar capabilities. After obtaining access to both Garros's plane, which had been forced down behind German lines, and Franz Schneider's prewar patent, Dutch designer Anthony Fokker quickly developed a synchronization gear that worked off the camshaft to interrupt the firing of either a Parabellum or Spandau machine gun. This was mounted and tested on one of his own monoplanes (the Fokker A.III). German pilots Oswald Boelcke and Max Immelmann both received the first prototypes, which were designated the Fokker E.I (dubbed the "Eindecker"), in early summer 1915. Although their 80 hp Oberursel UO rotary motor proved to be underpowered, both Boelcke and Immelmann succeeded in shooting down enemy aircraft. Convinced of its success, German authorities adopted it and Fokker rushed it into production.

Although only a few E.1 versions were built, 23 Fokker E.II fighters entered service in September 1915, before the most common variety, the E.III, of which approximately 150 were constructed, began to enter service in late 1915. Whereas the E.II and E.III were both powered by a 100 hp Oberursel U.I 9-cylinder rotary engine, the E.III featured some design modifications to strengthen its wings and improve its maneuverability. The E.III had a wingspan of 31 ft 2.75 in., a length of 23 ft 7.5 in., and a loaded weight of 1,342 lb. Its 100 hp Oberursel rotary motor could produce a maximum speed of 81 mph, could climb 1,000 m (3,281 ft) in 5 minutes, and had a service ceiling of approximately 3,500 m (11,482 ft). The Eindecker was a solid aircraft that featured the use of welded steel tubing for the fuselage frame. The wings, which were mounted to the side of the fuselage with two I-section main spars, were braced by cables that were attached to the undercarriage and a central pylon in front of the pilot's seat. An additional set of cables ran through pulleys and were attached to the control stick and wings to allow the pilot to warp the wings for lateral control. At first the Germans intended to use the Eindecker to provide protection for their own reconnaissance aircraft; consequently, they spread them out by placing two with each squadron. As Boelcke and Immelmann began to range out on their own and shoot down enemy aircraft, however, the Germans gradually began to concentrate them for greater effect during the winter of 1915–1916, a period that the Allies came to call the "Fokker Scourge." Even though the Eindecker owed much of its success to its synchronization gear, it must be noted that Allied aircraft at the time, particularly the R.A.F. B.E.2, which placed the armed observer in the front seat, were helpless when attacked from the rear. Nevertheless, it must be emphasized that Boelcke and Immelmann would use their Eindeckers to develop the basic fighting tactics and maneuvers that would remain standard throughout the war. By late spring 1916, new British and French biplanes, which were faster and more maneuverable, were eclipsing the Eindecker. Fokker attempted to extend their life by introducing the E.IV, which was slightly larger and powered by a two-row 160 hp Oberursel U III rotary engine. The increased weight and torque made it unsuccessful and only about 30 were produced.

As the Eindecker began to be outclassed by Allied biplanes, the Germans would turn to a series of biplanes in an effort to regain control of the skies. The first to enter service was the Halberstadt

D.II, which began to appear over the Western Front in the spring of 1916. These were based on the earlier Halberstadt D.I, which had seen limited production in late 1915. The primary difference was that the D.II was powered by a 120 hp Mercedes D.II inline motor instead of the D.I's 100 hp Mercedes inline engine. Although its fuselage used a wooden frame, the Halberstadt D-types did incorporate metal braces and steel tubing for the ailerons, elevators, and undercarriage. Armed with a synchronized Spandau, it was originally intended for escort service, but it was gradually concentrated in the first Jastas (fighter squadrons). An improved version, the D.III, was introduced in late 1916 with slightly longer ailerons and an improved exhaust manifold that was placed on the starboard side to improve visibility (it had originally vented upward) and make it more streamlined. With a wingspan of 28 ft 10.5 in., a length of 23 ft 11.5 in., and a loaded weight of 1,696 lbs, the D.III proved to be a nimble fighter, whose 120 hp Argus As.II inline motor could produce a maximum speed of 90 mph, climb to 3,000 m (9,843 ft) in 15 minutes, and provide a service ceiling of almost 6,100 m (20,013 ft). Approximately 200 D.IIs and D.IIIs entered service by the end of 1916, after which they began to be withdrawn from the Western Front and reallocated to the Eastern Front, the Balkans, and the Middle East. Two later versions, the D.IV and D.V, were introduced with twin-synchronized Spandaus in 1917 and appear to have been used by German units in the Balkans or sold to the Turks.

Having obtained success with its armed reconnaissance aircraft, the Roland C.II, Luftfahrzeug Gesellschaft (L.F.G.) introduced a streamlined, single-seat fighter, the Roland D.I biplane (dubbed the "Shark"), which entered service in the summer of 1916 and was quickly followed by the more numerous D.II later that fall. Both were armed with twin, synchronized Spandaus and were powered by a 160 hp Mercedes D.III inline engine, which produced a maximum speed of 105 mph and could climb to its service ceiling of 5,000 m (16,404 ft) in 23 minutes. The chief difference between the two was that the D.II featured a cutout in the fuselage and top wing to improve forward visibility. Both utilized a wooden-framed fuselage that was wrapped in thin sheets of plywood, then covered with fabric. With a wingspan of 29 ft 4 in., a length of 22 ft 9 in., and a loaded weight of 2,098 lbs, the D.II proved to be a disappointment, lacking the maneuverability of Albatros D-types that entered service at about the same time. In an attempt to improve performance, a modified version, the D.IIa, was introduced in early 1917, with a lighter loaded weight (1,749 lbs) and a more powerful 180 hp Argus As.III inline motor. These were quickly outclassed by new French and British fighters. As a result, most of the approximate 300 L.F.G. Roland D-types ended up being transferred from the Western Front to service on the Eastern Front, the Balkans, and the Middle East. They provide a good example of the problems that Germany faced in relying upon so many different design types.

Whereas the Halberstadt D.I and D.II, the Roland D.I and D.II, and the early Fokker D-types had proven to be outclassed by the French Nieuports and the British Airco D.H.2, the Germans would begin to regain air supremacy with the introduction of the Albatros D.I biplane in late summer 1916. Designed by lead Albatros engineer Robert Thelen, the D.I was similar to the successful C-type armed reconnaissance aircraft in that its fuselage was wooden framed and plywood covered, but the D.I and later D.II were more streamlined than the slab-sided C-types. Its wings were wooden framed and fabric covered with twin struts and wire-bracing. With a wingspan of 27 ft 10.75 in., a length of 24 ft 3 in., and a loaded weight of 1,976 lbs, the D.I was a compact, sturdy fighter that was capable of absorbing a lot of punishment, whereas its twin, synchronized Spandaus gave it a firepower advantage over contemporary Allied aircraft, which were fitted with just one gun. The D.II version, which was introduced in late 1916, was similar in design to the D.I, but featured a narrower gap between the fuselage and top wing to improve the pilot's forward and upward visibility. Whereas the first D.Is were powered by a 150 hp Benz Bz.III inline engine, the later production models and all of the D.IIs were powered by a 160 hp Mercedes D.III inline motor. The latter provided a maximum speed of 109 mph and could climb to 1,000 m (3,281 ft) in 5 minutes. Equally important to its performance characteristics, the Albatros D.I and D.II were introduced after the Germans had formed Jastas, thereby maximizing their impact by concentrating their numbers in fighter squadrons. Although a precise number of D.Is and D.IIs is not available, at least 250 were in service by January 1917.

By early 1917, Albatros was introducing the D.III, which was powered by the same engine as the D.II but had been totally redesigned by Robert Thelen, in part after the Nieuport 17, some of which had been captured by the Germans. Like the Nieuport, the Albatros D.III featured a sesquiplane layout in which the lower wing had a much narrower chord than the top wing. In addition, the wingspan was almost 2 ft longer at 29 ft 8 in., and steel-tube V-struts were used for bracing. Its 160 hp Mercedes D.IIIa inline motor featured a higher compression ratio that increased its performance at higher altitudes, giving it the same top speed of 108 mph as the D.II, but improving its climbing rate to 1,000 m (3,281 ft) in 4 minutes and increasing its service ceiling to slightly more than 5,846 m (18,000 ft), compared with 5,182 m (17,000 ft) for the D.II. The D.III's radiator had also been moved to the starboard side to prevent the pilot from being scalded if it was punctured (this had been a problem with the front mounting used for the D.I and D.II). Organized in Jastas, including Jasta 2, which was commanded by Manfred von Richthofen, the Albatros D.III enjoyed an almost absolute superiority over British and French aircraft in the spring of 1917, contributing to what the British called "Bloody April," after they lost 151 aircraft, including 75 between 4 and 8 April. By the end of April, however, the Albatros D.III was being outclassed by the R.A.F. S.E.5 and the SPAD VII. As in the case with the D.I and D.II, a precise total for the Albatros D.III is not available, but total production most likely approached 1,000 because there were still 446 serving on the Western Front in November 1917. As noted earlier, the Austro-Hungarian firm Oeffag produced 526 licensed-built versions of the Albatros D.III.

As the Allies regained air superiority during the summer of 1917, the Germans attempted to respond with a new version of its Albatros fighter—the Albatros D.V and D.Va. This was the most widely produced Albatros fighter of the war, with approximately 1,500 being constructed. Like the D.III, the Albatros D.V featured a sesquiplane layout and steel-tube V-struts to support the wings. It differed, however, in that its plywood fuselage was more rounded, giving it a more streamlined appearance. In addition, it was powered by either a 180 hp or 200 hp Mercedes D.IIIa inline engine,[6] which produced a maximum speed of 116 mph and gave it a service ceiling of 6,100 m (20,013 ft). The chief difference between the D.V and D.Va was that the former used a cable system that ran through the top wing to move the ailerons, whereas the latter used the same lower-wing cable system as the D.III. Although production ceased in February 1918, the Albatros D.V and D.Va remained in frontline service to the very end of the war, even though they were outclassed by the Sopwith Camel and SPAD XIII.

Another German fighter to enter service with somewhat mixed reviews in the summer of 1917 was the Pfalz D.III biplane. Having previously licensed-produced the L.F.G. Roland D.I and D.II fighter, Pfalz incorporated some of their features, as well as those of the Albatros D.III, into its own design. Like the Roland D.I and D.II, the Pfalz D.III used a wooden-framed fuselage that was covered with two thin sheets of plywood and then wrapped with fabric. Like the Albatros D.III, it featured a somewhat V-type strut whose base was wide enough to be attached to both spars of the lower wing, thereby providing greater support. Powered by a 160 hp Mercedes D.III inline motor, the Pfalz D.III was somewhat slow for its time at 103 mph, but it had a good rate of climb (1,000 m [3,281 ft] in 3 minutes 15 seconds). With a wingspan of 30 ft 10 in., a length of 22 ft 9.75 in., and a loaded weight of 2,056 lbs, it was considered less maneuverable than the Albatros D.V and D.Va. Because it was produced in Bavaria, it was supplied primarily to Bavarian aviation units, although it was found scattered in other German units as well. An improved version, the D.IIIa, was introduced in early 1918. It shared the same basic design features and armament (twin, synchronized Spandaus) as the D.III, but it sported a more powerful motor in the 180 hp Mercedes D.IIIa inline engine and more streamlined wing tips. Although it was outclassed by the last generation of British and French fighters, production of the Pfalz D.III and D.IIIa continued well into 1918, with a total of approximately 600 being produced.[7]

Perhaps the most famous German fighter to emerge during the First World War was the Fokker Dr.I triplane, which entered production in the summer of 1917 and began to appear on the Western Front in August 1917. Forever linked to Manfred von Richthofen, the Dr.I was a response to the British Sopwith Triplane, which had been introduced in the spring of 1917. Anthony Fokker, who had enjoyed success with the Eindecker but had obtained only minimal success with his first biplane fighters, the Fokker D.I–D.VI, turned to lead designer Reinhold Platz to fill the demand for a triplane. The resulting Dr.I utilized the same steel-tube construction as other Fokker aircraft and used plywood panels along the fuselage, which was then wrapped with fabric. The three wings were constructed of plywood from the leading edge to the central spar with fabric on the remainder, whereas the ailerons used steel-tube frames. The wings were of the same chord, but they were staggered in span with the top wing being the longest and extending approximately halfway forward of the bottom wing, which was the shortest. Although its 110 hp Oberursel rotary motor or Swedish-built (Thulin) Le Rhône rotary motor provided just 103 mph, which was comparatively slow for its time, the Dr.I was successful because its wingspan of 23 ft 7.5 in., length of 18 ft 11 in., and loaded weight of 1,290 lbs made it an agile, highly maneuverable fighter that could climb to 4,000 m (13,123 ft) in just 10 minutes.

The Dr.I's maneuverability, combined with its twin-synchronized Spandau machine guns, made it a lethal weapon in the hands of a skilled pilot. Indeed, upon being provided a Dr.I for testing on 28 August 1917, German ace Werner Voss would obtain twenty kills over the next 24 days. Voss's resulting overconfidence led him to challenge a patrol of seven British S.E.5s on 23 September 1917. Although he managed to shoot down two and hit all of the others, Voss was shot down and killed. It should be emphasized that the Dr.I was a demanding aircraft. After several wing failures resulted in crashes, the Dr.I was grounded during the fall of 1917 and did not reenter service until late December after its wings were strengthened. This delay limited construction to just 320 aircraft by the time production halted in May 1918. Despite its excellent maneuverability, the Dr.I was outclassed by the spring of 1918. Nevertheless, it remained the favored aircraft of Richthofen until he was shot down on 21 April 1918.

In addition to the fighters that they introduced in 1917, the Germans also began placing a new class of ground attack aircraft into service during the course of the year. Even though they were first intended for escort service, these heavily armed aircraft were soon concentrated in *Schlachtstaffeln* (Battle Flight) units that provided air support to German ground forces. The first of this type was the Halberstadt CL.II biplane. Designed by Karl Thies, the CL.II was relatively small for a two-seat aircraft, with a wingspan of 35 ft 4 in., a length of 23 ft 11.4 in., and a loaded weight of 2,493 lbs. Powered by a 160 hp Mercedes D.III inline engine, it could reach a maximum speed of 103 mph and could reach its service ceiling of 5,000 m (16,404 ft) in 39 minutes 30 seconds. The CL.II's wooden-framed fuselage was covered with thin plywood that was then wrapped with fabric, making it a fairly sturdy aircraft. Steel tubing was used with the ailerons, undercarriage, elevators, and wing struts. One of its most unique features was the use of a single cockpit in which the pilot and observer sat back to back, which improved communication and allowed for maximum use of its armament for ground strafing. In addition to the pilot's one to two forward-firing synchronized Spandaus and the observer's rear-firing, ring-mounted Parabellum, the CL.II came equipped with up to five 22-lb bombs and several antipersonnel grenades. In its ground support role, the CL.II would dive down and fly approximately 100 ft above the trenches, strafing enemy positions in advance of German ground forces. A combination of speed at low altitude and heavy firepower made it a difficult target for opposing ground troops. It was first used in this fashion during the successful German counterattack at Cambrai in November 1917. An improved version, the CL.IV, which was 2.5 ft shorter in length and approximately 100 lbs lighter, was introduced in time for the German spring offensive in 1918. The CL.IV also included improved forward visibility by lowering the top wing closer to the fuselage. Approximately 900 CL.IIs and 700 CL.IVs (including 250 of the latter produced by L.F.G. Roland) were produced by war's end.

Like Halberstadt, Hannoversche Waggonfabrik A.G. introduced an escort fighter, the Hannover CL.II, in summer 1917 that was soon pressed into ground attack duties. Hannover was a relative newcomer to aircraft production, having been forced by German authorities to add an aviation division to its existing railroad car manufacturing factories. After gaining experience with licensed-built versions of the Aviatik C.I and Halberstadt D.II, Hannover engineer Hermann Dorner designed the CL.II to meet the new two-seat fighter escort specifications that the German air service developed in 1917. With a wingspan of 38 ft 4.75 in., a length of 24 ft 10.5 in., and a loaded weight of 2,378 lbs, the CL.II proved to be fast and maneuverable for a two-seater with its 180 hp Argus As.III inline engine producing a maximum speed of 103 mph. Similar to the contemporary Halberstadt CL.II and CL.IV in its wooden-framed, plywood-covered, fabric-wrapped fuselage, it differed in its use of two cockpits (although they were placed close together with the pilot and observer sitting back to back) and a biplane tail, which allowed for a greater range of fire from the observer's ring-mounted, rear-firing Parabellum. It also used a forward-firing, synchronized Spandau. Slight modifications in the wing design resulted in two subsequent versions; the CL.III, which used a 160 hp Mercedes D.III inline motor, and CL.IIIa, which retained the 180 hp Argus inline motor. Total production of all three types exceeded 1,000 aircraft, with the most numerous being the CL.IIIa at 537 (including some that were licensed-built by L.F.G. Roland).

By far the most unique ground support aircraft built during the war was the nearly all-metal Junkers J.I biplane, which entered service in late 1917. Based on early all-metal prototypes developed by Dr. Hugo Junkers, the J.I featured a hexagon-shaped fuselage that was covered primarily with corrugated sheet metal. The nose and crew compartments were protected by .5 mm chrome-nickel sheet steel. Whereas the rear fuselage in early editions were covered in fabric, those built toward the end of the war were covered entirely with metal. The wings relied on steel spars and were covered with corrugated sheet metal. Instead of using cables to control the ailerons, elevator, and rudder, the J.I was one of the first aircraft to feature a direct linkage system of cranks and push-rods, all of which were enclosed to minimize damage from ground fire. The J.I, which was much larger than its Halberstadt and Hannover contemporaries, had a wingspan of 52 ft 6 in., length of 29 ft 10.4 in., and loaded weight of 4,787 lbs. Powered by a 200 hp Benz Bz.IV inline engine, it was capable of 96 mph. Although it took 32 minutes to climb 2,000 m (6,562 ft) and was not as maneuverable as the Halberstadts and Hannovers, the J.I excelled in ground attacks because it could absorb much punishment, while displaying great firepower with its twin forward-firing, synchronized Spandaus and its rear-firing, ring-mounted Parabellum. By war's end a total of 227 J.Is had entered service. It should be noted that Junkers introduced two other all-metal aircraft at the very end of the war, which were far advanced for their time. The Junkers CL.I was a low-wing monoplane designed for ground support duties and the Junkers D.I was a low-wing monoplane fighter. Although the 47 CL.Is and 41 D.Is came too late to make a difference in the war (the D.I most likely was not used at all), both would see action in 1919 against the Bolsheviks in the Baltic States.

Although the Allies had regained air superiority in late 1917, the Germans would introduce perhaps the best fighter of the war in the spring of 1918 with the Fokker D.VII biplane, which was intended as a replacement for the Fokker Dr.I. Whereas Fokker had produced a series of biplane fighters in 1916 and 1917, none proved to be very successful. With the D.VII, however, Reinhold Platz achieved a smashing success that exceeded the capabilities of any Allied fighter, including the Sopwith Camel and SPAD XIII. In many respects the D.VII utilized some of the same features as the earlier Dr.I, such as steel-tube framing for the fuselage, the use of plywood for the leading edge of the wings to the central spar with fabric on the remainder, and a solid or one-piece lower wing in which the spars ran through the fuselage and were bolted on tight. A combination of metal panels and plywood were used around the engine and cockpit with fabric used on the rear of the fuselage. With a wingspan of 29 ft 3.5 in., a length of 22 ft 11.6 in., and a loaded weight of 1,870 lbs, the D.VII proved to be a highly maneuverable, acrobatic aircraft that, unlike the Dr.I and Sopwith Camel, was easy to fly. Powered by either a 160 hp Mercedes D.III inline motor or a 185 hp BMW inline motor, it had a maximum speed of 116 mph, which was slower than the SPAD XIII and S.E.5a, but it outperformed them at high altitudes, having a service ceiling of almost 6,100 m (20,013 ft). It was particularly noted for its excellent turning ability—surpassed only by the Sopwith Camel—its fast climbing rate of 1,000 m (3,281 ft) in 3 minutes, and its ability to hang on its propeller and fire upward for a brief period without entering into a stall or spin. It was armed with twin, synchronized Spandaus. German authorities made every effort to rush it into production with approximately 1,000 being manufactured by Fokker, Albatros, and A.E.G. in the last 8 months of the war. Its advantage in quality could not make up for the Allied advantage in quantity.[8]

At approximately the same time that the Fokker D.VII entered service in April 1918, the prototype for the Fokker D.VIII monoplane (also known as the E.V) was entering testing. Designed by Reinhold Platz, it featured the same steel-tube construction of other Fokker aircraft, but its fuselage was entirely covered in fabric. Its parasol wing was made entirely out of fabric-covered plywood and used a thick chord with the ailerons being inset for a flush appearance, which provided greater aerodynamic stability in level flight and contributed to greater responsiveness. Tripod steel struts on each side of the fuselage were used to attach the wing. It was armed with twin, synchronized Spandaus. Although the Germans had moved primarily to inline engines, the D.VIII was designed to use the 110 hp Oberursel U.II rotary engine, primarily because of its availability at a time when Germany's supply of inline engines was being stretched to the limit. With a wingspan of 27 ft 4.4 in., a length of 19 ft 2.75 in., and a loaded weight of just 1,334 lbs, the D.VIII was a compact, lightweight fighter that was capable of a maximum speed of 127 mph and could climb 1,000 m (3,281 ft) in just 2 minutes and reach its service ceiling of 6,000 m (19,685 ft) in just 16 minutes. Attempts to rush it into production resulted in shoddy construction, leading to wing failures after it first appeared in numbers in August 1918 and halting construction so that the wings could be strengthened. As a result, the D.VIII did not see major combat until October 1918; however, in the short time that remained before the war's end, it established a reputation as an outstanding combat plane. A total of 289 were produced by the Armistice.

Even though the Fokker D.VII and D.VIII have received the most attention of Germany's last generation of World War I fighters, three others warrant mentioning: the L.F.G. (Roland) D.VIa and D.VIb biplane; the Pfalz D.XII biplane; and the Siemens-Schuckert D.III and D.IV biplane. Although they resembled the earlier L.F.G.

Roland D-types, the D.VIa and D.VIb (the former used the 150 hp Benz Bz.IIIa inline motor, whereas the latter used a 200 hp of the same type) were distinctive because of their "clinker" style of manufacture that used overlapping wedge-shaped strips of spruce in a manner similar to wooden boat construction. Even though it was not as maneuverable as its contemporaries, in part because it was slightly larger with a 30 ft 10 in. wingspan and 20 ft 8.75 in. length and slightly heavier at 1,892 lbs, it was relatively fast at 114 mph and could absorb a lot of punishment. The Pfalz D.XII was a marked improvement over the earlier Pfalz D.III, and some scholars consider it nearly equal to the Fokker D.VII. Its wooden-framed, plywood-covered, and fabric-wrapped fuselage and steel-tube framed wings made it a very sturdy aircraft that could outdive the Fokker D.VII. With a wingspan of 29 ft 6.4 in., a length of 20 ft 10 in., and a loaded weight of 1,973 lbs, it was capable of reaching a maximum speed of 106 mph with its 160 hp Mercedes D.IIIa inline engine. Introduced in September 1918, approximately 200 saw service before the war ended. Although the Siemens-Schuckert D.I had been considered a failure upon its introduction in 1916, late 1918 would see the Siemens-Schuckert firm produce one of the best, albeit unheralded, fighters of the war with the D.IV, which was powered by a 160 hp Siemens-Halske Sh.IIIa rotary motor and used a four-bladed propeller. Although relatively slow at 118 mph, it was an outstanding climber, able to rise to 1,000 m (3,281 ft) in 1 minute 45 seconds and 6,000 m (19,685 ft) in 20 minutes. More important, its service ceiling of 8,000 m (26,240 ft) gave it an advantage over any other fighter available at the time. With a wingspan of 27 ft 4.75 in., a length of 18 ft 8.5 in., and a loaded weight of 1,620 lbs, the D.IV was compact, agile, and acrobatic, but the tremendous torque produced by its rotary engine could induce fatal spins even though its wings were extended 4 in. longer on the right side than on the left in an effort to compensate for this. Nevertheless, it possessed the same right-turn advantage as did the Sopwith Camel. A total of 118 entered service by the end of the war.

ITALIAN FIGHTER AND ATTACK AIRCRAFT

Although Italy had been the first European power to use airplanes for military purposes during the Tripolitan War in 1911, it had relatively few aircraft when it entered the First World War on 23 May 1915. Whereas its Caproni bombers were more advanced that those of its French and British allies, the Italians had made no steps toward producing fighters. Although they at first purchased fighters from the British and French, they eventually began to produce a number of licensed-built aircraft. This was especially true of the Italian subsidiary of the Nieuport firm, Società Anonima Nieuport-Macchi, which would produce 240 Nieuport 10s, 450 Nieuport 11s, and 150 Nieuport 17s. In addition to these Nieuport designs, Nieuport-Macchi would produce approximately 900 licensed-built versions of the Hanriot HD.1, far in excess of the 100 produced in France. The Italian version of the HD.1 was slightly different from the French original in that the wingspan was slightly shorter at 27 ft 10.5 in., it was powered by a 110 hp Le Rhône rotary motor instead of the original 120 hp Le Rhône rotary motor, and its synchronized Vickers gun was centered in front of the pilot rather than being offset. The HD.1 provided outstanding service from its introduction in August 1917 to the end of the war.

By late 1917, Italy was able to introduce its first and only fighter of its own design into service, the Ansaldo A.1 Balilla (Hunter). Powered by a 220 hp SPA 6A inline engine, the A.1 was capable of a top speed of 137 mph and could climb to 3,048 m (10,000 ft) in just 8 minutes. Although it was well armed with twin, synchronized Vickers machine guns and regarded as easy to fly, it proved to be a disappointment. With a wingspan of 25 ft 2 in., a length of 22 ft 5.25 in., and a loaded weight of 1,951 lbs, the cumbersome A.1 was less maneuverable than the much lighter HD.1, which had a loaded weight of 1,323 lbs. As a result, only a few of the 108 that were produced saw front-line service, and then only as bomber or reconnaissance escort aircraft. Most were relegated to training duties or to home defense.

RUSSIAN FIGHTER AND ATTACK AIRCRAFT

Like Italy, Russia relied almost exclusively upon foreign-built or licensed-built aircraft, including fighters. The biggest handicap that Russian manufacturers faced was Russia's limited domestic engine industry. As a result, even though Russian factories, such as the Dux Company (Aktsionyernoye Obschchestvo Vozdukhoplavania), had the potential for a higher productive capacity, they were handicapped by their reliance upon French engines, which could not easily be shipped into Russia after Turkey entered the war. Although the Russians attempted to copy French engine designs, their performance was generally poor. Nevertheless, Russian companies produced almost 700 Nieuport fighters (the Nieuport 10 accounted for 325 of these and the Nieuport 11 accounted for 200). Dux would also build approximately 400 Morane-Saulnier Type L monoplanes, which were used as both armed reconnaissance aircraft and fighters, and approximately 100 SPAD VII fighters.

Having designed the world's first large, multiengine aircraft—the *Ilya Muromets* bomber—just prior to the war, Igor Sikorsky began work on a two-seat armed reconnaissance and escort fighter to work alongside it, eventually producing a successful prototype in early 1915. Production of the resulting Sikorsky S.16 began later in the year at the Russko-Baltiisky Vagon Zaved (R-BVZ, or Russo-Baltic Wagon Factory). With a wingspan of 27 ft 6 in., a length of 20 ft 4 in., and a loaded weight of 1,490 lbs, the S.16 was rather compact and lightweight for the time; unfortunately, it was underpowered because Russia lacked sufficient 100 hp Gnôme Monosoupape rotary engines, forcing it to be produced with an 80 hp Gnôme Monosoupape rotary motor, which was capable of producing a maximum speed of just 73 mph and reaching a service ceiling of 3,500 m (11,483 ft). Despite these deficiencies, it was one of the first Allied aircraft to be fitted with a forward-firing, synchronized machine gun, in this case a Colt machine gun. Because the Russian-designed synchronization gear had a high failure rate, most pilots rigged their own top-wing mounted gun. A total of 34 were produced prior to the Russian Revolution. Those that remained in place after the Bolsheviks seized power in the October Revolution of 1917 were soon pressed into service during the ensuing Russian Civil War, serving as fighters, reconnaissance aircraft, or as trainers.

U. S. FIGHTER
AND ATTACK AIRCRAFT

Although the United States had been the birthplace of the airplane and the U.S. Army Signal Corps had conducted some of the first experiments with firing a machine gun from an airplane, the United States would enter the First World War without fighters. As a result, the American Expeditionary Force (AEF) had to rely upon a variety of British and French aircraft, including the much-hated Nieuport 28. Although the U.S. Congress appropriated $640 million for aircraft construction, the results were meager. By the time the Thomas Morse S-4 became available in early 1918, it was already obsolete as a fighter, and was thus relegated to use as an advanced trainer. In an attempt to jump-start production, the army sought the input of French Captain George Lepere in designing a fighter. The result was the Packard-Lepere LUSAC 11 biplane, a two-seat fighter with a wingspan of 41 ft 7 in., a length of 25 ft 3 in., and a loaded weight of 3,746 lbs. Powered by a 425 hp Liberty V-type engine, it was capable of 133 mph and had a service ceiling of 21,500 ft (6,553 m). Although the army ordered 3,525, only 28 had been produced by the Armistice, resulting in a cancellation of the order. Had it entered service, it would have provided the AEF with a fighter similar to the Brisfit, since it carried four machine guns (two synchronized, forward-firing guns, and two ring-mounted rear-firing guns).

NOTES

1. Because the Austrian financier Camillo Castiglioni owned both the Hansa-Brandenburg firm as well as Phönix Flugzeugwerke and Ungarische Flugzeugwerke A.G. (Ufag), a number of sources have stated that Ufag also produced the Hansa-Brandenburg D.I. The most recent scholarship on Austro-Hungarian aircraft, however, asserts that there are no records to verify this. Peter M. Grosz, George Haddow, and Peter Schiemer, *Austro-Hungarian Army Aircraft of World War One* (Mountain View, CA: Flying Machines Press, 1993), 290.

2. Engine availability was the primary factor that contributed to the variation in series. Thus, even though the first series of Aviatik D.I fighters (the 38 series) was fitted with a 185 hp Austro-Daimler and the second series (the 138 series) was fitted with a 200 hp Austro-Daimler, the third series (the 238 series) was fitted with refurbished 160 hp Austro-Daimler engines because of the lack of other engines, leading to complaints from pilots.

3. MAG also produced 42 Fokker D.II fighters for the LFT.

4. It should be pointed out that the reputation of the A.1 was somewhat repaired after the war by such expert pilots as Charles Nungesser, who used them for aerial acrobatics.

5. Some sources put the number of SPAD VIIs produced at between 5,000 and 6,000.

6. These were the same as the 160 hp Mercedes D.IIIa inline engine, but they had higher compression and oversized cylinders.

7. Production of the Pfalz D.IIIa continued in part because Bavarian authorities had control over production and in part because the Germans were having to place a higher priority on quantity of aircraft, as opposed to quality of aircraft, in order to keep up with the huge increase in French and British production in 1918.

8. Fokker smuggled approximately 160 D.VII fighters into the Netherlands after the war and sold them to the Dutch government.

CHAPTER FIVE

Bomber Aircraft

EVER SINCE THE FIRST BALLOONISTS had succeeded in achieving manned flight, the idea of being able to fly (or float in the case of balloons) over one's enemies and drop bombs upon them had entered the minds of a few air enthusiasts and military planners. In 1792 Joseph Montgolfier had proposed using balloons to drop bombs on British forces and ships that had seized Toulon. A similar proposal was made by John Wise as the United States was planning its attack on Veracruz during the Mexican War in 1847. Neither proposal were seriously considered by military commanders. The closest example of an attempted aerial bombardment came in 1849 when the Austrians attempted to float small bomb-carrying balloons that had time fuses that were supposed to drop the bombs over Venice. A change of wind direction, however, resulted in failure with a few bombs dropping on the Austrians themselves. As a result, the idea of aerial bombardment had to await the development of the airship and the airplane before it could become reality—a reality that soon became a nightmare for many after the First World War broke out in August 1914.

From the very beginning of the war, aircraft were used to drop bombs or heavy steel darts on enemy forces. With the exceptions of Germany's use of zeppelins to drop bombs on Belgium and Britain's bombing of zeppelin sheds—the destruction of which were aided by the hydrogen within the ships—the results of bombing early in the war produced more of a nuisance than anything else because of the lack of effective bombs and the limited carrying capacity of most early aircraft. The war, however, soon proved the adage that necessity is the mother of invention, as all powers, with varying degrees of success, began developing a new class of aircraft—the bomber—whose sole or primary purpose was to drop bombs on enemy troops or strategic positions deep behind enemy lines. As a result, the nature of the battlefield changed, making it three-dimensional by adding the attack from above, and extending its depth. In addition, the bomber blurred the lines between combatants and noncombatants. Although attempts were made to develop bombsights, these were crude and largely ineffective, making strikes against an intended target more a matter of luck than anything else. These problems were compounded as bombers and zeppelins were forced to operate at night because of their vulnerability to fighters. To the extent that civilians became "fair game," the bomber helped usher in the era of total war.

AUSTRO-HUNGARIAN BOMBERS

Although Italy's declaration of war in 1915 confronted Austria-Hungary with an enemy that possessed an effective bomber (Russia had concentrated its *Ilya Muromets* against Germany), Austria-Hungary was slow to develop bombers of its own or to acquire such aircraft from its German ally. Indeed, during the first 3 years of the war, the *Luftfahrtruppen* (LFT) relied primarily upon B-type or C-type reconnaissance aircraft to carry out nighttime and daytime bombing missions, such as the daylight raid on Milan on 14 February 1916 by Lloyd and Lohner planes and the nighttime raid on the Ponte de Piave by a Brandenburg C-I later in the year. The limited carrying capacity of these aircraft resulted in minimal damage.

Beginning in the summer of 1915, the LFT began testing prototypes of a two-engine bomber designed by Hansa-Brandenburg chief engineer Ernst Heinkel. A series of modifications were required to improve the wing structure and overall performance of the aircraft before production of the Hansa-Brandenburg G.I biplane bomber began at Ufag in late 1916. Although great hopes were placed on the G.I, the same problems that plagued the prototypes persisted, leading to production being stopped in March 1917 with just 12 G.Is having been constructed. An additional 27 were purchased directly from Hansa-Brandenburg. The aircraft had a wingspan of 59 ft 0.6 in., a length of 32 ft 3 in., and a loaded weight of 6,042 lbs. Its twin 160 hp Austro-Daimler inline engines provided a maximum speed of 89 mph and the ability to climb to

1,000 m (3,281 ft) in 8 minutes and 3,000 m (9,843 ft) in 30 minutes. The G.I carried a three-man crew with the bombardier occupying a seat in the nose turret, which featured a ring-mounted machine gun, and the pilot and rear observer sitting in the rear section of the cockpit, with the observer having a rear-firing, ring-mounted machine gun. It was designed to carry a 726 lb-bomb load, consisting of five 110-lb bombs and four 44-lb bombs. Although only one mission was carried out in April 1917 before the G.Is were grounded because of their poor performance—primarily caused by wing stress failures—in early 1918 some 30 grounded models were refurbished for use as night bombers. Despite some added improvements, these still proved to have limited effectiveness. The primary difficulty posed by the G.I was that it was too tail heavy when carrying a bomb load and was consequently difficult to fly, especially in the mountainous terrain of the Italian Front. Although Aviatik and Oeffag would begin production of their own G-type bombers in late 1918 to replace the Hansa-Brandenburg G.I, the war ended before any of these could see service. As a result, Austria-Hungary came to rely almost exclusively upon imported German bombers, particularly the Gotha G.IV.

BRITISH BOMBERS

Even though the British successfully employed a variety of aircraft for bombing missions early in the war, including the use of a Sopwith Tabloid that destroyed a zeppelin (the Z-9) within its shed at Düsseldorf on 8 October 1914, these early aircraft had limited load capacity and had to use improvised means (sometimes an observer simply dropped the bomb over the side) to deliver their bomb load. In 1915 the Royal Aircraft Factory (R.A.F.) began development of the R.E.7 biplane, which was specifically designed to carry the R.A.F.'s new 336-lb bomb. Similar in design to the earlier R.E.5, the R.E.7 featured an upper wing with a span of 57 ft compared with just 42 ft for the lower wing, a length of 31 ft 10.5 in., and a rather large tail section that had a span of 16 ft. It was a sturdy aircraft that had a loaded weight of 3,450 lbs, which featured a forward fuselage constructed with steel-tube bracing, and which was equipped with an oleo-shock absorber undercarriage. Its wings were heavily braced with wires and two bay struts as well as angled outer struts that helped support the upper-wing extensions. Although a variety of engines were used in the R.E.7, most of the 250 produced came equipped with either a 160 hp Beardmore inline motor or 150 hp R.A.F. 4a inline motor with a maximum speed of 91 mph in the former and 84 mph in the latter. Most R.E.7s employed air brakes that were mounted on the side of the fuselage, and some used four-bladed propellers. The observer sat in the front cockpit, whereas the pilot sat in the rear cockpit, making it vulnerable to attack from the rear. As a result, a few were later redesigned as three-seaters and used for armed reconnaissance with the rear observer having a ring-mounted Lewis gun. Capable of carrying one 336-lb bomb (mounted directly under the fuselage) or two 112-lb bombs, the R.E.7 proved to be very effective in the early stages of the Battle of the Somme, striking German railway stations, railways, and ammunition depots. As the Germans shifted fighters (in particular the Fokker Eindecker) from Verdun to meet the British threat at the Somme, the R.E.7 proved to be vulnerable and were gradually withdrawn from the front by the end of 1916 and relegated to training duties.

Although originally intended as a long-range escort fighter when it was introduced in the spring of 1916, the Martinsyde G.100 biplane, dubbed the "Elephant" because of its large size, primarily saw service as a light bomber. Designed to have an endurance of 5 hours 30 minutes, the G.100 had a wingspan of 38 ft and length of 26 ft 6 in. to accommodate the added weight of its larger fuel tanks, which increased the total loaded weight to 2,424 lbs. Its 120 hp Beardmore inline engine provided a maximum speed of 95 mph and service ceiling of 14,000 ft (4,267 m), but the G.100 lacked the maneuverability needed for a fighter. Although it retained a top-wing mounted Lewis gun, it was fitted with bomb racks capable of one 112-lb bomb. Approximately 100 G.100s were produced. To increase its bombing capability, later models of the Elephant were equipped with the 160 hp Beardmore inline motor and designated as the G.102. Although its endurance was less at 4 hours 30 minutes, the G.102 could not only reach a maximum speed of 104 mph and a service ceiling of 16,000 ft (4,877 m), but also carry one 230-lb bomb or two 112-lb bombs or four 65-lb bombs. A total of 171 G.102s were constructed. Both versions of the Elephant remained in service on the Western Front until they were replaced by the Airco D.H.4 by the end of 1917. The British also employed them in Palestine and Mesopotamia until the end of the war.

Like the Martinsyde Elephant, the Sopwith 11/2 Strutter originally entered service in the spring of 1916 as a fighter, but ended up serving primarily as a light bomber and armed reconnaissance aircraft, making it one of the more versatile aircraft of the war. It saw service with Great Britain, Belgium, France, Russia, and the United States. Officially designated as Type 9700 by the Royal Naval Air Service (RNAS), it was quickly dubbed the "11/2 Strutter" because the center braces that attached the upper wing to the fuselage had the appearance of angled struts. The 11/2 Strutter was the first British aircraft to arrive at the front with a fixed, synchronized machine gun (Vickers). The observer fired a ring-mounted Lewis gun. Powered by a 110 hp Clerget rotary engine, the Sopwith 11/2 Strutter had a maximum speed of 106 mph and a service ceiling of 15,500 ft (4,724 m). With a wingspan of 33 ft 6 in., a length of 25 ft 3 in., and a loaded weight of 2,105 lbs, the Sopwith 11/2 Strutter proved to be more maneuverable than the Fokker Eindecker, but it was soon outclassed by the Halberstadt D.II biplane and Albatros D.I biplane fighters. As a result, the British and French switched it from use as a fighter to a light bomber, which was capable of carrying up to four 56-lb bombs. They continued in this role, often used to carry out reconnaissance missions and bomb targets of opportunity, until the end of the war, serving on the Western Front, the Eastern Front, and the Balkan Front. In addition, Sopwith 11/2 Strutters were used for antisubmarine patrols around the British Isles and in the Mediterranean. Of the estimated 6,000 produced, 75 percent were manufactured in France.

In an effort to produce an aircraft that could be used to strike German industrial sites, the British sought a bomber that could carry a heavier load and have a longer endurance. The first successful aircraft to meet this objective was the Short Bomber biplane, which entered service in late 1916. Adapted from the successful Short 184 floatplane, the Short Bomber was massive by single-engine standards with a wingspan of 85 ft, a length of 45 ft, and a loaded weight of 6,800 lbs. Its wings were braced by three sets of struts and wires, and the upper-wing extensions were braced by wires that were attached to king posts that were connected to the last set of struts. Powered by either a 225 hp Sunbeam inline motor or a 250 hp Rolls-Royce Eagle inline motor, the Short Bomber had a maximum speed of 77 mph, a service ceiling of 9,000 ft (2,743 m), and an endurance of 6 hours. It could carry either four 230-lb bombs or eight 112-lb bombs, and was protected by a ring-mounted Lewis gun fired by the observer from the rear cockpit. Although only 83 were built, they were used extensively by the RNAS to bomb German U-boat bases at Ostend and Zeebrugge during the winter of

1916–1917. Intended to be a major component of the RNAS's 3rd Wing, which targeted German industry in the Saar Basin, production shortages and transfers to the Royal Flying Corps (RFC) prevented it from serving in this role.

One reason for the Short Bomber's low production numbers was the introduction of the much larger Handley-Page 0/100 twin-engine biplane in the fall of 1916. With a wingspan of 100 ft (the lower wing was much shorter at 70 ft), a length of 62 ft 10 in., and a loaded weight of 14,000 lbs, the 0/100 was powered by two 250 hp Rolls-Royce Eagle II inline motors with four-bladed propellers. It had a maximum speed of 85 mph, a service ceiling of 7,000 ft (2,134 m), and an endurance of 8 hours. The 0/100 carried a crew of three to five members and either a special 1,600-lb blockbuster bomb or a variety of bombs up to a maximum load of 2,000 lbs. It was protected by three to five Lewis guns, but it proved to be too vulnerable to enemy fighters during the daytime and was soon relegated to night bombing. Although only 46 were built, the 0/100 was a step toward the strategic bombing force that Britain desired to use in retaliation for the German zeppelin raids. In one of the great ironies of the war, a 0/100 that was being delivered to its base in Dunkirk on 1 January 1917 mistakenly landed behind German lines. Although the British would later claim that the Gotha bombers were based on the British design, production of the Gothas had begun at least 2 months before this incident. Production of the 0/100 soon halted in favor of the Handley-Page 0/400, but 0/100s continued to serve until the end of war on the Western Front and at least one was based in the Aegean at Mudros from where it patrolled the eastern Mediterranean and carried out one bombing attack on Constantinople.

The Handley-Page 0/400 twin-engine biplane had the same wingspan of 100 ft and length of 62 ft 10 in. as the 0/100, but it featured a shorter nacelle for the crew and more powerful engines with two 360 hp Rolls-Royce Eagle VIII inline motors. Approximately 700 lbs lighter at a loaded weight of 13,300 lbs, it could carry the same bomb load as the 0/100. Its key differences lay in its performance with a maximum speed of 97.5 mph, a service ceiling of 8,500 ft (2,591 m), and an endurance of 8 hours. Although the 0/400 could have entered service much sooner, the Air Board did not decide to begin production until after the Gotha bomber raids on London in the summer of 1917. As a result, 0/400s did not begin to enter service until early 1918. Nevertheless, it played a leading role in the Royal Air Force's Independent Force, which conducted nighttime raids against German targets in western Germany. One 0/400 also participated in bombing exercises with the Australian Flying Corps in Palestine. In addition to approximately 400 produced in Britain by the Armistice, a total of 107 were constructed in the United States by the Standard Aircraft Corporation. The American-built versions used the 400 hp Liberty V-type engine. Although a few of the American models reached England for reassembly prior to the Armistice, none actually saw service in the war.

At the same time as the British were developing heavy bombers for strategic bombing, they introduced one of the best light bombers of the war with the Airco D.H.4. Designed by Geoffrey de Havilland, the D.H.4 was intended to be used as a daytime bomber that could act on its own without fighter escort. Although the British were forced to rely upon a variety of engine types because of shortages in production, most were powered by either a 230 hp B.H.P. inline motor or 250 h.p. Rolls-Royce III inline motor and all used a four-bladed airscrew. By 1918, however, the 375 hp Rolls-Royce Eagle VIII inline engine became its standard motor, providing a maximum speed of 143 mph and a service ceiling of 22,000 ft (6,706 m), which exceeded the capabilities of German fighters. With a wingspan of 42 ft 4 in., a length of 30 ft 8 in., and a loaded weight of 3,472 lbs, the D.H.4 was also surprisingly maneuverable. It was well defended with one or two forward-firing synchronized Vickers guns and one or two free-firing Lewis guns operated by the observer from the rear seat. The D.H.4 generally carried either two 230-lb bombs or four 112-lb bombs. Of the 1,449 produced in Britain, the bulk were used over the Western Front, but approximately 250 were used by the navy for antisubmarine patrols and home defense.[1] The D.H.4 was also licensed-produced in the United States and was the only American-built aircraft to see widespread service in the war.

Intended as an improvement to the D.H.4, so much so that many contracts for D.H.4s were canceled in its favor, the Airco D.H.9 proved to be a great disappointment. The chief failure of the D.H.9 was that its 230 hp Siddeley Puma inline engine proved to be under-powered, providing a maximum speed of just 111 mph and a service ceiling of just 15,500 ft (4,724 m), both well below the performance of the D.H.4. In other respects, the D.H.9 was virtually identical to its predecessor, with a wingspan of 42 ft 5 in. and a length of 30 ft 6 in. It was slightly heavier with a loaded weight of 3,669 lbs. The D.H.9 was equipped with one fixed, forward-firing, synchronized Vickers gun and came with either one or two ring-mounted Lewis guns. It carried either two 230-lb bombs or four 112-lb bombs that were mounted on racks under the wings. In one respect the design of the D.H.9 was an improvement over the D.H.4 in that the pilot and observer cockpits were closer together, making it easier to communicate. This allowed the fuel tank to be placed behind the engine rather than between the pilot and the observer, as was the case in the D.H.4. This improvement, however, came at the sacrifice of the pilot's forward and downward field of vision. Despite the obvious problems with the D.H.9, the British pressed forward with production, building a total of 3,204 by war's end—more than double the production of the better-performing D.H.4.[2] The D.H.9 was used primarily on the Western Front, but it also saw service on the Eastern Front, in the Mediterranean, and in the Middle East. A few D.H.9s were also supplied to the Whites during the Russian Civil War.

Although the D.H.9 had been a failure because of its underperforming engine, the Airco D.H.9A was introduced on the Western Front in June 1918. Powered by either a 375 hp Rolls-Royce Eagle VIII inline engine or a 400 hp Liberty V-type engine, the D.H.9A was capable of a maximum speed of 118 mph, a service ceiling of 16,000 ft (4,877 m), and an endurance of 3 hours 30 minutes in the former, and a maximum speed of 123 mph, a service ceiling of 16,500 ft (5,029 m), and an endurance of 5 hours 15 minutes in the latter. Both were capable of carrying a bomb load of up to 660 lbs. Similar in design to the D.H.9, the D.H.9A had a slightly longer wingspan of 45 ft 11 in., a length of 30 ft 3 in., and a loaded weight of 4,645 lbs. Like the D.H.9, it also came equipped with one fixed, forward-firing, synchronized Vickers gun and one or two ring-mounted Lewis guns in the rear cockpit. Although a total of 885 were produced by war's end, it was only during the last 2 months of the war that the D.H.9A saw action in any considerable numbers. It remained in service with the RAF until 1931, with an additional 2,500 being built after the war. A number of unlicensed versions that used a copy of the 400 hp Liberty V-type engine were built by the Soviet Union after the Russian Civil War.

Had the war continued into 1919, the British would have possessed three heavy bombers—the Airco D.H. 10 "Amiens," the Vickers F.B.27 "Vimy," and the Handley-Page V/1500—that would have enabled it to reach deep into Germany. The D.H.10 "Amiens" was a twin-engine biplane that had a wingspan of 65 ft 6 in., a length of 39 ft 7 in., and a loaded weight of 9,000 lbs. Its two 400 hp Liberty V-type engines gave it a maximum speed of 112 mph, a service ceiling of 17,000 ft (5,182 m), and a range of 600 miles. It could carry approximately 900 lbs of bombs and was well defended with ring-mounted Lewis guns in the nose and rear cockpits. A total of 223 were produced by the Armistice, with just 8 having arrived for service in France. After the war they were used for air mail service. The Vickers F.B.27 "Vimy" twin-engine biplane entered production just as the war came to a close. It had a wingspan of 68 ft, a length of 43 ft 6 in., and a loaded weight of 12,500 lbs. It could carry up to eighteen 112-lb bombs or two 230-lb bombs and had a maximum range of 900 miles. The Vimy remained in service with the RAF until 1930 with a total of 221 aircraft being produced. Over its years of service it used a variety of engines. The earliest models used two 200 hp Hispano-Suizas V-type engines, which provided a maximum speed of 89 mph and a service ceiling of 9,500 ft (2,896 m). Later versions would use two 360 hp Rolls-Royce Eagle VIII inline motors, which provided a maximum speed of 103 mph and a service ceiling of 10,500 ft (3,200 m). It was defended by ring-mounted Lewis guns that were placed in the nose and rear cockpits. Designed to give the RAF the ability to strike Berlin, the Handley-Page V/1500 was a massive aircraft with a wingspan of 126 ft (with a chord of 12 ft), a length of 62 ft, a height of 23 ft, and a loaded weight of approximately 24,000 lbs. It was powered by four 375 hp Rolls-Royce Eagle VIII inline engines, which sat back-to-back in a tractor-pusher configuration. With a maximum speed of 97 mph and a service ceiling of 10,000 ft (3,048 m), the V/1500 had a standard endurance of 6 hours and could carry thirty 250-lb bombs (7,500 lb-bomb load). Its endurance could be extended to 14 hours by sacrificing bombs for added fuel—an attack on Berlin would have carried a 1,000 lb-bomb load. It carried up to five ring-mounted or spigot-mounted Lewis guns for its four-man crew. Only six V/1500s had been completed by the Armistice. Although the RAF adopted the Vimy because it could be produced at less cost, a V/1500 was used by the British in bomb drops on Kabul in an attempt to suppress an Afghan uprising after the war.

FRENCH BOMBERS

After investing heavily in aircraft prior to the outbreak of the war, the French possessed a number of reconnaissance aircraft that were adapted for light bombing roles after the outbreak of the war. Among these were a series of Voisin pusher biplanes—designated Type 1 to Type 6 as more powerful engines were added—that were available at the outbreak of the war and entered service in the first 2 years of the war. Approximately 1,400 of all six types were produced in France, whereas Italy produced approximately 120 and Russia produced approximately 400. Of the Voisin types, the most commonly used for bombing purposes were the Type 3 and the Type 5, both of which had a wingspan of 48 ft 4.75 in. and a length of 31 ft 3.25 in. The Type 3 was powered by a 120 hp Salmson Canton-Unné radial motor, which produced a maximum speed of 62 mph, a ceiling of 2,743 m (9,000 ft), and an endurance of approximately 4 hours. It was armed with a Hotchkiss gun and could carry a bomb load of 330 lbs. The Type 5 was powered by a 150 hp Salmson Canton-Unné radial engine, which produced a maximum speed of 68 mph, a ceiling of 3,500 m (11,483 ft), and an endurance of 3 hours 30 minutes. Like the Type 3, it was armed with a Hotchkiss gun and could carry a bomb load of 330 lbs. Other reconnaissance aircraft that provided light bombing duties included the Nieuport 14 biplane, the Farman M.F.7 and M.F.11 pusher biplanes, and the twin-engine Caudron G.IV biplane.

The first French aircraft to see service primarily as a bomber was the Breguet-Michelin BrM4 biplane. It was based upon a Breguet BU.3 prototype that had been developed in early 1914 and had been selected for production by André and Edouard Michelet, who had offered to build and donate 100 bombers for the Aviation Militaire. The BrM4 had a wingspan of 61 ft 8 in., a length of 32 ft 6 in., and a loaded weight of 4,660 lbs. Fifty were powered by a 200 hp Salmson Canton-Unné radial motor, which provided a maximum speed of 77 mph, whereas the other fifty were powered by a 220 hp Renault 8Gd inline engine, which provided a maximum speed of 84 mph. Both had a service ceiling of approximately 3,870 m (12,697 ft) and were capable of carrying forty 16-lb bombs in underwing racks. The BrM4 was also protected with either a Hotchkiss gun or Lewis gun. It entered service in late 1915 and served into 1916 before being withdrawn from the front and used as a trainer. The French also developed a variant, designated as the BrM5, which came equipped with a .37 mm Hotchkiss cannon. It was produced in small numbers, with most being sold to the British for service with the RNAS.

After concentrating primarily on building reconnaissance and fighter aircraft during the first 2 years of the war, the French military finally conceded to parliamentary demands and began development of aircraft specifically designed for service as bombers. Among the first to emerge from this effort were the Voisin Type 8 and Type

10 pusher biplanes. Both had a wingspan of 61 ft 8 in. and a length of 36 ft 2 in., but the Type 8 had a loaded weight of 4,100 lbs, whereas the Type 10 had a loaded weight of 4,850 lbs. The difference in weight was a reflection of the differences in engine and resulting bomb load capacity. Entering service in November 1916, the Type 8 was powered by a 220 hp Peugeot 8Aa inline motor, which produced a maximum speed of 82 mph and service ceiling of 4,300 m (14,108 ft), provided an endurance of 4 hours, and carried a bomb load of approximately 400 lbs. Entering service in late 1917, the Type 10 was powered by a 280 hp Renault 12Fe inline engine, which produced a maximum speed of 84 mph and a service ceiling of 4,300 m (14,108 ft), provided an endurance of 5 hours, and carried a bomb load of 660 lbs. Most Type 8 and Type 10 bombers were protected with one or two Hotchkiss guns, but some were equipped with a .37 mm Hotchkiss cannon. Approximately 1,100 Type 8 bombers and 900 Type 10 bombers were produced during the war. Even though they carried relatively small bomb loads and had to be used at night, their numbers provided some success in carrying out tactical missions against German troop concentrations and strategic missions against German transportation systems.

Introduced in September 1917, the Breguet 14 biplane provided the French with their most successful daytime bomber of the war; a large number were also used for armed reconnaissance and a few were even used as air ambulance aircraft. Although some of the early Breguet 14s were fitted with a 220 hp Renault inline motor, most were powered by a 300 hp Renault inline engine, which produced a maximum speed of 121 mph and a service ceiling of 5,800 m (19,029 ft), provided an endurance of 2 hours 45 minutes, and carried a bomb load of up to 520 lbs. The Breguet 14 had a wingspan of 48 ft 9 in., a length of 29 ft 1.25 in., and a loaded weight of 3,891 lbs. It was protected by one fixed, forward-firing, synchronized Vickers gun and two ring-mounted Lewis guns. A few were also fitted with a downward-firing Lewis gun and used to provide close ground support. By war's end more than 3,500 Breguet 14s had been produced. An additional 5,000 were produced after the war until 1927. It remained in French service until 1932, seeing action in many colonial campaigns in North Africa and the Middle East. Numerous countries also purchased Breguet 14s for their air services in the 1920s.

Despite the pressure from French politicians, the French aircraft industry was slow to provide anything comparable to the heavy bombers being developed by other powers. This was partly because the army was more interested in fighters and reconnaissance air-craft and saw bombers as providing more of a supporting role for the infantry than a strategic role. Nevertheless, by late 1918 the French were experimenting with two prototype heavy bombers, the Caudron C.23 biplane and the Farman F.50 biplane. Although the former could carry a bomb load of approximately 1,750 lbs compared with the latter's bomb load of approximately 1,100 lbs, the F.50 was se-lected for production because of its superior climbing ability. Pow-ered by two 275 hp Lorraine 8Bd inline motors, the F.50 produced a maximum speed of 93 mph and could climb to 2,000 m (6,562 ft) in just 12 minutes 30 seconds. It had a service ceiling of 4,750 m (15,584 ft) and an endurance of 4 hours. The F.50 had a wingspan of 75 ft, a length of 39 ft 5 in., and a loaded weight of 6,834 lbs. F.50s began to enter service in early August 1918. Despite problems with the Lorraine engine, the F.50 provided useful service during the Allied counteroffensive by bombing train stations and ammu-nition depots in a series of nighttime raids in October 1918. Ap-proximately 50 were built by war's end. After the war a few were sold to foreign powers. Although it came too late to make much of a difference in the war, the F.50 did serve as the basis for the Far-man F.60 Goliath biplane, which was the main French bomber in the early 1920s.

GERMAN BOMBERS

Prior to the outbreak of the war, German zeppelins had captivated public attention and raised fears, fanned in part by the media, that these goliath airships would lay great cities to waste. Indeed, as indi-cated earlier, H. G. Wells had made the zeppelin the centerpiece of his 1908 book, *The War in the Air*. Although Germany possessed just nine airships when war broke out in August 1914, these were used in the opening stages of the German invasion through Belgium to drop bombs on Antwerp in an effort to force the Belgians to submit. Beginning in January 1915, the Germans launched their first at-tacks against Great Britain. The zeppelins used in these initial raids were carried out by the M-type, of which the naval zeppelin L-3 had been the first to enter service in May 1914. The airships in this class had a length of 518 ft 5 in., a diameter of 48 ft 8 in., and a gas vol-ume of 793,518 cubic ft, which provided a lifting capacity of 20,282 lbs and a service ceiling of 2,800 m (9,186 ft). They were powered by three 200 hp Maybach CX inline motors, which produced a maximum speed of 53 mph and gave them a range of 683 miles.

During the course of the war, the Germans would introduce three series of larger zeppelins in an effort to increase their bomb-carrying capacity, their service ceiling, and their range. The first class of zeppelins introduced during the war was the P-type, the first of which entered service in May 1915 as the L-10. It had a length of 536 ft 5 in., a diameter of 61 ft 5 in., and a gas volume of 1,126,533 cubic ft, which provided a lifting capacity of 35,715 lbs and a service ceiling of 3,900 m (12,795 ft). The P-type was powered by four 210 hp Maybach CX inline engines, which produced a maximum speed of 59 mph and gave it a range of 1,336 miles. In May 1916, Germany introduced the R-type or "super zeppelin," the first of which was designated the L-30. It had a length of 649 ft 7 in., a diameter of 78 ft 7 in., and a gas volume of 1,949,373 cubic ft, which provided a lifting capacity of 71,650 lbs and a service ceiling of 5,395 m (17,700 ft). The R-type was powered by six 240 hp Mabach HSLu inline motors, which produced a maximum speed of 64 mph and a range of 2,300 miles. In August 1917, the Zeppelin company introduced the last type to enter service during the war, the V-type, of which the L-59 is most famous for its November 1917 attempt to carry supplies from Bulgaria to Colonel Paul von Lettow-Vorbeck's forces in German East Africa. It had a length of 743 ft, a diameter of 78 ft 7 in., and a gas volume of 2,419,057 cubic ft, which provided a lifting capacity of 114,860 lbs and a service ceiling of 8,200 m (26,902 ft). The V-type was powered by five 240 hp Mabach Mb IVa inline engines, which produced a maximum speed of 67 mph and a range of 4,970 miles.

More than two-thirds of the 140 airships[3] used by Germany during the war were destroyed as the result of enemy fire or bombs, storms, or accidents, leading many historians to question whether the Germans had squandered precious resources that could have been poured into the development of bombers. It should be noted that, whereas the Germany Navy continued to invest heavily in zeppelins until the end of the war, the Germany Army began to turn toward bomber aircraft by 1915. These included a series of G-type light to medium bombers and the gigantic R-type (*Risenflugzeug*) heavy bombers.

In early 1915 Allgemeine Elektrizitäts Gesellschaft (A.E.G.) introduced the first of its series of G-types, the G.I twin-engine biplane. Production was limited because its two 100 hp Mercedes D.I inline motors proved to be underpowered. By the end of the year,

A.E.G. had introduced the G.II (powered by two 150 hp Benz inline engines and capable of carrying up to 440 lbs of bombs) and the G.III (powered by two 220 hp Mercedes D.IV inline engines and capable of carrying up to 660 lbs of bombs). Neither was produced in significant numbers; however, in late 1916 A.E.G. introduced the G.IV, which resembled the earlier versions, but was larger, better powered, and produced in greater numbers. With a wingspan of 60 ft 4.5 in., a length of 31 ft 10 in., and a loaded weight of 7,986 lbs, the G.IV was a sturdy bomber, utilizing steel-tube framing with a plywood nose section and fabric covering elsewhere. It was powered by two 260 hp Mercedes D.IVa inline motors, which produced a maximum speed of 103 mph and a service ceiling of 4,500 m (14,764 ft), provided an endurance of 4 hours 30 minutes, and carried a bomb load of up to 880 lbs. It was protected by two ring-mounted Parabellum machine guns—one in the forward cockpit and one in the rear cockpit. Because of its rather limited bomb load, the G.IV was used primarily for tactical bombing in support of ground troops. The G.IV most likely comprised more than 75 percent of the 542 total G-types built by A.E.G. Unlike other G-types produced by other manufacturers, all the A.E.G. G-types utilized a tractor-engine configuration instead of a pusher configuration.

Another early bomber that would lead to more successful versions was the Friedrichshafen G.II biplane, which entered service in limited numbers in 1916. Powered by two 200 hp Benz Bz.IV inline motors, which were configured as pushers, the G.II could carry a 1,000 lb-bomb load. In early 1917 Freidrichshafen introduced the G.III, which along with the Gotha G.IV and G.V, would serve as the primary German bombers during the last 2 years of the war. The G.III had a wingspan of 77 ft 9.25 in., a length of 42 ft, and a loaded weight of 8,646 lbs. Its wings consisted of a center section that was built around steel-tube spars and detachable outer sections that were constructed from spruce spars and braced with cables and steel tubes. This enabled it to be shipped easily by rail and reassembled. Powered by two 260 hp Mercedes D.IV inline engines, which were configured as pushers, the G.III could reach a maximum speed of 87 mph, climb to a service ceiling of 4,500 m (14,764 ft), and had an endurance of up to 5 hours. Well defended with two or three Parabellum machine guns and capable of carrying a bomb load of up to 3,300 lbs, the Friedrichshafen G.III was widely used on the Western Front. A total of 338 G.III and G.IIIa types (the later had a biplane tail unit for added stability) were produced in addition to less than 50 of the earlier G.II versions.

By far the most famous German bombers of the war were the Gotha G.IV and G.V biplanes, which carried out highly successful raids on London in the summer of 1917. They were derived from the earlier Gotha G.II and G.III, which were designed by Hans Burkhard and introduced in 1916. The former proved to be under-powered with its twin 220 hp Benz inline motors, limiting produc-tion to just ten aircraft. The latter, however, were powered by two 260 hp Mercedes inline engines and could carry a bomb load of ap-proximately 1,100 lbs. The G.III was also the first bomber that at-tempted to provide the tail gunner with the ability to fire downward as well as laterally and upward. Replaced on the Western Front fairly quickly by the much-improved G.IV, the G.III was transferred to the Balkans after Romania entered the war against Germany and Austria-Hungary.

The G.IV was introduced in late 1916 and formed the nucleus of Heavy Bomber Squadron No. 3, which by war's end was to drop more than 186,000 lbs of bombs on London in a series of raids that began with a daylight raid on 25 May 1917. With a wingspan of 77 ft 9.25 in., a length of 38 ft 11 in., and a loaded weight of 7,997 lbs, the G.IV was capable of carrying between 660 and 1,100 lbs of bombs, depending on the mission and the amount of fuel carried on board. In order to have maximum range for the attacks on London, for example, the G.IV carried just 660 lbs of bombs. One of the chief reasons for its success was that its twin 260 hp Mercedes D.IVa inline motors (configured in a pusher arrangement) enabled it to reach a maximum speed of 87 mph and to operate from a service ceiling of 6,500 m (21,325 ft)—a height that was beyond the capa-bilities of the home defense aircraft used by the British. As a result of the raids, the British were forced to divert top-of-the-line fighters to home defense, forcing the Gothas to switch to nighttime raids. The G.V was a heavier version that had a better center of gravity and featured an improved tail gunner firing arrangement. All versions of the Gothas had a three-man crew. Although precise production fig-ures are not available, it is estimated that 230 G.IVs entered service in 1917. Total production probably exceeded 400, of which forty air-frames produced by L.V.G. were supplied to Austria-Hungary and equipped by Oeffag with 230 hp Hiero inline engines.

At the same time that Germany began development of G-type bombers, a number of German manufactures—A.E.G., Deutsche Flugzeugwerke, Siemens-Schuckert-Werke, and Zeppelin Werke Staaken—attempted to develop huge R-type bombers. Although sev-eral difficulties had to be overcome to achieve a successful design, the most important were developing engines powerful enough to provide enough lift for takeoff and climbing, and an undercarriage system that could withstand the impact of landing such heavy aircraft. After the first prototypes appeared in late 1915, a process of trial and error eventually led to the production of R-types by Siemens-Schuckert and Zeppelin Staaken.

A total of seven production aircraft (the R.I through R.VII) were constructed by Siemens-Schuckert. All of them were powered by three engines that were housed within the front fuselage and used a chain and gear system to operate two tractor propellers that were installed on each side of the fuselage within the first bay opening between the upper and lower wings. The R.I had a wingspan of 91 ft 10 in., a length of 57 ft 5 in., and was powered by three 150 hp Benz Bz.III inline engines. The remaining Siemens-Schuckerts had wingspans in excess of 100 ft with the R.VII reaching 126 ft 1.5 in. Powered by three 260 hp Mercedes D.IVa inline motors, the R.VII was capable of a maximum speed of 81 mph, could climb to a service ceiling of 3,500 m (11,4843 ft), had an endurance of 7 hours, and could carry a bomb load of approximately 3,000 lbs. It was protected by up to three machine guns. Although the first three were used strictly for training, the last four saw service on the Russian Front in 1916 and 1917. Siemens-Schuckert was in the final stages of developing a massive R.VIII bomber that had a wingspan of 157 ft 6 in. and was to be powered by six 300 hp Mercedes inline engines, but the war ended before they were completed.

After achieving a successful flight with its R-prototype in April 1915, Zeppelin Staaken experimented with a variety of engines and configurations before finally beginning production of the R.VI, which entered service in June 1917. With a wingspan of 138 ft 5 in., a length of 72 ft 6.25 in., and a loaded weight of 26,066 lbs, the R.VI was the largest aircraft to see service in the war. Its undercarriage consisted of three chassis and a total of eighteen wheels. It was powered by either four 245 hp Maybach Mb.IV inline motors or four 260 hp Mercedes D.IVa inline motors, which were placed back to back in a tractor-pusher configuration. The R.VI had a maximum speed of 84 mph and a service ceiling of 4,320 m (14,173 ft). Its endurance varied from 7 to 10 hours depending upon the amount of fuel carried, which also resulted in a bomb load that varied from 1,650 to 4,400 lbs. It was also the first bomber to carry the huge 2,200-lb (1,000-kg) bomb, the largest used in the war. The R.VI was protected by four Parabellum machine guns. Noted for its rugged construction, which combined a wooden frame fuselage and steel-tube bracing and struts, the R.VI was used extensively on the Western Front and carried out numerous raids (some solo and others in conjunction with Gotha G.IV and G.V bombers) against Britain. In contrast to the Gothas, not a single R.VI was lost from enemy fire. A total of eighteen R.VI bombers were constructed. Of these, just one was built by Zeppelin Staaken; the other seventeen were licensed-built by Albatros, Aviatik, and Schütte Lanz.

ITALIAN BOMBERS

After conducting the world's first aerial bombardment from an airplane in November 1911 during the Tripolitan War against the Turks, the Italians were quick to recognize the potential for bombers. Indeed, Giulio Douhet's *Rules for the Use of Aircraft in War,* published in 1912, specifically called for the development of aircraft capable of dropping heavy bomb loads on enemy targets. Partly in response to Douhet's book, Giovanni Caproni began developing a large multiengine aircraft. His first attempt, the Caproni Ca 30 biplane, was successfully demonstrated in 1913. Its central nacelle housed three 90 hp Gnôme rotary engines, of which the front two used a gear system to power two tractor propellers on booms that extended from the fuselage, whereas the rear motor powered a pusher propellor at the back of the nacelle. This arrangement proved to be underpowered and awkward to operate, leading Caproni to alter his design by using three 100 hp Fiat A.10 inline engines, two of which were housed on the booms outside the fuselage and powered the tractor propellers directly, whereas the other was housed in the rear of the nacelle and powered a pusher propeller. This prototype, known as the Ca 32, was successfully demonstrated in October 1914.

After Italy entered the war in May 1915, the Italian military quickly placed orders for the Ca 32 prototype, which received the military designation as the Ca.1 type. It had a wingspan of 72 ft 10 in., a length of 35 ft 9 in., and a loaded weight of 7,280 lbs, including up to 1,000 lbs of bombs that were held in racks under the nacelle. Its three 100 hp Fiat A.10 inline motors provided a maximum speed of 72 mph, a service ceiling of 4,000 m (13,123 ft), and a range of 344 miles. The Ca.1 carried four crewmen, including a front gunner and tail gunner who operated two to four ring-mounted Revelli machine guns. The tail gunner had to stand in a raised cage from the back of the nacelle in order to fire above the arc of the propeller. Its wooden frame was covered with fabric and thin aluminum sheets protected the nacelle. Its landing gear consisted of two wheels that were attached by struts to the lower wing and two wheels that were suspended from the nose section of the nacelle. It was also distinctive with its twin booms that connected the nacelle and wings to the tail section, which used three rudders. The Ca.1 began arriving at the front in early August 1915. A total of 166 entered service before production ended in December 1916. During this same period a total of 9 Caproni Ca.2 biplane bombers also entered service. These were similar in all respects to the Ca.1 with the exception that they were powered by two 100 hp Fiat A.10 inline engines and one 150 hp Isotta-Fraschini V.4B V-type engine.

In late 1916 Caproni introduced his third series of bombers, the Ca.3 biplane, which used the same airframe and landing gear as the Ca.1 and Ca.2. It was powered by three 150 hp Isotta-Fraschini V.4B V-type motors, which increased its maximum speed to 86 mph and gave it an endurance of 3.5 hours. The added power enabled the Ca.3 to carry a bomb capacity of 1,760 lbs, which increased its total loaded weight to 8,400 lbs. It had a good climbing rate, which was an absolute necessity in the mountainous regions of the Italian Front, and had a service ceiling of 4,850 m (15,912 ft). Like the earlier Caproni bombers, the Ca.3 was well protected with two to four ring-mounted Revelli machine guns that were operated by a forward gunner and a tail gunner. In addition to its service as a bomber, the Ca.3 was also used as a torpedo bomber by the Italian Navy, which operated them out of coastal naval air stations. A total of 269 were produced in Italy between late 1916 and early 1918, eventually equipping 18 squadrons. Approximately 60 were licensed-produced in France by Établissements D'aviation Robert Esnault-Pelterie. Many of the Ca.3s that survived the war were adapted for mail and passenger service afterward.

In late 1917 Caproni introduced the Ca.4 bomber, which employed a unique triplane configuration. It had a wingspan of 98 ft (all three wings were of equal length), a length of 43 ft, and a loaded weight of 14,330 lbs, which included a bomb load of 3,000 lbs. The nacelle was attached to the central wing and provided seating for two pilots and a front gunner, who sat in the nose and operated two ring-mounted Revelli machine guns. A tail gunner was placed in each of the twin booms and was provided with one ring-mounted Revelli machine gun, making for a more comfortable arrangement than the standing position required in the earlier Capronis. The first few Ca.4 triplanes were powered by three 200 hp Isotta-Fraschini V-type engines, but these proved to be underpowered for such a heavy aircraft. As a result, most of the 38 Ca.4s that entered service were powered by either three 270 hp Isotta-Fraschini V-type motors or three 270 hp Fiat inline motors (a few were also powered by three 270 hp Liberty V-type engines). As in the earlier Capronis, two engines were placed in the forward part of the booms and one was placed in the rear of the nacelle. With performance varying with each engine type, most sources report an average of 87 mph and a service ceiling of 3,000 m (9,843 ft).

The final Caproni bomber of the war, the Ca.5 biplane, was introduced in early 1918 and remained in service until 1921. It had a wingspan of 77 ft, a length of 41 ft 4 in., and a loaded weight of 11,700 lbs, including a bomb load of 1,190 lbs. Like the Ca.4, the Ca.5 employed a variety of engines, using more powerful ones as they became available. The majority were powered by three 300 hp Fiat A.12 bis inline motors, two of which were placed in the front of the tail booms in a tractor configuration and one which was placed in the rear of the nacelle. The Ca.5 had a maximum speed of 95 mph and a service ceiling of 4,570 m (14,993 ft). It was protected by one or two ring-mounted Revelli machine guns in the nose section, and one or two ring-mounted Revelli machine guns in a raised turret of the rear nacelle. A total of 255 were built in Italy and at least 3 were produced in the United States by war's end.

In addition to its Caproni bombers, Italy, like other powers, used a number of its armed reconnaissance aircraft, such as the S.A.M.L. 1 and 2, the S.I.A. 7B2, and the Pompilio P-types, as light bombers. Italy also drew upon British and French bombers. It should also be noted that Italy had semi-ridge airships at its disposal and used approximately twenty of the M-type for bombing purposes during the course of the war. Indeed, on 26 May 1915, just 3 days after it declared war on Austria-Hungary, Italy used one of its M-type airships to bomb Sebenico. First introduced in 1912, the M-type was manufactured by Stabilimento Construzioni Aeronautiche. Unlike zeppelins, which were constructed with an outer and inner metal framework, and blimps, which used the pressure of the gas to keep their shape, the semi-rigid airships of the M-type utilized a central spine or keel that helped maintain its shape and support the engines and carriages. With a length of 272 ft 3 in., a diameter of 55 ft 9 in., and a gas volume of 473,750 cubic ft, the M-type could carry 2,200 lbs of bombs and reach altitudes of up to 4,570 m (14,993 ft). They were powered by two 250 hp Maybach inline motors, which could produce a maximum speed of 43 mph and an endurance of 6 hours.

RUSSIAN BOMBERS

Although Russia was not as industrially advanced as the other European powers, it would enter the First World War with the world's first four-engine aircraft, the Sikorsky *Ilya Muromets*. After achieving success with a number of smaller aircraft, Igor Sikorsky joined the Russo-Baltic Railroad Car Factory (Russko-Baltiisky Vagonny Zaved or R-BVZ) in the spring of 1912 and began designing a massive aircraft, the *Bol'shoi Bal'tisky* (the Great Baltic), which had a wingspan of 88 ft and a length of 65 ft. Sikorsky had originally intended to use just two 100 hp Argus inline engines. Although he managed to take off on 2 March 1913, the Great Baltic proved to be underpowered. Undeterred, Sikorsky added two additional motors, which were installed in tandem with the first two, thereby providing both a tractor and pusher configuration. Beginning in May 1913, Sikorsky made several test flights in the Great Baltic, after which he reconfigured all of the engines to be on the leading edge of the lower wing for a tractor design. This proved far more successful, as indicated by a 2 August 1913 flight in which he carried eight people aloft for more than 2 hours.

Sikorsky's next version, which served as the prototype of the wartime versions, was introduced in December 1913. It was similar to the Great Baltic, but it had a much larger fuselage that could accommodate up to sixteen passengers. By the spring of 1914, Sikorsky had developed the S-22B, dubbed the "Ilya Muromets" after a famous medieval Russian nobleman, it successfully completed a 1,600-mile round-trip flight between St. Petersburg and Kiev in June 1914.[4] With the outbreak of the war, the S-22B and a sister aircraft were mobilized for service. An additional five were constructed by December 1914 and organized as the *Eskadra Vozdushnykh Korablei* (EVK) or Squadron of Flying Ships.

Because the first *Ilya Muromets* types had been designed primarily to carry passengers, once the war began Sikorsky started work on a slightly smaller version, the V-type, that could be used as a bomber. Introduced in spring 1915, the V-type *Ilya Muromets* had a wingspan of 97 ft 9 in. and a length of 57 ft 5 in. Because of Russia's chronic shortage of engines, the R-BVZ was forced to rely upon a variety of engines for the V-type, including at least one that used different sets of engines; two 140 hp Argus and two 125 hp Argus inline engines. Of the thirty-two V-types produced, twenty-two were powered by four 150 hp Sunbeam inline motors, which provided a maximum speed of 68 mph. They had a loaded weight of 10,140 lbs, including a bomb load of approximately 1,100 lbs. Its crew of five to seven members were protected by free-firing machine guns. Three later versions were introduced during the war: the G-type and D-type introduced in 1916, and the E-type introduced in 1917. Of these, the E-type was the largest with a wingspan of 102 ft, a length of 61 ft 8 in., and a loaded weight of 15,500 lbs. Its four 220 hp Renault inline engines could produce a maximum speed of 80 mph. The E-type carried an eight-man crew, including two pilots, five gunners, and one mechanic. At least eight were constructed during 1917. The E-type went on to serve in the Red Air Force until 1924. The Sikorsky *Ilya Muromets* were sturdy, rugged aircraft. Of the approximate eighty that were built, only one was shot down by the enemy.

In addition to the *Ilya Muromets*, Russia used a number of British and French light bombers that were either imported or were licensed-built by Russian manufacturers. The most numerous was the Voisin Type 3, of which Russia purchased 800 from France and produced approximately 400 license-built versions. This included a total of ninety-eight produced by the Lebedev factory in the last 2 years of the war. A few remained in service with the Red Air Force as late as 1923.

U. S. BOMBERS

Although most of the efforts of the United States to produce aircraft for use in the war proved to be failures or came too late, its production of D.H.4 bombers equipped with the 400 hp Liberty V-12 engine was a success. The D.H.4 Liberty had a wingspan of 42 ft 5 in., a length of 29 ft 11 in., and a loaded weight of 4,297 lbs. Its 400 hp Liberty V-type engine produced a maximum speed of 124 mph, which exceeded the performance of all of the British versions, except those powered by the 375 hp Rolls-Royce Eagle VIII inline engine. The D.H.4 Liberty had a service ceiling of 19,500 ft (5,944 m) and a maximum range of 550 miles. It came equipped with two fixed, forward-firing, synchronized .30 caliber Marlin machine guns and two ring-mounted Lewis guns that were fired by the observer.

Its bomb racks were equipped to carry two 230-lb bombs or four 112-lb bombs. Although the D.H.4 Liberty had a reputation for catching fire because its fuel tank was placed between the pilot and observer and was consequently more exposed to enemy fire, it nevertheless played a prominent role in Brigadier General William "Billy" Mitchell's air plan for the St. Mihiel Offensive and the Meuse-Argonne Offensive. During this latter offensive, D.H.4 Liberties were used to drop supplies to the so-called Lost Battalion—the First Battalion, 308th Infantry, 77th Division—which had become isolated and surrounded by Germans, until it could be relieved by Allied troops. Two American crewman received the Congressional Medal of Honor for their efforts in this mission. A total of 4,844 were built by the time production was halted at the end of 1918. Of this number, 3,227 were produced by the Armistice, but only 628 saw combat in Europe. The D.H.4 Liberty remained in service in the United States until 1932.

NOTES

1. On 5 August 1918 a D.H.4 piloted by Major Egbert Cadbury shot down a zeppelin L-70, which was carrying Captain Peter Strasser, commander-in-chief of the Imperial German Naval Airship Service. Strasser's death brought an end to the German zeppelin raids.

2. The United States adopted plans to build 14,000 D.H.9s, which were to be powered by the 400 hp Liberty V-type engine, but production was halted after the Armistice with just 4 having been completed.

3. This included 22 Schütte-Lanz airships that were constructed with wooden and plywood airframes.

4. The trip included a stop each way for refueling. The aircraft was also serviced by its mechanics while in flight.

CHAPTER SIX

Naval Aircraft

WITH BALLOONS HAVING BEEN USED for observation purposes by the U.S. Navy in Mississippi during the siege of Island No. 10 in the American Civil War of 1861–1865, the Russian and Japanese navies in the Russo–Japanese War of 1904–1905, and the Italian Navy in the Tripolitan War of 1911–1912, it is not surprising that the major naval powers were quick to realize the advantage that aircraft could bring in extending vision beyond the immediate horizon and identifying enemy ship movements. Although successful experiments had been made in taking off and landing on ships prior to World War I, the limitations of both aircraft performance and ship design made ship-to-ship flight haphazard until the launching of the first purpose-built aircraft carrier, the Royal Navy's H.M.S. *Argus*, in 1918.[1] As a result, naval powers relied upon two main types of seaplanes: floatplanes employing externally attached floats or flying boats. These seaplanes operated either from coastal naval air stations or from ships, which either towed them or carried them onboard and used a winch and beam system to hoist them into or out of the water. During World War I, seaplanes would prove to have just as important an impact—albeit not as spectacular or as glamorous—upon naval warfare as did land airplanes upon land warfare. Seaplanes played an important role in transforming naval warfare by helping fulfill the traditional naval objective of establishing control or command of the seas, protecting coastlines and shipping lanes, and offering the possibility of projecting naval power inland through the air. Had the war continued into 1919, the British would have been able to mount carrier-based air attacks against the German Fleet. Such an ability was far beyond the capacity of 1914 seaplanes, thus demonstrating the impact that the war had upon technology.

AUSTRO-HUNGARIAN
NAVAL AIRCRAFT

Although Austria-Hungary lacked the aviation manufacturing resources that the other leading belligerents could call upon, the *Kaiserlich und Königlich Kriegsmarine* (the *KuK* or "Imperial and Royal Navy") entered the First World War with approximately the same level of naval aviation as Germany had. Its aviators had gained experience after being mobilized in 1913 for peacekeeping operations in Albania during the Second Balkan War. Upon the outbreak of war in 1914, the *KuK* provided much needed air support for the Austro-Hungarian Army during its advance into Serbia. More important, after Italy declared war on Austria-Hungary in May 1915, the *KuK's* aircraft enabled it to maintain control over the Adriatic until 1917.

Upon the outbreak of the war, Austria-Hungary possessed one of the best flying boats available in the Lohner Type E. Introduced in 1913 by Jacob Lohner Werke and Company, the Type E utilized a biplane configuration and carried a two-man crew. It had a wingspan of 53 ft 2 in., a length of 33 ft 8 in., and a loaded weight of 3,748 lbs. Powered by an 85 hp Hiero inline engine, which was placed in a pusher configuration between its upper and lower wing directly above the hull, the Type E could produce a maximum speed of 65 mph and reach a service ceiling of 4,000 m (13,123 ft). It had an endurance of 4 hours. Although it was intended primarily to operate over the Adriatic, where it was based in Austro-Hungarian naval bases, a few Type E flying boats were used to provide reconnaissance for the Austro-Hungarian Army's invasion of Serbia. Approximately forty Type E flying boats were produced. Some of these were later converted into Type S dual-control trainers.

In early 1915 Lohner introduced the Type L, which was designed as an armed reconnaissance flying boat. With a wingspan of 53 ft 2 in. and a length of 33 ft 8 in., it resembled the Type E, but it was more streamlined so that it had a similar total weight of 3,743 lbs, even though it had a larger, heavier engine and carried a 440-lb bomb load. The Type L was powered by either a 140 hp Hiero inline motor or a 160 or 180 hp Austro-Daimler inline motor set in a pusher configuration, which produced a maximum speed of approximately 70 mph, a service ceiling of 5,000 m (16,404 ft), and an endurance of 4 hours. It was also armed with a ring-mounted 7.62 mm Schwarzlose machine gun that was set on a rotating mounting. The pilot and observer sat side by side, with the former on the left and the latter on the right. Type L flying boats were also used for anti-submarine patrols in the Adriatic. The French submarine *Foucault* was forced to surface in September 1916 after Type Ls spotted it and dropped depth charges. A modified version, the three-seat Type R, was introduced in 1916 and was equipped for photo-reconnaissance. A captured Lohner Type L served as the basis for the first in a series of Macchi flying boats used by the Italian Navy. Approximately 160 Lohner Type L and 36 Type R flying boats were constructed during the war.

In addition to its Lohner flying boats, the Austro-Hungarian Navy also relied upon several German-designed floatplanes and flying boats. The most important of these was the single-seat Hansa-Brandenburg CC Flying Boat, which was designed by Ernst Heinkel and licensed-produced in Austria by Phönix Flugzeug-Werke. Where the Lohner flying boats had been used primarily for reconnaissance and maritime patrol, the Hansa-Brandenburg CC was designed to be used as a fighter. With a wingspan of 30 ft 6 in., a length of 25 ft 1 in., and a loaded weight of 2,989 lbs, it was much more maneuverable than those produced by Lohner. Powered by a 150 hp Benz Bz III inline engine set in a pusher configuration, the CC had a maximum speed of 109 mph and an endurance of 3 hours 30 minutes. It was armed with a fixed forward-firing 7.62 mm Schwarzlose machine gun. The Hansa-Brandenburg CC was also distinguished by its unique star-strutter wing braces in which four struts attached to the top wing and four struts attached to the bottom wing converged together in a central housing approximately midway in the gap between the wings, giving it the appearance of two pyramids joined together at the points. Of the approximately eighty that were constructed, about half were produced in Austria-Hungary.

BRITISH NAVAL AIRCRAFT

As the leading naval power at the turn of the century, the British had been quick to see the potential of incorporating air power into their naval arsenal. Upon becoming First Lord of the Admiralty in October

1911, Winston Churchill enthusiastically supported the incorporation of aircraft into the navy and played a leading role in the organization of the Royal Naval Air Service (RNAS), which began as the
Naval Wing of the Royal Flying Corps in 1912. As first director of the
Admiralty Air Department, Captain Murray Sueter, who had earlier
overseen construction of the navy's first airship, the *Mayfly*, played a
leading role in the development of the RNAS. Several leading naval
officers also promoted the cause of naval aviation. Vice Admiral Sir
John Jellicoe, destined to be named commander of the Grand Fleet
when Britain entered the war, was the navy's leading proponent of
airships. During the war, Jellicoe's successor, Sir David Beatty, called
for the construction of torpedo planes and aircraft carriers in order to
attack the German Navy while it was in the harbor.

Based on the prewar Short Folder, which featured folding wings
to make storage aboard ship easier, the Short 184 floatplane was introduced in early 1915 just in time to participate in the Royal Navy's
attempt to force the Dardanelles in the summer of 1915. On 12 August 1915 Commander Charles Edmonds succeeding in sinking a
Turkish ship by launching a 14-in. torpedo from his Short 184 floatplane. A few additional Turkish ships were similarly destroyed in the
days that followed. Short 184 floatplanes would also provide aerial
reconnaissance for the Royal Navy during the Battle of Jutland. The
Short 184 was powered by a 260 hp Sunbeam inline motor, which
provided a maximum speed of 88 mph, a service ceiling of 9,000 ft
(2,743 m), and a duration of 2 hours 45 minutes. With a wingspan
of 63 ft 6.25 in., a length of 40 ft 7.5 in., and a loaded weight of
5,363 lbs, the Short 184 proved to be somewhat difficult to fly.
When carrying a heavy torpedo between its two floats, it could at-
tain a ceiling of just 800 ft (244 m). It was protected by a free-firing
Lewis gun (later models had a ring mounting for the observer). Approximately 900 were built during the war.

Even though the Short 184 continued to be produced in large
numbers to the end of the war, the Short 320 floatplane was introduced in 1916 to meet the RNAS's requirements for a long-range
airplane that could carry its new 1,000-lb Mark IX 18-in. torpedo,
which was beyond the capabilities of the Short 184. The Short 320
was powered by a 320 hp Sunbeam Cossack inline engine, which
produced a maximum speed of 72.5 mph, a service ceiling of 3,000
ft (914 m), and an endurance of approximately 4 hours. When carrying two 230-lb bombs, instead of the torpedo, its performance increased to 79 mph, its service ceiling to 5,500 ft (1,676 m), and its
endurance to 6 hours. The Short 320 had a wingspan of 75 ft (the

lower wing was almost 30 ft shorter), a length of 45 ft 9 in., and a loaded weight of slightly more than 7,000 lbs. It was protected by a ring-mounted Lewis gun. Approximately 130 were constructed by war's end.

Like the Short 184, the Sopwith Schneider and Sopwith Baby were based on a prewar design that in April 1914 had won the Schneider Cup for the fastest seaplane. The prototype was basically a Sopwith Tabloid equipped with floats. After the war broke out, the RNAS placed an initial order for twelve that were to be armed with a Lewis gun mounted to fire at an upward angle over the propeller. With a wingspan of 25 ft 8 in., a length of 23 ft, and a loaded weight of 1,580 lbs, the Sopwith Schneider was a compact, agile aircraft. Its 100 hp Gnôme Monosoupape rotary motor provided a maximum speed of 92 mph, a service ceiling of 10,000 ft (3,048 m), and an endurance of 2 hours 15 minutes. After producing 136 of the Schneider version, Sopwith introduced a new version, the Baby, which used the same airframe but was powered by a 130 hp Clerget rotary engine. This increased its performance to a maximum speed of 100 mph. Total production of the Sopwith Baby was 456, with more than three-quarters of them constructed by subcontractors.

Although the Sopwith Pup is remembered primarily for its role as a fighter, it had originally been intended for service at sea. Of the 1,770 Pups produced, however, only 290 saw action with the RNAS. Nevertheless, the Pup was important for its experimental role in naval aviation. With a wingspan of 26 ft 6 in., a length of 19 ft 3.75 in., and a loaded weight of 1,225 lbs, the Pup did not require a long runway. Indeed, the Royal Navy soon learned that the Pup could take off from platforms built across the gun turrets of its battleships—a distance of just 20 ft. Landing was a more difficult task, but the Pup's excellent maneuverability allowed for a number of experiments to be carried out. On 2 August 1917, for example, Commander Edwin Dunning succeeded in landing on a special 228-ft flight deck that had been placed on top of the H.M.S. *Furious,* while the ship was under way. Five days later, however, Dunning was tragically killed when he attempted to land and his plane toppled overboard. Experiments were temporarily suspended until an afterdeck was attached to the *Furious,* extending its runway an additional 56 ft. In addition, the Pup's undercarriage was modified by replacing its wheels with skids and by adding a tail hook that was designed to catch arrester ropes upon landing. These modifications proved successful both on the *Furious* and the first British aircraft carrier, the H.M.S. *Argus,* which was commissioned in September 1918.

Introduced in 1917, the Fairey F.17 Campania floatplane was significant because it was the first seaplane specially designed to be launched from a seaplane carrier, specifically the ex-Cunard liner *Campania*, which had been converted by the British Navy to carry seaplanes.[2] The floats of the F.17 were placed on a wheeled cart for take off—the cart was then pulled back onboard. After completing its mission, the F.17 landed on the water, then pulled alongside to be hoisted back onboard. Although a variety of engines were used in the F.17, most were powered by either a 250 hp Sunbeam Maori II inline motor or the 345 hp Rolls-Royce Eagle VIII inline motor. Those powered by the latter had a maximum speed of 80 mph, a service ceiling of 5,500 ft (1,677 m), and an endurance of 3 hours. It had a wingspan of 61 ft 7.5 in., a length of 43 ft 1 in., and a loaded weight of 5,657 lbs. The F.17 was protected by a ring-mounted Lewis gun fired by the observer from the rear cockpit. It also carried up to 160 lbs of bombs. A total of sixty-two were built by war's end.

Introduced in 1917, the Felixstowe F.2A flying boat was based upon the Curtiss H-12 "Large America" design, but it had a far more hydrodynamic hull. Powered by twin 345 hp Rolls-Royce Eagle VIII inline engines set in a tractor configuration, the F.2A could reach a maximum speed of 95 mph and climb to a service ceiling of 9,600 ft (2,926 m). It had an endurance of 6 hours. With a wingspan of 95 ft 7.5 in., a length of 46 ft 3 in., and a loaded weight of 10,978 lbs, the Felixstowe was one of the largest flying boats of the war. Its four-man crew was well armed with four to seven Lewis guns, including a ring-mounted gun in the nose section, and it carried two 230-lb bombs. The F.2A was used primarily in the North Sea and proved to be effective against German submarines. It was a sturdy, rugged aircraft that was capable of absorbing a lot of punishment, while also providing a lot of firepower. On 4 June 1918, for example, a squadron of four F.2A flying boats were attacked by fourteen Hansa-Brandenburg W.29 floatplanes. Without losing a single flying boat, the British shot down six of the attacking W.29s. Approximately 100 F.2A flying boats were constructed by the end of the war. It remained in service with the Royal Air Force (RAF) until 1927.

Had the war continued into 1919, the Sopwith Cuckoo would have provided the British with carrier-based torpedo aircraft with which it could have attacked the German High Seas Fleet in its home base. Attempts to design such an aircraft dated back to 1915, but it was not until the summer of 1918 that a successful prototype had been tested and production was begun. The Cuckoo had a wingspan of 46 ft 9 in., a length of 28 ft 6 in., and a loaded weight of 3,883 lbs. Most were powered by a 200 hp Sunbeam Arab inline motor, which provided a maximum speed of 103 mph, a service ceiling of 12,100 ft, and an endurance of 4 hours. The Cuckoo was designed to carry the 1,000-lb Mark IX 18-in. torpedo. The first squadron of Cuckoos entered service onboard the H.M.S. *Argus* on 19 October 1918, but the Armistice came before they could be launched against the German Fleet. Although 350 had initially been ordered, the contract was canceled after the Armistice, with just 90 having entered service.

In addition to their flying boats and floatplanes, the British also relied heavily upon nonrigid airships (blimps) to carry out aerial patrols against German U-boats. The first of the Sea Scout Class airships entered service by March 1915. It used a gas envelope for lift and the fuselage of a B.E.2 aircraft suspended beneath for power. Each Sea Scout carried a bomb load of 112-lbs, a pilot, and wireless operator. The Sea Scout had a length of 143 ft, a diameter of 32 ft, and a volume of 70,000 cubic ft of gas. Because of the Sea Scout's limited range, the British Admiralty began development of the Coastal Class airship. The first airship of this design, the C.1, was 196 ft long, was powered by one pusher and one tractor engine, and was armed with two Lewis machine guns and four 112-lb or two 230-lb bombs. It was capable of up to 20 hours service at a maximum speed of 47 mph. In early 1917 the Admiralty introduced the North Sea Class, a nonrigid airship that was 262 ft long with a 35-ft-long cabin that provided for a crew of ten men. The North Sea Class was capable of 24-hour flights and carried heavier armament—three to five Lewis machine guns and six 230-lb bombs. In combination with the adoption of the convoy system, the British airships had a significant impact against the German U-boats. Whereas U-boats managed to sink 257 convoyed ships during the last 18 months of the war, only 2 of these ships were operating in convoys that were accompanied by aerial escort.

FRENCH NAVAL AIRCRAFT

Although the French Navy had been the first to dedicate a warship for carrying aircraft by converting the torpedo boat *Foudre* into a seaplane launcher in 1912, its air service possessed only eight seaplanes and no more than twelve other aircraft when war broke out in 1914. Assuming that the war would be short, the French suspended construction of further seaplanes, believing they would come too late to make a difference. Although this quickly proved to be wrong, the loss of its industrial centers in northeastern France to German occupation forced the French to shortchange naval aviation in order to meet the needs of its army air services and provide engines to its allies.

One of the first types of flying boats to be used in great numbers by the French was produced by the Franco-British Aviation firm (F.B.A.), which had sold three of its Type A flying boats to Austria-Hungary prior to the war. Although France had not acquired any of the Type A flying boats, it did purchase a majority of the 180 Type B flying boats that were built between 1914 and 1917. With a wingspan of 44 ft 11.75 in., a length of 29 ft 11.75 in., and a loaded weight of approximately 2,000 lbs, the Type B lacked maneuverability, and its 100 hp Gnôme Monosoupape rotary engine, which was set in a pusher configuration, provided just 60 mph. As a result, the Type B proved to be easy fodder for German fighters, in part because most were either unarmed or were armed with a single Lewis gun (a few models were armed with a .37 mm Hotchkiss cannon). Nevertheless, the Type B could carry two 330-lb bombs, which made it effective for patrols over the North Sea. An upgraded version, the Type C, powered by a 130 hp Clerget 9B rotary motor, entered production in early 1916. Most of these were sold to Italy and Russia. The most numerous version was the Type H, which used the same airframe as the Type B and C, but was powered by a 150 hp Hispano-Suiza 8A V-type engine, which gave it a maximum speed of 93 mph and service ceiling of 4,875 m (15,994 ft). Approximately 360 Type H flying boats were built in France, and an additional 982 were licensed-built in Italy by Società Idrovloanti Alta Italia.

In late 1916 the two-seat Tellier T.3 began entering service as a maritime patrol, antisubmarine flying boat. It had a wingspan of 51 ft 2 in., a length of 38 ft 9.75 in., and a loaded weight of 3,959 lbs. The T.3 was powered by a 200 hp Hispano-Suiza 8Ac V-type engine set in a pusher configuration, which produced a maximum speed of 84 mph, a service ceiling of 3,500 m (11,483 ft), and an endurance of 4 hours 30 minutes. It was protected by one ring-mounted Hotchkiss gun in its front nose. One of the key characteristics of the T.3 was its hydrodynamic hull, which allowed it to glide smoothly through the water before taking off. It also made it easy to land. A modified version, the T.6, was introduced in 1918. It was similar in all respects to the T.3, with the exception that it was armed with a

.47 mm Hotchkiss cannon, which made it ideal for escorting convoys. Approximately 190 T.3 and 55 T.6 flying boats were built by war's end.

Another flying boat to enter service in 1916 was the Donnet-Denhaut D.D.2 two seat flying boat. Like the Tellier T.3, the D.D.2 was intended to have a longer endurance in order to carry out anti-submarine maritime patrols. The first 36 D.D.2 flying boats were powered by the 160 hp Salmson Canton-Unné radial motor set in a pusher configuration, which provided a maximum speed of 93 mph, a service ceiling of 3,000 m (9,843 ft), and an endurance of 3 hours. The remaining 365 D.D.2 flying boats were powered by the 150 hp Hispano-Suiza 8Aa V-type engine, which provided a maximum speed of 99 mph, a service ceiling of 3,000 m (9,843 ft), and an endurance of 2 hours 45 minutes. The D.D.2 had a wingspan of 46 ft 7 in., a length of 35 ft 5 in., and a loaded weight of 3,042 lbs with the Salmson Canton-Unné or 3,196 lbs with the Hispano-Suiza. The hull of the D.D.2 extended far enough in front of the wings that both the pilot and observer sat forward, giving them an excellent range of vision. In addition to the observer's 7.7 mm Lewis or Hotchkiss gun, the D.D.2 carried up to 220 lbs of bombs and a radio. Approximately 400 were constructed.

In 1917 Donnet-Denhaut introduced a three-seat flying boat, the D.D.8, which was similar in design to the D.D.2. As in the D.D.2, the pilot sat in front of the wings, providing him an excellent range of vision. The front and rear observers fired ring-mounted Lewis or Hotchkiss guns, making the D.D.8 less vulnerable to an attack, especially from the rear. The D.D.8 had a wingspan of 53 ft 4.9 in., a length of 31 ft 2 in., and a loaded weight of 3,417 lbs. Its wings were slightly wider and more heavily braced to support the additional weight. The D.D.8 was powered by a 200 hp Hispano-Suiza 8B V-type engine set in a pusher configuration, which provided a maximum speed of 87 mph and an endurance of 3 hours 30 minutes. As with the D.D.2, it carried up to 220 lbs of bombs. Approximately 500 D.D.8 flying boats were built by the end of the war. They saw service from naval air stations along the English Channel and the Mediterranean.

Introduced by Hydravions Georges Levy in November 1917, the Georges-Levy 40 HB2 was a highly successful two- or three-seat maritime patrol flying boat. Unlike most of Levy's other flying boats, which were triplanes, the HB2 was a biplane. It had a wingspan of 60 ft 8.25 in., a length of 40 ft 8 in., and a loaded weight of 5,180 lbs. Powered by a 280 hp Renault 12Fe inline motor set in a pusher configuration, the HB2 had a maximum speed of 93 mph and an endurance of 6 hours 30 minutes. Its endurance, combined with its ability to carry 661 lbs of bombs (including the 176-lb G-bomb), made it ideal for use against submarines. It was also protected by a Lewis gun operated from the observer's nose seat. Approximately 100 were built by war's end. Finland purchased 12 HB2s after the war and used them in its struggle to maintain its independence after the Russian Revolution.

Because many of its seaplanes were susceptible to attacks by German fighters and therefore required land-based fighters to provide escort service, the French began a long search for a floatplane equivalent to a fighter. The French modified a number of licensed-built Sopwith 11/2 Strutters for service at sea, but it was the introduction of the SPAD XIV in early 1918 that finally gave France a seaplane worthy of a fighter. Designed by André Herbemont as a floatplane version of the earlier SPAD XII, the SPAD XIV had a wingspan of 32 ft 2 in., a length of 24 ft 3.25 in., and a loaded weight of 2,337 lbs. It was powered by a 220 hp Hispano-Suiza 8Cb V-type engine, which provided a maximum speed of 127 mph and a service ceiling of 5,000 m (16,404 ft). The SPAD XIV was well defended with a 7.7 mm fixed forward-firing synchronized Vickers machine gun and a twelve-round .37 cannon designed to fire through its hollow engine hub. A total of 40 were constructed by war's end, and all of them operated out of the French naval air station at Dunkirk.

Had the war continued into 1919, the Levy-Besson "High Seas" Flying Boat would have given the French a large flying boat similar in capabilities to the Felixstowe F.2A and Curtiss H.12 and H.16 "Large America." Although orders for 200 were issued, the contract was canceled shortly after the Armistice with just a few being built. Like its earlier flying boats, the "High Seas" Flying Boat used a triplane configuration. The top and center wings were of equal span, whereas the bottom was shorter and used a shoulder mounting on the hull. It had a span of 81 ft 8.25 in., a length of 58 ft 8.5 in., and a loaded weight of 15,873 lbs. Powered by three 350 hp Lorraine inline motors (the center engine was set in a pusher configuration, whereas the outer two were set in a tractor configuration), the Levy-Besson "High Seas" Flying Boat could reach a top speed of 96 mph and had an endurance of up to 12 hours. It carried a crew of four to five members, a radio set, and was armed with a thirty-five-round .75 mm cannon.

GERMAN NAVAL AIRCRAFT

Prior to the First World War, the German Navy had taken greater strides in developing naval aviation than any other power. In addition to its use of airships for long-range naval reconnaissance, the German Navy developed and used torpedo planes to a greater extent than did any other belligerent. It also experimented with using aircraft to lay mines and attack commercial shipping. As secretary of state of the Imperial Naval Office, *Grossadmiral* Alfred von Tirpitz, like Churchill, promoted research and development of seaplanes. Of equal importance, Wilhelm II's brother, *Grossadmiral Prinz* Heinrich, who had been one of the first in the German Navy to promote the use of zeppelins, would rely heavily upon seaplanes and torpedo planes as commander of the German Baltic Fleet during the war. Admirals Friedrich von Ingenohl, Hugo von Pohl, Reinhard Scheer, and Franz Hipper, who were successively commanders of the German High Seas Fleet, all saw the potential for aircraft as offensive weapons. The German Navy's failure to obtain sufficient numbers of naval aircraft during the war was not the result of a lack of understanding or support for aviation; rather, it was a result of the priority that the government gave to meeting the army's need for aircraft. One could also argue that the High Seas Fleet's zeppelin bombing campaign against Great Britain wasted scarce resources that could have been better used for naval aircraft.

With the exception of the Hansa-Brandenburg CC Flying Boat, approximately thirty-six of which served with the High Seas Fleet, Germany relied primarily upon floatplanes instead of flying boats. Introduced toward the end of 1914, the Friedrichshafen FF.33 proved to be the most widely produced German seaplane of the war, with almost 500 built in a number of varieties. Depending upon its version, it was used for reconnaissance, patrol, or fighter duties. Powered by a 150 hp Benz Bz.III inline motor, the FF.33 was capable of a maximum speed of 85 mph and had an endurance of 5–6 hours, depending on the version. The first in the series had a wingspan of 54 ft 11.5 in., a length of 34 ft 3.5 in., and a loaded weight of 3,636 lbs; whereas later versions (from version FF.33e onward) had a wingspan of 43 ft 7.5 in., a length of 28 ft 11.5 in., and a loaded weight of 3,020 lbs. Although the first four versions were unarmed, the FF.33e was armed with a ring-mounted Parabellum machine gun in the rear cockpit. The last three versions, beginning with the FF.33l, came equipped with an additional fixed forward-firing synchronized Spandau machine gun. One of the most famous

FF.33 floatplanes operated from the German auxiliary cruiser *Wolf* as it attacked shipping in the Pacific and Indian Oceans from November 1916 to February 1918. Dubbed the *"Wölfchen"* or "Wolf's cub," the FF.33 proved successful in identifying targets and using its wireless to signal the *Wolf* to come to its prey.

Even though the Friedrichshafen F.33 remained in production until late 1917, Friedrichshafen introduced a much larger two-seat armed reconnaissance floatplane earlier in that year with the FF.49c. It had a wingspan of 56 ft 3.25 in., a length of 38 ft 2.75 in., and a loaded weight of 4,723 lbs. Powered by a 200 hp Benz Bz.IV inline engine, the FF.49c had a maximum speed of 87 mph and an endurance of 5 hours 40 minutes. It was armed with one fixed forward-firing synchronized Spandau machine gun and one ring-mounted Parabellum machine gun in the rear cockpit. A total of 240 were produced by war's end, providing Germany with a highly successful armed reconnaissance aircraft that could also serve as a light bomber.

In 1916 the Germans would introduce a series of single-seat floatplane fighters in order to meet the challenge posed by British flying boats and seaplanes in the North Sea. The first of these to be introduced was the Albatros W.4, which followed the design of the Albatros D.I fighter but was larger (particularly in the span of the wings and the distance between the upper and lower wing). As in the D.I, the Albatros W.4 used a steel-tube framework and plywood covering around the fuselage, making it a rugged aircraft. It was powered by a 160 hp Mercedes D.III inline motor, which produced a maximum speed of 100 mph, a ceiling of 3,000 m (9,843 ft), and an endurance of 3 hours. The W.4 had a wingspan of 32 ft 2 in., a length of 27 ft 10.75 in., and a loaded weight of 2,354 lbs. It was armed with one or two fixed, forward-firing, synchronized Spandau machine guns. A total of 118 were produced through the end of 1917.

Like the Albatros W.4, the Hansa-Brandenburg K.D.W followed the design pattern of a land-based fighter; in this case the Hansa-Brandenburg D.I. Like its land-based counterpart, the K.D.W was designed by Ernst Heinkel and featured the unique star-strutter wing-brace system. It was powered by either a 150 hp Benz Bz.III inline engine or a 160 hp Maybach Mb.III inline engine, both of which produced a maximum speed of 106 mph and an endurance of 2 hours 30 minutes. Although slightly smaller than the Albatros W.4, with a wingspan of 30 ft 4.25 in., a length of 26 ft 3 in., and a loaded weight of 2,662 lbs, the K.D.W proved to be difficult to fly. As was the case with the Hansa-Brandenburg D.I, the star-strutter wing braces created additional drag. A total of fifty-eight K.D.W. float-planes were constructed, thirty-eight of which came equipped with a single fixed forward-firing synchronized Spandau machine gun. The last twenty were equipped with two Spandaus. The placement of the gun on the first thirty-eight was so far forward on the starboard side of the fuselage that it was virtually impossible for the pilot to access it in the event of a jam. This was corrected on the last twenty.

In early 1917 Hansa-Brandenburg introduced a two-seat fighter floatplane, the W.12, which quickly distinguished itself as a lethal fighting machine. With a wingspan of 36 ft 9 in., a length of 31 ft 6 in., and a loaded weight of 3,198 lbs, the W.12 was surprisingly maneuverable, yet easy to fly. Powered by either a 160 hp Mercedes D.III inline motor or a 150 hp Benz Bz.III inline motor, it could reach a maximum speed of 100 mph, climb to a service ceiling of 5,000 m (16,404 ft), and provide an endurance of 3 hours 30 minutes. It was armed with one or two fixed forward-firing synchronized Spandau machine guns and one ring-mounted Parabellum machine gun. With its wooden-framed construction and plywood-covered fuselage, the W.12 was capable of absorbing a lot of punishment while dishing out the same. Indeed, First Lieutenant Friedrich Christiansen, the leading ace of the High Seas Fleet, obtained thirteen kills in a W.12, including the shootdown of a British Coastal-Class airship on 17 December 1917.

Although the Hansa-Brandenburg W.12 had proven to be an effective two-seat fighter floatplane, the High Seas Fleet soon requested an upgraded version that would have greater endurance. The Hansa-Brandenburg W.19, introduced in January 1918, met this requirement by achieving an endurance of 5 hours compared with 3 hours 30 minutes of the W.12. To achieve this, engineer Ernst Heinkel designed what amounted to a larger version of the W.12, with the W.19 having a wingspan of 45 ft 3.4 in., a length of 34 ft 11.4 in., and a loaded weight 4,411 lbs. Despite the added size and weight, performance was not too adversely affected because the W.19 was powered by a 260 hp Maybach Mb.IV inline engine. This provided a maximum speed of 94 mph and a service ceiling of 5,000 m (16,404 ft). It was armed with one or two fixed forward-firing synchronized Spandau machine guns and one ring-mounted Parabellum machine gun.

The last major German seaplane to enter service was the Hansa-Brandenburg W.29, which was unique for its low-wing monoplane design. In many respects the W.29 was the same as the W.12 minus a wing. It used the same fuselage, the same engine, and the same wooden-framed, plywood construction. This naturally expedited production. The monoplane wing was longer in span and wider in chord, it was set at slightly more than 3 degrees dihedral (angled upward from the fuselage), and it was braced to the floats and fuselage. The W.29 had a wingspan of 44 ft 3.5 in., a length of 30 ft 8.5 in., and a loaded weight of 3,286 lbs. Powered by a 150 hp Benz Bz.III inline motor, the W.29 had a maximum speed of 109 mph, a service ceiling of 5,000 m (16,404 ft), and an endurance of 4 hours. It was armed with one or two fixed forward-firing synchronized Spandau machine guns and one ring-mounted Parabellum machine gun in the rear cockpit. A total of seventy-eight were produced by the end of the war.

ITALIAN NAVAL AIRCRAFT

The Italian Navy was the first to employ air power in a war when it used shipborne observation balloons to help its naval ships fire upon Turkish shore positions during the Tripolitan War of 1911–1912. Under *Capitano de Genio Navale* Allessandro Guidoni, the navy had also begun development of torpedo planes and experimented with employing seaplanes from the battleship *Dante Alighieri* and the cruisers *Amalfi* and *San Marco* prior to the outbreak of war in August 1914. By the time Italy entered the war 9 months later, it had established a series of naval air bases along its coasts and had converted the cruiser *Elba* into a seaplane carrier. Despite these early efforts, the Italian Navy possessed only around thirty aircraft when it entered the war.

After entering the war, Italy quickly began to manufacture some of the war's best seaplanes, including 982 licensed-built F.B.A. Type H flying boats that were produced by Società Idrovloanti Alta Italia (SIAI). These were slightly larger than the French original with a wingspan of 47 ft 8.75 in., a length of 33 ft 5.5 in., and a loaded weight of 3,086 lbs. They were powered by a 170 hp Isotta-Fraschini V-type engine set in a pusher configuration, which produced a maximum speed of 87 mph and a service ceiling of 5,000 m (16,404 ft). With an endurance of 3 hours 15 minutes, the Type H flying boat provided Italy ample coverage of the Adriatic.

Italy's best known series of flying boats were modeled after a captured Lohner Type L, which Italian forces managed to seize intact in May 1915. The Lohner L was handed over to Società Anomina

Nieuport-Macchi, which began production of copies in 1915, ultimately producing 140 Macchi L.1 flying boats and 200 Macchi L.3
flying boats that were only slightly different from the Lohner original. They had a wingspan of 52 ft 11.4 in., a length of 33 ft 7 in.,
and a loaded weight of 2,976 lbs. The L.1 was powered by a 150 hp
Isotta-Fraschini V-type engine set in a pusher configuration, which
produced a maximum speed of 68 mph, a service ceiling of 5,000 m
(16,404 ft), and an endurance of 4 hours. The L.3 was powered by a
160 hp Isotta-Fraschini V-type engine and featured a more streamlined design. It had a maximum speed of 90 mph, a service ceiling of
5,000 m (16,404 ft), and an endurance of 3 hours 5 minutes.

Introduced in 1918, the Macchi M.5 was distinctively different
from the earlier copies of the Lohner Type L. With a wingspan of 39
ft, a length of 26 ft 5 in., and a loaded weight of 2,138 lbs, the M.5
was smaller and more maneuverable than its Austrian opponents.
Although most were powered by a 160 hp Isotta-Fraschini V-4B
V-type engine set in a pusher configuration, which provided a maximum speed of 117 mph, some of the last to be produced were powered by a 250 hp Isotta-Fraschini V-type engine, which proved fast
enough at 130 mph to compete against land-based Austrian fighters.
Armed with two fixed forward-firing synchronized Fiat-Revelli machine guns and having an endurance of approximately 4 hours, the
M.5 played an important role in Italian efforts to secure control of
the Adriatic. A total of 344 were produced by war's end. The M.5 remained in service until 1923.

The last Italian flying boat to enter service before the end of the
war was the Macchi M.8, which was used primarily for armed reconnaissance and antisubmarine patrols. With a wingspan of 52 ft 6 in., a
length of 32 ft 8.4 in., and a loaded weight of 3,152 lbs, it was much
larger than the earlier M.5. Powered by a 170 hp Isotta-Fraschini
V-type engine set in a pusher configuration, the M.8 reached a maximum speed of 93 mph, climbed to a service ceiling of 5,000 m
(16,404 ft), and had an endurance of 4 hours. It was armed with one
forward-firing ring-mounted Revelli machine gun and carried four
110-lb bombs. A total of 57 entered service before the end of the war.

RUSSIAN NAVAL AIRCRAFT

By 1900 the Russian Imperial Navy had adopted balloons to en-
hance scouting of enemy vessels. In the aftermath of Russia's defeat

in the Russo–Japanese War of 1904–1905, during which its Pacific and Baltic Fleets had been virtually annihilated, Grand Duke Alexander Mikhailovich, an admiral in the navy and cousin to Tsar Nicholas II, saw aircraft as a means of rebuilding Russian naval power. Impressed by Louis Blériot's cross-Channel flight, Alexander reallocated funds that had been raised for building warships during the Russo–Japanese War to purchase airplanes from France, to train Russian pilots, and to build a naval air school in the Crimea. By 1912, the Russian Navy had organized air services for its Baltic and Black Sea Fleets.

By the time the war broke out in 1914, the Russians possessed a small number of Sikorsky S-10 Hydro floatplanes, which had entered service with the Baltic Fleet in the summer of 1913. The S-10 Hydro was based on a land-based racing prototype, but it had a slightly larger wingspan of 44 ft 11.3 in. (the top wing was approximately 16 ft longer than the bottom wing), a length of 26 ft 3 in., and a loaded weight of 2,381 lbs. Its 100 hp Argus inline motor could produce a maximum speed of 62 mph. They were used primarily for unarmed reconnaissance in the Baltic. Only sixteen were produced because the Russko-Baltiisky Vagonny Zaved placed a heavier priority on producing the Sikorsky *Ilya Muromets*.[3]

Even though Sikorsky had developed only one seaplane that entered production, one of his leading rivals, Dimitry Pavlovich Grigorovich, would build a series of flying boats while serving as chief engineer of the Shchetinin works in St. Petersburg. At first Shchetinin produced licensed-built Farman and Nieuport aircraft, but after making repairs to a Donnet-Leveque Type A flying boat, Grigorovich designed a version of his own that closely resembled it. After the Grigorovich M.5 flying boat was introduced in the spring of 1915, production moved beyond the prototype stage with approximately 100 M.5s being constructed. The M.5 had a wingspan of 44 ft 8 in., a length of 28 ft 3.25 in., and a loaded weight of 2,116 lbs. Powered by either a 100 hp Clerget rotary engine or 100 hp Gnôme Monosoupape rotary engine set in a pusher configuration, the M.5 could reach a maximum speed of 65 mph and climb to a service ceiling of 3,300 m (10,826 ft). It had an endurance of 4 hours. The observer sat in the front cockpit in the nose of the hull and operated a free-firing machine gun (various types were used). Small bombs were also carried onboard. It was used primarily with the Russian Black Sea Fleet, operating out of Russian coastal bases or from Russian seaplane carriers, the hydrocruisers *Imperator Nikolai I* and *Imperator Alexandr I*, both of which could carry six to eight M.5s. Its slow speed made in vulnerable to enemy fighters, ultimately forcing it to be reallocated for service as a trainer. It would continue in this latter role until 1925.

Introduced in early 1916, the M.9 was by far the most successful of Grigorovich's flying boats, with approximately 500 produced. With a wingspan of 52 ft 6 in., a length of 29 ft 6.25 in., and a loaded weight of 3,395 lbs, the M.9 was larger and heavier than the M.5. Because of Russia's chronic shortage of engines, a variety were used on the M.9. The most common was the 150 hp Salmson Canton-Unné radial motor, which was set in a pusher configuration. Although it could reach a maximum speed of just 68 mph and it had a service ceiling of just 3,000 m (9,843 ft), the M.9 was extremely seaworthy and proved to be highly effective for reconnaissance, patrolling, and light bombing duties. It saw service in both the Baltic Sea and the Black Sea, either operating from naval bases or from seaplane carriers. Although designed for a three-man crew, it normally carried just a pilot and one observer. It was protected with a pivot-mounted machine gun (a great variety were used) in the nose compartment, and it also carried small bombs. After the war, the M.9 was used effectively by the Red Army along the Volga during the Russian Civil War.

In 1917 Grigorovich introduced the M.11, which proved to be his last flying boat to be produced in great numbers. With a wingspan of 28 ft 8.4 in., a length of 24 ft 11 in., and a loaded weight of 2,041 lbs, the M.11 also provided some armor protection around the hull. Its 110 hp Le Rhône rotary engine, which was set in a pusher configuration, provided a maximum speed of 92 mph and an endurance of 2 hours 40 minutes. It would see service with both the Baltic Sea Fleet and the Black Sea Fleet. In addition, a few were modified with skis for use on frozen lakes. Approximately 75 were produced before the Russian Revolution disrupted production.

U. S. NAVAL AIRCRAFT

Although the United States had given birth to heavier-than-air flight, the U.S. Navy proved to be slow to respond to this new technology. By 1910, however, public pressure led Admiral of the Navy George Dewey to appoint Captain Washington Irving Chambers to investigate the possibilities of naval aviation. Over the next couple of years, Chambers initiated experiments that resulted in the first successful shipboard takeoff and landing and the first successful airplane catapult. Although many within the naval hierarchy considered these experiments a waste of precious resources, Captain Bradley A. Fiske, a member of the Navy's General Board, enthusiastically supported them. Indeed, in 1910 Fiske had even proposed defending the Philippines with a fleet of torpedo-carrying aircraft. Undaunted by the criticism of his superiors, Fiske received a 1912 patent for a device designed to carry and launch a torpedo from the air. In the meantime, a few junior naval officers had received flight training, which Rear Admiral Frank Jack Fletcher put to use for reconnaissance while leading naval forces in seizing Veracruz in April 1914. Despite Fletcher's commendation of their usefulness in the Veracruz operation, the navy's few aircraft were obsolete by European standards when the United States entered the First World War in April 1917.

Whereas the United States may not have possessed a large number of naval aircraft, it possessed one of the leading naval aircraft designers of the time in Glenn Curtiss. Prior to the war, Curtiss had begun trying to design a flying boat capable of crossing the Atlantic in hopes of winning a £10,000 prize offered by the London *Daily Mail* for the first nonstop trans-Atlantic crossing. Working with Royal Naval Commodore John C. Porte, Curtiss developed the first of his "America" series of flying boats. Although the outbreak of war prevented the trip, it put Curtiss in the business of supplying military versions of his "America" flying boat, designated as the H-4 "Small America," to the United States and Great Britain; however, its twin 100 hp Curtiss OX-5 inline engines proved to be too underpowered for effective use in maritime patrol. As a result, only about sixty were produced.

Curtiss enjoyed far greater success with the H-12 "Large America," which entered service with the RNAS in 1917 and became the first American-built aircraft to achieve a victory when it shot down a zeppelin over the North Atlantic. The British version of the H-12 was powered by twin 275 hp Rolls-Royce Eagle I inline motors, whereas the American version was powered by twin 330 hp Liberty 12 V-type engines (both types were set in a pusher configuration). The H-12 had a wingspan of 92 ft 8 in., a length of 46 ft 9 in., and a loaded weight of 7,989 lbs. It was capable of reaching 85 mph, had a service ceiling of 10,800 ft (3,292 m), and had an endurance of 6 hours, making it an effective maritime patrol aircraft. Its four-man crew was protected by three or four Lewis guns, and it could carry either two 230-lb bombs or four 100-lb bombs. A total of seventy were produced, with the British acquiring fifty and the U.S. Navy obtaining the rest. They remained in service until 1921.

In 1918 Curtiss introduced the H-16 "Large America," which was slightly larger and more powerful than the earlier H-12. The H-16 had a wingspan of 95 ft, a length of 46 ft 1 in., and a loaded weight of 10,900 lbs. Powered by two 400 hp Liberty V-type engines, which were set in a tractor configuration, the H-16 could reach a maximum speed of 95 mph and could climb to a service ceiling of 9,950 ft (3,033 m). It had an endurance of 4 hours.[4] Its four-man crew were well protected with five or six Lewis machine guns, and it carried four 230-lb bombs. With approximately 330 being produced, the H-16 was built in greater quantities than any other twin-engine Curtiss flying boat. The H-16 played a critical role in the Allied convoy system. Even though it did not sink any U-boats, it damaged several and successfully limited Allied shipping losses to just three ships in the areas it patrolled. It remained in service with the U.S. Navy until 1928.

In addition to his large twin-engine flying boats, Curtiss also produced the single-engine Curtiss HS flying boat, which was introduced in 1917. With a wingspan of 74 ft, a length of 39 ft, and a loaded weight of 6,432 lbs, it was surprisingly fast and maneuverable. Powered by a 350 hp Liberty V-type engine that was set in a pusher configuration, the Curtiss HS could reach a maximum speed of 82 mph, climb to a service ceiling of 5,200 ft (1,585 m), and have an endurance of up to 6 hours 20 minutes. It was used extensively for antisubmarine patrols from French naval air stations. Later versions were modified by extending the wingspan by 6 ft so that it could carry a heavier bomb to use against German U-boats. Its two-man crew was protected by one .30 caliber Marlin machine gun, and it carried two 230-lb bombs. A total of 673 were ultimately produced, and it remained in service until 1926.

In the same year that he introduced the HS flying boat, Curtiss introduced the N-9 floatplane, which was very similar to the more famous land-based JN-4 "Jenny." It had a wingspan of 53 ft 3 in., a length of 30 ft 10 in., and a loaded weight of 2,765 lbs. Powered by a 150 hp Hispano-Suiza 8A V-type engine, the N-9 had a maximum speed of 80 mph, a service ceiling of 9,850 ft (3,002 m), and an endurance of 3 hours. Approximately 560 were produced by war's end. It would continue to serve as the navy's primary floatplane trainer until 1926.

NOTES

1. American aviator Eugene Ely, a pilot for the Curtiss firm, successfully took off on 14 November 1910 in his 50 hp Curtiss Pusher from a special platform built on the cruiser *Birmingham*. Then, on 18 January 1911, Ely landed the same aircraft on the battleship *Pennsylvania*.

2. The F.17 was designed so that, when its wings were folded, it could fit within the hold of the *Campania*.

3. Sikorsky attempted to build a floatplane version of his *Ilya Muromets*, but the added weight of the floats made it difficult to fly.

4. Those purchased by the British were usually reequipped with twin 375 hp Rolls-Royce inline engines.

AIRCRAFT BY COUNTRY

Austro-Hungarian
Aviatik C.I
Etrich Taube
Hansa-Brandenburg C.I
Lloyd C Types
Lohner B Types and C.I
Phönix C.I
Phönix D-Series.

British
Airco D.H.2
Airco D.H.4
Airco D.H.9
Armstrong Whitworth F.K.8
Avro 504
Bristol Fighter F.2B "Brisfit"
Bristol Scout
Felixstowe F.2A and F.3
Handley-Page 0/100
Handley-Page 0/400
Martinsyde G 100 "Elephant"
Royal Aircraft Factory B.E.2 Series
Royal Aircraft Factory F.E.2 Series
Royal Aircraft Factory R.E.8
    "Harry Tate"
Royal Aircraft Factory S.E.5 and
    S.E.5a
Short 184
Sopwith 11/2 Strutter
Sopwith F.1 Camel
Sopwith Pup

Sopwith Tabloid
Sopwith Triplane
Vickers F.B.5 "Gun-Bus"

French
Blériot XI
Breguet 14
Caudron G.III and G.IV
Caudron R.11
Farman M.F.7 and M.F.11
Hanriot HD.1
Morane-Saulnier A.1
Morane-Saulnier L
Nieuport 11 and 16
Nieuport 17
Salmson 2A2
SPAD VII
SPAD XIII
Voisin Types 1–6
Voisin Types 8 and 10

German
A.E.G. C.IV
Albatros C.X and C.XII
Albatros D.V and D.Va
D.F.W. C-Types
Fokker D.VII
Fokker D.VIII
Fokker Dr.I
Fokker Eindecker

German, cont.
Friedrichshafen FF33 and FF49
Friedrichshafen G-Types
Gotha G.IV
Halbertstadt CL.II and CL.IV
Hannover CL.II and CL.IIIa
Hansa-Brandenburg W.29
Junkers CL.I
Junkers D.I
Junkers J.I
L.F.G. (Roland) C.II
L.V.G. C.V and C.VI
Pfalz D.III and D.IIIa
Rumpler C-Types
Siemens-Schuckert D.III and D.IV
Zeppelin (Staaken) R Types
Zeppelin P-Type Airship

Italian
Ansaldo A-I Balilla (Hunter)
Ansaldo S.V.A.5 "Primo"
Caproni Ca.1

Caproni Ca.5
Macchi M.5

Russian
Anatra D and DS
Grigorovich Flying Boats
Sikorsky *Ilya Muromets*
Sikorsky S-16

U. S.
Curtiss H-12 and H-16 Large
    America
Curtiss JN-4 "Jenny"
Wright *Military Flyer*

AIRCRAFT BY PRIMARY ROLE

Bomber Aircraft
Airco D.H.4
Airco D.H.9
Breguet 14
Caproni Ca.1
Caproni Ca.5
Caudron R.4 and R.11
Friedrichshafen G-Types
Gotha G.IV
Handley-Page 0/100
Handley-Page 0/400
Martinsyde G 100 "Elephant"
Sikorsky *Ilya Muromets*
Sopwith 11/2 Strutter
Voisin Types 1–6
Voisin Types 8 and 10
Zeppelin (Staaken) R Types
Zeppelin P-Type Airship

Fighter and Attack Aircraft
Airco D.H.2
Albatros D.V and D.Va
Ansaldo A-I Balilla (Hunter)
Bristol Fighter F.2B "Brisfit"
Fokker D.VII
Fokker D.VIII
Fokker Dr.I
Fokker Eindecker
Halbertstadt CL.II and CL.IV
Hannover CL.II and CL.IIIa

Hanriot HD.1
Junkers CL.I
Junkers D.I
Morane-Saulnier A.1
Nieuport 11 and 16
Nieuport 17
Pfalz D.III and D.IIIa
Phönix D.I, D.II, and D.III
Royal Aircraft Factory F.E.2-Series
Royal Aircraft Factory S.E.5 and
    S.E.5a
Siemens-Schuckert D.III
    and D.IV
Sikorsky S-16
Sopwith F.1 Camel
Sopwith Pup
Sopwith Triplane
SPAD VII
SPAD XIII
Vickers F.B.5 "Gun-Bus"

Naval Aircraft
Curtiss H-12 and H-16 Large
    America
Felixstowe F.2A and F.3
Friedrichshafen FF33 and FF49
Grigorovich Flying Boats
Hansa-Brandenburg W.29
Macchi M.5, M.7, and M.8
Short 184

Reconnaissance Aircraft
A.E.G. C.IV
Albatros C.X and C.XII
Anatra D and DS
Ansaldo S.V.A.5 "Primo"
Armstrong Whitworth F.K.8
Aviatik C.I
Avro 504
Bleriot XI
Bristol Scout
Caudron G.III and G.IV
Curtiss JN-4 "Jenny"
D.F.W. C-Types
Etrich Taube
Farman M.F.7 and M.F.11

Hansa-Brandenburg C.I
Junkers J.I
L.F.G. (Roland) C.II
L.V.G. C.V and C.VI
Lloyd C Types
Lohner B Types and C.I
Morane-Saulnier L
Phönix C.I
Royal Aircraft Factory B.E.2 Series
Royal Aircraft Factory R.E.8
   "Harry Tate"
Rumpler C-Types
Salmson 2A2
Sopwith Tabloid

AIRCRAFT IN ALPHABETICAL ORDER

A.E.G. C.IV

Courtesy of Art-Tech\Aerospace\M.A.R.S\TRH\Navy Historical.

COUNTRY OF ORIGIN: Germany

MANUFACTURER: Allgemeine Elektrizitäts Gellschaft

TYPE: Reconnaissance, Observation, and Light Bombing

CREW: 2

DIMENSIONS: Wingspan 44 ft 2 in.; Length 23 ft 5.5 in.; Height 10 ft 11.8 in.

LOADED WEIGHT: 2,464 lbs

POWER PLANT: 1 x 160 hp Mercedes D.III inline

PERFORMANCE: 99 mph maximum speed; 5,000 m (16,404 ft) service ceiling; 4 hour endurance

ARMAMENT: 1 x 7.92 mm fixed forward-firing, synchronized Spandau machine gun; 1 x 7.92 mm free-firing Parabellum machine gun

TOTAL PRODUCTION: Approximately 400

SERVICE DATES: 1916–1918

SUMMARY: Having been encouraged to enter the aircraft industry by the German High Command, Allgemeine Elektrizitäts Gellschaft (A.E.G.), which was Germany's leading electrical firm, had produced a small number of B-type and C-type reconnaissance aircraft prior to the introduction of its most widely produced model, the C.IV, in 1916. With the exception of the wood used for its wing ribs, steel-tube framing was used for all other parts of the aircraft—the airframe, struts, wing spars, ailerons, undercarriage, and tail structure. Whereas this made for a slow production process, the end result was a sturdy aircraft that performed well and could absorb a lot of punishment.

AIRCO D.H.2

Courtesy of Art-Tech\Aerospace\M.A.R.S\TRH\Navy Historical.

COUNTRY OF ORIGIN: Great Britain

MANUFACTURER: Aircraft Manufacturing Company

TYPE: Fighter (Pusher)

CREW: 1

DIMENSIONS: Wingspan 28 ft 3 in.; Length 25 ft 2.5 in.; Height 9 ft 6.5 in.

LOADED WEIGHT: 1,441 lbs

POWER PLANT: 1 x 100 hp Gnôme Monosoupape rotary or 1 x 110 hp Le Rhône rotary

PERFORMANCE: 93 mph maximum speed; 14,000 ft (4,267 m) service ceiling; 3 hour endurance

ARMAMENT: 1 x .303 caliber flexible-mounted Lewis machine gun

TOTAL PRODUCTION: Approximately 400

SERVICE DATES: 1915–1917

SUMMARY: Lacking a synchronized gear that would allow firing through the arc of the propeller, the British had relied upon a series of pusher types that allowed for a forward range of fire. Designed by Geoffrey de Havilland, the D.H.2 was a smaller single-seat fighter that was designed to end the so-called Fokker scourge. Although it was equipped with a movable Lewis gun, pilots had a difficult time trying to maneuver the D.H.2 and fire the gun at the same time, so they quickly improvised a method of fixing the gun in a forward-firing position. Their rotary engines also produced a tremendous amount of torque, which caused many an inexperienced pilot to enter a deadly spin. Crashes were almost always fatal because the engine and propeller were behind the pilot. Despite these hazards, the D.H.2 was more than a match for the Fokker Eindeckers. It was soon outclassed by German biplane fighters that began entering the war in mid-1916. Nevertheless, the D.H.2 remained in service on the Western Front until mid-1917.

AIRCO D.H.4

Courtesy of Art-Tech\Aerospace\M.A.R.S\TRH\Navy Historical.

COUNTRY OF ORIGIN: Great Britain

MANUFACTURER: Aircraft Manufacturing Company

TYPE: Bomber

CREW: 2

DIMENSIONS: Wingspan 42 ft 4.6 in.; Length 30 ft 8 in.; Height 10 ft 5 in.

LOADED WEIGHT: 3,472 lbs

POWER PLANT: 1 x 375 hp Rolls Royce Eagle VIII inline or 1 x 400 hp Liberty V-12

PERFORMANCE: 143 mph maximum speed; 22,000 ft (6,705 m) service ceiling; 3 hour 45 minute endurance

ARMAMENT: 1 or 2 x .303 caliber fixed forward-firing synchronized Vickers machine guns; 1 or 2 .303 caliber ring-mounted Lewis machine guns; 460 lbs of bombs

TOTAL PRODUCTION: 1,449 produced in Great Britain; 4,844 produced in the United States

SERVICE DATES: 1917–1932

SUMMARY: Designed by Geoffrey de Havilland, the D.H.4 is regarded as one of the best light bombers to serve in the war because its speed and maneuverability allowed it to be used in daylight, whereas most other bombers had to operate at night or with heavy escort. It was also one of the few designs that were mass produced in the United States in time to see action toward the end of the war. The D.H.4 did have one major drawback in that its fuel tank was placed between the pilot and observer, which made it difficult for them to communicate and provided a greater likelihood of the gas tank being struck and bursting in flame.

AIRCO D.H.9

Courtesy of Art-Tech\Aerospace\M.A.R.S\TRH\Navy Historical.

COUNTRY OF ORIGIN: Great Britain

MANUFACTURER: Aircraft Manufacturing Company

TYPE: Bomber

CREW: 2

DIMENSIONS: Wingspan 42 ft 4.6 in.; Length 30 ft 6 in.; Height 11 ft 2 in.

LOADED WEIGHT: 3,669 lbs

POWER PLANT: 1 x 230 hp B.H.P. Siddeley Puma inline

PERFORMANCE: 111 mph maximum speed; 15,500 ft (4,724 m) service ceiling; 4 hour 30 minute endurance

ARMAMENT: 1 x .303 caliber fixed forward-firing synchronized Vickers machine gun; 1 or 2 .303 caliber ring-mounted Lewis machine guns; 460 lbs of bombs

TOTAL PRODUCTION: 3,204

SERVICE DATES: 1917–1918

SUMMARY: Intended as an improvement to the D.H.4, the D.H.9 was in fact a poor substitute. Its chief problem was the 230 hp B.H.P. Siddeley Puma inline engine, which was known for being underpowered and for chronic breakdowns. A later version, the D.H.9a, was equipped with either a 375 hp Rolls-Royce Eagle VIII inline engine or the 400 hp Liberty V-12 engine. Their success proved that the basic design of the D.H.9 was fine; unfortunately, it came too late in the war to make a substantial difference.

ALBATROS C.X AND C.XII (PICTURED)

Courtesy of Art-Tech\Aerospace\M.A.R.S\TRH\Navy Historical.

COUNTRY OF ORIGIN: Germany

MANUFACTURER: Albatros Werke

TYPE: Reconnaissance and Artillery Observation

CREW: 2

DIMENSIONS: Wingspan 47 ft 1.5 in.; Length 30 ft 0.25 in.; Height 11 ft 1.8 in.

LOADED WEIGHT: 3,669 lbs

POWER PLANT: 1 x 260 hp Mercedes D.IVa inline

PERFORMANCE: 109 mph maximum speed; 5,000 m (16,404 ft) service ceiling; 3 hour 30 minute endurance

ARMAMENT: 1 x 7.92 mm fixed forward-firing synchronized Spandau machine gun; 1 x 7.92 mm free-firing Parabellum machine gun

TOTAL PRODUCTION: Approximately 400

SERVICE DATES: 1917–1918

SUMMARY: The Albatros C.X and C.XII were the last in a series of unarmed reconnaissance aircraft produced by Albatros Werke. Noted for its rugged construction, which relied upon a plywood covering of its fuselage, the C.X and C.XII were more streamlined than their predecessors, having a more curved, elliptical fuselage and nose section.

ALBATROS D.V (PICTURED) AND D.VA*

Courtesy of Art-Tech\Aerospace\M.A.R.S\TRH\Navy Historical.

COUNTRY OF ORIGIN: Germany

MANUFACTURER: Albatros Werke

TYPE: Fighter

CREW: 1

DIMENSIONS: Wingspan 29 ft 8.25 in.; Length 24 ft 0.6 in.; Height 8 ft 10.25 in.

LOADED WEIGHT: 2,061 lbs

POWER PLANT: 1 x 180 hp Mercedes D.IIIa inline

PERFORMANCE: 103 mph maximum speed; 6,250 m (20,505 ft) service ceiling; 2 hour endurance

ARMAMENT: 2 x 7.92 mm fixed forward-firing synchronized Spandau machine guns

TOTAL PRODUCTION: Approximately 1,500

SERVICE DATES: 1917–1918

SUMMARY: The Albatros D.V and D.Va were the most widely produced Albatros fighters. As with the earlier versions, it was noted for its plywood construction, which allowed it to absorb a great deal of punishment. In addition, the D.V and D.Va featured a more rounded, streamlined fuselage, a sesquiplane layout, and steel-tube V-struts to support the wings. Even though it was soon outclassed by the Sopwith Camel and SPAD XIII and ceased production in February 1918, it remained in service until the end of the war.

Captured Aircraft

ANATRA D AND DS* (PICTURED)
Courtesy of Art-Tech\Aerospace\M.A.R.S\TRH\Navy Historical.

COUNTRY OF ORIGIN: Russia

MANUFACTURER: Zavod A. A. Anatra

TYPE: Reconnaissance

CREW: 2

DIMENSIONS: Wingspan 40 ft 7 in.; Length 26 ft 6 in.; Height 10 ft 5 in.

LOADED WEIGHT: 2,566 lbs

POWER PLANT: 1 x 150 hp Salmson Canton-Unné radial

PERFORMANCE: 89 mph maximum speed; 4,300 m (14,108 ft) service ceiling; 3 hour 30 minute endurance

ARMAMENT: 1 x 7.7 mm fixed forward-firing synchronized Vickers machine gun; 1 x 7.7 mm ring-mounted Lewis machine gun

TOTAL PRODUCTION: Approximately 200 Anatra D and 100 Anatra DS

SERVICE DATES: 1916–1918

SUMMARY: Closely resembling German and Austro-Hungarian Aviatik fighters, the Anatra D and DS were the best Russian-designed and Russian-built reconnaissance aircraft of the war; unfortunately they had a tendency to be nose heavy, which sometimes resulted in crashes when power was reduced for landings. In addition, shortages of good lumber for the struts forced the Anatra company to manufacture wings spars out of two overlapping parts that were glued and taped together. Although these held up fine in stable flight, they were prone to fall apart when the aircraft was forced to undertake evasive maneuvers.

*Captured Aircraft

ANSALDO A-I BALILLA (HUNTER)

Courtesy of Art-Tech\Aerospace\M.A.R.S\TRH\Navy Historical.

COUNTRY OF ORIGIN: Italy

MANUFACTURER: Società Gio. Ansaldo & Cia.

TYPE: Fighter

CREW: 1

DIMENSIONS: Wingspan 25 ft 2.33 in.; Length 22 ft 5.25 in.; Height 8 ft 3.67 in.

LOADED WEIGHT: 1,951 lbs

POWER PLANT: 1 x 220 hp SPA.6A inline

PERFORMANCE: 137 mph maximum speed; 5,000 m (16,404 ft) service ceiling; 1 hour 30 minute endurance

ARMAMENT: 2 x 7.7 mm fixed forward-firing synchronized Vickers machine guns

TOTAL PRODUCTION: 150

SERVICE DATES: 1917–1918

SUMMARY: The Ansaldo A-I Balilla marked Italy's attempt to introduce a fighter of its own design. Even though its speed and climbing ability compared favorably with other fighters of its era, it lacked the maneuverability required for frontline service. As a result, the Italians were forced to relegate it to bomber escort duty.

ANSALDO S.V.A.5 "PRIMO"
Courtesy of Art-Tech\Aerospace\M.A.R.S\TRH\Navy Historical.

COUNTRY OF ORIGIN: Italy

MANUFACTURER: Società Gio. Ansaldo & Cia.

TYPE: Reconnaissance

CREW: 1 or 2

DIMENSIONS: Wingspan 29 ft 10.25 in.; Length 26 ft 6.8 in.; Height 10 ft 6 in.

LOADED WEIGHT: 2,315 lbs

POWER PLANT: 1 x 220 hp SPA.6A inline or 1 x 265 hp SPA.6A inline

PERFORMANCE: 143 mph maximum speed; 6,000 m (19,685 ft) service ceiling; 4 hour endurance

ARMAMENT: 2 x 7.7 mm fixed forward-firing synchronized Vickers machine guns

TOTAL PRODUCTION: Approximately 2,000 by 1927

SERVICE DATES: 1918–1929

SUMMARY: Originally intended to serve as a fighter, the Ansaldo S.V.A.5 lacked the maneuverability required for front-line service. As a result, most were reconfigured as two-seat armed reconnaissance aircraft and light bombers. The Primo was also used in one of the great propaganda feats of the war when a squadron of six Primos dropped leaflets over Vienna on 9 August 1918.

ARMSTRONG WHITWORTH F.K.8

Courtesy of Art-Tech\Aerospace\M.A.R.S\TRH\Navy Historical.

COUNTRY OF ORIGIN: Great Britain

MANUFACTURER: Sir W. G. Armstrong Whitworth Aircraft Ltd.

TYPE: Reconnaissance and Light Bomber

CREW: 2

DIMENSIONS: Wingspan 43 ft 6 in.; Length 31 ft; Height 11 ft

LOADED WEIGHT: 2,811 lbs

POWER PLANT: 1 x 160 hp Beardmore inline

PERFORMANCE: 95 mph maximum speed; 13,000 ft (3,962 m) service ceiling; 3 hour endurance

ARMAMENT: 1 x .303 caliber fixed forward-firing synchronized Vickers machine gun; 1 x .303 caliber free-firing Lewis machine gun; 160 lbs of bombs

TOTAL PRODUCTION: Approximately 1,500

SERVICE DATES: 1917–1918

SUMMARY: Nicknamed the "Big Ack," the Armstrong Whitworth F.K.8 was without question the best British C-type reconnaissance aircraft of the war. It was also one of the few nontraining aircraft of the time to be equipped with dual controls in the event that the pilot was injured in aerial combat. A rugged, strong aircraft, the "Big Ack" played a key role in providing close ground support, including laying down smoke screens during the Allied counteroffensive of 1918.

AVIATIK C.I

Courtesy of Art-Tech\Aerospace\M.A.R.S\TRH\Navy Historical.

COUNTRY OF ORIGIN: Austria-Hungary

MANUFACTURER: Oesterreichisch-Ungarische Flugzeugfabrik "Aviatik"

TYPE: Reconnaissance

CREW: 2

DIMENSIONS: Wingspan 27 ft 6 in.; Length 22 ft 6 in.; Height 7 ft 5 in.

LOADED WEIGHT: 2,152 lbs

POWER PLANT: 1 x 185 hp Austro-Daimler

PERFORMANCE: 111 mph maximum speed; 6,400 m (20,997 ft) service ceiling; 3 hour 30 minute endurance

ARMAMENT: 1 x 7.62 mm fixed forward-firing Schwarzlose machine gun; 1 x 7.62 ring-mounted Schwarzlose machine gun

TOTAL PRODUCTION: 167

SERVICE DATES: 1914–1918

SUMMARY: Designed by Julius von Berg, the Aviatik C.I was at first not well received by pilots because it was lighter and had more sensitive controls. Although this made it more difficult to fly, it also provided it greater maneuverability when challenged by enemy fighters; unfortunately, the first aircraft produced in the series placed the observer in the front seat, which did not offer a good range of defensive fire. This was later corrected in the C.III series. The Aviatic C type was also occasionally used as a single-seat photo-reconnaissance fighter because they proved as effective as the Aviatik D.I without the observer's weight.

AVRO 504

Courtesy of Art-Tech\Aerospace\M.A.R.S\TRH\Navy Historical.

COUNTRY OF ORIGIN: Great Britain

MANUFACTURER: A. V. Roe & Company

TYPE: Multipurpose (Reconnaissance, Light Bomber, Fighter, Trainer)

CREW: 1 or 2

DIMENSIONS: Wingspan 36 ft; Length 29 ft 5 in.; Height 10 ft 5 in.

LOADED WEIGHT: 1,660 lbs

POWER PLANT: 1 x 100 hp Gnôme Monosoupape rotary or 110 hp Le Rhône rotary

PERFORMANCE: 82 mph maximum speed; 12,000 ft (3,658 m) service ceiling; 4 hour 30 minute endurance (Gnôme); or 95 mph maximum speed; 16,404 ft (5,000 m) service ceiling; 3 hour endurance (Le Rhône)

ARMAMENT: None; 1 x .303 caliber fixed forward-firing synchronized Lewis machine gun; 80 lbs of bombs

TOTAL PRODUCTION: 8,970 in Great Britain; approximately 2,000 in the Soviet Union

SERVICE DATES: 1913–1933

SUMMARY: The Avro 504 ranks as the best multipurpose aircraft of the war, if not all time. Used primarily for reconnaissance and training purposes early in the war, it was gradually pressed into service as a fighter and light bomber to make up for aircraft shortages. In one of the most successful bombing raids of the war, a squadron of Avro 504s successfully dropped bombs on the German zeppelin hangers at Friedrichshafen.

BLÉRIOT XI

Courtesy of Art-Tech\Aerospace\M.A.R.S\TRH\Navy Historical.

COUNTRY OF ORIGIN: France

MANUFACTURER: Société des Avions Blériot

TYPE: Reconnaissance and Trainer

CREW: 1 or 2

DIMENSIONS: Wingspan 29 ft 7 in.; Length 25 ft 7 in.; Height 8 ft 5 in.

LOADED WEIGHT: 1,378 lbs

POWER PLANT: 1 x 70 hp Gnôme rotary

PERFORMANCE: 66 mph maximum speed; 914 m (3,000 ft) service ceiling; 3 hour 30 minute endurance

ARMAMENT: Rifle, pistols, flechetts (steel darts), up to 50 lbs of bombs

TOTAL PRODUCTION: Approximately 800

SERVICE DATES: 1910–1915

SUMMARY: Made famous by its 1909 flight across the English Channel, the Blériot XI played a key role in providing aerial reconnaissance during Italy's 1911 war against the Turks and during the opening stages of the First World War. Its low service ceiling unfortunately made it susceptible to ground fire, forcing it to be withdrawn from front-line service and relegated to training service.

BREGUET 14

Courtesy of Art-Tech\Aerospace\M.A.R.S\TRH\Navy Historical.

COUNTRY OF ORIGIN: France

MANUFACTURER: Société des Avions Louis Breguet

TYPE: Bomber and Reconnaissance

CREW: 2

DIMENSIONS: Wingspan 48 ft 9 in.; Length 29 ft 1.25 in.; Height 10 ft 9.8 in.

LOADED WEIGHT: 3,891 lbs

POWER PLANT: 1 x 300 hp Renault inline

PERFORMANCE: 121 mph maximum speed; 5,791 m (19,000 ft) service ceiling; 2 hour 45 minute endurance

ARMAMENT: 1 x 7.7 mm fixed forward-firing synchronized Vickers machine gun; 2–3 x 7.7 mm free-firing Lewis machine guns; 520 lbs of bombs

TOTAL PRODUCTION: 8,500 by 1927

SERVICE DATES: 1917–1932

SUMMARY: Without question the Breguet 14 was the most successful French daytime bomber of the war, making it very comparable to the contemporary Airco D.H.4. It was surprisingly fast and maneuverable for its size, and it possessed a tremendous amount of defensive firepower, making it able to hold its own against enemy fighters.

BRISTOL FIGHTER F.2B "BRISFIT"

Courtesy of Art-Tech\Aerospace\M.A.R.S\TRH\Navy Historical.

COUNTRY OF ORIGIN: Great Britain

MANUFACTURER: British & Colonial Aeroplane Company

TYPE: Fighter

CREW: 2

DIMENSIONS: Wingspan 39 ft 3 in.; Length 25 ft 10 in.; Height 9 ft 9 in.

LOADED WEIGHT: 2,779 lbs

POWER PLANT: 1 x 275 hp Rolls-Royce Falcon III inline

PERFORMANCE: 125 mph maximum speed; 20,000 ft (6,096 m) service ceiling; 3 hour endurance

ARMAMENT: 1 x .303 caliber fixed forward-firing synchronized Vickers machine gun; 1–2 x .303 caliber ring-mounted Lewis machine guns; 240 lbs of bombs

TOTAL PRODUCTION: Approximately 5,200

SERVICE DATES: 1918–1933

SUMMARY: The Brisfit is generally considered to be one of the best two-seat fighters of the war. At first British pilots made the mistake of flying it in tight formations, but they soon learned to rely upon its maneuverability and firepower to take on enemy fighters. With its synchronized forward-firing machine gun operated by the pilot and ring-mounted machine guns operated by the observer, the Brisfit had a tremendous advantage in firepower during aerial combat.

BRISTOL SCOUT

Courtesy of Art-Tech\Aerospace\M.A.R.S\TRH\Navy Historical.

COUNTRY OF ORIGIN: Great Britain

MANUFACTURER: British & Colonial Aeroplane Company

TYPE: Reconnaissance, Fighter, and Antizeppelin Patrol

CREW: 1

DIMENSIONS: Wingspan 24 ft 7 in.; Length 20 ft 8 in.; Height 8 ft 6 in.

LOADED WEIGHT: 1,440 lbs

POWER PLANT: 1 x 110 hp Clerget rotary

PERFORMANCE: 110 mph maximum speed; 16,404 ft (5,000 m) service ceiling; 2 hour endurance

ARMAMENT: 1 x .303 caliber fixed forward-firing synchronized Vickers machine gun

TOTAL PRODUCTION: 236

SERVICE DATES: 1914–1916

SUMMARY: Introduced shortly before the outbreak of the First World War, the Bristol Scout was one of the fastest aircraft available in the opening stages of the war. Although it was intended for reconnaissance, a few enterprising British pilots attached a Lewis gun to its top wing so that it could fire over the arc of the propeller. Had the British possessed a synchronization gear earlier enough, the Bristol Scout would have been far more lethal than the Fokker Eindeckers. By the time a synchronization gear became available in 1916, its capabilities as a fighter had already been surpassed.

CAPRONI CA.1

Courtesy of Art-Tech\Aerospace\M.A.R.S\TRH\Navy Historical.

COUNTRY OF ORIGIN: Italy

MANUFACTURER: Società di Aviazione Ing. Caproni

TYPE: Bomber

CREW: 4

DIMENSIONS: Wingspan 72 ft 10 in.; Length 35 ft 9 in.; Height 12 ft 2 in.

LOADED WEIGHT: 7,280 lbs

POWER PLANT: 3 x 100 hp Fiat A.10 in-line

PERFORMANCE: 72 mph maximum speed; 4,000 m (13,123 ft) service ceiling; 3 hour 30 minute endurance

ARMAMENT: 2–4 x 6.5 mm ring-mounted Revelli machine guns; 1,000 lbs of bombs

TOTAL PRODUCTION: 166

SERVICE DATES: 1915–1918

SUMMARY: With the exception of Russia, Italy was the only power to enter the First World War with a large multi-engine bomber. Designed by Giovanni Caproni, the Ca.1 had many unique features. Two of its engines, which were configured as tractors, were braced to the twin booms that connected the nacelle to the tail section. The remaining engine was housed in the rear of the nacelle and operated a pusher propeller. Its crew was well protected with ring-mounted machine guns that provided a good range of forward and rearward fire.

CAPRONI CA.5

Courtesy of Art-Tech\Aerospace\M.A.R.S\TRH\Navy Historical.

COUNTRY OF ORIGIN: Italy

MANUFACTURER: Società di Aviazione Ing. Caproni

TYPE: Bomber

CREW: 4

DIMENSIONS: Wingspan 77 ft; Length 41 ft 4 in.; Height 14 ft 8 in.

LOADED WEIGHT: 11,700 lbs

POWER PLANT: 3 x 300 hp Fiat A.12 bis inline

PERFORMANCE: 95 mph maximum speed; 4,572 m (15,000 ft) service ceiling; 4 hour endurance

ARMAMENT: 2–4 x 6.5 mm ring-mounted Revelli machine guns; 1,190 lbs of bombs

TOTAL PRODUCTION: 255

SERVICE DATES: 1917–1918

SUMMARY: Similar in design to the Ca.1, the Ca.5 was more powerful and could carry a slightly heavier load. Its rear gunner was placed in a raised turret at the back of the nacelle, which provided for unobstructed fire above the rear propeller.

CAUDRON G.III (PICTURED) AND G.IV

Courtesy of Art-Tech\Aerospace\M.A.R.S\TRH\Navy Historical.

COUNTRY OF ORIGIN: France

MANUFACTURER: Caudron Freres

TYPE: Reconnaissance and Training

CREW: 2

DIMENSIONS: Wingspan 43 ft 11 in.; Length 21 ft; Height 8 ft 5 in. (G.III); Wingspan 56 ft 4 in.; Length 23 ft 6 in.; Height 8 ft 5 in. (G.IV)

LOADED WEIGHT: 1,565 (G.III); 2,915 lbs (G.IV)

POWER PLANT: 1 x 90 hp Anzani rotary (G.III); 2 x 80 hp Le Rhône rotary (G.IV)

PERFORMANCE: 69 mph maximum speed; 3,962 m (13,000 ft) service ceiling; 3 hour endurance (G.III); 82 mph maximum speed; 4,300 m (14,108 ft) service ceiling; 4 hour endurance (G.IV)

ARMAMENT: None (G.III); 2 x 7.7 mm free-firing or ring-mounted Lewis or Vickers machine guns (G.IV).

TOTAL PRODUCTION: Approximately 2,400 G.III types and 1,358 G.IV types

SERVICE DATES: 1914–1917

SUMMARY: The Caudron G.III and G.IV were two early French reconnaissance aircraft that were produced in large numbers. Whereas the G.III was unarmed, the G.IV was introduced in 1915 with twin tractor-configured engines placed on each side of the nacelle. The chief advantage that this provided was allowing for unobstructed forward fire from the front nose seat. A few were also equipped with a Lewis gun mounted on the top wing and designed to fire to the rear to ward off attacks in that direction.

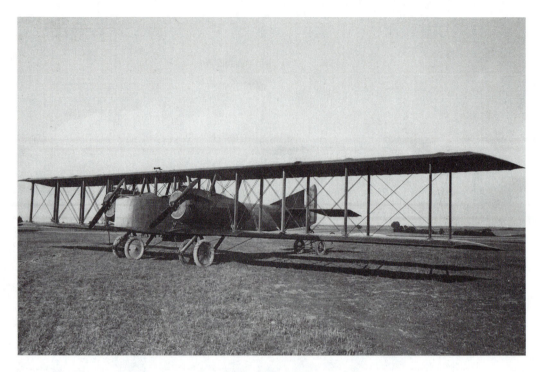

CAUDRON R.11

Courtesy of Art-Tech\Aerospace\M.A.R.S\TRH\Navy Historical.

COUNTRY OF ORIGIN: France

MANUFACTURER: Caudron Freres

TYPE: Fighter Escort

CREW: 3

DIMENSIONS: Wingspan 58 ft 9 in.; Length 36 ft 9 in.; Height 9 ft 2 in.

LOADED WEIGHT: 4,733 lbs

POWER PLANT: 2 x 215 hp Hispano-Suiza V-type

PERFORMANCE: 114 mph maximum speed; 5,950 m (19,521 ft) service ceiling; 3 hour endurance

ARMAMENT: 5 x 7.7 mm ring-mounted and free-firing Vickers machine guns

TOTAL PRODUCTION: 500

SERVICE DATES: 1918–1922

SUMMARY: Arriving in the spring of 1918, the Caudron R.11 was one of the most successful twin-engine fighter escort aircraft of the war. Its three-man crew had an ample range of forward and rearward fire. Although it could not outmaneuver German fighters, it could most definitely outgun them, as many a German pilot was to learn to his own detriment.

CURTISS H-12 (PICTURED) AND H-16 LARGE AMERICA
Courtesy of Art-Tech\Aerospace\M.A.R.S\TRH\Navy Historical.

COUNTRY OF ORIGIN: United States

MANUFACTURER: Curtiss Aeroplane and Motor Corporation

TYPE: Naval Antisubmarine and Reconnaissance Flying Boat

CREW: 4

DIMENSIONS: Wingspan 92 ft 8.5 in.; Length 46 ft 6 in.; Height 16 ft 6 in. (H-12); Wingspan 95 ft; Length 46 ft 1 in.; Height 17 ft 8 in. (H-16)

LOADED WEIGHT: 10,650 lbs (H-12); 10,900 lbs (H-16)

POWER PLANT: 2 x 275 hp Rolls-Royce Eagle I inline or 2 x 330 hp Liberty V-12 (H-12); 2 x 400 hp Liberty V-12 (H-16)

PERFORMANCE: 93 mph maximum speed; 10,800 ft (3,293 m) service ceiling; 6 hour endurance (Rolls-Royce Eagle I) or 85 mph maximum speed; 10,800 ft (3,293 m) service ceiling; 6 hour endurance (Liberty) in the H-12; 95 mph maximum speed; 9,950 ft (3,033 m) service ceiling; 4 hour endurance in the H-16

ARMAMENT: 3–4 x .303 caliber free-firing Lewis machine guns, or 3–4 x .30 caliber Lewis machine guns, and 472 lbs of bombs in the H-12; 5 x .30 caliber free-firing Lewis machine guns and 4 x 230-lb bombs in the H-16.

TOTAL PRODUCTION: 71 with Rolls-Royce Eagle I engines and 20 with Liberty engines (H-12); 334 (H-16)

SERVICE DATES: 1917–1921 (H-12); 1918–1928 (H-16)

SUMMARY: The H-12 and H-16 "Large America" series of flying boats were among the few American-made aircraft to see combat service during the First World War. The H-12, which was purchased in some quantity by the British, also served as the inspiration for the Felixstowe F.2a flying boat. Both proved to be highly useful in maritime patrol and antisubmarine warfare duties.

CURTISS JN-4 "JENNY"

Courtesy of Art-Tech\Aerospace\M.A.R.S\TRH\Navy Historical.

COUNTRY OF ORIGIN: United States

MANUFACTURER: Curtiss Aeroplane and Motor Company

TYPE: Trainer

CREW: 2

DIMENSIONS: Wingspan 43 ft 7 in.; Length 27 ft 4 in.; Height 9 ft 10.4 in.

LOADED WEIGHT: 2,030 lbs

POWER PLANT: 1 x 90 hp Curtiss OX-5 inline or 1 x 150 hp Wright-Hispano inline

PERFORMANCE: 75 mph maximum speed; 11,000 ft (3,353 m) service ceiling; 2 hour 15 minute endurance (Curtiss OX-5); 93 mph maximum speed; 10,525 ft (3,208 m) service ceiling; 3 hour endurance (Wright-Hispano)

ARMAMENT: None

TOTAL PRODUCTION: Approximately 5,000 military versions and 2,000 civilian versions

SERVICE DATES: 1915–1927

SUMMARY: One of the most popular and well-known aircraft of the World War I era, the JN-4 "Jenny" served as one of the primary trainers for American and British airmen. An earlier version, JN-3, had accompanied American troops in the Punitive Expedition into Mexico following Pancho Villa's raid on Columbus, New Mexico. It was one of the first aircraft to use a single-stick controller to operate the ailerons, elevator, and rudder.

D.F.W. C-TYPES
Courtesy of Art-Tech\Aerospace\M.A.R.S\TRH\Navy Historical.

COUNTRY OF ORIGIN: Germany

MANUFACTURER: Deutsche Flugzeug-Werke

TYPE: Reconnaissance

CREW: 2

DIMENSIONS: Wingspan 43 ft 7 in.; Length 25 ft 10 in.; Height 10 ft 8 in.

LOADED WEIGHT: 3,146 lbs

POWER PLANT: 1 x 200 hp Benz Bz IV in-line

PERFORMANCE: 100 mph maximum speed; 5,000 m (16,404 ft) service ceiling; 3 hour 30 minute endurance

ARMAMENT: 1 x 7.92 mm fixed forward-firing synchronized Spandau machine gun and 1 x 7.92 mm free-firing Parabellum machine gun

TOTAL PRODUCTION: 2,340 of all C-types by D.F.W.

SERVICE DATES: 1916–1918

SUMMARY: Even though they are not as well remembered as the Albatros and Fokker aircraft of the First World War, the D.F.W. C-type armed reconnaissance aircraft were the most widely produced German aircraft of the war. Noted for their rugged plywood construction and stable flying characteristics, the D.F.W. was widely used for photo-reconnaissance. Indeed, a few were equipped with special high-compression motors that allowed them to operate at well above 20,000 ft for extended periods.

ETRICH TAUBE

Courtesy of Art-Tech\Aerospace\M.A.R.S\TRH\Navy Historical.

COUNTRY OF ORIGIN: Austria-Hungary

MANUFACTURER: Lohner Werke, Albatros Werke, Deutsche Flugzeug-Werke, and others

TYPE: Reconnaissance and Training

CREW: 2

DIMENSIONS: Wingspan 47 ft 1 in.; Length 32 ft 3.75 in.; Height 10 ft 4 in.

LOADED WEIGHT: 1,918 lbs

POWER PLANT: 1 x 100 hp Mercedes D.I inline

PERFORMANCE: 71 mph maximum speed; 3,000 m (9,843 ft) service ceiling; 4 hour endurance

ARMAMENT: None

TOTAL PRODUCTION: Approximately 500

SERVICE DATES: 1909–1914

SUMMARY: Even though Austria-Hungary was well behind the other powers in aviation, it nevertheless produced one of the most widely used reconnaissance aircraft of the earlier stages of the war. Because it was licensed-produced by such a variety of manufacturers, the performance standards and dimensions vary widely. The Taube was noted for being easy to fly and for maintaining its stability in flight; unfortunately, this also meant that it lacked maneuverability, which quickly led to it being withdrawn from front-line service.

FARMAN M.F.7 (PICTURED) AND M.F.11
Courtesy of Art-Tech\Aerospace\M.A.R.S\TRH\Navy Historical.

COUNTRY OF ORIGIN: France

MANUFACTURER: Société Henri et Maurice Farman

TYPE: Reconnaissance, Bombing, and Training

CREW: 2

DIMENSIONS: Wingspan 50 ft 11 in.; Length 37 ft 9.5 in.; Height 11 ft (M.F.7) Wingspan 53 ft; Length 30 ft 8 in.; Height 10 ft 4 in. (M.F.11)

LOADED WEIGHT: 1,885 lbs (M.F.7); 2,046 lbs (M.F.11)

POWER PLANT: 1 x 70 hp Renault inline (M.F.7); 1 x 130 hp Renault 8C inline (M.F.11)

PERFORMANCE: 60 mph maximum speed; 4,000 m (13,123 ft) service ceiling; 3 hour 15 minute endurance (M.F.7); 80 mph maximum speed; 3,810 m (12,500 ft) service ceiling; 3 hour 45 minute endurance (M.F.11)

ARMAMENT: 1 x 7.7 mm free-firing Lewis or Hotchkiss machine gun (M.F.7); 1 x 7.7 mm free-firing Lewis or Hotchkiss machine gun and 288 lbs of bombs (M.F.11)

TOTAL PRODUCTION: 380 M.F.7 types and several thousand M.F.11 types

SERVICE DATES: 1914–1918

SUMMARY: Designed by Maurice Farman, the M.F.7 and M.F.11 were pusher biplanes that were used for reconnaissance and light bombing duties. Although its pusher configuration gave its observer an unobstructed forward line of fire, the M.F.7 and M.F.11 both proved vulnerable to attack from the rear. As a result, by 1916 their primary duty shifted from reconnaissance and day bombing to nighttime bombing, a role that they would continue to perform until the end of the war.

FELIXSTOWE F.2A AND F.3 (PICTURED)

Courtesy of Art-Tech\Aerospace\M.A.R.S\TRH\Navy Historical.

COUNTRY OF ORIGIN: Great Britain

MANUFACTURER: The Aircraft Manufacturing Company, Ltd.

TYPE: Naval Antisubmarine and Maritime Patrol Flying Boat

CREW: 4

DIMENSIONS: Wingspan 95 ft 7 in.; Length 46 ft 3 in.; Height 17 ft 6 in.

LOADED WEIGHT: 10,978 lbs

POWER PLANT: 2 x 345 hp Rolls-Royce Eagle VIII inline

PERFORMANCE: 95 mph maximum speed; 9,600 ft (2,926 m) service ceiling; 7 hour 15 minute endurance

ARMAMENT: 4–7 x .303 caliber free-firing Lewis guns; 920 lbs of bombs

TOTAL PRODUCTION: Approximately 100

SERVICE DATES: 1917–1927

SUMMARY: Influenced by the Curtiss H-12 "Large America" flying boat, the Felixstowe F.2A and F.3 featured a superior hull design that was more hydrodynamic. It became available at the height of the German U-boat campaign in 1917 and may have been responsible for sinking or damaging several U-boats, though evidence is inconclusive. At a minimum, however, the Felixstowe flying boats disrupted U-boat activity.

FOKKER D.VII

Courtesy of Art-Tech\Aerospace\M.A.R.S\TRH\Navy Historical.

COUNTRY OF ORIGIN: Germany

MANUFACTURER: Fokker Flugzeug-Werke

TYPE: Fighter

CREW: 1

DIMENSIONS: Wingspan 29 ft 3.5 in.; Length 22 ft 11.6 in.; Height 9 ft 2.25 in.

LOADED WEIGHT: 1,870 lbs

POWER PLANT: 1 x 160 hp Mercedes D.III inline or 1 x 185 hp B.M.W. inline

PERFORMANCE: 116 mph maximum speed; 6,100 m (20,013 ft) service ceiling; 2 hour endurance

ARMAMENT: 2 x 7.92 fixed forward-firing synchronized Spandau machine guns

TOTAL PRODUCTION: Approximately 1,000 (including those built by subcontractors)

SERVICE DATES: 1918

SUMMARY: The Fokker D.VII is generally considered the best German fighter of the war and ranks among the best fighters from any country. Its combination of speed, agility, and firepower made it a lethal weapon. In particular, it was noted for being able to hang on its propeller for a brief period before stalling, a maneuver that could catch an opponent by surprise. Unfortunately for Germany, the D.VII came too late in the war and in too few numbers to make a difference.

FOKKER D.VIII

Courtesy of Art-Tech\Aerospace\M.A.R.S\TRH\Navy Historical.

COUNTRY OF ORIGIN: Germany
MANUFACTURER: Fokker Flugzeug-Werke
TYPE: Fighter
CREW: 1
DIMENSIONS: Wingspan 27 ft 4.4 in.; Length 29 ft 2.75 in.; Height 8 ft 6.4 in.
LOADED WEIGHT: 1,334 lbs
POWER PLANT: 1 x 110 hp Oberursel U.II rotary
PERFORMANCE: 127 mph maximum speed; 6,100 m (20,013 ft) service ceiling; 1 hour 30 minute endurance
ARMAMENT: 2 x 7.92 fixed forward-firing synchronized Spandau machine guns

TOTAL PRODUCTION: 289
SERVICE DATES: 1918
SUMMARY: Had the war continued into 1919, the Fokker D.VIII or E.V monoplane fighter would have outclassed anything that the Allies had available. Its light weight and rotary engine gave it a turning ability second only to the Sopwith Camel, and it could climb rapidly, reaching its service ceiling in just 16 minutes. Although it employed the same steel-tube framework as earlier Fokker aircraft, it was covered by fabric instead of plywood.

FOKKER DR.I
Courtesy of Art-Tech\Aerospace\M.A.R.S\TRH\Navy Historical.

COUNTRY OF ORIGIN: Germany
MANUFACTURER: Fokker Flugzeug-Werke
TYPE: Fighter
CREW: 1
DIMENSIONS: Wingspan 23 ft 7.5 in.; Length 18 ft 11 in.; Height 9 ft 8 in.
LOADED WEIGHT: 1,290 lbs
POWER PLANT: 1 x 110 hp Oberursel UR.II rotary
PERFORMANCE: 103 mph maximum speed; 6,100 m (20,013 ft) service ceiling; 1 hour 30 minute endurance
ARMAMENT: 2 x 7.92 mm fixed forward-firing synchronized Spandau machine guns

TOTAL PRODUCTION: 320
SERVICE DATES: 1917–1918
SUMMARY: Perhaps no other aircraft of the First World War is better known than the Fokker Dr.I Triplane, if for no other reason than it was the favored aircraft of Manfred von Richthofen, the Red Baron. Although it was comparatively slow for its time period, the Dr.I more than compensated with its acrobatic maneuverability. Stress fractures of the wings resulted in a delay in production and ultimately caused Fokker to shift to the more reliable D.VII.

FOKKER EINDECKER

Courtesy of Art-Tech\Aerospace\M.A.R.S\TRH\Navy Historical.

COUNTRY OF ORIGIN: Germany
MANUFACTURER: Fokker Flugzeug-Werke
TYPE: Fighter
CREW: 1
DIMENSIONS: Wingspan 31 ft 2.75 in.;
   Length 23 ft 11.3 in.; Height 9 ft 1.75 in.
LOADED WEIGHT: 1,400 lbs
POWER PLANT: 1 x 100 hp Oberursel U.I
   rotary
PERFORMANCE: 87 mph maximum speed;
   3,500 m (11,483 ft) service ceiling;
   2 hour 45 minute endurance
ARMAMENT: 1 x 7.92 mm fixed forward-
   firing synchronized Parabellum or Spandau machine gun
TOTAL PRODUCTION: Approximately 220
   of all types
SERVICE DATES: 1915–1916
SUMMARY: Although the Fokker Eindecker
   was not particularly fast or maneuverable compared with many opposing Allied aircraft, it had the technological advantage of being the first aircraft
equipped with a interrupter gear synchronized to allow a machine gun to fire
through the arc of the propeller. As a result, Germans pilots flying an Eindecker
had a firepower advantage that would
not be matched by the Allies until the
summer of 1916. Although only a few
Eindeckers were available at any one
time and they were scattered across the
Western Front rather than concentrated
into squadrons, they had a dispropor-
tionate impact upon Allied aircraft, leading to what contemporaries referred to
as the "Fokker Scourge" from the fall of
1915 to the spring of 1916.

FRIEDRICHSHAFEN FF.33 AND FF.49

Courtesy of Art-Tech\Aerospace\M.A.R.S\TRH\Navy Historical.

COUNTRY OF ORIGIN: Germany

MANUFACTURER: Flugzeugbau Friedrichshafen

TYPE: Naval Reconnaissance Patrol/ Fighter Floatplane

CREW: 2

DIMENSIONS: (FF.33) Wingspan 54 ft 11.5 in.; Length 34 ft 3.5 in.; Height 12 ft 2.6 in.; (FF.49) Wingspan 56 ft 3.25 in.; Length 38 ft 2.75 in.; Height 14 ft 9.25 in.

LOADED WEIGHT: (FF.33) 3,637 lbs; (FF.44) 4,723 lbs

POWER PLANT: (FF.33) 1 x 150 hp Benz Bz.III inline; (FF.49) 1 x 200 hp Benz Bz.IV inline

PERFORMANCE: (FF.33) 74.5 mph maximum speed; 4,420 m (14,501 ft) service ceiling; 5–6 hour endurance; (FF.49) 87 mph maximum speed; 4,420 m (14,501 ft) service ceiling; 5–6 hour endurance

ARMAMENT: (FF.33) majority none, some with 1 x 7.92 mm fixed forward-firing synchronized Spandau machine gun and 1 x 7.92 mm free-firing Parabellum machine gun; (FF.49) 1 x 7.92 mm fixed forward-firing synchronized Spandau machine gun and 1 x 7.92 mm free-firing Parabellum machine gun

TOTAL PRODUCTION: (FF.33) Approximately 300; (FF.49) Approximately 240

SERVICE DATES: 1915–1918

SUMMARY: The Friedrichshafen FF.33 and FF.49 were the most widely used German floatplanes of the First World War. The first few series of FF.33s were unarmed reconnaissance types used for patrol duties in the North Sea. Later versions were equipped with both forward-firing synchronized machine guns and free-firing machine guns, as well as radio transmitters. One of the most famous of these aircraft was an FF.33l that worked in concert with the German commerce raider, the *Wolf,* helping it identify targets and avoid enemy warships during a 16-month tour of service in the Indian and Pacific Oceans.

FRIEDRICHSHAFEN G-TYPES

Courtesy of Art-Tech\Aerospace\M.A.R.S\TRH\Navy Historical.

COUNTRY OF ORIGIN: Germany

MANUFACTURER: Flugzeugbau Friedrichshafen

TYPE: Bomber

CREW: 3

DIMENSIONS: Wingspan 77 ft 11 in.; Length 42 ft 2 in.; Height 12 ft

LOADED WEIGHT: 8,686 lbs

POWER PLANT: 2 x 260 hp Mercedes D.IVa inline

PERFORMANCE: 88 mph maximum speed; 4,510 m (14,797 ft) service ceiling; 5 hour endurance

ARMAMENT: 2–3 x 7.92 mm free-firing Parabellum machine guns and up to 3,300 lbs of bombs

TOTAL PRODUCTION: 338

SERVICE DATES: 1917–1918

SUMMARY: Although it is not as well remembered as the Gotha bombers that attacked London, the Friedrichshafen G-types actually had a much higher bomb load capability than did the Gothas. They were used exclusively on the Western Front, but evidently never in attacks on Britain.

GOTHA G.IV

Courtesy of Art-Tech\Aerospace\M.A.R.S\TRH\Navy Historical.

COUNTRY OF ORIGIN: Germany

MANUFACTURER: Gothaer Waggonfabrik

TYPE: Bomber

CREW: 3

DIMENSIONS: Wingspan 77 ft 9.25 in.; Length 38 ft 11 in.; Height 14 ft 1.25 in.

LOADED WEIGHT: 7,997 lbs

POWER PLANT: 2 x 260 hp Mercedes D.IVa inline

PERFORMANCE: 87 mph maximum speed; 6,500 m (21,325 ft) service ceiling; 4–6 hour endurance

ARMAMENT: 2 x 7.92 mm free-firing Parabellum machine guns and up to 1,100 lbs of bombs

TOTAL PRODUCTION: Approximately 400

SERVICE DATES: 1916–1918

SUMMARY: The Gotha bombers are without question the most well-remembered bombers of the First World War because of a series of highly successful daylight raids on London beginning in May 1917. Although the Gothas ultimately had to resort to nighttime attacks, they had an important impact upon the British, forcing them to divert fighters from the Western Front to home defense and contributing to the decision to organize the Royal Air Force as an independent branch of service.

GRIGOROVICH FLYING BOATS

Courtesy of Art-Tech\Aerospace\M.A.R.S\TRH\Navy Historical.

COUNTRY OF ORIGIN: Russia

MANUFACTURER: Shchetinin

TYPE: Naval Reconnaissance, Patrol, and Bomber Flying Boat

CREW: 2

DIMENSIONS: Wingspan 52 ft 6 in.; Length 29 ft 6 in.

LOADED WEIGHT: 3,549 lbs

POWER PLANT: 1 x 150 hp Salmson Canton-Unné radial

PERFORMANCE: 68.3 mph maximum speed; 3,000 m (9,843 ft) service ceiling; 5 hour endurance

ARMAMENT: 1 x 7.7 mm free-firing Lewis machine gun

TOTAL PRODUCTION: Approximately 500

SERVICE DATES: 1916–1921

SUMMARY: Of the series of flying boats designed by Dimitry Pavlovich Grigorovich, the M.9 was the most successful and widely reproduced of the war. It was used in the Baltic and Black Seas, operating out of coastal bases or from seaplane carriers. After the war it would be used during the Russian Civil War by the Bolsheviks against the Whites along the Volga River. It later led to the M.24, which is pictured above.

HALBERTSTADT CL.II AND CL.IV (PICTURED)
Courtesy of Art-Tech\Aerospace\M.A.R.S\TRH\Navy Historical.

COUNTRY OF ORIGIN: Germany

MANUFACTURER: Halberstadt Flugzeug-Werke

TYPE: Fighter and Ground Attack

CREW: 2

DIMENSIONS: Wingspan 35 ft 4 in.; Length 23 ft 11.4 in. (CL.II) and 21 ft 5 in. (CL.IV); Height 9 ft 0.25 in.

LOADED WEIGHT: (CL.II) 2,493 lbs; (CL.IV) 2,393 lbs

POWER PLANT: 1 x 160 hp Mercedes D.III inline

PERFORMANCE: 103 mph maximum speed; 5,000 m (16,404 ft) service ceiling; 3 hour endurance

ARMAMENT: 1–2 x 7.92 mm fixed forward-firing synchronized Spandau machine guns, 1 x 7.92 mm rear-firing Parabellum gun; 110 lb; of bombs or grenades

TOTAL PRODUCTION: Approximately 900 CL.IIs and 700 CL.IVs

SERVICE DATES: 1917–1918

SUMMARY: Originally intended for service as an escort fighter, the Halberstadt CL.II and CL.IV came to be used primarily to provide close ground support. It was a sturdy aircraft that could absorb a lot of punishment, while expending a lot of firepower itself. Its single cockpit allowed the pilot and observer/tail gunner to sit back to back, which made communication easy. It also allowed them a perfect vantage point for strafing enemy troop positions.

HANDLEY-PAGE 0/100

Courtesy of Art-Tech\Aerospace\M.A.R.S\TRH\Navy Historical.

COUNTRY OF ORIGIN: Great Britain

MANUFACTURER: Handley Page Ltd.

TYPE: Bomber, Heavy

CREW: 3–5

DIMENSIONS: Wingspan 100 ft; Length 62 ft 10 in.; Height 22 ft

LOADED WEIGHT: 14,000 lbs

POWER PLANT: 2 x 250 hp Rolls-Royce Eagle II inline

PERFORMANCE: 85 mph maximum speed; 7,000 ft (2,134 m) service ceiling; 8 hour endurance

ARMAMENT: 3–5 x .303 caliber free-firing Lewis machine guns and 1 x 1,600-lb bomb or 2,000 lbs of bombs

TOTAL PRODUCTION: 46

SERVICE DATES: 1916–1918

SUMMARY: Although produced in small numbers, the Handley-Page 0/100 marked an attempt by the British to develop a heavy bomber that would be capable of striking German targets in retaliation for the German zeppelin raids against Great Britain. Even though it was protected by 3–5 machine guns, it proved to be too vulnerable to German fighters for use as a daytime bomber. As a result, it was relegated to nighttime bombing.

HANDLEY-PAGE 0/400
Courtesy of Art-Tech\Aerospace\M.A.R.S\TRH\Navy Historical.

COUNTRY OF ORIGIN: Great Britain

MANUFACTURER: Handley Page Ltd. and Standard Aircraft Corporation

TYPE: Bomber, Heavy

CREW: 3–5

DIMENSIONS: Wingspan 100 ft; Length 62 ft 10 in.; Height 22 ft

LOADED WEIGHT: 13,300 lbs

POWER PLANT: 2 x 360 hp Rolls-Royce Eagle VIII inline or 2 x 400 hp Liberty V-12

PERFORMANCE: 97.5 mph maximum speed; 8,500 ft (2,591 m) service ceiling; 8 hour endurance

ARMAMENT: 3–5 x .303 caliber free-firing Lewis machine guns and 1 x 1,600-lb bomb or 2,000 lbs of bombs

TOTAL PRODUCTION: Approximately 400 in Great Britain and 107 in the United States

SERVICE DATES: 1918–1920

SUMMARY: Based on the same airframe as the Handley-Page 0/100, the Handley Page 0/400 was faster, more maneuverable, and able to operate from a higher service ceiling. It was used extensively as part of the Royal Air Force's Independent Bombing Force's strategic campaign against targets in Western Germany. Had the war continued into 1919, a large number of American-built versions would have entered the conflict.

HANNOVER CL.II AND CL.IIIA

Courtesy of Art-Tech\Aerospace\M.A.R.S\TRH\Navy Historical.

COUNTRY OF ORIGIN: Germany

MANUFACTURER: Hannoversche Waggon-fabrik

TYPE: Fighter and Ground Attack

CREW: 2

DIMENSIONS: Wingspan 38 ft 4.75 in.; Length 24 ft 10.5 in.; Height 9 ft 2.25 in.

LOADED WEIGHT: 2,378 lbs

POWER PLANT: 1 x 180 hp Argus As.III inline or 1 x 160 hp Mercedes D.III inline

PERFORMANCE: 103 mph maximum speed; 5,000 m (16,404 ft) service ceiling; 3 hour endurance

ARMAMENT: 1 x 7.92 mm fixed forward-firing synchronized Spandau machine gun and 1 x 7.92 mm free-firing Parabellum machine gun

TOTAL PRODUCTION: Approximately 1,000

SERVICE DATES: 1917–1918

SUMMARY: Like the Halberstadt CL.II and CL.IV, the Hannover CL.II and CL.IIIa were originally intended for service as escort fighters for German bombers and reconnaissance aircraft. By late 1917, however, they became an integral part of the German Army's plan for close air support of ground forces. By strafing enemy positions and dropping grenades, the CL-types were to help pin the enemy down and help German troops advance. This proved to be critical to the early successes of the German spring offensive of 1918.

HANRIOT HD.1

Courtesy of Art-Tech\Aerospace\M.A.R.S\TRH\Navy Historical.

COUNTRY OF ORIGIN: France

MANUFACTURER: Aeroplanes Hanriot de Cie; Nieuport-Macchi

TYPE: Fighter

CREW: 1

DIMENSIONS: Wingspan 28 ft 6 in.; Length 19 ft 2 in.; Height 8 ft 4.5 in.

LOADED WEIGHT: 1,335 lbs

POWER PLANT: 1 x 120 hp Le Rhône rotary or 1 x 110 hp Le Rhône rotary

PERFORMANCE: 114 mph maximum speed; 6,300 m (20,670 ft) service ceiling; 2 hour 30 minute endurance

ARMAMENT: 1 x 7.7 mm fixed forward-firing synchronized Vickers machine gun

TOTAL PRODUCTION: Approximately 100 in France and 900 in Italy

SERVICE DATES: 1917–1918

SUMMARY: Although designed for service with France, the Hanriot HD.1 was rejected in favor of the SPAD VII. Nevertheless, Hanriot sold approximately 100 HD.1 fighters to Belgium and Italy. In addition, Nieuport-Macchi built approximately 900 licensed-built versions, which served as the chief Italian fighter through the end of the war.

HANSA-BRANDENBURG C.I

Courtesy of Art-Tech\Aerospace\M.A.R.S\TRH\Navy Historical.

COUNTRY OF ORIGIN: Austria-Hungary

MANUFACTURER: Phönix Flugzeug-Werke, Ungarische Flugzeugwerke

TYPE: Reconnaissance, Light Bombing, and Artillery Observation

CREW: 2

DIMENSIONS: Wingspan 40 ft 2.25 in.; Length 27 ft 8.6 in.; Height 10 ft 11 in.

LOADED WEIGHT: 2,888 lbs

POWER PLANT: 1 x 160 hp Austro-Daimler inline

PERFORMANCE: 87 mph maximum speed; 5,791 m (19,000 ft) service ceiling; 3 hour endurance

ARMAMENT: 1 x 7.62 mm fixed forward-firing Schwarzlose machine gun; 1 x 7.62 mm ring-mounted Schwarzlose machine gun

TOTAL PRODUCTION: 1,258

SERVICE DATES: 1916–1918

SUMMARY: Although Hansa-Brandenburg was a German company, the Hansa-Brandenburg C.I biplane was unique in that it was constructed only within Austria-Hungary. With a total of 1,258 built under license in eighteen different series by Phönix and Ufag, the Hansa-Brandenburg C.I was Austria-Hungary's most widely produced and used reconnaissance aircraft during the war. Designed by Ernst Heinkel, who would gain greater fame for his World War II–era aircraft, the C.I was a high-powered aircraft that was more than capable of evading enemy fighters and defending itself. In addition, its ability to carry a 200-lb bomb load made it useful as a light bomber. It also proved to be an effective ground attack plane because of its forward- and rear-firing machine guns and because it could carry eight fragmentation bombs under its wings.

HANSA-BRANDENBURG W.29

Courtesy of Art-Tech\Aerospace\M.A.R.S\TRH\Navy Historical.

COUNTRY OF ORIGIN: Germany

MANUFACTURER: Hansa und Brandenburgische Flugzeug-Werke

TYPE: Naval Maritime Patrol Floatplane

CREW: 2

DIMENSIONS: Wingspan 44 ft 3.5 in.; Length 30 ft 8.5 in.; Height 9 ft 10.1 in.

LOADED WEIGHT: 3,287 lbs

POWER PLANT: 1 x 150 hp Benz Bz.III inline

PERFORMANCE: 109 mph maximum speed; 5,000 m (16,404 ft) service ceiling; 4 hour endurance

ARMAMENT: 1–2 x 7.92 mm fixed forward-firing synchronized Spandau machine guns and 1 x 7.92 mm free-firing Parabellum machine gun

TOTAL PRODUCTION: 78

SERVICE DATES: 1918

SUMMARY: Introduced in the last year of the war, the Hansa-Brandenburg W.29 was the last major seaplane to by produced by Germany. It stood out from its predecessors because of its low-wing monoplane design, which made it faster and more maneuverable.

JUNKERS CL.I

Courtesy of Art-Tech\Aerospace\M.A.R.S\TRH\Navy Historical.

COUNTRY OF ORIGIN: Germany

MANUFACTURER: Junkers Flugzeug-Werke

TYPE: Fighter and Ground Attack

CREW: 2

DIMENSIONS: Wingspan 39 ft 6 in.; Length 25 ft 11 in.; Height 7 ft 9 in.

LOADED WEIGHT: 2,310 lbs

POWER PLANT: 1 x 180 hp Mercedes D.IIIa inline

PERFORMANCE: 100 mph maximum speed; 6,000 m (19,685 ft) service ceiling; 2 hour endurance

ARMAMENT: 2 x 7.92 mm fixed forward-firing synchronized Spandau machine guns and 1 x 7.92 mm free-firing Parabellum machine gun

TOTAL PRODUCTION: 47

SERVICE DATES: 1918

SUMMARY: Although it came too late in the war to make a difference, the Junkers CL.I was one of the best ground attack aircraft to appear in the war. Its all-metal construction and low monoplane design gave it little in common with other World War I aircraft. Had the war continued into 1919, it would have provided the Germans with a great advantage because its rugged construction could absorb a great deal of punishment. Although it is unclear whether or not it served on the Western Front, it was used against the Bolsheviks in the Baltic States after the war.

JUNKERS D.I

Courtesy of Art-Tech\Aerospace\M.A.R.S\TRH\Navy Historical.

COUNTRY OF ORIGIN: Germany
MANUFACTURER: Junkers Flugzeug-Werke
TYPE: Fighter
CREW: 1
DIMENSIONS: Wingspan 29 ft 6 in.; Length 23 ft 9 in.; Height 7 ft 4 in.
LOADED WEIGHT: 1,835 lbs
POWER PLANT: 1 x 185 hp B.M.W. inline
PERFORMANCE: 118 mph maximum speed; 6,000 m (19,685 ft) service ceiling; 1 hour 30 minute endurance
ARMAMENT: 2 x 7.92 mm fixed forward-firing synchronized Spandau machine guns

TOTAL PRODUCTION: 41
SERVICE DATES: 1918
SUMMARY: Like the CL.I, the Junkers D.1 was a low-wing monoplane of all-metal construction that had little resemblance to other World War I–era aircraft. It was surprisingly lightweight, yet rugged and agile. The D.I unfortunately appeared too late in the war for the Germans. Indeed, it most likely did not see combat prior to the Armistice. Afterward, they were used to assist the Baltic States against the Bolsheviks.

JUNKERS J.I

Courtesy of Art-Tech\Aerospace\M.A.R.S\TRH\Navy Historical.

COUNTRY OF ORIGIN: Germany

MANUFACTURER: Junkers Flugzeug-Werke

TYPE: Reconnaissance and Ground Support

CREW: 2

DIMENSIONS: Wingspan 52 ft 6 in.; Length 29 ft 10.4 in.; Height 11 ft 1 in.

LOADED WEIGHT: 4,787 lbs

POWER PLANT: 1 x 200 hp Benz Bz.IV in-line

PERFORMANCE: 96 mph maximum speed; 4,000 m (13,123 ft) service ceiling; 2 hour endurance

ARMAMENT: 2 x 7.92 mm fixed forward-firing synchronized Spandau machine guns and 1 x 7.92 mm free-firing Parabellum machine gun

TOTAL PRODUCTION: 227

SERVICE DATES: 1917–1918

SUMMARY: From as early as 1915, Dr. Hugo Junkers had been experimenting with an all-metal aircraft, ultimately introducing the Junkers J.I biplane in early 1917. It was ideal for providing close ground support because its all-metal construction, which included thicker armor around the floor of the fuselage, gave the pilot and observer/tail gunner ample protection from small arms fire while flying at low altitudes.

L.F.G. (ROLAND) C.II

Courtesy of Art-Tech\Aerospace\M.A.R.S\TRH\Navy Historical.

COUNTRY OF ORIGIN: Germany

MANUFACTURER: Luftfahrzeug Gesellschaft

TYPE: Reconnaissance and Escort

CREW: 2

DIMENSIONS: Wingspan 33 ft 9.5 in.; Length 25 ft 3.25 in.; Height 9 ft 6 in.

LOADED WEIGHT: 2,824 lbs

POWER PLANT: 1 x 160 hp Mercedes D.III inline

PERFORMANCE: 103 mph maximum speed; 4,572 m (15,000 ft) service ceiling; 4–5 hour endurance

ARMAMENT: 1 x 7.92 fixed forward-firing synchronized Spandau and 1 x 7.92 ring-mounted Parabellum machine gun

TOTAL PRODUCTION: Approximately 275

SERVICE DATES: 1916–1917

SUMMARY: Dubbed the "Walfisch" or Whale because of its rather bloated-looking fuselage, the L.F.G. Roland C.II was a precursor to the later CL-type ground support aircraft. Its wings were supported by a large "I"-shaped strut, which was designed to minimize drag and thereby improve its performance. Its unique semi-monocoque fuselage involved painstakingly wrapping several layers of plywood veneer strips around its wooden frame before covering it with fabric. This resulted in a smoothed curved surface with a high strength-to-weight ratio that held up well in combat conditions and adverse weather. Its one major defect was that the pilot's seat was so low in the fuselage that he had to land almost blindly.

LLOYD C-TYPES

Courtesy of Art-Tech\Aerospace\M.A.R.S\TRH\Navy Historical.

COUNTRY OF ORIGIN: Austria-Hungary

MANUFACTURER: Ungarische Lloyd Flugzeug und Motorenfabrik

TYPE: Reconnaissance and Training

CREW: 2

DIMENSIONS: Wingspan 45 ft 11 in.; Length 29 ft 6 in.; Height 11 ft 2 in.

LOADED WEIGHT: 2,888 lbs

POWER PLANT: 1 x 160 hp Austro-Daimler inline

PERFORMANCE: 83 mph maximum speed; 6,000 m (19,685 ft) service ceiling; 3 hour 30 minute endurance

ARMAMENT: 1 x 7.62 mm ring-mounted Schwarzlose machine gun

TOTAL PRODUCTION: Approximately 100

SERVICE DATES: 1916–1918

SUMMARY: The most numerous of the various C-types produced by Lloyd, the C.III was noted for its superb climbing ability, which was a prerequisite for crossing the Alps and serving in the mountainous terrain of the Italian Front. Its sweptback wings were also a unique feature that was not shared by many aircraft of the time. One main drawback was that its engine and radiator partially obstructed the pilot's forward view. In addition, it lacked the speed and maneuverability required for escaping from the last generation of Allied fighters, resulting in it being relegated to service as a trainer.

LOHNER B-TYPES (PICTURED) AND C.I

Courtesy of Art-Tech\Aerospace\M.A.R.S\TRH\Navy Historical.

COUNTRY OF ORIGIN: Austria-Hungary

MANUFACTURER: Lohnerwerke

TYPE: Armed Reconnaissance

CREW: 2

DIMENSIONS: (B.VII) Wingspan 50 ft 6 in.; Length 36 ft 9 in.; Height 12 ft 4 in.; (C.I) Wingspan 40 ft 9.75 in.; Length 30 ft 4.2 in.; Height 9 ft 9.75 in.

LOADED WEIGHT: (B.VII) 3,177 lbs; (C.I) 2,681 lbs

POWER PLANT: 1 x 160 hp Austro-Daimler inline

PERFORMANCE: 75–82 mph maximum speed; 3,500 m (11,483 ft) service ceiling; 3 hour 15 minute endurance

ARMAMENT: 1 x 7.62 mm ring-mounted Schwarzlose machine gun and up to 485 lbs of bombs

TOTAL PRODUCTION: 98 B-Types and 40 C-Types

SERVICE DATES: 1915–1917

SUMMARY: Based on a prewar design that finally entered production in 1915, the Lohner B.VII and C.I provided the Austro-Hungarian Army with both an excellent armed reconnaissance aircraft as well as a light bomber. With its ability to take off and land on short airfields, it was ideally suited for the mountainous terrain of the Italian Front. It was gradually replaced by more powerful aircraft, such as the Hansa-Brandenburg C.I and Phönix C.I, and relegated to service as trainers.

L.V.G. C.V AND C.VI (PICTURED)

Courtesy of Art-Tech\Aerospace\M.A.R.S\TRH\Navy Historical.

COUNTRY OF ORIGIN: Germany

MANUFACTURER: Luft-Verkehrs Gesellschaft

TYPE: Reconnaissance, Light Bombing, and Ground Attack

CREW: 2

DIMENSIONS: Wingspan 44 ft 8.5 in.; Length 26 ft 5.75 in.; Height 10 ft 6 in.

LOADED WEIGHT: 2,888 lbs

POWER PLANT: 1 x 200 hp Benz Bz.IV inline

PERFORMANCE: 106 mph maximum speed; 6,477 m (21,250 ft) service ceiling; 3 hour 30 minute endurance

ARMAMENT: 1 x 7.92 mm fixed forward-firing synchronized Spandau machine gun; 1 x 7.92 mm ring-mounted Parabellum machine gun; and up 250 lbs of bombs

TOTAL PRODUCTION: Approximately 1,200

SERVICE DATES: 1917–1918

SUMMARY: Although intended for armed reconnaissance, the L.V.G. C.V and C.VI's firepower and ability to carry up to 250 lbs of bombs made it well suited for ground support service. The chief drawback of the C.V was that its engine cowling and radiator obstructed the pilot's forward view. This was corrected in the C.VI version. In addition, the C.VI featured a reduced gap between the upper and lower wings, which were also set at a slight stagger to improve observation of the ground while in flight.

MACCHI M.5

Courtesy of Art-Tech\Aerospace\M.A.R.S\TRH\Navy Historical.

COUNTRY OF ORIGIN: Italy

MANUFACTURER: Società Anonima Nieuport-Macchi

TYPE: Naval Fighter and Maritime Patrol Flying Boat

CREW: 1

DIMENSIONS: Wingspan 39 ft 0.5 in.; Length 26 ft 5.3 in.; Height 10 ft 4.25 in.

LOADED WEIGHT: 2,138 lbs

POWER PLANT: 1 x 160 hp Isotta-Fraschini V-4B inline

PERFORMANCE: 117 mph maximum speed; 4,600 m (15,092 ft) service ceiling; 3 hour 15 minute endurance

ARMAMENT: 2 x 6.5 mm fixed forward-firing Fiat Revelli machine guns

TOTAL PRODUCTION: 240

SERVICE DATES: 1918–1923

SUMMARY: Although the original Macchi flying boats closely followed the design of a captured Lohner L-type flying boat, the M.5 marked a distinctively different design that was smaller and more maneuverable. It proved to be crucial in allowing Italy to seize control of the air space over the Adriatic and was more than capable of holding its own against land-based Austro-Hungarian fighters.

MARTINSYDE G.100 "ELEPHANT"

Courtesy of Art-Tech\Aerospace\M.A.R.S\TRH\Navy Historical.

COUNTRY OF ORIGIN: Great Britain

MANUFACTURER: Martin and Handasyde Ltd.

TYPE: Fighter, Bomber, and Reconnaissance

CREW: 2

DIMENSIONS: Wingspan 38 ft; Length 26 ft 6 in.; Height 9 ft 8 in.

LOADED WEIGHT: 2,424 lbs

POWER PLANT: 1 x 160 hp Beardmore inline

PERFORMANCE: 104 mph maximum speed; 16,404 ft (5,000 m) service ceiling; 4 hour 30 minute endurance

ARMAMENT: 2 x .303 caliber fixed forward-firing synchronized Lewis guns and up to 260 lbs of bombs

TOTAL PRODUCTION: Approximately 100 G.100s and 171 G.102s

SERVICE DATES: 1916–1918

SUMMARY: Originally intended to serve as a long-range escort fighter, the Martinsyde G.100, nicknamed the "Elephant" because of its size, saw service primarily as a light bomber. The Elephant remained in service on the Western Front until it was replaced by the Airco D.H.4 by the end of 1917. The British also employed them in Palestine and Mesopotamia until the end of the war.

MORANE-SAULNIER A.1

Courtesy of Art-Tech\Aerospace\M.A.R.S\TRH\Navy Historical.

COUNTRY OF ORIGIN: France

MANUFACTURER: Aeroplanes Morane-Saulnier

TYPE: Fighter and Trainer

CREW: 1

DIMENSIONS: Wingspan 27 ft 11 in.; Length 18 ft 6 in.; Height 7 ft 10 in.

LOADED WEIGHT: 1,431 lbs

POWER PLANT: 1 x 150 hp Gnôme Monosoupape rotary

PERFORMANCE: 129 mph maximum speed; 7,000 m (22,966 ft) service ceiling; 1 hour 30 minute endurance

ARMAMENT: 1–2 x 7.7 mm fixed forward-firing synchronized Vickers guns

TOTAL PRODUCTION: 1,210

SERVICE DATES: 1918

SUMMARY: Although produced in large numbers after being introduced in late 1917, the A.1 monoplane proved to be a failure as a fighter plane because the immense torque produced by its 150 hp Gnôme Monosoupape rotary engine made it prone to deadly spins. As a result, they were relegated to use as primary trainers with their wings being "clipped" to prevent them from flying, turning them into so-called penguins in which students learned the basics by taxiing at high speed.

MORANE-SAULNIER L

Courtesy of Art-Tech\Aerospace\M.A.R.S\TRH\Navy Historical.

COUNTRY OF ORIGIN: France

MANUFACTURER: Aeroplanes Morane-Saulnier

TYPE: Reconnaissance and Fighter

CREW: 1–2

DIMENSIONS: Wingspan 33 ft 9 in.; Length 20 ft 9 in.; Height 10 ft 4 in.

LOADED WEIGHT: 1,499 lbs

POWER PLANT: 1 x 80 hp Gnôme rotary or 1 x 80 hp Le Rhône rotary

PERFORMANCE: 71 mph maximum speed; 4,000 m (13,123 ft) service ceiling; 4 hour endurance

ARMAMENT: 1 x 7.7 mm fixed forward-firing Lewis or Hotchkiss machine gun

TOTAL PRODUCTION: Approximately 600 in France and 400 in Russia

SERVICE DATES: 1913–1916

SUMMARY: Originally serving as a reconnaissance aircraft upon the outbreak of the First World War, the Type L was transformed into a fighter in the spring of 1915 when pilot Roland Garros and designer Raymond Saulnier used the expedient of affixing metal wedges to the propellers and found that five of six rounds passed through with the other one being deflected. Beginning on 1 April 1915 Garros quickly proved the advantage of forward fire by shooting down five German aircraft in a 3-week period. They continued to serve in this role until they were replaced by Nieuport fighters in 1916.

NIEUPORT 11 AND 16 (PICTURED)

Courtesy of Art-Tech\Aerospace\M.A.R.S\TRH\Navy Historical.

COUNTRY OF ORIGIN: France

MANUFACTURER: Société Anonyme des Établissements Nieuport

TYPE: Fighter

CREW: 1

DIMENSIONS: Wingspan 24 ft 8 in.; Length 18 ft 1 in.; Height 8 ft

LOADED WEIGHT: 1,058 lbs

POWER PLANT: (Nieuport 11) 1 x 80 hp Le Rhône rotary; (Nieuport 16) 1 x 110 hp Le Rhône rotary

PERFORMANCE: 100–102 mph maximum speed; 5,000 m (16,404 ft) service ceiling; 2 hour 30 minute endurance

ARMAMENT: 1 x 7.7 mm fixed forward-firing Lewis machine gun mounted to the top wing

TOTAL PRODUCTION: Approximately 2,000 (including 540 built in Italy and 200 built in Russia)

SERVICE DATES: 1915–1917

SUMMARY: The Nieuport 11 was the first French aircraft specifically designed to serve as a fighter. Nicknamed the *Bébé* (Baby) because of its compact size, it was faster and more maneuverable than the Fokker Eindeckers. Because the French still lacked a synchronization gear, it had to rely upon a top-wing–mounted Lewis gun or Hotchkiss gun. It played a critical role in bringing an end to the Fokker Scourge and giving the Allies control of the skies over Verdun and the Somme. The Nieuport 16 used the same airframe as the Nieuport 11, but it sported a larger engine. It was also among the first Allied aircraft to have a synchronized gun.

NIEUPORT 17

Courtesy of Art-Tech\Aerospace\M.A.R.S\TRH\Navy Historical.

COUNTRY OF ORIGIN: France

MANUFACTURER: Société Anonyme des Établissements Nieuport

TYPE: Fighter

CREW: 1

DIMENSIONS: Wingspan 26 ft 9 in.; Length 19 ft; Height 7 ft 7.75 in.

LOADED WEIGHT: 1,234 lbs

POWER PLANT: 1 x 110 hp Le Rhône rotary or 1 x 130 hp Clerget 9B rotary

PERFORMANCE: 102 mph maximum speed (Le Rhône) and 118 mph maximum speed (Clerget); 5,300 m (17,388 ft) service ceiling; 2 hour endurance

ARMAMENT: 2 x 7.7 mm fixed forward-firing Lewis machine guns mounted on the top wing or 2 x 7.7 mm fixed forward-firing synchronized Vickers machine guns

TOTAL PRODUCTION: Approximately 2,000 (including 150 in Italy)

SERVICE DATES: 1916–1918

SUMMARY: Introduced in late spring 1916, the Nieuport 17 was the best wartime fighter produced by the Nieuport firm. Numerous Allied aces, such as Georges Guynemer, Edward Mannock, and Francesco Baracca, scored victories while flying the Nieuport 17. Like the Sopwith Camel, its rotary engine enabled it to make sharp right-degree turns, which gave it an advantage over German and Austro-Hungarian fighters.

PFALZ D.III AND D.IIIA (PICTURED)
Courtesy of Art-Tech\Aerospace\M.A.R.S\TRH\Navy Historical.

COUNTRY OF ORIGIN: Germany

MANUFACTURER: Pfalz Flugzeug-Werke

TYPE: Fighter

CREW: 1

DIMENSIONS: Wingspan 30 ft 10 in.; Length 22 ft 9.75 in.; Height 8 ft 9 in.

LOADED WEIGHT: 2,056 lbs

POWER PLANT: 1 x 160 hp Mercedes D.III inline

PERFORMANCE: 103 mph maximum speed; 5,182 m (17,000 ft) service ceiling; 2 hour 30 minute endurance

ARMAMENT: 2 x 7.92 mm fixed forward-firing synchronized Spandau machine guns

TOTAL PRODUCTION: Approximately 600

SERVICE DATES: 1917–1918

SUMMARY: Even though German pilots did not rate the Pfalz D.III and D.IIIa as highly as they did its contemporary Albatros and Fokker fighters, it was actually a very sturdy, capable fighter. In particular, its wings could withstand a steep dive better than its more-illustrious counterparts. This made it very well suited for carrying out attacks on Allied balloons.

PHÖNIX C.I

Courtesy of Art-Tech\Aerospace\M.A.R.S\TRH\Navy Historical.

COUNTRY OF ORIGIN: Austria-Hungary
MANUFACTURER: Phönix Flugzeug-Werke
TYPE: Reconnaissance
CREW: 2
DIMENSIONS: Wingspan 36 ft 1 in.; Length 24 ft 11.2 in.; Height 9 ft 8 in.
LOADED WEIGHT: 2,734 lbs
POWER PLANT: 1 x 230 hp Hiero inline
PERFORMANCE: 109 mph maximum speed; 5,235 m (17,175 ft) service ceiling; 3 hour 30 minute endurance
ARMAMENT: 1 x 7.62 fixed forward-firing synchronized Schwarzlose machine gun and 1 x 7.62 ring-mounted Schwarzlose machine gun
TOTAL PRODUCTION: 98 by Phönix and an additional 32 by Sweden after the war.
SERVICE DATES: 1918–1935

SUMMARY: The Phönix C.I was without question the best-armed reconnaissance aircraft produced by Austria-Hungary during the war and compares favorably with those produced by other powers. Well armed, fast at high altitudes, and highly maneuverable, the C.I could hold its own against enemy fighters. Because it closely resembled the Phönix D.I from a distance, many an enemy pilot made the mistake of coming on too close before realizing their mistake. It is believed that is what resulted in the loss of Italy's leading ace, Francesco Baracca. The C.1, unfortunately for Austria-Hungary, came too late and in too few numbers to make a difference in the war.

PHÖNIX D-SERIES

Courtesy of Art-Tech\Aerospace\M.A.R.S\TRH\Navy Historical.

COUNTRY OF ORIGIN: Austria-Hungary

MANUFACTURER: Phönix Flugzeug-Werke

TYPE: Fighter

CREW: 1

DIMENSIONS: Wingspan 32 ft 1.8 in.; Length 22 ft 1.8 in.; Height 9 ft 5 in.

LOADED WEIGHT: 2,097 lbs

POWER PLANT: 1 x 230 hp Hiero inline

PERFORMANCE: 115 mph maximum speed; 6,800 m (22,308 ft) service ceiling; 1 hour 45 minute endurance

ARMAMENT: 2 x 7.62 mm fixed forward-firing synchronized Schwarzlose machine guns

TOTAL PRODUCTION: 213 during the war and 38 purchased or produced by Sweden after the war

SERVICE DATES: 1917–1933

SUMMARY: The Phönix D-series of fighters were noted for being sturdy, well-built aircraft whose plywood fuselage could absorb a lot of punishment. The first type in the series proved to be a slow climber and lacked good maneuverability. Later types corrected this deficiency, giving Austria-Hungary a fighter that could hold its own against anything that the Allies had; unfortunately, they were in limited supply and came too late in the war.

ROYAL AIRCRAFT FACTORY B.E.2 SERIES
Courtesy of Art-Tech\Aerospace\M.A.R.S\TRH\Navy Historical.

COUNTRY OF ORIGIN: Great Britain

MANUFACTURER: Royal Aircraft Factory and several subcontractors

TYPE: Reconnaissance, Multipurpose

CREW: 2

DIMENSIONS: Wingspan 40 ft 9 in.; Length 27 ft 3 in.; Height 11 ft

LOADED WEIGHT: 2,100 lbs

POWER PLANT: 1 x 90 hp RAF 1a rotary

PERFORMANCE: 70 mph maximum speed; 10,000 ft (3,048 m) service ceiling; 3 hour endurance

ARMAMENT: 1 x .303 caliber spigot-mounted Lewis machine gun

TOTAL PRODUCTION: 3,535

SERVICE DATES: 1912–1918

SUMMARY: Although it was an able aircraft when it was introduced in 1912 and provided good reconnaissance service in the opening stages of the First World War, the B.E.2 proved to be easy prey for German fighters by 1915 because its inherent stability, which made it easy to fly, gave it little maneuverability. Rather than recognize the basic design problems of the B.E.2, the British simply attempted to add ever-more powerful motors. Although this increased its speed, it did little to make it a more nimble aircraft. As a result, more British pilots would be shot down in a B.E.2 than in any other aircraft.

ROYAL AIRCRAFT FACTORY F.E.2 SERIES

Courtesy of Art-Tech\Aerospace\M.A.R.S\TRH\Navy Historical.

COUNTRY OF ORIGIN: Great Britain

MANUFACTURER: Royal Aircraft Factory and several subcontractors

TYPE: Fighter, Reconnaissance, Night Bomber (Pusher)

CREW: 2

DIMENSIONS: Wingspan 47 ft 9 in.; Length 32 ft 3 in.; Height 12 ft 7 in.

LOADED WEIGHT: 2,970 lbs

POWER PLANT: 1 x 120 hp Beardmore inline

PERFORMANCE: 80 mph maximum speed; 9,000 ft (2,743 m) service ceiling; 3 hour endurance

ARMAMENT: 1 x .303 forward-firing Lewis machine gun; 1 x .303 rear-firing Lewis gun mounted on the top wing; and up to 350 lb of bombs

TOTAL PRODUCTION: Approximately 2,000

SERVICE DATES: 1915–1918

SUMMARY: Based on a prewar design by Geoffrey de Havilland, the F.E.2 series of two-seat pusher aircraft provided able service as a fighter until the British could develop a synchronized gear for a tractor-configured airplane. It proved to be a good climber and was surprisingly maneuverable despite its size and pusher configuration. The F.E.2 had an advantage over the Fokker Eindecker because its observer, who sat in the front of the nacelle, both operated a forward-firing, bracket-mounted Lewis gun and could stand and fire to the rear with a Lewis gun that was mounted to fire over the top wing and the arc of the propeller.

ROYAL AIRCRAFT FACTORY R.E.8 "HARRY TATE"
Courtesy of Art-Tech\Aerospace\M.A.R.S\TRH\Navy Historical.

COUNTRY OF ORIGIN: Great Britain

MANUFACTURER: Royal Aircraft Factory and several subcontractors

TYPE: Reconnaissance and Escort Fighter

CREW: 2

DIMENSIONS: Wingspan 42 ft 7 in.; Length 32 ft 7 in.; Height 11 ft 4 in.

LOADED WEIGHT: 2,869 lbs

POWER PLANT: 1 x 150 hp RAF 4a inline

PERFORMANCE: 103 mph maximum speed; 13,500 ft (4,115 m) service ceiling; 4 hour endurance

ARMAMENT: 1 x .303 caliber fixed forward-firing synchronized Vickers machine gun and 1 x .303 caliber ring-mounted Lewis machine gun

TOTAL PRODUCTION: Approximately 4,000

SERVICE DATES: 1917–1918

SUMMARY: Nicknamed the "Harry Tate" after a contemporary vaudeville comedian, the R.E.8 was a marked improvement to the B.E.2 in terms of firepower and speed; unfortunately, it lacked the maneuverability of the contemporary Armstrong-Whitworth F.K.8 and was therefore vulnerable to the last generation of German fighters. Even though it suffered a much higher casualty rate, the British inexplicably pressed on with production until the very end of the war.

ROYAL AIRCRAFT FACTORY S.E.5 (PICTURED) AND S.E.5A

Courtesy of Art-Tech\Aerospace\M.A.R.S\TRH\Navy Historical.

COUNTRY OF ORIGIN: Great Britain

MANUFACTURER: Royal Aircraft Factory and several subcontractors

TYPE: Fighter

CREW: 1

DIMENSIONS: Wingspan 26 ft 7.4 in.; Length 20 ft 11 in.; Height 9 ft 6 in.

LOADED WEIGHT: 1,988 lbs

POWER PLANT: 1 x 200 hp Hispano-Suiza V-type

PERFORMANCE: 138 mph maximum speed; 19,500 ft (5,944 m) service ceiling; 2 hour 30 minute endurance

ARMAMENT: 1 x .303 caliber fixed forward-firing synchronized Vickers machine gun; 1 x .303 caliber forward-upward-firing Lewis machine gun; and up to 100 lbs of bombs

TOTAL PRODUCTION: 5,205

SERVICE DATES: 1917–1918

SUMMARY: The Royal Aircraft Factory's S.E.5 and S.E.5a ranks second only to the Sopwith Camel as Britain's best fighter of the war. In some respects it was even better in that it was easy to fly, yet remained maneuverable, whereas the Camel had a tendency to enter a deadly spin. The S.E.5 and S.E.5a (the latter came with a 200 hp Hispano-Suiza) also possessed a unique firing system, using one fixed forward-firing synchronized Vickers gun and a Lewis gun that was attached to a Foster mounting for firing at an upward angle. The latter gun proved useful against Germany zeppelins and often caught opposing pilots by surprise. Of his seventy-three victories, British ace Edward Mannock achieved fifty while flying an S.E.5.

RUMPLER C-TYPES

Courtesy of Art-Tech\Aerospace\M.A.R.S\TRH\Navy Historical.

COUNTRY OF ORIGIN: Germany

MANUFACTURER: Rumpler Flugzeug-Werke

TYPE: Reconnaissance and Photo-Reconnaissance

CREW: 2

DIMENSIONS: Wingspan 41 ft 6 in.; Length 27 ft 7 in.; Height 10 ft 8 in.

LOADED WEIGHT: 3,373 lbs

POWER PLANT: 1 x 260 hp Mercedes D.IVa inline or 1 x 240 hp high-compression Maybach Mb.IV

PERFORMANCE: 106 mph maximum speed; 6,400 m (20,997 ft) service ceiling (24,000 ft with Maybach); 3 hour 30 minute endurance

ARMAMENT: 1 x 7.92 mm fixed forward-firing synchronized Spandau machine gun; 1 x 7.92 mm ring-mounted Parabellum machine gun; and up to 220 lbs bombs

TOTAL PRODUCTION: Approximately 500 of all Rumpler C-types

SERVICE DATES: 1917–1918

SUMMARY: Although many C-types were used for photo-reconnaissance, the Rumpler C-types were especially well suited for this role because of their ability to fly at high altitudes for long periods. Indeed, the C.VII "Rubilt" was powered by a special high-compression 240 hp Maybach Mb.IV inline engine, which allowed it to operate at a service ceiling of 7,315 m (24,000 ft), well beyond the reach of Allied fighters. It came equipped with oxygen and heated uniforms for its pilot and observer.

SALMSON 2A2

Courtesy of Art-Tech\Aerospace\M.A.R.S\TRH\Navy Historical.

COUNTRY OF ORIGIN: France

MANUFACTURER: Société des Moteurs Salmson

TYPE: Reconnaissance

CREW: 2

DIMENSIONS: Wingspan 38 ft 7 in.; Length 27 ft 11 in.; Height 9 ft 6.3 in.

LOADED WEIGHT: 2,798 lbs

POWER PLANT: 1 x 260 hp Salmson Canton-Unné radial

PERFORMANCE: 115 mph maximum speed; 6,250 m (20,505 ft) service ceiling; 3 hour endurance

ARMAMENT: 1 x 7.7 mm fixed forward-firing synchronized Vickers machine gun and 2 x 7.7 mm ring-mounted Lewis machine guns

TOTAL PRODUCTION: Approximately 3,200

SERVICE DATES: 1917–1918

SUMMARY: The Salmson 2A2 is generally considered one of the best-armed reconnaissance aircraft of the war and certainly the best produced by France. It was fast, highly maneuverable, and more than capable of defending itself. It was also widely used for photo-reconnaissance and artillery observation. Almost 25 percent of those that were produced were purchased by the United States for service with the American Expeditionary Force.

SHORT 184

Courtesy of Art-Tech\Aerospace\M.A.R.S\TRH\Navy Historical.

COUNTRY OF ORIGIN: Great Britain

MANUFACTURER: Short Brothers Ltd.

TYPE: Naval Torpedo Bombing and Reconnaissance Seaplane

CREW: 1–2

DIMENSIONS: Wingspan 63 ft 6.25 in.; Length 40 ft 7.5 in.; Height 13 ft 6 in.

LOADED WEIGHT: 5,363 lbs

POWER PLANT: 1 x 260 hp Sunbeam inline

PERFORMANCE: 88 mph maximum speed; 9,000 ft (2,743 m) service ceiling; 2 hour 45 minute endurance

ARMAMENT: 1 x .303 caliber free-firing Lewis machine gun and 1 x 14 in. diameter torpedo or up to 520 lbs of bombs

TOTAL PRODUCTION: Approximately 900

SERVICE DATES: 1915–1918

SUMMARY: Introduced in 1915, the Short 184 floatplane proved to be one of the most successful British seaplanes of the First World War. During the Dardanelles Campaign of 1915, a Short 184 became the first aircraft to sink an enemy ship, launching a 14-in.-diameter torpedo that sunk a Turkish cargo steamer. Because it had a limited range and altitude when carrying the heavy torpedo, the British would develop the Short 320 and the Sopwith Cuckoo to take over that responsibility, leaving the Short 184 to provide reconnaissance duty for the British Navy.

SIEMENS-SCHUCKERT D.III AND D.IV (PICTURED)

Courtesy of Art-Tech\Aerospace\M.A.R.S\TRH\Navy Historical.

COUNTRY OF ORIGIN: Germany

MANUFACTURER: Siemens-Schuckert Werke

TYPE: Fighter

CREW: 1

DIMENSIONS: Wingspan 27 ft 4.75 in.; Length 18 ft 8.5 in.; Height 8 ft 11 in.

LOADED WEIGHT: 1,620 lbs

POWER PLANT: 1 x 160 hp Siemens-Halske Sh.IIIa rotary

PERFORMANCE: 118 mph maximum speed; 8,000 m (26,240 ft) service ceiling; 2 hour endurance

ARMAMENT: 2 x 7.92 mm fixed forward-firing synchronized Spandau machine guns

TOTAL PRODUCTION: 118

SERVICE DATES: 1918

SUMMARY: Although it was relatively slow by 1918 standards, the Siemens-Schuckert D.III and D.IV was an outstanding climber, able to reach 6,100 m (20,013 ft) in just 20 minutes. Indeed, its service ceiling of 8,000 m (26,240 ft) gave it a tremendous advantage over lower-flying Allied fighters. Its 160 hp rotary engine, however, produced so much torque that its wings were extended 4 in. on the right side in an attempt to compensate. Inexperienced pilots often entered a deadly spin, but experienced pilots found that it had an outstanding right-turn advantage, similar to that enjoyed by the Sopwith Camel. The Siemens-Schuckert D.III and D.IV, unfortunately for the Germans, came too late and in too few number to make a difference in the war.

SIKORSKY *ILYA MUROMETS*

Courtesy of Art-Tech\Aerospace\M.A.R.S\TRH\Navy Historical.

COUNTRY OF ORIGIN: Russia

MANUFACTURER: Russko-Baltiisky Vagonny Zaved

TYPE: Bomber, Heavy

CREW: 4–8

DIMENSIONS: Wingspan 97 ft 9 in.; Length 57 ft 5 in.; Height 15 ft 6 in. (V-type)

LOADED WEIGHT: 10,140 lbs

POWER PLANT: 4 x 150 hp Sunbeam inline

PERFORMANCE: 68 mph maximum speed; 2,000 m (6,562 ft) service ceiling; 4–5 hour endurance

ARMAMENT: 4–7 x 7.7 mm free-firing Lewis machine guns and approximately 1,100 lbs of bombs

TOTAL PRODUCTION: Approximately 80 of all types

SERVICE DATES: 1914–1924

SUMMARY: Although Russia was far less industrially advanced than the other European powers, it would enter the First World War with the world's first four-engine aircraft in the Sikorsky *Ilya Muromets*. Even though the Russians had to rely upon a variety of engines, sometimes using different types on the same aircraft, the Sikorsky *Ilya Muromets* bombers performed well, exceeding the capabilities of anything that others powers would possess until the last 2 years of the war. They proved to be durable and rugged, with only one of the eighty produced being shot down. A few would survive the war and serve with the Bolsheviks during the Russian Civil War.

SIKORSKY S-16
Courtesy of Art-Tech\Aerospace\M.A.R.S\TRH\Navy Historical.

COUNTRY OF ORIGIN: Russia

MANUFACTURER: Russko-Baltiisky Vagonny Zaved

TYPE: Fighter, Reconnaissance

CREW: 1–2

DIMENSIONS: Wingspan 27 ft 6 in.; Length 20 ft 4 in.; Height 9 ft 1 in.

LOADED WEIGHT: 1,490 lbs

POWER PLANT: 1 x 80 hp Gnôme Mono-soupape rotary

PERFORMANCE: 73 mph maximum speed; 3,500 m (11,483 ft) service ceiling; 2 hour 30 minute endurance

ARMAMENT: 1 x 7.62 mm fixed forward-firing synchronized Colt machine gun and 1 x 7.62 mm ring-mounted Colt machine gun

TOTAL PRODUCTION: 34

SERVICE DATES: 1916–1924

SUMMARY: Even though Russia had to rely primarily upon foreign imports or for-eign-designed, licensed-built fighters, the Sikorsky 16 was one of the few Rus-sian-designed aircraft to see service in the war. Used for both armed-recon-naissance and as a fighter, the Sikorsky was highly maneuverable, but its 80 hp rotary engine made it too slow for 1916 standards. Its Russian-designed syn-chronization gear also proved to be so prone to malfunction that many pilots rigged the forward-firing gun to fire over the top wing to avoid the risk of shoot-ing off their propeller. The few Sikorsky 16s that survived the First World War saw service with the Bolsheviks in the Russian Civil War and served as trainers with the Red Air Force thereafter.

SOPWITH 11/2 STRUTTER

Courtesy of Art-Tech\Aerospace\M.A.R.S\TRH\Navy Historical.

COUNTRY OF ORIGIN: Great Britain

MANUFACTURER: Sopwith Aviation Company and several subcontractors

TYPE: Fighter, Bomber, and Reconnaissance

CREW: 1–2

DIMENSIONS: Wingspan 33 ft 6 in.; Length 25 ft 3 in.; Height 10 ft 3 in.

LOADED WEIGHT: 2,105 lbs

POWER PLANT: 1 x 110 hp Clerget rotary

PERFORMANCE: 106 mph maximum speed; 15,500 ft (4,724 m) service ceiling; 4–5 hour endurance

ARMAMENT: 1 x .303 caliber fixed forward-firing synchronized Vickers machine gun; 1 x .303 caliber ring-mounted Lewis machine gun; and 4 x 56-lb bombs

TOTAL PRODUCTION: Approximately 1,500 in Great Britain and 4,500 in France

SERVICE DATES: 1916–1918

SUMMARY: The Sopwith 11/2 Strutter was one of the most successful multirole aircraft of the war. Although it was originally intended for service with the Royal Naval Air Service, it was pressed into service with the Royal Flying Corps as a fighter during the Battle of the Somme in 1916 because it was one of the first British airplanes equipped with a synchronized forward-firing machine gun. As more agile fighters became available, its role was changed to provide service for armed-reconnaissance, artillery observation, and light bombing.

SOPWITH F.1 CAMEL
Courtesy of Art-Tech\Aerospace\M.A.R.S\TRH\Navy Historical.

COUNTRY OF ORIGIN: Great Britain

MANUFACTURER: Sopwith Aviation Company

TYPE: Fighter

CREW: 1

DIMENSIONS: Wingspan 28 ft; Length 18 ft 9 in.; Height 8 ft 6 in.

LOADED WEIGHT: 1,453 lbs

POWER PLANT: 1 x 130 hp Clerget rotary

PERFORMANCE: 113 mph maximum speed; 19,000 ft (5,791 m) service ceiling; 2 hour 30 minute endurance

ARMAMENT: 2 x .303 caliber fixed forward-firing synchronized Vickers machine guns

TOTAL PRODUCTION: 5,490

SERVICE DATES: 1917–1919

SUMMARY: Dubbed the "Camel" because its twin Vickers guns were covered, giving it the appearance of a hump, the Sopwith F.1 Camel was without question the best-known and best-performing British fighter of the First World War. Historians have long debated whether it or the Fokker D.VII was the best fighter of the war. In terms of individual performance, the D.VII was slightly faster, a better climber, and more maneuverable at higher altitudes, whereas the torque produced by the Camel's 130 hp rotary engine gave it the advantage of making a tight 360-degree right circle in the same time that it took opponents to turn 90 degrees. The Camel was unforgiving in the hands of an average pilot, however, because the torque of its engine made it prone to enter a deadly spin. In terms of sheer numbers produced and approximately 1,300 victories attained, the Camel was definitely the more prolific killer.

SOPWITH PUP

Courtesy of Art-Tech\Aerospace\M.A.R.S\TRH\Navy Historical.

COUNTRY OF ORIGIN: Great Britain

MANUFACTURER: Sopwith Aviation Company

TYPE: Fighter

CREW: 1

DIMENSIONS: Wingspan 26 ft 6 in.; Length 19 ft 3.75 in.; Height 9 ft 5 in.

LOADED WEIGHT: 1,225 lbs

POWER PLANT: 1 x 80 hp Le Rhône, Gnôme, or Clerget rotary

PERFORMANCE: 111 mph maximum speed; 17,500 ft (5,334 m) service ceiling; 3 hour endurance

ARMAMENT: 1 x .303 caliber fixed forward-firing synchronized Vickers or Lewis machine gun and 8 x Le Prieur rockets

TOTAL PRODUCTION: 1,770

SERVICE DATES: 1916–1918

SUMMARY: Dubbed the "Pup" because it was a smaller version of the Sopwith 11/2 Strutter, the Sopwith Pup was one of the first British fighters to be equipped with a synchronized machine gun. Although it was originally intended for service with the Royal Naval Air Service, the vast majority served as fighters over the Western Front, where they were noted for their maneuverability and high performance at high altitudes. Approximately 290 Pups saw service with the Royal Naval Air Service, which used them in experiments with taking off and landing onboard ship. Those serving aboard ship were eventually fitted with skids instead of wheels.

SOPWITH TABLOID

Courtesy of Art-Tech\Aerospace\M.A.R.S\TRH\Navy Historical.

COUNTRY OF ORIGIN: Great Britain

MANUFACTURER: Sopwith Aviation Company

TYPE: Reconnaissance, Light Bomber

CREW: 1

DIMENSIONS: Wingspan 25 ft 6 in.; Length 20 ft 4 in.; Height 8 ft 5 in.

LOADED WEIGHT: 1,120 lbs

POWER PLANT: 1 x 80 hp Gnôme rotary

PERFORMANCE: 93 mph maximum speed; 15,000 ft (4,572 m) service ceiling; 3 hour 15 minute endurance

ARMAMENT: None officially; small arms and light bombs

TOTAL PRODUCTION: Approximately 50

SERVICE DATES: 1913–1915

SUMMARY: The Sopwith Tabloid was one of the fastest aircraft available at the outbreak of the war. Although produced in small numbers, they provided good service as reconnaissance aircraft in the first 2 years of the war. Because of their extended endurance, Tabloids also carried out some of the war's most spectacular early bombing raids, including one on 8 October 1914 in which First Lieutenant Reggie Marix succeeded in destroying a zeppelin L-9 in its Düsseldorf shed.

SOPWITH TRIPLANE

Courtesy of Art-Tech\Aerospace\M.A.R.S\TRH\Navy Historical.

COUNTRY OF ORIGIN: Great Britain
MANUFACTURER: Sopwith Aviation Company
TYPE: Fighter
CREW: 1
DIMENSIONS: Wingspan 26 ft 6 in.; Length 18 ft 10 in.; Height 10 ft 6 in.
LOADED WEIGHT: 1,541 lbs
POWER PLANT: 1 x 130 hp Clerget rotary
PERFORMANCE: 117 mph maximum speed; 20,500 ft (6,248 m) service ceiling; 2 hour 45 minute endurance
ARMAMENT: 1–2 x .303 caliber fixed forward-firing synchronized Vickers machine guns

TOTAL PRODUCTION: 140
SERVICE DATES: 1916–1917
SUMMARY: Nicknamed the "Tripehound" because of its resemblance to the Sopwith Pup, the Sopwith Triplane had an important impact despite its rather short service. Indeed, German pilots were so impressed by its performance, specifically its outstanding climbing ability and maneuverability, that their demands for a similar aircraft led to the introduction of the Fokker Dr.I. It should be noted that the Sopwith Triplane served only with Royal Naval Air Service units.

SPAD VII

Courtesy of Art-Tech\Aerospace\M.A.R.S\TRH\Navy Historical.

COUNTRY OF ORIGIN: France

MANUFACTURER: Société Anonyme Pour l'Aviation et ses Derives

TYPE: Fighter

CREW: 1

DIMENSIONS: Wingspan 25 ft 8 in.; Length 20 ft 3 in.; Height 7 ft

LOADED WEIGHT: 1,550 lbs

POWER PLANT: 1 x 150 Hispano-Suiza 8Aa V-type or 180 hp Hispano-Suiza 8Ab V-type

PERFORMANCE: 119 mph (150 hp Hispano) or 131 mph (180 hp Hispano) maximum speed; 5,490 m (18,012 ft) service ceiling; 2 hour 15 minute endurance

ARMAMENT: 1 x 7.7 mm fixed forward-firing synchronized Vickers machine gun

TOTAL PRODUCTION: Approximately 3,500 (some sources indicate 5,000–6,000)

SERVICE DATES: 1916–1918

SUMMARY: Where the French had relied heavily upon aircraft powered by rotary engines, the SPAD VII was among the first fighters to be powered by the V-type Hispano-Suiza, which provided a performance similar to rotary engines, but without the dangerous torque that had made them prone to enter deadly spins. Upon being introduced, the SPAD VII was supplied to France's most famous squadron, *Les Cigognes* (the *Storks*), and it soon won the favor of such aces as René Fonck and Georges Guynemer. Indeed, the latter's suggestion led to the introduction of a modified version, the SPAD XIII, which included extra armament with a .37 mm cannon that fired through its hollow engine hub. In addition to its excellent performance, the SPAD VII was noted for its sturdy construction, which allowed it to absorb a lot of punishment.

SPAD XIII

Courtesy of Art-Tech\Aerospace\M.A.R.S\TRH\Navy Historical.

COUNTRY OF ORIGIN: France

MANUFACTURER: Société Anonyme Pour l'Aviation et ses Derives

TYPE: Fighter

CREW: 1

DIMENSIONS: Wingspan 27 ft; Length 20 ft 8 in.; Height 7 ft 11.75 in.

LOADED WEIGHT: 1,808 lbs

POWER PLANT: 1 x 200 hp Hispano-Suiza 8Ba V-type or 1 x 230 hp Hispano-Suiza 8Be V-type

PERFORMANCE: 131 mph maximum speed (200 hp) and 140 mph (230 hp); 6,645 m (21,801 ft) service ceiling; 2 hour endurance

ARMAMENT: 2 x 7.7 mm fixed forward-firing synchronized Vickers machine gun

TOTAL PRODUCTION: Approximately 8,400

SERVICE DATES: 1917–1923

SUMMARY: Introduced as a successor to the SPAD VII, the SPAD XIII was faster than the contemporary Sopwith Camel and Fokker D.VII. Although it lacked the turning ability of the Camel and the climbing ability of the Fokker D.VII, the SPAD XIII more than made up for these minor shortcomings in the sheer numbers in which it was produced. Its quantity proved critical to the Allies seizing and maintaining control of the skies over the Western Front in 1918.

VICKERS F.B.5 "GUN-BUS"

Courtesy of Art-Tech\Aerospace\M.A.R.S\TRH\Navy Historical.

COUNTRY OF ORIGIN: Great Britain

MANUFACTURER: Vickers Ltd.

TYPE: Fighter (Pusher)

CREW: 2

DIMENSIONS: Wingspan 26 ft 2 in.; Length 27 ft 2 in.; Height 11 ft 6 in.

LOADED WEIGHT: 2,050 lbs

POWER PLANT: 1 x 100 hp Gnôme Monosoupape rotary

PERFORMANCE: 70 mph maximum speed; 9,000 ft (2,743 m) service ceiling; 4 hour endurance

ARMAMENT: 1 x .303 caliber forward-firing Vickers machine gun

TOTAL PRODUCTION: 200

SERVICE DATES: 1914–1916

SUMMARY: Introduced in late 1914 and appearing on the Western Front in early 1915, the Vickers F.B.5, nicknamed the "Gun-Bus," was the first British aircraft specifically designed as a fighter. Designed as a pusher so that its front-seat observer could have the advantage of a full range of forward fire, the F.B.5 enjoyed great success even though it was relatively slow and lacked maneuverability. The introduction of the faster, more maneuverable Fokker Eindecker in the fall of 1915 quickly revealed the F.B.5's vulnerability to rear attack. It was relegated to training status by 1916.

VOISIN TYPES 1–6

Courtesy of Art-Tech\Aerospace\M.A.R.S\TRH\Navy Historical.

COUNTRY OF ORIGIN: France

MANUFACTURER: Compagnie Gabriel Voisin

TYPE: Bomber and Ground Attack (Pusher)

CREW: 2

DIMENSIONS: Wingspan 48 ft 4.75 in.; Length 31 ft 3.25 in.; Height 11 ft 11 in.

LOADED WEIGHT: 2,513 lbs

POWER PLANT: 1 x 150 hp Salmson Canton-Unné radial (Type 5)

PERFORMANCE: 65 mph maximum speed; 3,500 m (11,483 ft) service ceiling; 3 hour 30 minute endurance

ARMAMENT: 1 x 7.7 mm forward-firing Hotchkiss machine gun and 330 lbs of bombs

TOTAL PRODUCTION: Approximately 1,920 of all types, including 120 produced in Italy and 400 produced in Russia

SERVICE DATES: 1914–1918

SUMMARY: From the opening of the war to its end, the Voisin Type 1 to Type 6 pusher biplanes (each type was signified by more powerful motors) provided the French an aircraft that performed multiple roles, ranging from reconnaissance to light bombing. Types 3 and 5 could carry a 330-lb bomb load and were used primarily for light bombing. Because of their vulnerability to enemy fighters, they were used primarily at night.

VOISIN TYPES 8 AND 10 (PICTURED)

Courtesy of Art-Tech\Aerospace\M.A.R.S\TRH\Navy Historical.

COUNTRY OF ORIGIN: France

MANUFACTURER: Compagnie Gabriel Voisin

TYPE: Bomber (Pusher)

CREW: 2

DIMENSIONS: Wingspan 61 ft 8 in.; Length 36 ft 2 in.; Height 11 ft 5.75 in.

LOADED WEIGHT: (Type 8) 4,100 lbs; (Type 10) 4,850 lbs

POWER PLANT: (Type 8) 1 x 220 hp Peugeot 8Aa inline; (Type 10) 1 x 280 hp Renault 12Fe inline

PERFORMANCE: 82 mph maximum speed (Type 8) and 84 mph maximum speed (Type 10); 4,300 m (14,108 ft) service ceiling; 4–5 hour endurance

ARMAMENT: 1–2 x 7.7 mm forward-firing Hotchkiss machine gun or 1 x .37 mm Hotchkiss cannon; and 400 lbs of bombs (Type 8) or 660 lbs of bombs (Type 10)

TOTAL PRODUCTION: 1,100 Type 8 and 900 Type 10

SERVICE DATES: 1916–1918

SUMMARY: Intended as a replacement for the earlier Voisin Types 1–6, the Type 8 and Type 10 were designed to carry a heavier bomb load and to have a longer endurance. Although they also had to be used at night, their extended range allowed them to be used to strike strategic targets in Western Germany. They were also used to carry out reconnaissance and bomb targets of opportunity.

WRIGHT MILITARY FLYER

Courtesy of Art-Tech\Aerospace\M.A.R.S\TRH\Navy Historical.

COUNTRY OF ORIGIN: United States

MANUFACTURER: Wright Brothers Aeroplane Company

TYPE: Reconnaissance

CREW: 2

DIMENSIONS: Wingspan 36 ft 6 in.; Length 28 ft 11 in.; Height 7 ft 10.5 in.

LOADED WEIGHT: 1,200 lbs

POWER PLANT: 1 x 35 hp inline

PERFORMANCE: 44 mph maximum speed; 1,000 ft (305 m) service ceiling; 1 hour endurance

ARMAMENT: None

TOTAL PRODUCTION: 1

SERVICE DATES: 1909–1911

SUMMARY: The *Wright Military Flyer* was designed to meet specifications that the U.S. Army Signal Corps had set in December 1907 for an aircraft that would have a range of 125 miles, possess an average speed of 40 mph, and be easy to disassemble and reassemble for transportation. Orville demonstrated the *Military Flyer* in several flights at Fort Meyers, Virginia, in September 1908. Despite a crash that killed his passenger, Lieutenant Thomas E. Selfridge—the world's first aircraft casualty—and destroyed the prototype, the War Department accepted the Wrights' bid of $25,000. Unlike their original flyers, the *Military Flyer* (Type A) possessed two seats, allowing the pilot and passenger to sit upright. It was otherwise fairly similar to the earlier versions, in that it placed the elevator in the front of the aircraft (canard configuration) to minimize stalls, utilized a pusher configuration (with the engine and propeller in the rear), and required the use of a drop-weight launching. It remained in service until 1911 and trained many of the army's first pilots.

ZEPPELIN (STAAKEN) R TYPES

Courtesy of Art-Tech\Aerospace\M.A.R.S\TRH\Navy Historical.

COUNTRY OF ORIGIN: Germany

MANUFACTURER: Zeppelin Werke Staaken; Automobil und Aviatik; Ostdeutsche Albatros-Werke; and Luftfahrzeugbau Schütte-Lanz

TYPE: Bomber, Heavy

CREW: 4

DIMENSIONS: Wingspan 138 ft 5 in.; Length 72 ft 6.25 in.; Height 20 ft 8 in.

LOADED WEIGHT: 26,066 lbs

POWER PLANT: 4 x 245 hp Maybach Mb.IV inline or 4 x 260 hp Mercedes D.IVa inline

PERFORMANCE: 84 mph maximum speed; 4,320 m (14,173 ft) service ceiling; 7–10 hour endurance

ARMAMENT: 4 x 7.92 mm free-firing Parabellum machine guns and 1,650–4,400 lbs of bombs

TOTAL PRODUCTION: 18

SERVICE DATES: 1917–1918

SUMMARY: After demonstrating a prototype in April 1915, Zeppelin Staaken spent the next 2 years experimenting with a variety of engines and configurations before beginning production of the R.VI model in June 1917. The largest aircraft to see service in the war, the R.VI's four engines were configured in a back-to-back pusher-tractor configuration. Depending on the mission and the amount of fuel carried, its endurance ranged from 7 to 10 hours with a bomb load of 1,650–4,400 lbs. It was also the first bomber to carry Germany's huge 1,000-kg (2,200-lb) bomb, the largest used in the war. Noted for its rugged construction, the R.VI was used extensively on the Western Front and carried out numerous raids (some solo and others in conjunction with Gotha G.IV and G.V bombers) against Britain. Not a single R.VI was lost from enemy fire. Just one of the eighteen constructed was built by Zeppelin Staaken.

ZEPPELIN P-TYPE AIRSHIP
Courtesy of Art-Tech\Aerospace\M.A.R.S\TRH\Navy Historical.

COUNTRY OF ORIGIN: Germany

MANUFACTURER: Zeppelin Werke Staaken

TYPE: Bomber Airship, Long Range

CREW: 21

DIMENSIONS: Length 536 ft 5 in; Diameter 61 ft 5 in.; Volume 1,126,533 cubic ft

LOADED WEIGHT: 35,715 lbs

POWER PLANT: 4 x 210 Maybach CX inline

PERFORMANCE: 59 mph maximum speed; 3,900 m (12,795 ft) service ceiling; 1,336 mile range

ARMAMENT: Up to 2,500 lbs of bombs

TOTAL PRODUCTION: 20 out of 118 zeppelins used in the war

SERVICE DATES: 1915–1917

SUMMARY: The P-type airship was the first class of zeppelin produced in the war, beginning with the introduction of the L-10 in May 1915. Compared with the M-type that had entered service in early 1914, the P-type's gas capacity had an additional 333,015 cubic ft of gas, which increased its lifting capacity from 20,282 to 35,715 lbs, and its service ceiling from 9,200 to 12,800 ft. In addition, the P-type's range was almost twice that of the M-type; 1,336 miles compared with just 683. Even though this gave the Germans an airship that was more than capable of striking Great Britain, its service ceiling soon proved to be too low, making it an easy target for British fighters armed with incendiary bullets.

GLOSSARY OF TERMS

Aerofoil   A cross-section shape of a wing

Aileron   A part of the wing that controls roll left or right

Altitude Conversion Chart (meters / feet)

1,000 m	3,281 ft
2,000 m	6,562 ft
3,000 m	9,842 ft
4,000 m	13,123 ft
5,000 m	16,404 ft
6,000 m	19,685 ft
7,000 m	22,965 ft
8,000 m	26,247 ft
9,000 m	29,526 ft
10,000 m	32,808 ft

Anhedral   The downward angle of the tips of the wings in relation to where the wings are attached to the fuselage

Aspect Ratio   Division of the wingspan by chord line

Attack Aircraft   Aircraft designed to strike small targets at short distance and support ground troops

Bomber   An aircraft designed to drop bombs on distant targets

Camber   The degree of curvature of an aerofoil shape; greater camber provides greater lift, but it also creates drag

Canard   A horizontal stabilizer extending in front of the wings; often described as a tail-first design

Chord   The width of a wing from the leading edge to the trailing edge

Cockpit   The area housing the controls and where the pilot sits; an area for such other crew members as observers or tailgunners

Dihedral   The upward angle from which the tips of the wings are in relation to where the wing attaches to the fuselage

Drag   The aerodynamic forces that resists an aircraft's movement through the air

Elevators   Located on the tail section to set the pitch (up and down motion) of the aircraft

Elevons   A combination of elevators and ailerons

Fighter   An aircraft designed to shoot down other aircraft

Flaps   A part of the wing that can be lowered to decrease speed; sometimes referred to as air brakes

Fuselage   The long, narrow body of an aircraft, going down its center and housing its engine and cockpit or cockpits

Gap   Distance between the wings

Inline Engine   Stationary engine in which the pistons are set in a straight row

Loaded Weight   The normal weight of an aircraft at takeoff, comprising the aircraft, fuel, crew, and armament.

Monocoque   A construction method in which the fuselage is built around wooden hoops—usually using plywood strips—providing for a smooth rounded surface

Nacelle   A shortened fuselage that houses the crew; normally found on twin-engine aircraft or on pushers with the engine being in the rear of the nacelle

Nonrigid Airship   An airship (blimp) whose shape is provided by the pressurized gas envelope

Nose   The front section of the fuselage

Observation   Aircraft used within a closer range, usually to assist artillery

Pitch   Movement of the aircraft up and down; controlled by the elevator

Pivot-Mounted Gun   A machine gun mounted on a pivot on the side or to the rear of the observer's seat, which allows for the gun to be moved up or down or side to side at an opposing plane

Pusher Configuration   An aircraft whose engine and propeller are located behind the wings

Radial Engine   Stationary engine in which pistons are set in a circular or star pattern around the crankshaft

Reconnaissance   Aircraft used for viewing or photographing enemy positions

Rigid Airship   An airship whose shape is established by a metal or wooden framework

Ring-Mounted Gun   A machine gun mounted on a circular ring around the observer's seat, which allows for a smooth movement and aiming of the gun

Roll   Moving the aircraft on a left or right roll by the ailerons

Rotary Engine   An engine in which the crankshaft is stationary and the engine revolves around it

Rudder   A part of the tail section that moves the aircraft from left to right, generally operated by foot pedals

Semi-Rigid Airship   An airship that has a central keel to which the envelope and engine compartments are attached

Service Ceiling   Highest altitude at which an aircraft normally operates

Sesquiplane   Aircraft in which the lower wing is much smaller than the upper wing in either chord or span or both

Slip   Movement whereby the pilot sets the ailerons and rudder in opposite directions so that the aircraft moves forward at an angle; useful for reducing speed quickly by increasing drag

Spin   Caused when an aircraft stalls and begins to spin or rotate around its vertical axis

Stagger   A biplane or triplane in which the wings are staggered rather than being in line on the fuselage; the lower wing is normally placed further back

Stall   Caused when an aircraft's angle of attack exceeds its critical angle, resulting in airflow no longer going over the wing, and thus causing the plane to fall

Sweptback   When the wings of an aircraft are affixed so that leading edge is at a backward angle rather than a 90-degree angle to the fuselage

Synchronized Gun   A gun that is fixed to the fuselage and equipped with an interrupter gear that is synchronized with the engine so that it will not fire when a bullet would hit the propeller

Tail   The rear section of an airplane that houses the rudder and elevators

Tractor Configuration   An aircraft whose engine and propeller are located in front of the wings

Trainer   Aircraft designed or used to train pilots, sometimes with dual controls for instructor and students

V-Type Engine   Stationary engine in which the pistons are set in a v-pattern, with two being beside each other

Wingspan   Distance of aircraft between the tips of the longest wing

Wing-Warping   Method of warping the ends of the wings to control rolling motion

Yaw   Movement of the aircraft left and right; controlled by the rudder

A SELECTIVE BIBLIOGRAPHY
OF MILITARY AIRCRAFT,
ORIGINS TO 1918

Abate, Rosario. *Aeroplani Caproni: Gianni Caproni and His Aircraft, 1910–1983*. Trento, Italy: Museo Caproni, 1992.

Andrews, C. F., and E. B. Morgan. *Vickers Aircraft since 1908*. London: Putnam, 1988.

Baker, David. *Manfred von Richthofen: The Man and the Aircraft He Flew*. London: Outline, 1990.

Barnes, C. H. *Bristol Aircraft since 1910*. London: Putnam, 1988.

_____. *Handley Page Aircraft since 1907*. London: Putnam, 1987.

Bickers, Richard Townshend. *The First Great Air War*. London: Hodder & Stoughton, 1988.

Bowen, Ezra. *Knights of the Air*. Alexandra, VA: Time-Life Books, 1980.

Bowers, Peter M. *Curtiss Aircraft, 1907–1947*. Annapolis, MD: Naval Institute Press, 1979.

Boyne, Walter J. *The Influence of Air Power upon History*. Gretna, LA: Pelican Publishing Company, 2003.

Bruce, J. M. *British Aeroplanes, 1914–18*. London: Putnam & Co., Ltd., 1957; reprint, New York: Funk & Wagnalls, 1969.

———. *Nieuport Aircraft of World War One*. London: Arms and Armour Press, 1988.

———. *The Aeroplanes of the Royal Flying Corps (Military Wing)*. London: Putnam, 1982.

———. *The Sopwith Fighters*. London: Arms and Armour Press, 1986.

Campbell, Christopher. *Aces and Aircraft of World War I*. New York: Greenwich House, 1984.

Castle, H. G. *Fire over England: The German Air Raids in World War I*. London: Putnam, 1982.

Christienne, Charles, and Pierre Lissarrague. *A History of French Military Aviation*. Washington: Smithsonian Institution Press, 1986.

Clark, Alan. *Aces High: The War in the Air over the Western Front, 1914–18*. New York: Putnam, 1973.

Conners, John. *Albatros Fighters in Action*. Carrollton, TX: Squadron/Signal Publications, 1981.

———. *SPAD Fighters in Action*. Carrollton, TX: Squadron/Signal Publications, 1989.

Cooke, James J. *The U.S. Air Service in the Great War, 1917–1918*. New York: Praeger Publishers, 1996.

Cooksley, Peter. *German Bombers of World War I in Action*. Carrollton, TX: Squadron/Signal Publications, 2000.

Cooper, Malcolm. *The Birth of Independent Air Power: British Air Policy in the First World War*. London: Allen & Unwin, 1986.

Crouch, Tom D. *First Flight: The Wright Brothers and the Invention of the Airplane*. Washington: U.S. Department of Interior, 2002.

———. *The Bishop's Boys: A Life of Wilbur and Orville Wright*. New York: W. W. Norton & Co., 1989.

Davilla, James J., and Arthur M. Soltan. *French Aircraft of the First World War*. Mountain View, CA: Flying Machines Press, 1997.

Driver, Hugh. *The Birth of Military Aviation: Britain, 1903–1914*. Woodbridge, U.K.: Royal Historical Society, 1997.

Durkota, Alan, Thomas Darcey, and Victor Kulikov. *The Imperial Russian Air Service: Famous Pilots and Aircraft of World War One*. Mountain View, CA: Flying Machines Press, 1995.

Eckener, Hugo. *Count Zeppelin—the Man and His Work*. London: Massie Publishing, 1938.

Ege, Lennart A. T. *Balloons and Airships*. Translated and edited by Kenneth Munson. New York: The Macmillan Company, 1974.

Fitzsimons, Bernard. *Warplanes and Air Battles of World War I*. New York: Beekman House, 1973.

Flammer, Philip M. *The Vivid Air: The Lafayette Escadrille*. Athens: University of Georgia Press, 1981.

Franks, Norman L. R. *Dog Fight: Aerial Tactics of the Aces of World War I*. London: Greenhill, 2003.

———. *The Storks: The Story of Les Cigognes, France's Elite Fighter Group of World War I*. London: Grub Street, 1998.

Fredette, Raymond H. *The Sky on Fire: The First Battle of Britain, 1917–1918*. New York: Harcourt, Brace, and Jovanovich, 1966.

Fredriksen, John C. *International Warbirds: An Illustrated Guide to World Military Aircraft, 1914–2000*. Santa Barbara, CA: ABC-CLIO, Inc., 2001.

———. *Warbirds: An Illustrated Guide to U.S. Military Aircraft, 1915–2000*. Santa Barbara, CA: ABC-CLIO, Inc., 1999.

Gibbs-Smith, Charles H. *The Invention of the Aeroplane, 1799–1909*. London: Faber & Faber, 1966.

Gray, Peter, and Owen Thetford. *German Aircraft of the First World War*. London: Putnam, 1962.

Grosz, Peter M., George Haddow, and Peter Schiemer. *Austro-Hungarian Army Aircraft of World War One*. Mountain View, CA: Flying Machines Press, 1993.

Grosz, Peter M. *German Aircraft of World War I*. Stamford, CT: Flying Machines Press, 1999.

———. *Gotha I-V*. Aircraft in Profile No. 115. Windson, U.K.: Profile Publications, 1967.

———. *Pfalz: World War I Aircraft*. Glendale, CA: Aviation, 1975.

Gurney, Gene. *Flying Aces of World War I*. New York: Random House, 1965.

Haddow, G. W., and Peter M. Gross. *The German Giants*. London: Putnam & Co., 1962.

Hallion, Richard P. *Rise of the Fighter Aircraft, 1914–1918*. Annapolis, MD: Nautical and Aviation Publishing Co., 1984.

———. *Strike from the Sky: The History of Battlefield Air Attack, 1911–1945*. Shrewsbury, U.K.: Airlife Publications, 1989.

———. *Taking Flight: Inventing the Aerial Age from Antiquity through the First World War*. New York: Oxford University Press, 2003.

Hare, Paul R. *Aeroplanes of the Royal Aircraft Factory*. Marlborough, U.K.: Crowood, 1999.

Hart, Clive. *The Prehistory of Flight*. Berkeley: University of California Press, 1985.

Hegener, Henri. *Fokker: The Man and His Aircraft*. Letchworth, U.K.: Harleyford Publications, 1961.

Hezlett, Sir Arthur. *Aircraft and Sea Power*. New York: Stein and Day, 1970.

Higham, Robin. *100 Years of Air Power & Aviation*. College Station: Texas A & M University Press, 2003.

Hudson, James L. *The Hostile Skies: A Combat History of the American Air Service in World War I*. Syracuse, NY: Syracuse University Press, 1968.

Imrie, Alex. *Fokker Fighters of World War One*. London: Arms and Armour Press, 1987.

Jackson, A. J. *De Havilland Aircraft since 1909*. London: Putnam, 1987.

Jackson, Robert. *Fighter Pilots of World War I*. New York: St. Martin's Press, 1977.

Kennett, Lee. *The First Air War, 1914–1918*. New York: The Free Press, 1991.

Kilduff, Peter. *Germany's First Air Force, 1914–1918*. Osceola, WS: Motorbooks International Publishers, 1991.

King, Brad. *Royal Naval Air Service, 1912–1918*. Aldershot, U.K.: Hikoki Publications, 1997.

King, H. F. *Sopwith Aircraft, 1912–1920*. London: Putnam, 1980.

Kosin, Rudiger. *The German Fighter since 1915*. London: Putnam, 1988.

Lamberton, W. M., and E. F. Cheesman. *Fighter Aircraft of the 1914–1918 War*. Fallbrook, CA: Aero Publications, Inc., 1960.

———. *Reconnaissance & Bomber Aircraft of the 1914–1918 War*. Los Angeles: Aero Publishers, Inc., 1962.

Lawson, Eric, and Jane Lawson. *The First Air Campaign: August 1914–November 1918*. Conshohocken, PA: Combined Books, 1996.

Layman, R. D. *Naval Aviation in the First World War: Its Impact and Influence*. Annapolis, MD: Naval Institute Press, 1996.

Lewis, Bruce. *A Few of the First: The True Stories of the Men Who Flew in and before the First World War*. London: Leo Cooper, 1997.

Lewis, Gwiylm, and Chaz Bowyer. *Wings over the Somme*. Wrexham, U.K.: Bridge Books, 1994.

Longstreet, Stephen. *The Canvas Falcons: The Story of the Men and Planes of World War I*. New York: Barnes & Noble Books, 1995.

Mason, Herbert Molloy. *High Flew the Falcons: French Aces of World War I*. Philadelphia: Lippincott, 1965.

Morris, Joseph. *The German Air Raids on Great Britain, 1914–1918*. Dallington, U.K.: The Naval and Military Press, 1993.

Morrow, John Howard, Jr. *Building German Airpower, 1909–1914*. Knoxville: University of Tennessee Press, 1976.

————. *German Air Power in World War I.* Lincoln: University of Nebraska Press, 1982.

————. *The Great War in the Air: Military Aviation from 1909 to 1921.* Washington: Smithsonian Institution Press, 1993.

Munson, Kenneth. *Aircraft of World War I.* Garden City, NY: Doubleday and Company, Inc., 1968.

————. *Bombers, Patrol, and Reconnaissance Aircraft, 1914–1919.* New York: The Macmillan Company, 1968.

————. *Fighters, Attack, and Training Aircraft, 1914–1919.* New York: The Macmillan Company, 1968.

Murray, Williamson. *War in the Air, 1914–45.* London: Cassell Publishers, 1999.

Neumann, George P. *The German Air Force in the Great War.* London: Hodder & Stoughton, Ltd., 1921.

Norman, Aaron. *The Great Air War.* New York: The Macmillan Company, 1968.

Norris, Geoffrey. *The Royal Flying Corps: A History.* London: Muller, 1965.

Owers, Colin A. *De Havilland Aircraft of World War I.* 2 vols. Boulder, CO: Flying Machines Press, 2001.

Penrose, Harald. *British Aviation: The Great War and Armistice, 1915–1919.* London, Putnam, 1969.

————. *British Aviation: The Pioneer Years, 1903–1914.* London: Putnam, 1967.

Pisano, Dominick A., Thomas J. Dietz, Joanne M. Gernstein, and Karl S. Schneide. *Legend, Memory, and the Great War in the Air.* Seattle: University of Washington Press in association with the National Air and Space Museum, Smithsonian Institution, 1992.

Reynolds, Quentin. *They Fought for the Sky.* New York: Holt, Rinehart, and Winston, 1957.

Rimmell, Raymond L. *The German Air Service in World War One.* London: Arms and Armour Press, 1988.

Robertson, Bruce., ed. *Air Aces of the 1914–1918 War*. Letchworth, U.K.: Harleyford Publications, 1959.

Robinson, Douglas H. *The Zeppelin in Combat*. Atglen, PA: Schiffer Publishing Company, 1994.

Rolt, L. T. C. *The Aeronauts: A History of Ballooning, 1783–1903*. Brunswick, U.K.: 1985.

Stansbury, Haydon F. *Aeronautics in the Union and Confederate Armies*. 2 vols. Baltimore: Johns Hopkins University Press, 1941.

Taylor, John William Ransom, and Fred T. Jane. *Jane's Fighting Aircraft of World War I*. 1919; reprint, New York: Military Press, 1990.

Thetford, Owen. *British Naval Aviation since 1912*. London: Putnam, 1977.

Treadwell, Terry C., and Alan C. Wood. *Airships of the First World War: Images of Aviation*. Stroud, U.K.: Tempus Publishing Limited, 1999.

Treadwell, Terry C. *America's First Air War: The United States Army, Naval and Marine Air Services in the First World War*. Shrewsbury, U.K.: Airlife Publishing Ltd., 2000.

Whitehouse, Arthur George Joseph. *Decisive Air Battles of the First World War*. New York: Duell, Sloan, and Pearce, 1963.

Williams, Ray. *Armstrong-Whitworth Aircraft*. Stroud, U.K.: Chalford Publishing, 1988.

Winter, Denis. *The First of the Few: Fighter Pilots of the First World War*. Athens: University of Georgia Press, 1983.

Wohl, Robert. *A Passion for Wings: Aviation and the Western Imagination, 1908–1918*. New Haven: Yale University Press, 1994.

Wood, Alan C. *Aces and Airmen of World War I*. London: Brassey's, 2002.

Wragg, David. *Wings over the Sea: A History of Naval Aviation*. New York: Arco Publishing, Inc., 1979.

INDEX

ABOUT THE AUTHOR

Justin D. Murphy, Ph.D., is professor of history and Director of the Douglas MacArthur Academy of Freedom Honors Program at Howard Payne University, Brownwood, Texas. He has published numerous articles and book reviews in scholarly journals and encyclopedias and served as associate editor of *The European Powers in the First World War: An Encyclopedia* and *Encyclopedia of American Military History*.